Politics
of the
Russian Nobility,
1881–1905

Politics
of the
Russian Nobility
1881 – 1905

G. M. Hamburg

Rutgers University Press
New Brunswick, New Jersey

85929

The author wishes to thank George Allen and Unwin for permission to quote from "The Last Peasant Poet" in *Modern Poems from Russia* by Gerald Shelley (1977), p. 59:ll. 9–13; Walter Arndt for permission to quote from "Vol'nost'" in *Pushkin Threefold* (1972), pp. 4–5:ll. 57–64; Faber and Faber Ltd. and Random House, Inc. for permission to quote from "Not Palaces" in *Selected Poems* by Stephen Spender (1964), ll. 1–12; *Russian Review* for permission to quote from the article, "The Russian Nobility on the Eve of the 1905 Revolution," in *Russian Review* 38 (July 1979): 323–338; *Slavic Review* for permission to quote from the article, "Portrait of an Elite: Russian Marshals of the Nobility, 1861–1917," in *Slavic Review* 40 (Winter 1981): 585–602; and Viking Penguin and Sir Charles Johnston for permission to quote from *Eugene Onegin* by Alexander Pushkin, translated by Sir Charles Johnston (1977).

Library of Congress Cataloging in Publication Data

Hamburg, Gary M.
  Politics of the Russian nobility, 1881–1905.

  Bibliography: p.
  Includes index.
  1. Soviet Union—Politics and government—1881–1894. 2. Soviet Union—Politics and government—1894–1917. 3. Soviet Union—Nobility—History.   I. Title.
DK240.H35   1984   947.08   83-3234

ISBN 0-8135-1009-0

*For Nancy and
my grandmother, Eunice Oard*

Contents

Tables

Acknowledgments

I wish to thank IREX and the administrators of the Fulbright-Hays Fellowships for funding my research in the USSR in 1975–1976; the Maybelle MacLeod Lewis Foundation for its support in 1976–1977, when the original version of this account was written; and the History Department at the University of Notre Dame for a research leave in 1981, when the final version of the manuscript was completed.

This work was read by many people who offered constructive comments: Nancy Ickler, Fredrick Pike, Samuel C. Ramer, Richard Teichgraeber, J. Robert Wegs. Special thanks are in order to Roberta Thompson Manning who read the manuscript for Rutgers Press and who has shared her expertise on the nobility with me and other scholars; to William J. Rosenberg, the second reader for Rutgers Press, whose demanding criticism led me to rethink and reshape the entire book; to Herbert Mann, the former director of Rutgers Press, who encouraged me in many ways during the completion of the book; and to Marlie Wasserman, senior editor at Rutgers Press, by whose kindness and careful reading of the manuscript I have profited greatly.

I owe a considerable debt to four Soviet scholars: P. A. Zaionchkovsky who suggested that I undertake a collective biography of the noble marshals; B. V. Anan'ich who helped me with several difficult problems in economic history and who made numerous suggestions to further my research; Iu. B. Soloviev whose books provide the first and best guide to the complexities of noble politics before 1905; and S. G. Sakharova, archivist at the Central State Historical Archive (TsGIA) in Leningrad, for her energy and skill in locating important documents.

My deepest gratitude goes to Terence Emmons, who has devoted countless hours to discussions of the nobility and whose erudition has been a vital resource to me at every stage of my research and writing.

Introduction

The last hundred years have been hard on nobility. Stephen Spender expressed the spirit of our age in his dismissal of gilded privilege. "Not palaces, an era's crown / Where the mind dwells, intrigues, rests. . . ." "It is too late for rare accumulation, / For family pride, for beauty's filtered dusts. . . ."[1] Nowhere has the century been more hostile to family tradition and wealth than in Russia. In the spring and summer of 1917 Russian peasants organized themselves, seized land owned by the nobility, and, in many cases, drove the local *barin* out of his ancestral home. The peasant revolution of 1917 was so widespread in scale, so elemental in its force, that the weak Provisional Government of Kerensky could not resist it.[2] One of the Russian Revolution's most conspicuous effects was its root-and-branch extirpation of the Russian nobility.

The simplest explanation of this rural revolution is that when central control over the provinces was rendered utterly ineffectual by the war and the February Revolution, the Russian peasants took advantage of the situation to dispossess the nobility on whose land they had long had designs. Peasants acted rationally and in faith to a vision of social utopia much like that of the Diggers in seventeenth-century England. They believed that land should be equally distributed and that social barriers should be stricken down. Land should be the property of those who tilled it. Indeed, two decades before the 1917 revolution Russian peasant egalitarianism was already so universal that many sensitive Russians anticipated the coming of a rural revolt. There is a brilliant scene in Vladimir Nabokov's

1

memoirs where Nabokov's father is called away from lunch to re-solve a grievance of local peasants. To show their gratitude for Na-bokov père's action, the peasants playfully picked him up and tossed him up and down in celebration. The family governess, "a primly pessimistic lady," watched this ritual and observed prophetically: "Un jour ils vont le laisser tomber."[3] And so, metaphorically, the peasants did in 1917.

Yet to claim that the rural revolution of 1917 was the product of peasant land hunger and hatred for the nobility is to oversimplify. In fact, the fate of the Russian nobility was sealed not so much by the breakdown of government authority and the passions of the revolutionary year, as by economic change and a long process of internal disintegration within the nobility. The Russian nobility actually lost its firm hold on landownership decades before the rev-olution. The internal cohesion of the nobility as a social formation broke down in the nineteenth century. And by the turn of the cen-tury the nobles suffered from what Lawrence Stone, in another con-text, called a "crisis of confidence"; they lacked faith in the future of their own privileges. By the first decade of the twentieth century, Nabokov remembers "the old and the new, the liberal touch and the patriarchal one, fatal poverty and fatalistic wealth got fantasti-cally interwoven."[4]

This book is an attempt to discuss what I believe to have been the crucial period in the history of the modern Russian nobility—the years from roughly 1881 to the revolution of 1905, the revolu-tion Trotsky saw as a "dress rehearsal for 1917." In this period the nobility engaged in unsuccessful economic and political competi-tion with the other social groups. Representatives of the nobility debated their place in the Russian polity but were unable to agree on a single definition of their proper position. Their economic griev-ances were brought to the government's attention, but no positive and effective responses were forthcoming. Resentment against the government and political tensions within the nobility contributed to the revolutionary upheaval in 1905 and helped shape the political and economic circumstances that lasted until 1917.

I have divided the book into three sections. Part One is an intro-duction to the nobility and politics before 1881. It explores the valid-ity of class analysis as a methodology for studying the Russian no-bility, and concludes that such a conceptual approach is seriously flawed. Much, though not all of the evidence cited in this section will be familiar to other historians. My contribution is to clear the ground of obstacles to understanding. Part Two is the heart of the book, a discussion of noble politics between 1881 and 1905. This discussion is not a comprehensive treatment of all matters affecting the Russian nobility, but rather a series of case studies designed to illuminate the nobility's response to economic and political challenge.[5] I have tried to show how complex and contradictory was this response, and how it was connected with the economic, social, and political diversity of the First Estate. Almost all of Part Two depends on archival research, firsthand examination of statistical sources, or reinterpretation of primary materials presented by other historians. The Conclusion places the history of Russian noble politics in a comparative perspective.

METHODOLOGY

One of the social historian's thorniest problems is how to divide complicated societies into groups large enough to facilitate the study of social relations, yet not so large as to preclude meaningful generalizations about individuals. Many historians, Marxist and non-Marxist, have accepted social classes as the appropriate units of analysis for these purposes. Orthodox Marxists continue to believe that an individual's public identity is best understood as a function of his relationship to the means of production, and that the historical progress of a society is best understood as the result of class antagonisms. Many non-Marxists are disposed to employ the categories of class analysis as useful, indeed indispensable labels in their work, even when they reject class struggle as the motive force in history. For these historians, class is a heuristic device that enables a scholar to impose order on an otherwise chaotic social universe.

But class analysis has not been without critics. Certain influential historians of France have been particularly outspoken in their rejection of it. Richard Cobb has flatly rejected any sociological abstraction or quantitative study that effaces from historical narratives the record of individual lives.[6] And in his massive, two-volume interpretation of France since 1848, the Oxford historian Theodore Zeldin has insisted that individuals are the proper subjects for the historian and that individuals are so complex that no single theory will explain their behavior. "Other disciplines may develop 'general theories,'" writes Zeldin, "but historians fool themselves if they try to do this. Historical analysis inescapably finds the individual the object of many different pressures and often presenting a different face to each of these; he can behave, depending on the circumstances in which he finds himself, in ways which appear contradictory, and he hardly ever becomes quite predictable."[7] Having abandoned class analysis and all general theories, Zeldin suggests that historians adopt his method of *pointillisme*, a metaphor for impressionistic depiction of societies through tiny individual dots of color.

Some Marxist scholars have also been critical of past uses of class analysis. The English historian E. P. Thompson has denied that class is purely, or even primarily, an economic category; it is, instead, a living relationship created through acts of will and shared historical experience. Thus, in Thompson's view, it would be possible for a group of workers to bear a common relationship to the means of production without constituting a class. The existence of a class presupposes deep cultural ties, even a common Weltanschauung.[8] Thompson's empirical Marxism has tended to corrode the orthodox Marxian assumption that class is a relatively straightforward phenomenon, apprehensible in economic terms. Meanwhile, the French socialist François Furet has attacked the class interpretation of the French Revolution. To most French Marxists, the French Revolution represents the triumph of the bourgeoisie over the aristocracy, of capitalism over feudalism; the French Revolution is the test case for Marxian historical sociology as well as the font of modern history. But to Furet, the origin of the French Revolution is found in a struggle within the French elite, a struggle not polarized along class lines. In a polemic against the orthodox Marxism of Albert Soboul, Furet has referred to Soboul's class interpretation of the French Revolution as a pious "revolutionary catechism" bearing little relationship to historical fact.[9] Although Furet's original intention in criticizing class analysis was to construct a more sophisticated Marxian theory of social development, he has weakened the orthodox theory of class antagonism as a motor of social change and sown doubts about how much of orthodox class analysis can be salvaged.

Quite apart from their work on specific historiographical issues, the Marxist and non-Marxist critics of class analysis have had a more general impact on historians of Western Europe. By encouraging greater precision in the use of the term "class" and demanding more attention to individual historical actors who may not fit into classes as traditionally defined, the critics have forced their fellow historians to begin rethinking the problem of social analysis. For example, Peter Stearns has confessed that social historians "toss the term class about with gay abandon" and have not been sensitive enough to complexity in social stratification.[10] Stearns's attempts to redefine class may be first steps toward a new methodological consensus.[11]

4

In light of the debate among Western Europeanists, it is time for Russian historians to reexamine the utility of class as a historical category, especially in describing the Russian nobility. There are three related problems that deserve historians' attention. First, both Western and Soviet scholars have tended to use the legal term *dvorianskoe soslovie* ("noble Estate") as a synonym for *dvoriansky klass* ("noble class").[12] This easy equation ignores a distinction made by Marx himself between *Stand* ("Estate") and *Klass*, and it is an accurate equation only if all Russians who belonged de jure to the nobility also met the historical criteria for class membership. This usage of terms requires careful scrutiny.

Second, historians have not been rigorous in defining the category of class as applied to the nobility. On the one hand, they have referred to the noble class as a unitary sociopolitical formation—as a single "ruling class" or as a social group characterized by its "parasitic essence." On the other hand, these scholars have shown a certain awareness of the social, economic, and political differentiation of the nobility. Thus, the brilliant Soviet scholar Iu. B. Soloviev has written on the same page that the nobility was "parasitic" by nature, but that "the nobility itself was not a single whole," and "the distinctions that had always characterized the landowning class became even more noticeable" after the turn of the century.[13] What is lacking in the scholarly literature is a long look at the extent of differentiation among nobles and a systematic inquiry into whether this differentiation can be reconciled with the notion of class. In this context it is also appropriate to ask whether E. P. Thompson's criterion for a class's existence—a living relationship characterized by deep historical ties or a common Weltanschauung—was fulfilled by the Russian nobility.

Third, there is as yet no agreement among scholars about the relationship of Russian nobles to the autocracy. Certain Soviet scholars have asserted that the nobility constituted Russia's ruling class until February 1917.[14] Other Soviet scholars have seen the tsarist government under Stolypin as a kind of Bonapartist regime in which the central government balanced between two unitary classes—the declining nobility and the rising bourgeoisie.[15] Some Western historians have denied that the nobility had political power at all: for them the state was an independent force emancipated from and standing above a more or less helpless society.[16] These fundamental disagreements prompted P. G. Ryndziunsky to complain in a recent article: "One is forced to state that the autocracy as a political institution has been characterized on the whole incompletely. The first item on the agenda is a comprehensive investigation of the autocracy's political profile."[17] To the extent that understanding the nobility's relationship to the state is central to an investigation of the autocracy's political profile, the obvious question to ask is whether they really did act as Russia's ruling class until 1917.

In pressing these questions, I have kept in mind J. H. Hexter's claim that historians may be divided into two camps: the "splitters" who like to point out divergences, to perceive differences, to draw distinctions, to reject systems of history; and the "lumpers" who prefer systematic histories with great logical coherence. In temperament I am a splitter, as the following pages will attest. But I also think it possible, indeed necessary, for the social historian to "lump" on occasion. Therefore, after criticizing the general theories of other historians by drawing necessary distinctions, I have offered generalizations of my own.

Jorge Luis Borges has written a magnificent story in which the narrator is lured by a half-mad poet into the cellar of a house on Garay Street in Buenos Aires; there, by lying motionless in the total darkness and fixing his eyes on the nineteenth step of the cellar stairs, the narrator saw the wondrous Aleph. The Aleph revealed to its observer the unity and diversity of the world: all the inhabitants of the earth, past and present, coexisted in the Aleph, occupying the same space without blending into each other; all the actions of the historical past and present occurred simultaneously in the Aleph, whose time was the eternal now. Having experienced the Aleph, the narrator left the cellar in a state of awe and unaccountable anger with his host, the poet. Later, in a postscript, the narrator informed his readers that he believed the Aleph of Garay Street to have been a false Aleph.

In a sense, the search of the social historian is a search for the Aleph—for a vision of social reality that portrays the whole of society while not effacing the identity of individuals. This search may be frustratingly utopian—Borges is slyly silent about that. But in any case let us hope that, like the narrator of the story, we may at least recognize a false Aleph when we see one.

PART ONE

A Prologue

She enjoys the stately orchestration
of oligarchical converse,
pride's icy calm, the combination
of ranks and ages so diverse.
—A. S. Pushkin, **Eugene Onegin,**
Canto VIII

C H A P T E R   1
The Nobility
as a Social Formation

Russian society under the old regime was divided legally into *sosloviia*, a word best translated in French as *états*, in German as *Stände*, in English as Estates. The privileged Estate in Russia was the *dvorianstvo*, or the nobility. According to the *Code of Laws of the Russian Empire*, membership in the nobility was either "a consequence of virtue" or of "having forebears who have distinguished themselves by services to the crown." In practice, one could enter the nobility by three avenues: by command of the monarch; by rising to an ennobling rank in the civil or military service; or by receiving an award, usually a medal, for long or distinguished service.[1] Thus, it should be clear that the nobility in Russia was a legally delimited social formation, membership in which conferred privilege on people from various backgrounds—military, bureaucratic, courtly, and provincial. Nobles did not necessarily share the same relationship to the means of production, or a common attitude toward the world. The Russian nobility was an Estate, not necessarily a class.

The most important legal subdivision within the nobility was that between the hereditary and nonhereditary nobility. Hereditary nobles could pass on their privileged status to all their legitimate children. Hereditary nobility could be forfeited only if an individual was found guilty of a serious crime and the Senate prescribed loss of noble status as a punishment for the offense. Nonhereditary nobility, also called personal nobility, was usually attained in the course of government service; it carried with it all privileges otherwise per-

9

taining to membership in the nobility, but it could not be conferred on one's children.

By 1897 in the fifty provinces of European Russia there were 885,754 hereditary nobles and 486,963 personal nobles.[2] The total population of the Empire in that year was roughly 93,443,000; so the nobility at the turn of the century comprised about 1.5 percent of the population.[3] The dimensions of the nobility increased rapidly in the last twenty-five years of the nineteenth century. The earlier period from the end of the Napoleonic wars until 1870 was one of relative stability for the noble population; the general trend was characterized by a slowly rising population curve punctuated by a small decline in the number of nobles from 1834 to 1850 and a sharp decline from 1863 to 1870.[4] After 1870 the noble population began to increase rapidly. The hereditary nobility increased by nearly 63 percent between 1870 and 1897, while the personal nobility grew almost 54 percent over the same period.[5]

This apparently unprecedented rapid rise in the noble population at the end of the nineteenth century is difficult to explain. Certainly part of the increase was due to the expansion of the central bureaucracy. Officials who attained the top ranks in the administration were awarded noble status. Since promotions were made on the basis of merit, thousands of commoners reached personal and hereditary noble status by official advancement. The receipt of medals also contributed to the growth of the nobility. Military men who served twenty years and earned a St. Anne ribbon of the second class automatically became hereditary nobles. Officials who served thirty-five years in the central government were automatically awarded a St. Vladimir ribbon and hereditary nobility. Between 1875 and 1896 some 37,000 individuals attained hereditary noble status through promotion or decoration.[6]

The bulk of the noble population increase must, however, have been the result of demographic expansion. Why the population increase should have been so swift at the end of the nineteenth century is puzzling, since this was a period of economic contraction, at least in the agrarian sector. Historians know too little about marriage and fertility patterns among the nobility to explain the seeming paradox of demographic expansion during an economic downturn. More investigation of this problem seems warranted.

One further complication of the noble growth pattern should be mentioned: population growth was subject to regional variations. The nine western provinces were affected significantly by the Polish rebellion of 1863 and its suppression. Noble population statistics show a precipitous drop for the years 1863 to 1870. The central industrial and central agricultural regions did not experience any significant population decreases in the second half of the nineteenth century. The statistics show a smooth progression, with the rate of population increase accelerating after 1870.

The one region in which population trends were most erratic was the Right-bank Ukraine, an area including the three provinces of Kiev, Volynia, and Podolia. Here there were forty years of relative population stability (1795–1834), followed by a period of rapid decline lasting thirty-six years (1834–1870), and then an upswing in population after 1870. The reason for this precipitate fall in the noble population in the Ukraine was that many nobles there had sympathized with the Polish rebels in 1831/32 and lost their noble status as a punishment. In the three southwestern provinces a special commission had been appointed to confirm grants of nobility; between 1845 and 1850 the commission confirmed only 581 persons in noble status, referred 22,000 claims for further study, and rejected 81,000 claims.[7]

ETHNIC AND RELIGIOUS COMPOSITION OF THE NOBILITY

In a monographic article A. P. Korelin has examined the national composition of the nobility in the Russian Empire between 1861 and 1904.[8] Korelin found that 53 percent of hereditary nobles spoke Russian as their native language. Over 28 percent spoke Polish, almost 6 percent Georgian languages, 5 percent Tatar, 3 percent Lithuanian, and 2 percent German. Almost nine out of ten Russian-speaking nobles lived in the provinces of European Russia; 4 percent lived in the Caucasus, 2 percent lived in Poland, and the rest in Siberia and Central Asia. Surprisingly, only about one-third of Polish-speaking hereditary nobles lived in Poland; almost 65 percent of them resided in the nine western provinces of Russia, an area that had been a part of the Polish cultural domain up to the middle of the seventeenth century. About three-fourths of the Turkic- and Tatar-speaking nobles lived in the Caucasus and Central Asia, and the other quarter were scattered throughout European Russia. Nearly 81 percent of personal nobles were classified as Russians, and 10 percent were Polish.[9]

The distinctiveness of national groups among the nobility was accentuated by religious affiliation. Almost all the Russian nobles who were not atheists were Russian Orthodox. Catholicism dominated among the Poles, Lutheranism was prevalent in the Baltic states, and Islam was strong in southern Russia and Central Asia. The Armenian-Gregorian faith was encountered chiefly in the southern and steppe regions.

The nobility of the Russian Empire made up an ethnic and religious mosaic, especially outside the center of the Russian state. Historians too often forget the extent to which nationality and confession could be factors in noble politics. For example, the Georgian nobility in Transcaucasia resisted the government's first attempts to impose an emancipation from serfdom similar to the one decreed in Russia itself. A Georgian noble named Kipiani argued that the Russian crown was obligated by treaty to respect the Georgian law code of Vakhtang VI which stated that the nobility had clear authority over everything the peasants had. The final emancipation settlement in Georgia was more favorable to the nobility than the settlements for other parts of the Empire.[10] Politics in the nine western provinces were especially affected by national and religious antagonisms. I have already noted that after the Polish rebellion of 1863, Polish nobles were considered "untrustworthy" by the crown. Consequently, noble institutions were not extended to these provinces, and noble marshals were appointed by the tsar rather than elected. The Noble Land Bank was not opened to farmers in the nine western provinces until after the turn of the century. Polish nobles clearly resented this economic discrimination.[11] The so-called western zemstvo crisis was one of the major turning points in Duma politics in 1909–10.[12] Moreover, traditional Catholic and Orthodox anti-Semitism was intensified by the agrarian crisis at the end of the nineteenth century, and was especially noticeable in the western region. Many right-wing factions with noble members sponsored the monarchist cause and deliberately enflamed resentment against Jews.[13] It should be remembered that one of the most rabid conservatives of the Duma period, V. M. Puriskevich, a man who showed his contempt for Russian democracy by walking into a session of the Duma with a red carnation in his fly, was a landowner from the province of Bessarabia.

There was also a special relationship between the crown and the nobility in the three Baltic provinces. It was in the Baltic states that serfdom was first abolished in the Empire. Alexander I had decreed peasant emancipation in Estland in 1811, in Courland in 1817, and in Lifland in 1819. At the time Alexander thought of the Baltic emancipations as models for the rest of the Empire and even asked Arakcheev to prepare a plan based on the Baltic experience. Nothing ever came of the Arakcheev proposal. The Baltic nobility also seemed to play a disproportionately important role in the making of government policy, and to have an inordinately high representation in the central bureaucracy. This "German influence" over policy was resented by certain Russian nobles, and it may have contributed to the strong current of antibureaucratic thought among self-styled Russian Slavophiles.

LANDOWNING, SERVICE,
AND OCCUPATION

One of the characteristics of increasingly sophisticated and complicated modern societies is that individuals derive much of their social personae and identity from their occupations. Hierarchically ordered societies, on the other hand, value birth and restrict occupational choices to a few familiar possibilities. Nineteenth-century Russian society was in the midst of a transition from the *Ständestaat* of Peter the Great, with its relatively rigid social and occupational structure, to the much more fluid and complicated society that existed under Nicholas II.

For nobles in Petrine Russia, occupation was almost an irrelevant question, because Peter devised an elaborate set of institutions to compel members of the nobility to do government service. The principle of compulsory service theoretically effaced the distinction between mere landowners and noble servitors, although in practice many nobles contrived to avoid government service or to reduce their service careers to short intervals. When Peter III abolished compulsory service in 1762, the nobility were liberated from their obligations to the state, and perhaps, as Marc Raeff has suggested, the government "declared its independence" of the nobility.[14] The 1762 emancipation certainly hastened the development of a landowning nobility divorced from the state, and it made of state service an occupational choice. However, there was never a complete break between state service and landowning, partly because it was easy for landowners working in the civil or military service to place their estates under the direction of relatives or trusted bailiffs. Moreover, there may have been something like a normative career pattern for certain well-to-do landowners which specified that postadolescent males do several years of service, then marry, and ultimately find their way back to their estates.

By the reign of Nicholas I choice of occupation, still limited mainly to service or agriculture, began to be influenced by ideological factors. The apparently tidy relationship between the government and the serfowning nobility was disrupted, first by the Decembrist uprising, and then by Nicholas's bitterly reactionary policies and his incompetent supervision of the rapidly growing bureaucratic apparatus. As Nicholas Riasanovsky put it, there was a "parting of the ways" between the government and educated society under Nicholas I. Some of the bitterness felt by the nobility was expressed by Boris Chicherin, who wrote:

> And how could I, in the political conditions of the time, be enticed by service? To become a direct tool of the government, which was repressing mercilessly every thought and all enlightenment, and which I hated for that from the bottom of my soul; to crawl slavishly up the service ladder, pleasing superiors, never expressing my convictions, often doing what seemed to me the greatest evil—such was the service perspective that opened up in front of me. I turned away from it with indignation, but there was no other solution in sight.[15]

The deep anger toward the tsar may have kept hundreds of nobles out of government employment. Late in the 1840s a report by the Ministry of Internal Affairs revealed that nearly half the nobility—122,426 persons out of 253,068—"had never been in any branch of the service."[16] Yet for all the resentment felt by some toward the government, there were other nobles willing to fill government posts. In fact, the high bureaucracy under Nicholas remained an almost exclusive preserve of wealthy serfowners. P. A. Zaionchkovsky has discovered that in 1853 fully forty of fifty-five members of the State Council, all eighteen ministers, and eighty-four of one hundred and ten senators were noble landowners. Many of these held more than one thousand serfs on their estates.[17]

By the end of the nineteenth century the Russian social structure had become more flexible than ever before, and the relationship between landowners and bureaucrats had changed dramatically. Relying on data collected in 1903, Zaionchkovsky has noted that only forty-six of eighty-three members of that year's State Council, ten of twenty-four ministers, and eighty-five of one hundred and eighty-three senators had landed estates. In addition, the dimensions of their properties were not as great as those of their predecessors under Nicholas I.[18] Thus, the control of large landowners over government—if we judge only from statistical information—seemed to be slipping. Simultaneously, more career options were opening up for educated Russian nobles. At the end of the century the nobility were more active in provincial service than before. The zemstvos now hired large staffs in agronomy, statistics, civil engineering, medicine, and other fields which earlier landed nobles would have avoided, but which were now considered worthy occupations. By the late nineteenth century what we today call the "knowledge industry" was a source of occupations for nobles and non-nobles alike. The book-publishing trade expanded rapidly from the time of Nicholas I; by midcentury it was a relatively dependable, if sometimes difficult, field of employment for the educated elite. The university professoriate and the scientific-technical intelligentsia were expanding rapidly at midcentury. In the 1860s, as Alexander Vucinich has written, more than 80 percent of the leading scientists in Russia came from the nobility, from affluent commercial families, or from the families of well-placed bureaucrats.[19] Finally, I must mention the profession of writers. Someone has said that Pushkin was the first Russian to make a living by his pen. Once he had shown the way in the first third of the century, hundreds of other Russians—including many nobles—followed his example.

What I want to stress is that by the end of the nineteenth century, choice of occupation had become so important for young nobles that it may have been more crucial to defining their identities than was the accident of birth into a privileged Estate. Of course, this very choice of occupation was, in a sense, a luxury of the wealthy, or one by-product of birth into the nobility at a time of rapid social and economic change. I am not asserting that Russia was a fully "bourgeois" or "modern" society under Nicholas II—whatever the terms "bourgeois" and "modern" may mean. I am arguing that occupational choice by the end of the nineteenth century had become a factor distinguishing one noble from another, that like economic wherewithal, occupational choice split the nobility into smaller groups, into strata. Occupation, like all the other social indices considered above, makes it difficult, if not impossible, to speak of the Russian nobility as a unified social class.

DIFFERENTIATION
OF THE NOBILITY BY WEALTH

The economic differentiation of the nobility had deep roots in the Russian past. From the fifteenth to the late eighteenth century autocrats granted hundreds of thousands of desiatins of land to loyal servitors, the wealthiest of whom possessed estates of enormous size and resources. Yet some of the descendants of these wealthy servitors were practically penniless by the middle of the nineteenth century. Respect did not automatically attach, for example, to a person named Prince Golitsyn; everything depended on whether the prince was rich or poor.

TABLE 1.1
Stratification of Noble Landownership, 1877

Size of estate	Number of owners	Percent of total	Area in 1,000 des.	Percent of total
Petty (to 100 des.)	56,551	49.3	1,924.4	2.6
Middling (101 to 1,000 des.)	44,827	39.3	16,264.7	22.4
Magnate (over 1,000 des.)	13,388	11.4	54,976.4	75.0
TOTAL	114,716	100.0	73,163.5	100.0

SOURCE: N. A. Proskuriakova, "Razmeshchenie i struktura dvorianskogo zemle-vladeniia Evropeiskoi Rossii v kontse XIX–nachale XX v.," p. 68.

The Soviet historian N. A. Proskuriakova has studied the distribution of land owned by the nobility in the second half of the nineteenth century. Her study yields a breakdown of noble landowner-ship by size of estate owned (see Table 1.1).

At the top of the economic scale were the magnates, a mere 11 percent of the number of landowners who collectively owned three-fourths of the total noble land fund. And among these thirteen thousand owners was a tiny group of landowners from 102 families, who, according to the historian Minarik, themselves held one-fifth of the privately owned land in Russia.[20] This was perhaps the same elite group about which Gogol sighed in *Dead Souls*: "Alas, fat men know better than thin men how to manage their affairs in this world." The formidable strength of the hundred families was based upon 16.2 million desiatins of agricultural and forest land concentrated in the Ural region, in central Russia, in Belorussia and the Right-bank Ukraine, but the wealth of these families was not exclusively derived from agriculture. The largest group of landowners, clustered in the Urals, owned 8.1 million desiatins of land. Part of this land was cultivated, but most was exploited by the owners who operated the enormous mining and metallurgical industries of the region.[21] In Belorussia and the Ukraine landed magnates invested much capital in sugar factories. Thirteen families had large sugar-processing plants.[22] Other families invested in the wine, flour, forestry, textile, glass, paper, machine-building, fishing, and gold-mining industries. This diversification of investments in landed and un-

TABLE 1.2

Size of Landed Estates Belonging
to Largest Landowners, 1890–1905

Size of estate	Number of estates	Percent of total	Area in 1,000 des.	Percent of total
Up to 1,000 des.	81	13.0	46.9	0.3
1,000 to 10,000 des.	301	47.9	1,222.8	7.9
10,000 to 50,000 des.	166	26.4	3,766.0	23.9
50,000 to 100,000 des.	41	6.5	2,620.4	16.6
Over 100,000 des.	39	6.2	8,079.6	51.3
TOTAL	628	100.0	15,733.7	100.0

SOURCE: L. P. Minarik, *Ekonomicheskaia kharakteristika krupneishikh zemel'nykh sobstvennikov Rossii kontsa XIX–nachala XX v.*, p. 76.

landed holdings protected the hundred families from adverse secular trends in agriculture late in the nineteenth century when the nobility faced a dangerous economic situation.

Yet if the hundred families had income from many sources and often from nonagricultural sectors, their greatest assets were still landed estates. Even the Ural magnates, who in the early nineteenth century had been content with their mining and metallurgical enterprises, showed greater interest in purely agricultural pursuits in the post-Emancipation period. While a single landowner might possess estates of varying sizes in a number of provinces, the estates owned by members of the hundred families tended to be large latifundia. The Soviet historian L. P. Minarik studied 628 estates of large landowners and concluded that just under half the total (246 estates) were latifundia of 10,000 or more desiatins (see Table 1.2). According to Minarik, eighty estates, each over 50,000 desiatins, accounted for 10.6 million desiatins of the approximately 85.9 million desiatins of privately owned land in Russia. These data illustrate the tremendous weight of the hundred families' estates compared to those of the nobility at large.

There were three reasons for the extraordinary concentration of landed resources in certain of the hundred families' holdings. The first reason was that land was originally acquired from the government in huge blocks. Although the size of these parcels diminished over time because of inheritance and sale, the estates were still substantial in the post-1861 period. For example, in 1558 and 1568

Ivan IV granted to the Stroganovs 3.8 million and 4.9 million desiatins respectively; in 1692 the Stroganov estates were unified
under Grigory Dmitrievich Stroganov. By 1902, despite some fragmentation, the Perm estates of Sergei Alexandrovich Stroganov still
encompassed 1.1 million desiatins.[23] A second reason for estate concentration was legislation that permitted the creation of entailed
manors, so-called *maioraty*. The Statute on Entailed Inherited Estates,
promulgated on 16 July 1845, permitted estate owners to found
permanently entailed estates if they had a parcel of land between
10,000 and 100,000 desiatins or an average annual income from an
estate of not less than 12,000 and not more than 200,000 rubles.
These estates could not be sold for debts, and, in the case of huge
unpaid obligations on the death of the *maiorat* owner, the state
treasury would assume the estate obligations. At the end of the
nineteenth century there were 153 estates, encompassing 3,338,875
desiatins, registered as *maioraty*.[24] Other legislation permitted large
estate owners to borrow at special rates from the Noble Land Bank,
to borrow directly from the treasury, to pay low land taxes.[25] A third
reason for the high concentration of land among the hundred families was that the great prestige and economic might of the families
facilitated strategic *mariages de convenance*. A magnate wanting to
round out his estate could often do so through matrimony.

At the other extreme of the economic continuum were poor nobles
who had to scrounge a living from scarce resources. These impoverished nobles were often uneducated and illiterate. In 1767 Russian
nobles submitted more than one hundred *nakazy*, or instructions, to
the Legislative Commission convened by Catherine II. After a careful examination of the *nakazy*, one historian has concluded that 160
out of 951 signatories (or one in six) were illiterate.[26] Several of the
1767 *nakazy* complained about the abject poverty in which poor nobles lived, and listed various duties and taxes that were difficult
to pay.

The rate of illiteracy stayed high in the nineteenth century among
this stratum of the nobility, and many noble families stayed poor.[27]
Richard Pipes has argued that "the great majority of imperial *dvoriane*
remained destitute. Their incomes were so small they could not
educate their children or afford any of the amenities associated with
the aristocratic life to which they now began to aspire."[28] Pipes's argument is confirmed by several sources. On the eve of the emancipation 44 percent of serfowners had less than twenty-one souls (male
serfs); this group of petty owners held only 3 percent of all the
souls in Russia. Economic historians usually argue that serfowning
was not really profitable unless the owner held at least fifty souls.

Thus, by this crude accounting virtually half of the serfowning nobility before 1861 lived in a state approaching poverty. A government report submitted to Nicholas I in 1843 found that 9,287 descendants of hereditary gentry families in five provinces (Smolensk, Riazan', Simbirsk, Kaluga, and Vologda) had little land, no serfs, and a style of life "virtually indistinguishable from the peasantry."[29] A final confirmation of Pipes's argument may be found in *Dead Souls* in Gogol's amusing caricatures of down-and-out nobles, like Korobochka and Pliushkin. Although one should be chary of treating *Dead Souls* as a sociological source, its comedy would surely have been lost on contemporary readers if Gogol's descriptions of different types of nobles did not roughly correspond to recognizable social types. There is certainly no reason to assume that the deplorable condition of these petty nobles changed after the emancipation; in fact, the loss of the little serf labor once available to this stratum of nobles and the increased competitive demands of post-emancipation agriculture only made their situations worse.[30]

Some historians believe that the most important stratum in the nineteenth-century nobility may have been the middling nobility, or gentry—roughly 40 percent of landowners who held over 22 percent of the privately owned land in Russia in 1877. These were people who lived well enough to support themselves in comfort, to educate their children, and to participate in cultural and public affairs. Indeed, Pipes has asserted that Russian culture is to a very large extent the product of this group.[31]

It is true that noble politics in the late nineteenth century was a province in which this stratum of nobility made a very significant contribution. Zemstvo institutions and noble assemblies were dominated numerically by representatives of the gentry, even if the leaders of these institutions were often drawn from what Proskuriakova would classify as the magnates. The agricultural depression of the 1880s and 1890s certainly stimulated the gentry to increased political activity, although this political activity, as we shall see later, was not very well organized or coordinated.

It should be noted that by Proskuriakova's reckoning, the middling and petty nobility were most important economically in the central blacksoil, central industrial, Left-bank Ukraine, and Lithuanian regions. These groups owned from one-third (Left-bank Ukraine) to one-half (central blacksoil) of all noble lands in their regions. The middle and petty nobility were least important economically in the Baltic, Ural, and southeast regions. Thus, differentiation of the nobility into strata was not uniform throughout Russia, but was, to a certain extent, a regional phenomenon.[32]

19

A thinker in a desert mission,
he changed the corvée of tradition
into a small quit-rent, and got
his serfs rejoicing at their lot.
But, in a fearless huff, his thrifty
neighbor was sure, from this would flow
consequences of hideous woe;
another's grin was sly and shifty,
but all concurred that, truth to speak,
he was a menace and a freak.
—A. S. Pushkin, **Eugene Onegin,**
Canto II

C H A P T E R   2
Land and Economy

As a social formation the Russian nobility lacked coherence. They were ethnically and religiously diversified, divided by occupational allegiances, and stratified by income and extent of landownership. But did they still constitute a class because of their common relationship to the means of production? Did the nobility's activity as estate owners, producers of agricultural commodities, and exploiters of the peasantry make them a unified class despite their social diversity?

There is a strong case for viewing the pre-emancipation nobility as an economically united class. After all, since the 1785 charter on the nobility, one of the privileges of Russian nobles had been the ownership of "populated lands"—that is, lands on which serfs lived. Moreover, the nobility had a virtual monopoly on serfownership; after 1762 when Peter III prohibited the purchase of serfs by merchants for employment in factories, and excepting the brief period from 1798 to 1816 when this prohibition temporarily lapsed, nobles exclusively controlled the destinies of Russian peasants, and they alone profited from serf labor. Of course, not all nobles were serfowners in fact, but they could become serfowners if they had the will and resources to do so. And even those who preferred to work in the government rather than on the land might be seen as tacit supporters and beneficiaries of serfdom; clearly, serfdom could not continue without the approval of the government, and without the sanction of most noble bureaucrats within the government. Since the existence of serfdom was arguably the most important fact of Russian life before 1861, one might be inclined to regard the nobility's privileged status before the emancipation as sufficient evidence that they did constitute a class.

The case for viewing the pre-emancipation nobility as a class demands that we ignore or consider of secondary importance the obvious distinctions in wealth of the serfowning nobility. It also requires that we disregard the ways in which the serf economy operated in various regions of Russia. For example, if we accept the class interpretation, we must think of southern estate owners who required three days a week of compulsory labor from their serfs as essentially like northern estate owners who required money dues that might be earned through handicrafts or work outside the estate in an industrial town. What is important in the class interpretation is the exploitative nexus between seigneur and serf, not the form of dues paying, the nature of seigneurial work supervision, the relative cruelty or benevolence of the owner—all factors which varied from estate to estate, and to a certain extent, from region to region in Russia. Whether we agree or disagree with the class interpretation, careful study of the pre-1861 nobility demonstrates, in Daniel Field's words, that "the nobility was a coherent whole only in that almost every nobleman benefited, or believed that he benefited, from the exploitation of servile labor."[1]

Yet if a dominant position in the serf system was the only thing that made the pre-emancipation nobility coherent, what united nobles after the abolition of serfdom? This question can be answered only if we analyze the impact of the emancipation on the nobility and comment on their commercial activity in the first decades after the end of serfdom.

Post-emancipation Land Settlements and Agriculture

A century ago the English journalist Donald Mackenzie Wallace visited the estates of Russian landowners in order to discover how the nobility lived and how they had reacted to the end of serfdom. Wallace had no difficulty being admitted to high society. "Of all the foreign countries in which I have traveled," he wrote, "Russia certainly bears the palm in the matter of hospitality. Every spring I found myself in the possession of a large number of invitations from landed proprietors in different parts of the country—far more than I could possibly accept—and a great part of the summer was generally spent in wandering about from one country house to another."[2] Wallace was perhaps uniquely favored with the chance to gather eyewitness testimony on the impact of the emancipation, and he took advantage of his opportunity to write brilliant portraits of his noble acquaintances. But Wallace did not succeed at first in drawing any firm conclusions from his observations: "After roaming around the country for five years (1870–1875) collecting information from the best available sources, I hesitated to draw any conclusions, and my state of mind at the time was naturally reflected in the early editions of this work [*Russia*]."[3] Although Wallace attributed his initial confusion to the unreliability of economic record-keeping before 1861 and to the biases of his informants, one suspects that the very complexity of the agricultural situation after 1861 made confident generalization almost impossible for him.

If Wallace, with all his acuity, was puzzled by the situation of the nobility after the emancipation—indeed, overwhelmed by its complications—we should not expect the situation to appear much simpler after a century of historical research. Maybe the best way to sort out the thorny problems of noble agriculture is to analyze the emancipation's impact in general terms and then to focus on the nobility in particular regions of Russia.

The immediate problem presented by the emancipation was how the former seigneury would be divided among newly liberated serfs and noble landowners. This difficulty was partly resolved by the emancipation legislation itself which fixed the maximum, or "prescribed," allotments to be given to peasants. In cases where the peasantry had tilled less than one-third of the maximum allotment before 1861, landowners were obliged to increase the peasants' holdings to at least one-third of the maximum allotment. If, before 1861, peasants had tilled allotments greater than the maximum allotments, then nobles could cut the peasants' permanent allotments to the size of the maximum allotment fixed by law. In general, if peasant allotments fell within the statutory maxima and minima, then their pre-emancipation allotments were to be regarded as permanent allotments. These general guidelines functioned subject to several exceptions. If peasant allotments before 1861 were collectively more than twice as large as the demesne, then nobles could increase their demesne to one-third the total size of the estate, regardless of how this affected the peasants' allotments. In steppe areas, nobles could increase their holdings to one-half the total size of the pre-emancipation estate.[4] Nobles were also allowed to keep woods, most meadowlands, and waterways.

One result of the emancipation was a net decrease of 4.1 percent in the amount of land tilled by the peasantry after 1861.[5] Another result was bitterness among the peasants over land settlements that, on balance, seemed to favor the nobility. This bitterness was reflected in the more than six hundred peasant disorders that occurred in the first four months after the announcement of the emancipation; in nearly five hundred cases, soldiers were required to suppress riotous peasants.[6] The emancipation agreement seemed so obviously unfair and the bloody suppression of peasants so unjust that Alexander Herzen, regarded in 1861 as the conscience of Russian society, published the initial reports of peasant uprisings in his London-based newspaper almost without editorial comment.[7]

One should not suppose that the land settlements were equally favorable to nobles throughout the Empire, nor that divisions of old estates proceeded everywhere according to identical principles. In the western and Right-bank Ukrainian provinces where Polish opponents of tsarism had found support among the predominantly Polish nobility, the government changed the terms of the emancipation to favor the peasantry. The architect of the change, Minister of Internal Affairs P. A. Valuev, wrote that "in such circumstances there is only one option: by the granting of new concessions [*l'got*] to solidify behind ourselves the rural population of the northwestern provinces which has heretofore believed in and been so loyal to the government."[8] Thus, in the five provinces of Kov'no, Vil'no, Grodno, Minsk, and Vitebsk, the peasants' allotments were increased by over 750,000 desiatins, or 24 percent.[9] In Kiev, Volynia, and Podolia the increase in peasant allotments was 18 percent.[10] This enormous increase in the land peasants tilled for their own use was the economic price that the western nobility paid for disloyalty in 1863/64.

In the provinces of the central nonblacksoil area, peasants also received frequent allotments equal to or even exceeding the "maximum" allotment prescribed by law. For example, in El'ninsk district, Smolensk province, 92 percent of peasants received allotments equal to or greater than the allotment maximum. Of course, the land received was usually of inferior quality, and landowners in the nonblacksoil provinces counted on other forms of reimbursement from the peasantry than use of peasant land cutoffs [*otrezki*].[11] Meanwhile, in the fertile blacksoil provinces of the central agricultural region and in southern provinces from Ekaterinoslav to Samara, the reduction in land allotted to peasants was more than 25 percent of the pre-emancipation total.[12] Thus, measured in terms of net land allotted to peasants, the nobility of central and southern Russia were the beneficiaries of the emancipation, while the nobility in the western provinces were losers.

Even within these regions there were wide variations in the principles on which nobles divided their estates. Some nobles who were interested in farming grain attempted to create consolidated estates on which arable might easily be tilled. Consolidation of seigneurial land required not only a redrawing of boundaries on arable land, but frequently the moving of entire villages. The historian D. I. Budaev counted 427 villages moved in Smolensk province alone— 222 of them against the peasants' wills.[13] But consolidation was not the only guiding principle in land settlements. Other nobles tried to draw land boundaries in such a way that their own lands would surround, or interlard, peasant lands. These nobles hoped to force peasants to pay fees for use and transit rights. As the populist agronomist A. N. Engel'gardt noted: "In evaluating the estate they [*pomeshchiki*] look not at the quality of land, not at the tools, but at how land is situated in relation to adjoining villages: does it support them; is it necessary for the peasants; can they [the peasants] get along without it or not."[14] For example, in Volokolamsk district, Moscow province, peasants complained that the landowner Liasvotovich "divided allotments in such a way that all land is surrounded from three sides by his land, so that from all sides we will always have problems with pasturing cattle and with other inconveniences. For the village Putiatina he made an allotment with mixed boundaries [*nadel cherespolosny*], land inside ours he gave to himself, and to us he gave the lands outside it, so that we have to cross his land to get to ours. . . ."[15]

Two points deserve emphasis here. First, land settlements differed so much from region to region, indeed within individual provinces, as to constitute a new factor dividing the nobility or, at the very least, making simple descriptions of the nobility after 1861 impossible. Second, land settlements that appeared favorable to the nobility in 1861 would later seem shortsighted, even unfavorable. Nobles who drew allotments with mixed boundaries in order to increase income in the short run would find that *cherespolosnost'* was a barrier to efficient agriculture and a source of serious peasant grievances.[16]

The fixing of new estate boundaries was only part of the overall land settlement outlined in the 1861 emancipation charter. From the noble point of view, compensation for the loss of former lands was equally significant. For the short term the government guaranteed landowners' incomes by requiring peasants to acquit old *barshchina* (labor) and *obrok* (money or in kind) obligations for allotments; this was tantamount to the continuation of serfdom. These obligations were to be met until the conclusion of so-called "redemption agreements" on allotted lands whereby peasants would pay off, or "redeem," lands granted to them under the emancipation. Transfer to redemption was not obligatory under the 1861 law, but it could occur under two circumstances: first, peasants could reach voluntary agreements with landowners to transfer allotments to redemption; or second, the landowner could demand the beginning of redemption. In the former instance the landowner would receive a capital payment equal to his yearly *obrok* payment multiplied by 16 2/3; the government paid (as a loan to the peasant) between three-fourths and four-fifths of this land compensation to the *pomeshchik*, and peasants paid the balance. In the latter instance the landowner received compensation from the government, but forfeited additional capital from the peasants. In both cases the peasants were to redeem their loans by paying back the treasury over a period of forty-nine years.

In general, the transfer of peasants to redemption was accomplished rapidly since landowners were eager to receive monetary reimbursement for the land allotted to the peasants. But the transfer was not popular everywhere; in the nonblacksoil provinces of central Russia the rate of transfer to redemption payments lagged behind the national average. Apparently certain landowners preferred, whether for economic or social and psychological reasons, that their peasants remain temporarily obligated to them—that is, that serfdom continue. For whatever reason, in 1881, twenty years after the emancipation, there were 837,500 souls who still lived in states of temporary obligation to the nobility. Throughout the spring of 1881 the government debated what to do about these "temporarily obligated" souls, and finally, after repeated urging from Finance Minister Abaza, the government declared all peasants must be transferred to redemption by 1 January 1883.[17]

Transfer to redemption brought the nobility a huge financial windfall. Because of the way that redemptions were computed, payments substantially exceeded the free-market value of the land. In the blacksoil provinces of central and southern Russia net allotment redemption value exceeded the net sale value of allotment lands by 123 million rubles; in the nonblacksoil provinces of the center and north the excess value of compensation to the nobility over free-market prices of allotment land was 187 million rubles. Only in the western provinces were allotment values approximately equal to the free-market prices of land.[18]

The strange thing about this windfall was how quickly the money seemed to disappear and how angrily some nobles complained about it. The complaints can be explained by three factors. First, the government deducted the nobility's pre-emancipation mortgage debt from their total compensation. In 1881 the noble debt equaled over 300 million rubles, while the compensation for peasant allotments was 750 million rubles. Thus, 40 percent of the nominal value of the land ceded to peasants was applied to debt cancellation. Second, the government did not pay the nobility in cash, but rather in redemption bonds. The idea behind the government's issuance of bonds was that nobles would hold their assets for long periods in securities and that the value of these securities would remain stable, or even rise, because of the anticipated slow turnover. The government's plan was not very perspicacious: one might have predicted that nobles would rush to convert bonds to cash and that this rush to cash in bonds would drive down the real value of the bonds. In fact, the redemption bond market was very damaging for the nobility. It proved not only very unstable, but at one point a flooded market meant bonds could be cashed only at a loss of 30 percent in nominal value.[19]

The third reason for complaints about redemption had nothing to do with the mechanics of payment, rather it was connected to the undeveloped state of the rural economy. Before 1859 nobles who wished to mortgage their serfs could apply to the State Loan Bank, but this institution closed in 1859 because of the coming emancipation. There was at the time no other reliable land mortgage bank in Russia. In the 1860s and 1870s a handful of new banks were founded to provide agricultural credit: the Kherson Land Bank (1864), the Mutual Land Credit Society (1866), and eleven joint stock banks (1871–1872). With one exception these banks operated at a strictly local or provincial level so that most nobles in the 1860s and 1870s had no solid sources of credit at all. Furthermore, because of the high demand for loans and the absence of competition from other banks, these banks could command high interest rates. The absence of a credit network in the years after the emancipation doubtless accounts in part for many complaints from the nobility about the amount of redemption compensation received from the government.

After land boundaries had been redrawn and redemption payments had commenced, there remained yet another problem for noble landowners: what to do with their estates and how to treat the now-liberated peasantry. In a sense, this was the most complicated and significant problem presented by the new era. The government guided and, to a limited extent, oversaw both land settlements and monetary compensation; these two problems were bureaucratically manageable. The government could not manage noble lands, however, once the emancipation's terms had been fulfilled, nor could the government interfere in the quotidian relationships among landlords and peasants, except, of course, to enforce criminal law. Yet the sum of decisions about how to run estates and how to treat local peasants could literally determine the fate of rural Russia. And it was in this realm that the discretionary authority of *pomeshchiki* was widest.

The response of many *pomeshchiki*, faced for the first time with the necessity to run estates without serf labor, was to sell their lands. In the late 1870s the Mutual Land Credit Society, the only land bank in Russia with a national clientele, announced in newspapers all over the country a public sale of 2,000 estates.[20] This announcement caught the eye of Tambov journalist S. N. Terpigoriev who resolved to investigate the reasons for the auction. In his amusing account *Oskudenie (Impoverishment)* Terpigoriev contended that the nobility under serfdom had never thought seriously about farming at all, and thus could hardly have been expected to devise new farming techniques after the emancipation. "Remembering those days, one has to admit the undoubted fact that *pomeshchiki* were occupied to a much greater extent with the preservation of their stomachs, and even with their personal rights and prerogatives [*preimushchestva*] than with the economic side of the reforms. . . . It strikes me that this was because at that time there was no farming in the sense that farming is now understood, even here in this country. Yes, there was no farming. There was an insane waste of animal and human labor, almost for no return, without any accounting, without any theory, without any system, to say nothing of any scientific preparation, or the application of any scientific laws."[21] Terpigoriev also complained about the spirit in which the nobility received word of the emancipation and adapted themselves to it. Initial fear of revolution after the announcement that the government had decided to emancipate the serfs was displaced by spiteful pettiness toward the peasants in drawing new land boundaries, then by the utopian hope that one's male heir, if properly and expensively educated, could put right the new estate. All the while, as nobles tried to adjust to new conditions, they spent money recklessly—on furtive pleasures, on bribing officials, on new homes in provincial capitals. Thus, redemption money was quickly spent, nobles found themselves again in debt or desirous of credit, and, meanwhile, nothing substantive had been done to make the new estate a profitable economic operation. The solution to this "hopeless" situation was to auction the estate.[22]

Terpigoriev's attempt to explain estate sales in the 1860s and 1870s as a function of the nobility's moral weaknesses and ignorance of farming sounds exaggerated to the modern ear, but other contemporary observers of rural life offered similar explanations. In his *Pis'ma o provintsii* (*Provincial Sketches*) Saltykov-Shchedrin contended that three of the crucial barriers to rural progress were: the ignorance of the old nobility; their irrational negative attitude toward the emancipation; and parasitism—the custom of living off present labor. These vices were accompanied by habits of frivolous spending and conspicuous consumption that drained the purses of the old nobility.[23] One should also remember Lev Tolstoy's portrait of Stiva Oblonsky in *Anna Karenina*. Oblonsky was embarrassed not only by his adulteries, but by massive debts piled up at the English Club and other social haunts. He decided to sell a forest on his wife's lands to discharge these debts. Oblonsky was more than a fictional creation; in post-emancipation Russia he was a social type frequently encountered in the salons of Petersburg and Moscow.

Thus, one of the results of the emancipation was the free choice of many nobles, ignorant of agriculture and accustomed to carefree spending, to sell their estates. By 1877/78, when the government surveyed landownership in the Empire, the nobility owned only 73.2 million desiatins of land. Peasants had purchased more than 5 million desiatins to supplement their allotments, while merchants and burghers owned 11.7 million desiatins.[24]

Yet nobles who sold their entire estates were a minority. Most members of the landed elite chose to cultivate their lands in one of a variety of ways. The boldest course was to make a complete break with the past by imposing "rational" farming practices on one's estate. Rational farming, in the parlance of the 1860s, meant the introduction of sophisticated crop rotation schemes and modern machinery. Rational agriculture was much criticized in literature and popular journalism because many of the techniques and machines being introduced by the nobility had been borrowed from foreign nations and not properly adapted to Russian conditions. Terpigoriev, for instance, reported a Tambov noble who spent his redemption money on expensive foreign equipment that proved completely impractical in Russia.[25] Wallace also described this kind of not too farsighted landowner in his *Russia*. Wallace's Victor Alexandr'ich bought German ploughs that were too heavy to be pulled by small

Russian horses. "These may be very well for the Germans, but they won't do for us," the peasants remarked.[26] We should not think, however, that these examples of noble improvidence typified those who wished to introduce scientific farming in Russia.[27] Many estates, particularly in southern Russia, were successfully converted, in whole or in part, to mechanized agriculture. These estates included those with large-scale sugar beet refineries, distilleries, and potato mills; there were also smaller-scale operations devoted to the mechanical cultivation and export of wheat. As one might have expected, farming machinery became more rather than less popular with time. Liashchenko noted that the number of Russian factories producing farm equipment increased from 52 in 1862 to 340 factories in 1879. If we add the value of imported equipment to that of domestic machinery, the farm equipment business grossed over 7 million rubles by 1880.[28]

Yet far into the twentieth century most agricultural labor in Russia was done not by machines, but by men, women, and draft animals. One of the ways animate power could be employed on an estate was the hiring of laborers on the free market and the provision to these laborers of farming tools and draft animals. Because the hiring of laborers and the fixing of wages occurred in the free market, Soviet historians think of this kind of land cultivation as "progressive" and capitalistic, although it is difficult to see anything very progressive about conditions of employment. On one estate in the 1870s workers were recruited from all over Russia to work from May to the fall harvest, a period of four and one-half months. Wages were as little as seventeen rubles for the whole growing season in which stewards sometimes forced laborers to work as many as sixteen hours a day. Contemporary testimony suggests that the work was in some ways just as trying as serf labor: overseers could treat summer laborers almost as arbitrarily as they had serfs, and there was evidently the same kind of sexual exploitation of female workers by overseers that had occurred with female serfs and bailiffs before 1861.[29]

Low wages and difficult working conditions perhaps account in part for high turnover in the work force and for problems in recruiting necessary labor from year to year. Indeed, the largest problem with hired labor from the noble perspective was the comparative shortage in labor supply in the 1860s and 1870s. Statistics on the number of peasants given passports for periods of more than one year suggest that the agricultural labor market was miniscule in the 1860s compared to the 1890s.[30] In the early 1870s there were complaints by nobles to the Valuev Commission about shortages of labor and uncertainty in the labor market.[31] Despite the difficulties with hiring labor, many nobles preferred wage labor to other arrangements. Once a harvest was over, landowners no longer had to maintain any relationships with their workers. The work relationship became, to a certain degree, depersonalized, and laborers were transformed, in the landowner's eyes, into commodities.

Both "rational" mechanized agriculture and the free-market hired labor system required landowners to radically change their approaches to cultivating land. But there were other means of tilling the soil than these—namely, the various systems of land renting— which were closer to land tenure as practiced under serfdom. One of the most common forms of land rent was sharecropping, in which the landowner permitted peasants to cultivate his lands in exchange for a portion of the crop harvested. Sharecropping was usually regulated by short-term contracts which gave the peasants the right to half the total harvest on a *pomeshchik*'s land (*ispol'naia sistema; arenda ispolu*) or even a lesser fraction. Another common type of rent was called *otrabotka*, or labor service, under which landowners leased land in return for peasant cultivation of the landowner's estate with peasant tools. The type of rent least onerous for the peasants (but probably least common immediately after the emancipation) was simple money rent—a lease of land for a flat fee per desiatin.

In his book *The Development of Capitalism in Russia*, Lenin argued that both sharecropping and *otrabotka* resembled *barshchina*, or work dues paid under serfdom, because the peasant had to discharge labor duties for the landowner in return for the privilege of cultivating land for an income. In theory, sharecropping and *otrabotka* differed from work dues because they were relationships entered into freely by peasants and were governed by written contracts; in practice, however, peasants were often compelled by the small and inferior allotments given them after the emancipation, or by the natural growth of their families, to enter into these contracts. Contemporaries seem to have been well aware of how closely these arrangements resembled *barshchina*. One correspondent for the Department of Agriculture noted that in Orel province "ex-serfs continue to rent land from their former landlords, and in return till the landowners' land. Such villages continue to bear the name of '*barshchina*' of such-and-such landlord."[32] Money rents can be said to resemble *obrok* payments by a similar logic.

Land rent in its main variants was appealing to noble landowners for many reasons: it imposed no radical changes on the actual operation of the estate because the use of labor was so similar to that under serfdom; it required virtually no capital investment on the noble's part; it guaranteed a return in money or in kind (unless there was a complete crop failure), and virtually all of this return was profit. These advantages were all short-term advantages of great magnitude—just the kind that would appeal to nobles who were hardpressed for cash, rather unimaginative and unenterprising. The disadvantages of land rent were mostly long-term: every negotiation over the terms of rent raised tensions between the landlord and local peasants; the system of production was static and, therefore, would mean that well-run scientific farms had a growing competitive edge.

It is impossible to determine from existing statistical sources exactly how many estates employed land rent and how many hired laborers only. It is even unclear whether the amount of rented land grew after 1877. The only thing that existing sources enable us to say with certainty is that rent was quite widely used. According to data on estates mortgaged to the Noble Land Bank between 1886 and 1890, Liashchenko has calculated that 39 percent of estates had leases on a sharecropping basis, 40 percent were run by landowners themselves (presumably with hired labor), while 21 percent of estates had a mixture of the two systems.[33] Other scholars who have investigated rent from the peasant perspective calculate that at the end of the century peasants rented between 10 million and 50 million desiatins; the best American scholar, Geroid Tanquary Robinson, believed that the peasants rented about 19.5 million desiatins in 1900, whereas the most recent Soviet scholar to write on the issue, A. M. Anfimov, accepted a range between 32 and 37 million desiatins.[34]

THE EMANCIPATION'S REGIONAL IMPACT

In the first part of this discussion I treated the general complexities of the emancipation's impact on the nobility and mentioned regional distinctions only in passing. It should be emphasized, however, that the post-emancipation rural economy can be understood accurately only if these regional differences are clearly outlined. The Soviet historian N. M. Druzhinin recently proposed that Russian agricultural activity following the end of serfdom had different characteristics in four broad regions or zones.[35] Druzhinin's description can be taken as the basis for a discussion of the phenomenon of regional noble differentiation in the economic sphere.

The first zone described by Druzhinin was the nonblacksoil area, including provinces of the central industrial region (Moscow, Kostroma, Iaroslavl', Tver', Kaluga, Vladimir, Nizhny Novgorod, plus the northern districts of Riazan'), the northwest (Petersburg, Novgorod, Pskov), and the northern province Vologda. Although this zone included both capital cities, Moscow and Petersburg, and much of Russia's nascent industrial capacity, it was not a thriving region in rural areas. In the north and northwest barely 14 percent of the soil was arable, the rest being covered with forests (49 percent), meadows and pastures (14 percent), and marshes or wasteland. In the central industrial region about 35 percent of the soil was arable, and 40 percent was forested.[36] Throughout the zone soils were relatively unproductive unless heavily fertilized and carefully drained—both expensive operations rarely undertaken on noble estates. Most estates in the zone were farmed on some kind of rent basis, usually on sharecropping or labor-service arrangements. Hired labor in agriculture was infrequently encountered because the existing surplus peasant population was drawn heavily into industry and nobles could not match wages paid at large urban factories.[37] Few estates in the zone were mechanized.

A recent study of agricultural production in nineteenth-century Russia demonstrated that grain grown in this zone was not sufficient to feed the indigenous population. The northern and northwestern provinces had large grain deficits in the 1860s and 1870s, while the central industrial provinces had a small surplus in the 1860s (not enough to make up for the deficits in the north and the northwest) and a substantial average deficit in the 1870s.[38]

Given the general poverty of the zone, its backward farming techniques and poor grain production, we should not be surprised to find that noble land here was rapidly sold to peasants and merchants. By 1877 about 29 percent of noble land in the central industrial region and 17 percent in the north had been sold to other *sosloviia*, the highest percentages of sale anywhere in Russia.[39] In that year noble land in the nonblacksoil zone constituted 19.7 percent of the national noble land fund in area, but only 13.9 percent of the total in value.[40] It is no wonder that Druzhinin's word for the nobility's agriculture activity in this first zone was "joyless" [*bezradostnaia*].

Druzhinin's second zone comprised most of the blacksoil belt, including provinces of the central agricultural region (Orel, Kursk, Tambov, Voronezh, Tula, and the southern districts of Riazan'), the Mid-Volga (Kazan', Simbirsk, Saratov, Penza), and Left-bank Ukraine (Poltava, Khar'kov, Chernigov). This zone constituted an agricultural unit because the relatively favorable soil and climatic conditions had made it the breadbasket of pre-emancipation Russia. The central agricultural provinces were almost exclusively rural, and two-thirds of their total area was arable. The Left-bank Ukraine was also rural and highly cultivated. In both areas pasture, meadowland, and forests were fast disappearing under the plough. In the Mid-Volga provinces slightly over half the land was arable, and there was a larger forest area than elsewhere in the zone—about 25 percent of these provinces was wooded.[41]

Despite, or perhaps because of, the relatively favorable natural conditions, agriculture in this zone did not quickly adopt the most modern techniques and machinery. The nobility had done well in the past with the traditional three-field system of crop rotation, and soil in most of the zone was still fertile enough so as not to require constant fertilization. In the central agricultural provinces the nobility had succeeded in retaining their pre-emancipation arable and had reduced peasant allotments by 25 percent. This achievement was a blessing for the nobility, but also a curse because the poor peasants in the region were torn between work for the local nobility on the rent system and leaving the region to work for higher wages in New Russia and the south. In the 1860s the average yearly wage of a peasant working in the central agricultural provinces was between thirty and sixty rubles, whereas a peasant could make between sixty and ninety rubles in the south. Thus, one of the biggest problems for *pomeshchiki* here was finding enough workers to cultivate the land.[42]

In the Left-bank Ukraine most noble estates were farmed by local peasants on a sharecropping or *otrabotka* basis, and the three-field system also continued there. One of the few districts where more advanced techniques of agriculture were practiced was Konstantinograd district in Poltava province, the site of a large peasant uprising in 1902. Konstantinograd district employed large numbers of hired workers along with local peasants working on *otrabotka*.[43] Through most of the Left-bank Ukraine shortages of manpower were not a serious problem in agriculture because the local population was dense enough to compensate for peasants who left for better jobs in the cities or the south.

The Mid-Volga provinces were different from the central agricultural and Left-bank Ukrainian provinces. The climate in the Mid-Volga was unsuited to stable agriculture; rainfall was uneven, and the whole area, especially Saratov, suffered from periodic drought. Indeed, climatic conditions here combined with other factors to produce a devastating famine in 1891/92. However, much of the soil in the Mid-Volga was practically virgin land, and its incredible fertility almost made up for climatic shortcomings. As in other blacksoil provinces, estates in the Mid-Volga were farmed mostly by peasants on money rent or sharecropping bases, and the prevailing crop rotation was on the three-field system.

Grains were the money crops through most of the blacksoil zone, and generally provinces in this zone produced large surpluses for the national and international markets. The central agricultural provinces produced the biggest net surpluses of any region in Russia in the 1860s and 1870s, and the Mid-Volga provinces also did well despite periodic shortfalls. The Left-bank Ukraine suffered a small net grain deficit during the 1860s, but had recovered by the 1870s when it showed an impressive surplus.[44] In much of the blacksoil zone wheats of lower quality were grown for the internal market and export; these wheats had high seed-yield ratios compared to other grains, and good prices could be gotten on the London exchange. Rye continued to be the major grain of the zone. By the 1870s potatoes were being grown more often in the central agricultural provinces, but the total land area farmed with potatoes was less than 4 percent of the arable land.[45]

The economic activity of the nobility made an important contribution to the rural economy of the entire blacksoil zone. In his study of harvests, Nifontov reported that in the central agricultural provinces, noble land accounted for 27.6 percent of the total grain produced in the 1860s and 33.9 percent of the total in the 1870s. In the Left-bank Ukraine the noble contribution to the total harvest was 35.4 percent in the 1860s and an average of 37.3 percent in the 1870s. High productivity made estates in this zone quite valuable.[46] Collectively, estates in this region constituted 24 percent of the nobility's total land fund by area, and 43 percent of its monetary value. The high productivity and economic strength of the nobility in the blacksoil zone were reflected in the comparatively low percentages of nobles' land sold to commoners before 1877. Only 12 percent of the noble land fund in the central agricultural provinces and barely 10 percent in the Left-bank Ukraine was sold to members of other *sosloviia*.[47] The real dangers for the nobility in the blacksoil zone were all long-run: the growing problem of soil depletion in the central agricultural region and frequent droughts in the Mid-Volga provinces; the potential problem of indebtedness to private land banks (six of the eleven private land banks founded after the emancipation operated in this region); the problem of worker shortages in the central agricultural region; and social antagonisms between nobles and peasants. At the end of Alexander II's reign all these problems seemed manageable, and the nobility appeared relatively secure.

Druzhinin's third zone was the southern steppes, comprising the provinces of New Russia (Kherson, Tauride, and Ekaterinoslav), the Don Oblast', and the Lower Volga Basin (Samara and Ufa). The southern steppes possessed much rich soil, a warm climate, and proximity to southern ports—all advantages in the production and marketing of grain. However, the southern steppes had two fundamental problems as a producing region. The first was a susceptibility to severe drought, especially in the Lower Volga Basin. A famous casualty of drought in this area was Lev Tolstoy, who in 1871 bought an estate in Samara province. Tolstoy lost 20,000 rubles in his first two years farming the estate. Then in 1873 the whole area was hit by drought-caused famine, during which Tolstoy engaged in relief work. In 1874, according to Tolstoy's own account, "there was a very abundant harvest throughout the whole Samara province, and, as far as I know, the only place in the whole Samara province that was missed by rains was my estate, and I had again sowed a big area and again suffered a big loss."[48]

The second difficulty was underpopulation that led to a chronic shortage of labor. Estate owners tried to solve this problem by paying the highest wages in Russia for hired labor. By the 1880s the result was an annual inundation of the south by poor peasants seeking high-paying jobs. To get to Kherson province some peasants walked "hundreds and thousands of versts along railroad tracks and navigable rivers," while others rode on large boats called *dubi* that were packed dangerously full with fifty to eighty workers each. Once in Kherson prospective workers gathered at commercial villages, towns, and railway stations for labor markets at which the overseers of noble estates could hire them. As many as nine thousand workers gathered at one place in Kherson. In Tauride province in the Kakhovka township as many as forty thousand workers sometimes congregated for the labor market.[49] Estate owners combined this army of manual laborers with a stock of modern machinery from reapers to steam ploughs to threshers. Lenin's descriptions of how thousands of peasants worked alongside swiftly operating agricultural machines create a colorful impression of how the large southern steppes estates looked at harvest time.[50] Most historians of Russian agriculture rank the southern steppes as the locus of the most advanced agricultural technology and most intense commercial farming in the Empire by the late 1880s.[51] Yet in the late 1870s the southern steppes still bore traces of more primitive labor and market systems; on some estates, for example, sharecropping and money rent were still practiced.

Nifontov has shown that there were substantial grain surpluses for the 1860s and 1870s in the Lower Volga Basin, and a small surplus in the New Russia, Don Oblast' area.[52] These surpluses would continue to grow until the southern steppes supplanted the blacksoil center as the breadbasket of Russia in the 1890s.[53] The pride of the region was high quality wheats grown mainly for export. In addition, the steppes were ideal for growing fruits and vegetables, and also for the domestic wine industry. The nobility of this region could supplement their earnings from grain by devoting part of their estates to these other valuable crops.

In the southern steppes the nobility seemed to have held intact their economic position vis-à-vis other *sosloviia* after the emancipation. By 1877 the noble land fund had declined only 12 percent.[54] Like their counterparts in the blacksoil zone, the southern nobility faced several long-term challenges: the possibility of exhausted soils and a chronic susceptibility to drought; serious shortages of manpower that could be remedied only by very high wages; a tendency for noble farmers to go deep into debt (four of the eleven private land banks operated here); direct exposure to the effects of international market fluctuations as wheat plantings increased in the region. Not all these problems would be as easy to eradicate as the tough grass that had once covered the steppes.

Druzhinin's fourth zone was the western periphery from the Baltic Sea in the north to the mouth of the Danube in the south. It included the Baltic provinces (Estland, Lifland, Courland), the western region comprised of Belorussia and Lithuania (Mogilev, Minsk, Vitebsk, Kov'no, Grodno, Vil'no), the Right-bank Ukraine (Kiev, Podolia, Volynia), and Bessarabia. Soil conditions in this zone varied from the poor soil of Belorussia to the excellent blacksoil in the Right-bank Ukraine, and ways of farming estates varied just as widely. Druzhinin apparently grouped these provinces into one zone partly because of the mixed character of agriculture here. These provinces also fall into a group because they were exceptions in the emancipation legislation: peasants in the Baltic provinces had been freed by Alexander I; peasants in the western region and Right-bank Ukraine had fallen subject to special legislation in the 1860s, partly because of unique political circumstances surrounding the Polish uprising; peasants in Bessarabia had been liberated under the law of 1868, which was quite favorable to them.

The western region of Belorussia and Lithuania was part of the nonblacksoil area and its agriculture resembled that of the nonblacksoil zone. Just over one-fourth of the land of Belorussia was arable, and nearly 40 percent was forested. Land there was farmed by peasants, usually on long-term rent contracts. The three-field system of crop rotation prevailed, although four-field rotations also existed.[55] Because of the social and climatic conditions in Belorussia, the area was a net grain importer in most years. By the late nineteenth century, Belorussian nobles were trying to diversify farming by growing more potatoes and raising livestock. Lithuania was better situated for cereal culture, although a backward farming technology was used there as well as in Belorussia. If one takes the Belorussian and Lithuanian areas together, statistics show a net regional grain deficit in the 1860s, followed by an average surplus in the 1870s.[56]

Like the western region, the Baltic provinces had relatively poor soils for agriculture—mostly sand and light clays. Yet social conditions in the Baltic were more advantageous than further south. The peasantry included prosperous owners of as many as fifty desiatins. Other peasants were landless, but they could receive very high wages as yearly workers for local landlords. The social structure in this area seemed relatively cohesive, and the countryside prosperous and quiescent. Baltic landowners, often of German extraction, farmed their lands with modern techniques: multifield rotations, constant fertilization, good drainage of land, and a mixture of long-term labor service and hired labor. Grain production showed consistent surpluses in the 1860s and 1870s.[57]

In the Right-bank Ukraine and Bessarabia soil conditions and climate were propitious for agriculture. In the Right-bank Ukraine high-grade wheat and sugar beets were grown, along with other cereals and potatoes. In Bessarabia wine grapes, assorted fruits, wheat, and corn were cultivated. In both areas there was a mix of advanced and primitive farming. Estate owners in the Ukraine often resorted to sharecropping and labor rent, and the three-field rotation was still used; yet by the 1870s four-field rotations, machine cultivation, and hired labor were becoming commoner. On sugar beet farms there were enormous refineries, and these farms were often run like factories. In Bessarabia wealthier estate owners ran their farms according to advanced techniques, but they spent much money on hired labor, which was in chronic short supply. These expenditures were so high that some nobles preferred to rent estates on a long-term basis. After small average grain deficits in the 1860s, the Right-bank Ukraine showed consistent surpluses in cereal production through the 1890s.[58]

Because of the timing and peculiarities of peasant emancipations in the western periphery, it does not make sense to compare post-1861 sales of estates there to those in other regions of Russia. Nor does the internal heterogeneity of the western periphery permit firm generalizations about the economic strength of the nobility in this zone compared with that of other zones. We may do well to accept Druzhinin's argument that the western periphery was an area of sharp contrast between more- and less-advanced methods of production, and between different types of social arrangements.

The emancipation's impact on the nobility differed significantly according to the nature of land settlements between nobles and peasants, the amount and timing of redemption payments, the kinds of land tenure adopted after 1861, and regional conditions. These differences helped generate an agrarian economy in which there were competitive, even antagonistic relationships among noble landowners. Hypothetically, a former *pomeshchik* in Orel province might be perfectly content to maintain personal patriarchal ties with his former serfs and to conclude with them a rent contract, but he might lose much of his labor force to a Kherson landowner willing to pay higher wages to hired labor. The Orel landowner would have an interest in economic stasis, in keeping his ex-serfs dependent on him and living on the land; the Kherson landowner would be a proponent of economic change, an opponent of patriarchal ties. Both landowners might concur that the nobility's economic superiority over the peasantry should be maintained, but their different economic circumstances would require them to defend their economic superiority in different ways. If asked by a governmental commission about the economic problems confronting the nobility, our two hypothetical landowners might agree only that nobles faced hard times; their descriptions of local problems and suggested solutions would diverge radically.

The emancipation destroyed the economic coherence of the Russian nobility by eliminating the only economic factor the nobles had in common—serf labor. It is true that many nobles retained certain economic privileges and continued to exploit peasant labor, but once the personal nexus between lord and bondsman had been replaced by the immense variety of more-impersonal relationships possible in the new agrarian order, the economic identity of the nobility became so complicated that not even Wallace could do it justice. There was no longer a common relationship to the means of production among Russian nobles.

In a grandee must always be
A mind sound, a heart educated.
A worthy servant, he should be
To his sacred station dedicated:
He is the instrument of power,
Of tsarist buildings the foundation;
In all his thoughts, words, and action
Must be—loyalty, glory, honor.
—G. Derzhavin, "Vel'mozhu"

Yes, I abhor thee and thy throne,
Oh, miscreant in despot's clothing!
Thy doom, thy children's dying groan,
I witness them with mirthful loathing.
Upon thy brow one reads the sign
Of subject peoples' execration,
World's horror, blemish of creation,
Reproach on earth to the Divine.
—A. S. Pushkin, "Vol'nost'"

CHAPTER 3
Traditional Politics

An English traveler to Russia in the reign of Catherine the Great wrote that "the sovereign of the Russian Empire is absolute and despotic in the utmost latitude of these words and master of the lives and properties of all his subjects who, though they are the first nobility . . . may nevertheless for the most trifling offense be seized upon and sent to Siberia."[1] A vision of the tsar as absolute ruler with powers unequaled by other European sovereigns has strong support in Western historiography and, like the eighteenth-century Englishman quoted above, Western historians have tended to conclude that the nobility were without real political power—so many subjects under the tsar's arbitrary sway. There is, of course, much evidence to support the contention that the nobility were insignificant in power compared to the monarch. There were only two real attempts by members of the post-Petrine nobility to compel the crown to change its policies: the first during the succession crisis of 1730, and the second in the 1825 Decembrist rebellion. Both incidents witnessed collisions of the autocracy with small groups of upper-crust nobles who did not have very wide support among the provincial nobility. Both rebellions ended with victories for the crown.

One's impression of the weakness of the nobility is also supported by the contempt with which the court camarilla regarded the *dvorianstvo*. Pavel Stroganov, a member of Alexander I's "Unofficial Committee," said of them: "Neither rights, nor justice, nor anything else can generate in them the idea of even the most minor resistance."[2] Most outspoken of all about the weakness of the nobility were radicals of the generation of the 1830s and 1840s. Alexander Herzen bitterly noted: "West European aristocracy is indeed so completely alien to us that all accounts of our grandees may be reduced to stories of savage luxury, of banquets in which a whole town takes part, of innumerable houseserfs, of tyrannizing over peasants and inconsiderable neighbors, together with slavish subservience before the Emperor and the Court."[3]

Soviet historians have been rather inconsistent in their treatment of the relationship between the nobility and the autocracy. Some have argued, on the one hand, that the Russian government was nothing but the tool of the nobility and government policy was little but their formulated class interest.[4] The tsar himself was simply the wealthiest of the feudal lords. Thus, the government struck down peasant rebels and everywhere fortified the nobles' control over serfs. The government also suppressed the liberal opposition among the nobility, arresting Radishchev and crushing the Decembrists precisely because they did not understand the true class interests of the nobility. On the other hand, some Soviet historians have seen Russian absolutism in the eighteenth century as the product of a situation in which the autocrat balanced between the declining nobility and the rising bourgeoisie, and emerged as all-powerful arbiter of Russia's destiny without being identified with any one class.[5] More-recent Soviet historians have emphasized the autocrat's discretionary authority and the distance between the autocrat and the class interests of the nobility.[6] These historians recognize that the state itself possessed a certain historical force independent of its class basis. Except for its emphasis on the rising bourgeoisie, this second Soviet view seems almost to converge with the main Western interpretation in underlining the despotic powers of the crown.

Which of these interpretations is correct? How do we reconcile the Western perception of noble powerlessness with the first Soviet view that the nobility and the state were powerful and inseparable twins, the Dioscuri of the Russian political constellation? And did the nobility find in politics, as they never did in social structure and economic behavior, a coherent class program and identity? Or was a lack of corporate spirit the determining characteristic of Russian noble politics, as Stroganov and Herzen observed? To answer these questions we need to analyze the modes of political activity open to the nobility, the background of politically active nobles, the intellectual traditions that informed political activism, and the substance of nobles' political activity at midcentury.

THE MODES OF POLITICAL ACTIVITY

In order to understand the nature of imperial Russian politics, one must distinguish between two fundamentally different modes of political decision making, each with its own characteristic avenues of political activity. The first mode of political decision making might be called the deliberative constitutional mode. This mode provides formal avenues whereby the wishes of the executive are necessarily subjected to the scrutiny and deliberation of other agencies which may place limitations on them. Political power in the deliberative constitutional mode is legally or customarily distributed amongst the executive and other agencies of government. The second mode of political decision making might be called the consultative bureaucratic mode. This way of decision making provides informal and formal agencies which the executive may consult before he formulates his will as law. Consultative bureaucratic agencies have no constituted power to restrain the executive; they may alter the executive's will only by urging on him the opinions of the public, of an elite, of a single class or individual. Executive decisions may then emerge in consensus with opinion. Formal political power in a consultative bureaucratic system is concentrated in the executive, although informal power, derived mainly from access to the executive, may be distributed quite widely. Limits on executive power exist in a consultative bureaucratic system to the extent that the executive is determined to govern in the interests of an elite, or within the limits imposed by public opinion.

In most modern Western states political decision making generally follows the deliberative constitutional mode. Constitutional charters separate executive power from legislative authority and allow legislatures to limit and block the executive will. Of course, in specific areas of policy and in political emergencies, power may be vested almost entirely in the executive. For example, many constitutions have clauses like that in the Weimar Constitution which confers on the president of a republic the power to rule by decree in the event of national danger. In other states the president may be allowed extraordinary control over appointments in the civil service and judiciary, and over the making of foreign policy. In all these instances decisions will follow the consultative bureaucratic mode. Thus, political systems as a whole can and do incorporate both modes of decision making.

What distinguished imperial Russian politics from politics of other European nations was the remarkable absence of deliberative constitutional decision making. The post-Petrine Russian state was an extreme variant of European absolutism. In theory, all secular power derived from God and reposed in the tsar whose will, formulated in decrees, was the law of the Empire. "In the Christian world," as the poet Zhukovsky put it, "autocracy is the highest level of power; it is the last link between the power of man and the power of God."[7] This model of state theoretically left no room for opposition to the tsar by social classes or individuals, nor did it allow for economic or social corporations to infringe on the tsar's prerogatives to set policy and make law.

There is some evidence that before Peter I agencies existed that might have formed the basis for a constitutional representative government, if Peter and his successors had allowed them to grow. The Soviet historian Cherepnin has contended that between 1549 and 1683 there were fifty-seven meetings of the zemsky sobor, or assembly of the land, in which the clergy, military service class, merchants, townsmen, and even peasants met in response to civil disorders, military danger, and financial crisis. In 1613 a zemsky sobor elected Mikhail Romanov to wear the Russian crown, and other assemblies voted for new laws, higher taxes, and even on the question of war. Cherepnin compared the zemsky sobor to Western representative institutions like Parliament.[8]

But the zemsky sobor was never firmly rooted in Russia. Although some members of the post-Petrine nobility argued that reinstitution of the zemsky sobor would solve the nation's political problems without necessarily infringing on monarchical prerogatives, it is clear that no autocrat ever seriously contemplated this political course. Moreover, there was no widespread support within the nobility for constitutional limitations on the monarch, as demonstrated by the failed revolution in 1730 and the hostility toward the Decembrists' political program.

Thus, post-Petrine nobles were servitors and landowners who had no access to deliberative constitutional decision-making procedures, who had no legal way of restraining the tsar. This is what Western historians mean when they argue that the nobility were "powerless," and it was this "powerlessness" that so exercised Herzen and amused Pavel Stroganov.

The Russian state operated as a consultative bureaucratic system. Yet within this framework for political activity, the nobility had substantial influence on the making of policy. Policy did not spring full blown from the tsar like Athena from the brow of Zeus; policy was formulated by the tsar in consultation with advisers, virtually all of whom were noble. A persuasive noble with access to the ear of the sovereign might therefore be seen as possessing power *in posse*. Such power could easily be transformed into patronage. During the reign of a weak autocrat—and the whole period from 1725 to 1760 was one of weak heads of state—a favorite of the tsar or a group of courtier nobles virtually ruled the nation; one thinks of the enormous influence wielded by Menshikov immediately after Peter I's death, or of the authority of Bühren under Anna Ivanovna. Yet, even under a strong sovereign, patronage systems run by favorites, or by courtier factions—"parties" as David Ransel has called them— were an inherent feature of the governmental system.[9] As the Russian government was systematized, as the bureaucracy became more regularized, the scope of patronage politics was reduced, though patronage was never rooted out altogether. Indeed, one might argue that the bureaucracy was itself nothing but a gigantic patronage system operating in a routinized fashion within certain arbitrarily defined legal norms.

One result of patronage politics was that Russian manners were based to a considerable extent on considerations of rank and social status. In an amusing and perceptive aside in *Dead Souls* Gogol commented on the effects of bureaucracy and patronage in Russia:

> It must be said that if we in Russia have not caught up with foreigners in some things, we have far outstripped them in the art of behavior. It is quite impossible to enumerate all the shades and subtleties of our manners. No Frenchman or German will ever grasp or even suspect their peculiarities and distinctions. . . . We have clever fellows who talk in quite a different way to a landowner with two hundred serfs and to one with three hundred serfs; and to one with three hundred they will talk differently again from the way they will talk to one with five hundred, and in a different way again from one with eight hundred—in short, even if the number were to grow to a million they would still find different shades for it. Let us, for instance, imagine some government office—not here but in some Ruritanian kingdom— and let us also suppose that this office has a chief. Please have a look at him as he sits among his subordinates—why, you would be so awe-stricken that you would not be able to utter a word! Pride and

nobility and what else does not his face express? All you have to do
is to pick up a brush and paint him—a Prometheus, a veritable
Prometheus! Looks like an eagle, walks with measured, smooth steps.
But that very eagle, when he has left his office and is approaching the
office of his own chief, scurries along like a partridge with papers
under his arm, as fast as his legs will carry him. In society and at an
evening party, if everyone is of a lower rank, our Prometheus remains
a Prometheus, but if they are ever so little above him, our Prometheus
undergoes a metamorphosis such as even Ovid never thought of: a
fly, less than a fly, he has reduced himself to a grain of sand![10]

The very significance of rank and the power associated with it
gave rise to a society in which knowledge of family histories, economic circumstances, and recent promotions within ministries was
itself valuable, for this knowledge could be turned to one's personal
and familial advantage. In the first scene of *The Idiot* Dostoevsky
introduces us to a bureaucrat who is part of that group of people
Dostoevsky dismisses as *"gospoda vseznaiki"*—roughly "Mister Know-
It-Alls." The *vseznaika* knows "in what department so-and-so serves,
who are his friends, which his income is, where he was governor,
who his wife is and what dowry she brought him, who are his first
cousins and who are his second cousins, and everything of that
sort."[11] What is more, some *vseznaiki* were smart enough to make
careers out of exploiting this knowledge. How else are we to understand that type of noble represented by Anna Pavlovna Scherer in
War and Peace? Salons were vital organs of power and influence in
hierarchical absolutist societies, and the successful organizer of a
salon was highly valued.

Much, but by no means all, of the nobility's political power derived
from control over patronage. Another avenue for the exercise of
power was consultative institutions established by autocrats on an
ad hoc basis. The best example of ad hoc monarchical consultation
for the late eighteenth century was the Legislative Commission of
1767 to which Catherine II submitted her famous *Nakaz*. Although
Catherine did not allow the nobles assembled to reach a conclusion
in their deliberations, opinions expressed at the Legislative Commission gave Catherine solid indications that the nobility supported
serfdom and did not support sweeping reforms of the governmental
structure. The Legislative Commission may have had something to
do with Catherine's increasing caution and conservatism. In the
nineteenth century the best example of monarchical consultation
may have been the committees established by Alexander II to consider the proper form and scope of the emancipation legislation. In

1858 Alexander ordered each province to select a committee to work out reform proposals; these proposals were to be coordinated by a national agency called the Editorial Commissions. In the end, the provincial committees had a definite impact on the size of land settlements made with the peasantry, although the extent of their influence on other aspects of the emancipation is questionable. The autocracy easily accommodated these unusual consultative mechanisms because they were convoked and dismissed at the will of the sovereign, and because they were exceptional measures. However, the regime resisted regularized national consultations and any suggestion that the nobility had the right to be consulted on issues of extraordinary moment to the nation.

The regime did establish institutions that allowed the nobility to meet regularly at the local and provincial level to formulate complaints about government policy. These institutions were created under the Charter of the Nobility in 1785, a document which became the keystone of provincial noble power until the end of the old regime.[12] The charter set up provincial societies of nobles in each province as well as political organs called noble assemblies. These assemblies scheduled regular meetings at three-year intervals, but "extraordinary sessions" could be called in emergencies with permission from the provincial governor and the Ministry of Internal Affairs. The assemblies generally attended to the internal business of the nobility as a *soslovie*—that is, to the election of officers, the keeping of the official genealogy in a province, and the collection of funds used for corporate purposes. But assemblies also had the right to petition provincial bureaucrats, the Minister of Internal Affairs, and the tsar himself for redress of corporate grievances, or to demand the "end of local abuses and amelioration of problems noticed in local administration even if they stem from general policy directives." Petitions were to be sent through elected officers, known as "marshals," or through specially chosen deputations. In the interim between assemblies provincial marshals could act as spokesmen for the noble assemblies in their respective province. This provincial structure was duplicated at the district level, where district assemblies met at the same intervals and also elected marshals.

Noble assemblies and their elected marshals played no important role in national politics in the first half of the nineteenth century. Their statutory authority was over corporate affairs at the provincial and district levels, and their petition power was largely redundant in a polity where patronage already guaranteed the nobility sufficient influence. Thus, for most of the first half of the century noble assemblies were sparsely attended, and it cannot be said that the assemblies were zealous about defending corporate rights that were already seemingly well protected at the ministerial level.

Three other avenues by which the nobility exercised political influence should be mentioned. One was the press, which had been limited in circulation in the eighteenth century and subjected to strict censorship under Nicholas I, but which under Alexander II had been allowed a measure of autonomy. In the post-reform period conservative opinion was published in papers like *Vest'*, Mikhail Katkov's *Moskovskie vedomosti*, and Prince Meshchersky's *Grazhdanin*. Liberal opinion had outlets in fat journals like *Vestnik Evropy*. In the second half of the century these organs carried sharp debates on the role of the nobility in the state, and implied criticism of government policy. Another avenue for noble politics was the zemstvos, founded in 1864. Although formally all-Estate institutions, the zemstvos were dominated through most of their history by the nobility. Indeed, they served the nobility as convenient means to meddle in local politics after the emancipation, and as another fulcrum against which demands on the government could be pressed. It must be said, however, that the ethos of the zemstvos was different from that of noble assemblies; in the zemstvos the ideal of serving all groups in society and even the leveling notion of individual equality were regarded seriously. Finally, noble influence could be channeled through voluntary organizations like the Moscow Society for Farmers, and the Southern Russian Society of Farmers, or through private groups like the Beseda circle. In each instance, the extent of impact on government policymakers depended on the expertise or collective prestige of the individuals involved.

Given all the channels through which noble opinion might be articulated, it should be evident that the nobility might exert significant political influence on the crown. Because the crown preserved its absolute prerogatives, of course, and because society itself was arranged hierarchically, the style of politics in Russia was deferential. But one should not confuse deference and outward submissiveness with lack of influence over policy. Deferential politics, though comical in some ways, can be an extraordinarily efficient way of discovering policy consensus and maintaining the prestige of the sovereign and his supporters. To the extent that the autocrat is seen as the personal font of justice and mercy, his majesty will be respected; to the extent that the sovereign's retainers can influence the exercise of justice and mercy, they too will be respected. So long as nothing affects the basic symbiotic relationship between the autocrat and the nobility, the political system will function smoothly.

Indeed, for most of the eighteenth century and the first half of the nineteenth century there seemed to be a relatively clear consensus among monarch, servitors, and landowners on the principle that the nobility and crown were interdependent and on the major policy issue that serfdom should not be abolished by monarchical decree. This consensus was threatened briefly by Alexander I in his early reformist period, by liberal nobles in 1825 during the Decembrist rebellion, and by the strains imposed on the educated nobility by Nicholas I. Yet the alliance between nobility and crown stayed intact until the emancipation.

Recognition of the close relationship between the nobility and the crown has led certain Soviet historians to assert that the nobility had enormous political power and to speak of the nobility as a ruling class. The Soviet interpretation sees consultative bureaucratic politics as the way in which economic privilege was maintained. The absence of positive legal power for individual nobles and the noble corporation as a whole and the absence of a constitution are treated as irrelevant to control over the real font of power—that is, over the means of production, land. Thus, it should be obvious that Soviet historians and Western historians disagree about the "power" of the nobility within the state because they mean by "power" two different things.

The emancipation, of course, destroyed the alliance, or consensus, between nobles and the crown at its most fundamental level, and in so doing raised the issue of how the nobility could adapt politically to the new economic and social realities of rural Russia. This issue was less pressing for mere noble servitors who owned no land than for those who earned their living from agriculture. Thus, the most urgent rethinking of political assumptions was done by the landed nobility. The struggle for adaptation to new conditions, led by noble landowners, comprises the substance of noble politics between 1861 and 1905.

The Political Actors

In the section above we have discussed the relationship of the landed nobility to the crown and the avenues of noble political influence in very general terms. We must look more carefully at the social composition of provincial political institutions—especially the noble assemblies and marshals of the nobility.

The right to participate in noble assemblies was not guaranteed to all nobles, but rather to those who belonged to the hereditary nobility and who met specified income and property-owning qualifications. In the pre-emancipation period, assembly members had to own at least 100 serfs or 3,000 desiatins of "unpopulated" land. High-ranked civil servants and military officers had to own merely five serfs or 150 desiatins of unpopulated land. Those who owned less than the specified requirements had only one-twentieth of a vote, but, by banding together with others, they could be represented in assemblies. After the emancipation the rules for property qualifications were changed twice—once in 1870 and once in 1896. The 1870 regulations allowed those who owned from 200 to 300 desiatins in the blacksoil areas and from 300 to 600 desiatins in the nonblacksoil and steppe provinces to vote in noble assemblies. Civil servants and military men could vote if they had pensions of at least 900 rubles. The petty nobles were counted as before— one-twentieth of a vote. The 1896 regulation lowered the property requirements slightly, to between 150 and 200 desiatins in the blacksoil provinces, and between 300 and 500 desiatins in most other areas.[13]

The significance of these regulations is that noble assemblies were dominated not by the petty nobles who were so numerous compared to other strata, but rather by the gentry and the landed magnates. At the end of the nineteenth century the Special Commission on the Nobility studied actual attendance at noble assemblies in twenty-six provinces. It discovered that of 276,177 eligible hereditary nobles only 58,707 attended assembly meetings. Among participants 9 percent owned less than the specified property requirement, 76 percent owned between one and ten times the requirement, and 15 percent owned more than ten times the statutory minimum. Thus, the largest representation was enjoyed by the gentry, who with the landed magnates commanded large majorities everywhere.[14]

Although the statistical data pertained to the mid-1890s, the picture of noble assemblies dominated by the gentry and magnates seems constant throughout the post-reform era. In the mid-1860s Terpigoriev visited several noble assemblies in his native Tambov, and in *Oskudenie* he recorded his memories of a "typical" assembly.

> It was already December. This was the year of the election and one had to travel to the provincial capital. Here was a legal pretext to break out of "this prison," if only for a week or two, to breathe, to refresh oneself. The palate anticipated the taste of caviar and salmon; the odor of steaming meat and vegetable soup tantalized the nose. . . . There, midst the clouds of tobacco smoke, one could see the off-duty military officer playing billiards. On the way to the provincial town, of course, almost everyone had to stop off at the district capital to see

his creditor and borrow some money against next year's harvest, or sell some family heirloom. Many nobles could not go at all; they lacked the hundred or two hundred rubles for the road and expenses in town. . . . Finally we arrived. We made our usual visits to the governor, the provincial marshal and the bishop. The assembled swore an oath of allegiance to the tsar, the bishop made a speech most appropriate to the occasion. Then, of course, we all left to spend two or three hours in the restaurants and hotels.[15]

Terpigoriev's description of the (expensive) recreation and food enjoyed by the nobles who could attend, and his reference to the poverty of those who could not, suggest that noble assemblies in the 1860s, like those in the 1890s, were populated by the financially secure and well-to-do, and by those with good credit.

The climax of noble assemblies was usually the election of a marshal, the key figure in corporate life whose office, next to the governorship, was the most important post in the provinces. Under the 1785 charter, provincial marshals were responsible for the following duties: acting as treasurers of the provincial noble assemblies, as keepers of the provincial genealogy registers, and as spokesmen for the nobility in the periods when assemblies were not in session. Marshals also discharged administrative duties in the provincial bureaucracy: they were members of the bureaus on peasant, zemstvo, and municipal affairs as well as chairmen of the provincial commission on land assessments, and they would soon be ex officio chairmen of provincial zemstvo assemblies and provincial education councils. At the *uezd* level, district marshals chaired the bureau on peasant affairs, district zemstvo assemblies, and the committees on temperance and public health; after 1889 the district marshals would head the assemblies of land captains.[16] This formidable list of corporate and bureaucratic duties suggests that noble marshals occupied a strategic position in Russian politics: they were simultaneously intermediaries between the landed nobility and the bureaucracy, between the bureaucracy and the peasantry, between the nobility and the peasantry.

In choosing someone for such a responsible position, nobles at assemblies made wealth an important criterion. As Terpigoriev recalled: "It was now our difficult task to elect a man who could simultaneously satisfy all our 'parties' and the requirements of the marshal's rank—that is, a man who was strong and intelligent, who stood head and shoulders above the rest; if such a man could not be found, a colorless person would do. In either case, our marshal would have to be a man of means, if not a rich man."[17]

TABLE 3.1

Souls (Male Serfs) Owned by Provincial Marshals, 1861–1881

Number of serfs	Number of marshals
0–10	0
11–50	7
51–100	1
101–500	22
501–1,000	18
1,001–5,000	24
over 5,000	9

SOURCE: Marshals' service records found in TsGIA, fond 1343, opisi 16–36, *raznye dela.*

Just how wealthy were the marshals of the nobility? The only convenient source for measuring the wealth of many gentry marshals is the service record preserved in the central government archive. Many service records of marshals who served before 1880 list wealth only in the number of male serfs (or temporarily obligated peasants) on the estate of the marshal. The immediate families of eighty-three provincial marshals of the nobility whose service records were located possessed 194,630 souls—an average of more than 2,300 souls per family (see Table 3.1). Even after the top nine owners are excluded from the list, the average number of male serfs owned was still over one thousand.[18]

In 1858 only 3 percent of all serfowners in Russia possessed five hundred or more serfs, while only 1 percent possessed a thousand or more. Therefore, provincial marshals *as a group* were representative of the very top stratum of the nobility. However, aggregate statistics can be very misleading since they obscure the distribution of wealth within a goup. When one examines the distribution of serfowning, the picture that emerges is quite different. If one takes serfownership as an index of wealth, marshals were generally, but by no means universally, well-to-do.

Sometime after the emancipation, service records began to list wealth in terms of landownership. A sample of thirty-seven provincial marshals, roughly 10 percent of the total, showed a wide disparity in ownership. Even after one excludes the wealthiest twelve proprietors from the group for statistical reasons, one finds the average marshal owned nearly four thousand desiatins.[19] The extremes in ownership are striking; one marshal farmed only 709 desiatins, while another owned 1,067,017 desiatins. Nearly all the marshals in this small sample were large landowners by contemporary stan-

TABLE 3.2
Land Owned by District Marshals, 1895

Number of desiatins	Number of marshals
0–100	0
101–500	6
501–1,000	33
1,001–5,000	66
5,001–10,000	9
over 10,000	11

SOURCE: *Vsia Rossiia. Russkaia kniga promyshlennosti, torgovli, sel'skogo khoziaistva i administratsii. Adres-kalendar' rossiiskoi imperii* (1895 edition).

dards, but the diversity within the group should not be overlooked.

A second estimate of landownership may be made on the basis of published records. In 1895 one source listed the size of twenty-two marshals' estates which averaged over 5,500 desiatins.[20] The estates varied in size from 626 desiatins to 75,000 desiatins. Among district marshals, about whom there was information in 125 cases, the average estate was almost 3,500 desiatins[21] (see Table 3.2). The distribution of landownership among district marshals was revealing. Both provincial and district marshals were wealthy, if the sole criterion of wealth is landownership. However, as the distribution figures indicate, neither group was completely homogeneous. On the contrary, there were wide differentials in wealth within both groups.

The marshals' service backgrounds were not untypical of the diversity of the First Estate. There were at least three different career patterns followed by men who became marshals: national service with the central government, military service, and provincial service. A good example of a national servitor who became a provincial marshal was Apollon Dmitrievich Kholodkovsky, a minor bureaucrat who worked his way up the service ladder to become provincial marshal in Orenburg province in the mid-1880s. Kholodkovsky was from a relatively poor family—his father owned only sixty desiatins—and his first job had been an insignificant post in the Department of Taxation and Collections. But Kholodkovsky had the good fortune to transfer to the Accounting Department of the Ministry of Internal Affairs just when the Ministry began to seriously concern itself with reforms. Kholodkovsky was both decorated and promoted for his work on the peasant reforms. He sat on a series of important committees, including one that finally drafted the Zemstvo

Statute in 1864. Kholodkovsky's hard work with the central government led to excellent assignments in Orenburg province where he was for a time acting head of the governor-general's office, and to an award of nearly 3,000 desiatins of land. Finally, after leaving the central government altogether, Kholodkovsky was elected provincial marshal of the nobility.[22]

An example of a career combining military and provincial service was that of Penza provincial marshal Alexander Nikolaevich Arapov, who joined the cavalry in 1817, fought against the first Polish rebellion in 1831 and the Hungarian revolution in 1849, and rose to the rank of lieutenant general before his retirement from the army. Arapov apparently gained a reputation as a "man of law and order." During the tense period of the Crimean War and the preparation of the peasant reforms, the Penza nobility elected him provincial marshal. Arapov served six consecutive terms as marshal.[23]

One of the most outspoken nobles in Russia, Leonid Matveevich Muromtsov, was a provincial servitor throughout his career. Muromtsov was the child of a Riazan' landowner who had over three thousand desiatins of land and of Princess E. K. Golitsyna who possessed a large estate of her own in Tula province. Muromtsov entered Moscow University and graduated with a candidate's degree in 1846. He entered service as a junior assistant to Moscow's military governor and was reassigned to the Moscow Treasury Board and the Department of Liquor Taxation. In 1851 Muromtsov became a deputy in the Dankovsky district assembly of Riazan' province, and in 1853 he was elected district marshal. In the next twenty-five years Muromtsov served both at the provincial level (as justice of the peace and trustee of Zaraisky educational district) and in a minor capacity in the central bureaucracy (as a member of the Economic Board of the Holy Synod). Finally in 1878, Muromtsov was elected Riazan' provincial marshal—a post he would retain until the turn of the century.[24]

There is nothing unique about the careers of Kholodkovsky, Arapov, and Muromtsov—examples of careers running along similar paths could be multiplied almost ad infinitum.[25] What is noteworthy about these three marshals is that they had almost nothing in common besides their election as marshals. Kholodkovsky had spent his early career in a ministry, while Arapov was in the army. Muromtsov had nothing to do with the military and little connection with the central government. The nineteenth-century nobility were sociologically diverse; this diversity was reflected in the economic and occupational backgrounds of the noble marshals. As a group the marshals were wealthier than the nobility as a whole, but there was still a wide variation in wealth. The marshals' careers were perhaps more distinguished than those of most nobles, but the career choices of marshals mirrored the choices available to the nobility as a whole. Given the marshals' diverse backgrounds, one would not expect them to impose common assumptions on the corporate politics of the nobility or a common program during the post-emancipation period which would demand so many difficult choices.

For comparative purposes it is interesting to note that the noble representation and leadership in the zemstvo were quite similar to those of noble assemblies. Property restrictions in the post-emancipation assemblies followed zemstvo property restrictions quite closely; thus, both zemstvos and assemblies were dominated by the middle and upper strata of the nobility. Zemstvo leadership was heavily weighted toward middle and large landowners. In a recent study of 991 zemstvo *glasnye* from twenty-four provinces, the Soviet historian N. M. Pirumova counted 864 hereditary nobles. In her sample, 61 percent of the *glasnye* owned more than 500 desiatins ·of land, 28 percent had estates between 200 and 500 desiatins, and 3 percent held less than 200 desiatins. Pirumova pointed out that in the central agricultural and southern steppes zemstvos, the prevalence of large landowners was even higher than elsewhere in the country.[26] One difference between noble marshals and zemstvo *glasnye* was the degree of commitment of *glasnye* to provincial politics. Whereas many marshals did service with the national government and the military and seem to have had a more encompassing commitment to the nobility in all its aspects, the zemstvo leadership evidently concentrated its attention on the provinces. Two-thirds of zemstvo *glasnye* in 1893 held provincial offices outside the zemstvo.[27] The articulate zemstvo leadership seemed dedicated to provincial self-government as the solution to Russia's problems, whereas the ideology of self-government was less firmly rooted in the noble assemblies. Nevertheless, social differences between the noble assemblies and zemstvos were differences of degree, not kind: both agencies were dominated by people from roughly the same differentiated middle- and upper-noble background.

INTELLECTUAL TRADITIONS

What intellectual traditions informed the political activity of nobles after the emancipation? Were their political positions closely enough related one to another that ideological diversity within the First

Estate was minimal? Did there exist among the nobility the kind of group identity that E. P. Thompson would consider necessary for a class? These questions may be partially clarified by ranging noble ideologies along the political spectrum from left to right.

We must begin, however, with an important caveat: one of the most remarkable features of the corporate politics of nobles was that petitions of the government generally had very little manifest intellectual content. The traditions of Russian social thought—say, liberalism or various forms of Slavophilism—rarely had a direct influence in the politics of noble assemblies. There are several reasons for the apparent divorce between intellectual movements and everyday corporate political affairs.

The first reason was the nature of discourse in government agencies and among the nobility. This discourse was characterized by pompous circumlocutions, decorous artifice, and formalized phraseology, all of which reflected the hierarchical ordering of government and society. In a bitter passage Saltykov-Shchedrin commented on the oddity of this discourse in the bureaucracy: "To many people it seemed that authority would be seriously shaken if, instead of 'I have the honor most humbly to request,' one would write simply, 'I ask,' or if, instead of, 'as regards the following, please do not reserve to yourself the information,' one wrote, 'please inform me.' It was assumed that saving labor would lead to idleness, idleness would engender disrespect, and disrespect rebellion."[28]

Language not only reflected patterns of hierarchy in government and society, but itself constituted an obstacle to the expression of a full range of political ideas. The language of noble petitions was a language of supplication: once a supplicatory mode of address was adopted, a petition writer would find it hard to criticize the tsar even indirectly or to justify a proposal on untraditional grounds. Noble assemblies pleaded with the tsar to exercise his mercy, his charity; these requests, even when made at some length and with urgency, had to be expressed humbly and in such a way as not to pressure the tsar, not to presume on his kindness. Such presumption would constitute a derogation of the monarch's person, and would, therefore, be an infringement on autocracy itself.

The formalized language of supplication persisted well into the second half of the nineteenth century. For example, in December 1883, the Orel provincial noble assembly addressed a petition to the tsar asking for a change in credit policies. The petition began with a typical formalized invocation of the right to petition, traced this right to earlier tsarist decrees, and directed the monarch's attention to the issues at hand. "Employing the invaluable right granted to the Russian nobility by the Sovereign ancestors of Your Imperial Majesty, we make bold to proffer to Your Most Gracious attention, Your Highness, this most loyal supplication. . . ." The strongest language of the petition was a prediction of the results that would attend the nobility if the petition were rejected. "If the Sovereign will of your Majesty does not come to our aid, then the time is not far off when the nobility will lose the possibility of remaining the leading Estate that directs the people on the path toward social improvement and agricultural success."[29] Even this passage, with all its urgency, did not upbraid the tsar for his wrong-minded policies; the tone of the passage, like that of the rest of the petition, was the supplicatory tone of vassals speaking to their feudal lord. Of course, in a consultative bureaucratic type of political system one would expect no less.

A second reason for the divorce between intellectual movements and everyday politics was that Russian social thought was the product of an educated minority whose ideas were often so abstract as to make their application to politics difficult. Russian thinkers in the first half of the nineteenth century wrote abstractly partly because of fear of censorship, and partly because they were creatures of the drawing room, the university, the capitals, and were thus cut off from provincial concerns. The Polish historian Andrzej Walicki has pointed to the abstract, pre-political nature of the controversy between Westernizers and Slavophiles. "An analysis of the essential content of Slavophilism and Westernism leads to the conclusion," wrote Walicki, "that the two systems were not so much political ideologies with concrete, limited, and attainable ends, as two types of *Weltanschauung*, two utopias, equally 'transcendent' in relation to existing social realities. They were doomed to remain at this pre-political stage because the Russia of Nicholas I allowed no outlet for political action." Walicki then noted that as soon as Westernism and Slavophilism began to face concrete political problems (the revolution of 1848 in Europe and then the peasant reforms), they disintegrated as philosophical movements.[30] In the second half of the nineteenth century when censorship was less restrictive and when there were more outlets for political expression than before (the press, zemstvos, voluntary societies), political thinking became less abstract and the rift between intellectual life and politics decreased. The intellectual content of noble petitions was greatest in times of national crisis like the reform period in the late 1850s and early 1860s, or the terrorist crisis from 1878 to 1882, or the constitutional crisis before the 1905 revolution. But generally speaking, the grand intellectual traditions did not make themselves much felt in the everyday politics of the nobility; they were still too abstract to provide aid in following pressing local issues.

A final reason for the separation between intellectual movements and everyday political affairs was that marshals of the nobility in many cases were products of national service who intended to return some day to national service. There was no personal advantage for an ambitious marshal to earn a reputation as an ideologue when such a reputation might block a future appointment to a governorship or a ministry, especially since one might speak effectively in behalf of the local nobility in the stylized nonideological language of supplication.

Recognizing the divorce between intellectual tradition and politics helps one understand a peculiarity of most provincial political activity: in Russia provincial politics, and to a lesser extent, national politics tended to be what political scientists call "interest politics." Petitions frequently were nothing more than defenses of the local landowners' immediate concerns. Nobles in a given province petitioned for a change in regulations or in the distribution of goods that would benefit their province. They understood that their claims might infringe on the interests of local peasants, merchants, or perhaps on nobles not represented in the provincial assembly. But justification of these petitions did not necessarily require appeal to philosophical tenets underpinning the state, or to the kind of observations about ideal political society that one would find in the works of Khomiakov. A summary of local problems and, perhaps, a ritualized reference to the role of the nobility as "leading Estate" were thought sufficient justification for petitions.

Interest politics was tailored perfectly to a nobility that was stratified, differentiated by region, and presided over by leaders whose own backgrounds were heterogeneous; it was theoretically a fine mechanism for the solution of purely local problems or for the satisfaction of a particular stratum of nobles. But interest politics in Russia was not well suited to defending the whole nobility *as a class.* How, after all, could the landowners in Orel province speak for landowners in Khar'kov, or for unlanded bureaucrats in St. Petersburg? Even if the rhetoric of a petition adopted in Orel referred to dangers confronting the nobility as a class, the tsar would not necessarily read the passage in question as a dictum of the entire First Estate, but rather as an expression of a majority opinion in one provincial assembly. Only a consistent, coordinated defense of the landed interest, one that crossed provincial lines and united existent political factions, could be regarded as clear evidence of a unified class consciousness. Such coordination was hard to achieve because the autocracy did not permit interprovincial meetings of the nobility, because the coincidence of noble interests throughout the Empire was rare indeed, and because, as we shall see below, the nobility was anything but a coherent political formation.

Thus far I have argued that, except in times of crisis, the traditions of Russian social thought had little direct effect on provincial politics. Now we must look at the intellectual traditions which did affect noble politics, either directly during a political crisis, or indirectly. Immediately after the death of Nicholas I there was a burst of political activity unparalleled in previous Russian history. The journals published in the first years of Alexander II's reign and the letters of contemporaries betrayed an extraordinary excitement not only about the substantive issues being discussed, but about the very fact that true debate took place. The historian M. P. Pogodin wrote in 1856:

> The Russian man has awakened (deeply he slept!) and crossed himself, he has started to look around, to listen, to think seriously. . . .
> The Russian man has opened his eyes! All his emotions are engaged: compassion, indignation, joy, shame, spite, anger, outraged honor, the desire for revenge, sadness, national pride, memories of past glory agitating the soul. His entire psyche is in turmoil.[31]

In a letter to V. P. Botkin, Lev Tolstoy remarked, somewhat petulantly, on the unusual political activism:

> We—i.e. Russian society—are in an unprecedented muddle, brought on by the question of emancipation. Suddenly and unexpectedly everybody has been caught up in political life. However little prepared he may be for such a life, everybody feels the need for activity. And whatever they say and do, it's getting dreadful and disgusting. . . .
> As far as the public's concerned, there is positively no place now for belles lettres. . . . I've grown tired of talk, arguments, speeches, etc.[32]

In this atmosphere of political ferment the radical left was represented by the faction popularly known as the nihilists. Historians have tended to think of the nihilists as *raznochintsy*, members of an inchoate social formation that existed somewhere between the nobility and the merchantry. However, a recent study of the nihilists by Daniel Brower has demonstrated that a substantial portion of the nihilists came from noble backgrounds. Between 1855 and 1869, 41 percent of the radicals in St. Petersburg originated in the landowning nobility, and 23 percent in the bureaucratic nobility; surprisingly, only 2 percent of these radicals were *raznochintsy*.[33] Before

Brower's study historians were misled by two leaders of the nihilists, Chernyshevsky and Dobroliubov, who were priests' sons. It was too often forgotten that the third major literary critic who inspired St. Petersburg youth was Dmitry Pisarev, a man whose father was a provincial "Don Juan" with a sizable estate on which he often entertained local nobles, both male and female.[34]

The strong representation of nobles within the nihilists may account for certain characteristic features of nihilist ideology and social conduct. Crucial to nihilist thinking was a rejection of the nobility as a privileged caste who had contributed nothing positive to the national welfare and who stood as an enormous encumbrance to a more rationally organized society. The vehemence of the nihilists' assault on the First Estate may be centrally linked to guilt over many radicals' privileged social origins. One of the clearest expressions of the nihilist attitude toward the nobility was provided by none other than Pisarev in a political allegory called "Bees" ("*Pchely*"), written in 1862 and published posthumously. Pisarev used the organization of beehives as a vehicle to express his hatred for hierarchical society:

> The entire population of the hive falls into three castes, distinguished each from the other by external signs. At the head of the hive stands the queen bee, or tsaritsa, the sole female having the ability and the right to lay eggs; she may literally say; l'état c'est moi, because she brings into the world everything that lives and moves in the hive. The rear section of her body is significantly longer than that of the workers; her sexual organs are more developed, therefore, her wings are shorter; as a result, the tsaritsa rarely leaves the hive and spends her whole life in the enjoyment of prepared food and in the satisfaction of her strongly developed sexual drives. She flies out only to give herself to a beloved drone midst flowering nature or to concede her place to a lucky competitor.
>
> Behind the tsaritsa follow the drones, or males, who far surpass the workers in length of body; these drones do not work, they do not carry weapons for defense, they eat a lot, impregnate the tsaritsa by turns and aside from this, they know neither cares nor obligations.
>
> Worker-bees are females incapable of bearing children; in their **incapacity nature is not to blame but upbringing; insufficient food** retards the development of their reproductive system and condemns them to a laboring life, lacking enjoyment. Not having the possibility to live for themselves, the workers turn their activity toward the raising of larvae borne by the tsaritsa; all the honey collected by them from flowers goes to feed the larvae, the drones and the tsaritsa. . . . Worker bees are woeful pariahs who do not feel their humiliation, who are incapable of escaping it, and who hold in this

humiliation the next generation, which in its turn will act in this
disgraceful conservative spirit, and so on forever. This is a proletariat,
crushed by the existing order of things, bound in hopeless slavery,
turning in the eternal circle and without any consciousness of a
better situation.[35]

As if this criticism weren't already clear enough, Pisarev added
another section referring to the drones "understanding their Estate
[*soslovnye*] privileges," to the drones' "laziness," to their "competition to show profound loyalty, or at least, fervent love to the
queen."[36] This almost obsessive preoccupation with and hatred
of hierarchy and privilege were typical of the Russian radicals from
the nihilists, to the Jacobin populists like Tkachev, to anarchists
like Bakunin.

The second aspect of the radical assault on the nobility was a rejection in practice of courtly "style"—of aristocratic behavior, dress,
and courtly language. Turgenev saw at once that the refinements
so important in high society could not be reconciled with "nihilism."
Bazarov's rudeness was not the result of personal preference but of
a necessary, philosophically grounded rejection of that which had
no utility.[37] Chernyshevsky's character Lopukhov in *What Is to Be
Done?* pushed aristocrats off sidewalks—a deliberate inversion of
the social code, and Chernyshevsky himself took pride in a blunt-
ness of address he knew to be offensive to the older generation.
The American historian Abbott Gleason has even argued that the
younger generation's rejection of Herzen was based less on ideological differences than on stylistic ones: Herzen was too much the
"flower of the conservatory" to suit the young.[38] Gleason probably
lays too much stress on the issue of style; he is arguing, in semiotic
terms, that clothing and language were "signs" distinguishing the
young from the old, when actually they were mere "signifiers" of
more deeply rooted differences in ideology and in generational experience. Is it not likely that many young radicals, ridden with
guilt over their own privileged origins, sought clear external forms
of speech, dress, and behavior that would divide them from their
parents' generation?

Nihilist thought, born of the political crisis during the debate over
emancipation, passed into a wider and more sophisticated radical
current in the 1870s known as populism. Like the radicals of the
1860s, a substantial number of populists were of noble origin.
Brower's study of the period from 1870 to 1875 showed that in
St. Petersburg 33 percent of radicals were from the landowning
nobility and 19 percent were from bureaucratic noble backgrounds; a

mere 5 percent of the Brower sample were *raznochintsy*.[39] The ideology of populism was strongly affected by the presence of so many radicals from noble backgrounds. The phenomenon of the "repentant noblemen" made its appearance in the 1870s as an outgrowth of the social thought of P. L. Lavrov and N. K. Mikhailovsky, both of whom were from gentry families, and both of whom were convinced that the privileged elite should work for the obliteration of social distinctions. In his *Historical Letters* Lavrov tried to convince young Russians that their personal educations had been purchased "by the blood, sufferings, or toil of millions" of peasants, and that the young were morally bound to discharge their debt to the masses.[40] Mikhailovsky was an especially forceful defender of Lavrov's view, and Mikhailovsky went even farther than Lavrov in justifying an end to social privilege. "Serving the people above all you serve no privilege, no exclusive interest, you serve simply labor, and as a result, incidentally, your own self."[41] Among the thousands of young Russians who heeded Lavrov and Mikhailovsky in the "Going to the People" were several hundred students from noble backgrounds.

The existence of an articulate radical left with many members drawn from noble families influenced the corporate politics of nobility both directly and indirectly. After the promulgation of the emancipation legislation, radicals pushed hard for the development of representative institutions in Russia. This effort, originating both from *Kolokol* in London and from the nihilists in the capital, encouraged the left liberal constitutional campaign in noble assemblies, especially Tver' province. As Terence Emmons has pointed out, there was a clear coincidence of political demands in 1861 and 1862, with Chernyshevsky, Herzen, and liberals like Tver' marshal Unkovsky lining up behind the same basic program of reform.[42] The influence of the radical left proved short lived, however; it collapsed in the wake of the St. Petersburg fire, the Polish rebellion, and government repression. In the late 1870s there was a brief revival of radical influence on noble politics. In 1878 the left liberals I. I. Petrunkevich and A. F. Lindfors were moved to conduct negotiations with members of the Land and Liberty populist revolutionary faction over a possible united front against the autocracy; Petrunkevich later persuaded the Chernigov zemstvo to send an address to the crown that had clear constitutionalist implications. Aside from these cases of direct influence in crisis situations, the radical left influenced noble politics by forcing nobles to define programs of social reform or defenses of the landed interests against the background of revolutionary alternatives. In short, radicals lent to noble corporate politics an urgency that might not otherwise have been present; the radicals provided an important part of the political context in which corporate political deliberations took place.

The liberal camp in the emancipation period was represented by the lineal descendants of the Westernizers and the Slavophiles. For a time adherents of both the old tendencies seemed to be in agreement on a general program to change Russian society; in fact, the program they followed was designed to accommodate people "from all spheres, all classes, all tendencies." The main demands of liberals in 1856 were: freedom of conscience, freedom from serfdom, freedom of public opinion, freedom of the press, freedom of teaching, public discussion of the national budget and government programs "harmful to the state," and public conduct of legal procedures.[43] However, as debate moved from general to specific, as liberals attended to concrete political issues raised by the prospective abolition of serfdom—the form of the emancipation, the exact division of land between nobles and peasants, and, perhaps most divisive of all, the future role of the nobility in Russian political society—their unity of purpose began to disintegrate. There were so many possible solutions to these problems that the intellectual movements of the pre-reform period splintered into a host of contending schools. For example, the three leading "liberal Slavophiles"—A. I. Koshelev, V. A. Cherkassky, and Iu. F. Samarin—were political allies and proponents of emancipation before 1858; thereafter they found themselves quarreling over the role of the nobility in the future polity. Koshelev became a partisan of a semiconstitutional regime led by nobles; he believed that unrestrained bureaucracy was leading Russia to ruin, and that the nobility, meeting in a zemsky sobor, could solve the nation's problems.[44] Cherkassky thought the nobility inimical to self-government.[45] Samarin found himself hoping that a fusion between tsar and people would be effected by the crown. Samarin was the lone member of this group who managed to profess faith in the state.[46] Both Cherkassky and Samarin wound up politically isolated, while Koshelev found support among liberal constitutionalists. It should be noted that Koshelev's "semiconstitutional" program contributed to the later movement of liberal Slavophilism, or neo-Slavophilism, led by the Moscow zemstvo chairman Dmitry Shipov at the turn of the century.[47]

The emancipation debates also resulted in the fragmentation of the Westernizer camp. V. A. Kitaev's study of B. N. Chicherin, K. D. Kavelin, and M. N. Katkov illustrated the swiftly growing discord that accompanied the open political discussion that began in 1855.[48] Chicherin quickly announced himself as an admirer of French centralized republicanism, a system of rule in which the government acted as a leveller of class distinctions and at the same time served as a guarantor of social order. Chicherin argued that the Russian state should follow the French republican path of development and destroy class privilege by decree. Yet the autocracy should also "prepare society for independence and prepare the soil on which its [society's] internal strength can develop freely and harmoniously."[49] Chicherin was, therefore, a defender of peasant reforms introduced from above by a powerful state; he looked forward to liberty and the end of juridical inequality in the distant future, and distrusted the nobility as a political force.

Katkov was a defender of the peasant reforms, but he also believed in decentralized local self-government led by the nobility. Katkov thought that decentralized self-government was somehow compatible with monarchical government and he pointed to England as an example. As Kitaev has noted, Katkov was influenced in his Anglomania by the appearance of Alexis de Tocqueville's *Old Regime and the French Revolution*.[50]

Unlike Chicherin, Kavelin was no admirer of the Russian state: "Visit the kitchen where state policies and laws are prepared, listen to these gentlemen, and you will be seized with terror. No, better a peasant from behind the plow, better a huckster from the bazaar than these———, who are worthless except for petty intrigue."[51] Yet Kavelin had little faith in self-government led by the nobility and was a strong opponent of constitutionalism. He was forced reluctantly to hope that the autocracy would grant wise reforms, but he had no solid reason to trust the crown and his ideology kept him from reliance on other forces in society.[52] It might be added that Herzen, who was once a member of the Westernizer camp, moved from cooperation with Chicherin and Kavelin to a personal break with them. By 1862 the whole Westernizer camp had disintegrated, just as the Slavophiles had.

If we categorize the distinct political tendencies represented after 1861 by this mere handful of former adherents to Westernism and Slavophilism, we see how quickly the number of political ideologies grew in the reform period. Separate categories might include semiconstitutional Slavophilism (Koshelev), anticonstitutional Slavophilism (Cherkassky), anticonstitutional statism (Samarin), anticonstitutional monarchism (Katkov), skeptical liberal monarchism (Kavelin), and skeptical democratic socialism (Herzen).

This proliferation of political tendencies within the liberal intellectual elite was mirrored to a certain extent by the growth of factions in noble assemblies during the emancipation debate. The left liberals were numerous in the Tver' and Kherson provincial assemblies; they supported an end to noble privileges in the economic realm, an emancipation settlement more favorable to the peasantry than the one adopted by the government, and the creation of a constitutional representative system. There were other assemblies in which a kind of moderate liberalism predominated: these liberals wanted to retain most of the privileges deriving from noble status, although they were willing to consider a constitutional system with a representative element if representation was weighted substantially in favor of large property holders.[53]

Thus, Russian liberalism, as a consequence of the emancipation debates and the constitutional campaign of the early 1860s, lost much of its programmatic unity and social cohesiveness. All Russian liberals worked in their own ways for the *raskreposhchenie obshchestva*, for the "unbinding of society," but they worked toward this very general goal by urging on the government specific ideas that were often incompatible. The differences in the liberal camp reflected both the increasing political sophistication of Russian high society and, to a lesser extent, differences in economic circumstance resulting from the differentiation of the Russian nobility.

In the middle of the political spectrum was an area where liberalism and conservatism blended together in a way that one finds difficult to categorize. One example from this politically gray area was the aristocratic constitutionalist tendency among the nobility in the 1860s and 1870s. During the emancipation debate there formed around N. A. Bezobrazov, and Counts P. P. Shuvalov, F. E. Paskevich, and V. P. Orlov-Davydov a group of frondeurs who opposed land redemption as a step that would undercut the rights of the nobility and who argued for an emancipation to be fashioned by the provincial nobility alone, without the interference of government bureaucrats. In 1861/62 these aristocrats began to push for the election of two noble delegates from each province "to gather in one of the capitals, as a general or state assembly."[54] The intention of the aristocrats was to secure a new foothold in the political decision-making process that would better enable them to protect the future interests of the First Estate. Aristocratic constitutionalism had support in Voronezh, St. Petersburg, Moscow, Tula, and Tambov provinces, although there was nothing approaching majority support in these assemblies. In the late 1860s and the early 1870s the aristocratic constitutionalist movement was championed by a powerful group within the central government apparatus, a group led by Chief of Gendarmes P. A. Shuvalov. The political platform of the Shuvalov group was formulated by the former Samara district and provincial marshal of the nobility, B. P. Obukhov, who wished "to call together and unite the very considerable number of conservative elements, the development and strengthening of which will provide a center of gravity for society and will be a corrective in its direction of development." Put in clear language, the Shuvalov program was a call for an English-style parliament with representation mainly for the propertied; Shuvalov also depended upon the conservatism of the majority of noble marshals who were to have an important role in the transitional stages of Shuvalov's program. The Shuvalov plan, like its predecessors, failed because it was interpreted as an infringement of the emperor's power.[55]

The difficulty of classifying the aristocrat constitutionalists as "liberal" or "conservative" should be apparent from these cases. The frondeurs were conservative in that they acted to preserve the power of the nobility; they were liberal in that they proposed reform of the state apparatus in the direction of the English model as the means of conservation.

The conservative camp itself was occupied by individuals who were ideological defenders of autocratic absolutism and a *Ständestaat* —men like St. Petersburg journalist V. P. Meshchersky—and by other individuals who saw themselves dependent on a strong autocracy and who were suspicious of any change in a liberal direction that might threaten the crown or the nobility's position vis-à-vis the crown. These latter unreflective conservatives constituted the base of the crown's social support through much of the second half of the century, and among them were many likely supporters of petitions written with a view to protect their own provinces or districts. For them the only ideology that mattered was self-interest conceived in the narrowest terms. They were the group described so acutely by Saltykov-Shchedrin in the late 1860s:

> Talk to any one of the provincial *historiografs*, and what will you hear from him? You will hear complaints that his position is not sufficiently solid; you will hear importunate pleas for shoring up this position; you will hear arrogant threats that the universe will burst asunder if the most efficacious and energetic measures are not taken immediately.[56]

Just as the left end of the political spectrum included radicals hostile to the nobility, the right end of the spectrum was populated by extremists who were also very critical of the First Estate. One thread of radical rightist thought was represented by what Abbott Gleason has called "the new right"—that group of thinkers which grew into existence after the emancipation and spent most of its energy in the fight against nihilism, but which also reserved much critical ammunition for the nobility. The best-known example of an anti-nihilist with a powerful disdain for the nobility was Dostoevsky, who, interestingly enough, was himself a second-generation *dvorianin*, but who all his life had felt insecure in the role of nobleman. Dostoevsky's attack on the First Estate had three components. First, Dostoevsky saw the Russian nobility as one source of the spiritual weakening of Russia. The characters Svidrigailov in *Crime and Punishment*, Fedor Pavlovich in *The Brothers Karamazov*, and a host of others illustrate Dostoevsky's conviction that noble country life was ridden with spiritual decay. Second, Dostoevsky saw courtly manners as a needless source of confusion and as a symptom of a rotten social order. In *The Idiot* Prince Myshkin's befuddlement by drawing-room society was a perfect example of the ill effects of "aristocratic" manners on a simple pure soul. In other novels, particularly *The Possessed*, Dostoevsky's scandal scenes are dependent on a deliberate inversion or rejection of the behavioral code of polite society. On the question of courtly manners, Dostoevsky's criticisms obviously coincided with those of the radical left. Third, Dostoevsky thought genuine nobility was not something achieved by membership in a social caste, rather it was a quality of spiritual goodness and "broadness" of character forged inside an individual's soul. This last idea was expressed in *The Adolescent* in the conversation between Versilov, who defended "an aristocracy of the spirit," and Prince Sergei, whose pride was fixed on mere title.[57]

Another thread of extreme rightism was the Christian anarchism, or libertarianism, of Lev Tolstoy. The self-transformation of Tolstoy from serfowner and novelist to Christian proponent of popular literature and inveterate opponent of the state was the right-wing equivalent of the appearance of the "repentent noblemen" among the populists. Tolstoy's conversion was no dramatic affair, but a painstaking process of reflection and moral rebuilding which ended in the rejection of social privilege and the full acceptance of human brotherhood.

The clearest evidence of Tolstoy's new attitude toward the nobility may be found in *Anna Karenina* and in the religious tracts of the early 1880s, especially in *Confession*. In *Anna Karenina* Tolstoy made his characters confront the proliferation of political schools that had followed the emancipation. Oblonsky had to choose between the liberalism that fitted so easily with his way of life, and conservatism. Levin had to decide at first how much sympathy to give to zemstvo liberalism, and later in the book he had to vote in a noble election for marshal where the contest was between an old honest conservative and a young liberal with big plans for provincial government.[58]

It is clear from the colorful account of the noble election that this confrontation with ideology produced in Levin nothing but aversion to politics: he left the hall before the end of the balloting which elected a marshal known as Nevedovsky—a name hinting at the ignorance (*nevezhestvo*) of its bearer and his electors. Tolstoy also forced Levin to come to terms with nihilism in the person of his brother Nikolai; Levin agreed with his brother's passionate condemnation of social institutions, especially with the criticism of social privilege, although he could not accept Nikolai's radical solutions. Tolstoy also demonstrated an awareness of the arbitrariness of the social code governing proper behavior in aristocratic circles: "The code categorically determined that though the card sharper must be paid, the tailor need not be; that one may not lie to a man, but might to a woman; that one must not deceive anyone, except a husband; that one must not forgive an insult but may insult others, and so on. These rules might be irrational and bad but they were absolute."[59] Levin rejected this social code for a higher code—that of Christianity.

The action of the novel finally led Levin to see that the privileged elite in Russia was an anachronism. Levin confided to an acquaintance: "I must confess to you that I only imperfectly understand the meaning of these noble elections." The acquaintance replied: "But what is there to understand? It has no meaning whatsoever. The nobility is an obsolete institution which continues to act through inertia. Look at the uniforms! They tell the tale: this is an assembly of Justices of the Peace, permanent officials, and so on, but not of nobles."[60] By the time Tolstoy had finished writing his *Confession* in 1880, his conviction of the obsolescence of the First Estate had **turned into a profound revulsion for the nobility's unchristian ways** of life and a wholehearted embrace of peasant religion.[61]

Thus, examination of ideologies defended by members of the Russian nobility between 1855 and 1880 shows that there was no clearly dominant intellectual position informing noble politics. Debates about the nobility's fate took place against a fragmented political background, with noble ideologies ranging all the way from nihilism to Christian anarchism. In fact, if there was anything characteristic of Russian noble politics in this period it was the absence of a coherent politics, or rather of a coherent intellectual tradition in terms of which all political proposals might be understood.

The fragmentation of Russian intellectual life and of Russian political debates was the logical result of the increasing sophistication of the educated elite, of the transition from a *Ständestaat* to a more fluid and complicated social structure, and of the growing diversity within the nobility. Once serfdom had been abolished, nobles lost the one institution they had had in common, and the raison d'être of the noble Estate was called into question. In a sense, all the ideologies current among educated Russians between 1855 and 1880 can be seen as responses to the problem of the nobility's continued existence in a radically changed social order. While moderate variants of liberalism and aristocratic conservatism suggested different means of accommodating nobles to the new situation, the radical ideologies of the left and right denied that the nobility should have a place in the new order at all. Because the lines of demarcation between ideological camps were so clearly drawn and the issues of the debate on the nobility so passionately contested, there could be no possibility of compromise between the disputants. Therefore, the birth of political debate in civil society around 1855 meant the genesis of permanent ideological divisions within the Russian nobility. Like Osiris's body, dismembered and scattered by the winds over the earth, the self-satisfied pre-emancipation consensus of the nobility was shattered beyond repair.

THE PROBLEM OF CLASS RECONSIDERED

At the beginning of this book I asked whether class analysis was an appropriate method to use in describing the Russian nobility. In Chapter 1 I argued that the nobility was a legally delimited social Estate whose members where ethnically and religiously diversified, divided by occupational allegiance, and stratified by income and extent of landownership. In Chapter 2 I suggested that after the abolition of serfdom, the Russian nobility had no common relationship to the means of production in the countryside. The emancipation settlement dictated sharp differences in the nature of land settlements between nobles and peasants; differences in the amount, timing, and impact of redemption payments; an assortment of land-tenure relationships between nobles and peasants; and a regional differentiation in agriculture and noble-peasant relationships. In the present chapter I have asserted that the institutional political leadership of the landed nobility, the noble marshals, was economically and socially heterogeneous, that this leadership had followed at least three career paths, and that to a considerable degree the marshals mirrored the diversity of the nobility as a whole. I have also asserted that there was no ideology common to politically active nobles, that the emancipation and other developments had wrought an end to consensus. Thus, the weight of the evidence indicates that the Russian nobility lacked a common identity, and that class analysis is generally inappropriate to the study of the First Estate after the emancipation.

Of course, it is true that Russian nobles were privileged with respect to other *sosloviia*. Doubtless the poorest noble had a higher social status than peasants living around him, even if his economic position was the same as that of the neighboring peasants. Without question there did exist an exploitative nexus between many landed nobles and the peasantry. And while nobles had at their disposal a number of political mechanisms by which they could influence the crown, mechanisms including voluntary societies, the press, patronage ties, the zemstvos, and the noble assemblies, the peasantry were denied access to all these means of influencing the autocrat, save one—the zemstvos. But privilege in the form of status, a favorable economic position, and political influence does not *in and of itself* constitute the existence of a class. If the differences between the upper reaches of a social formation and its lowest depths are so great as to make incommensurable distinctions between members of that formation, if the nature of economic privilege varies vastly from region to region and from individual to individual, if political influence cannot be brought to bear in any reasonably coherent manner, then privilege may exist but historians ought not denominate it as class privilege.

I believe that the only way to understand the politics of the nobility between 1881 and 1905 is to discard the terminology of class analysis and to study the activity of noble assemblies as interest politics. It was chiefly through the deferential language of petitions, passed by noble assemblies and submitted to the government by marshals of the nobility, that local nobles brought their grievances to the attention of the national government. Even though these petitions sometimes spoke of the fate of the Russian nobility as a class and in terms easily susceptible to Marxian analysis, the post-1881 petitions are best understood as fundamentally nonideological instruments for adjusting local grievances. Only when one sees interest politics as a primarily local and nonideological phenomenon, can one comprehend the frustrating inability of the nobility to unite themselves in the face of the grave crisis from 1881 to 1905. Interest politics could not overcome the social, economic, and intellectual differences among nobles; it could only reflect and magnify these differences.

PART TWO

Mounting Tensions, 1881–1905

A moment earlier, inspiration
had filled this heart, and detestation
and hope and passion; life had glowed
and blood had bubbled as it flowed;
but now the mansion is forsaken;
shutters are up, and all is pale
and still within, behind the veil
of chalk the window panes have taken.
The lady of the house has fled.
Where to, God knows. The trail is dead.
  —*A. S. Pushkin,*
  Eugene Onegin, *Canto VI*

C H A P T E R 4
Terrorism,
the Great Depression,
and Noble Politics

wo historical developments of the late 1870s and early 1880s shaped a generation of Russian noble politics. The first was the appearance of the terrorist movement within populism and the assassination of Alexander II; the second was the beginning of the Great Depression which contributed to the crisis of Russian agriculture. Previous historians, including Zaionchkovsky and Soloviev, have missed an important perspective on Russian noble politics by viewing these developments as separate phenomena. In this chapter I shall describe in general terms the combined impact of both terrorism and the Great Depression on Russian noble politics. Subsequent chapters will recount the nobility's specific attempts to change government policies and show why these attempts were only partially successful.

TERRORISM AND THE
POLITICAL CRISIS, 1878–1882

On 1 May 1879 P. A. Valuev wrote in broken English his verdict on Alexander II and on the Russian imperial government: "Not two years purchats. . . ." Valuev believed that Alexander possessed a "trivial soul" and operated with divided political loyalties: "wholeness in relation only to himself." Of the government, Valuev said: "There are fragments of a government. There is no whole. It [the government] is an idea, an abstraction."[1] During the next twenty-two months—the period of the Temporary Governors-General, the Supreme Administrative Commission, and the "dictatorship of the heart"—Valuev remained pessimistic. In no less than six diary entries he referred explicitly to the vulnerability of the government, and on 8 September 1880 he even quoted his own prophecy giving the regime but two years of life.[2] The assassination of the tsar on 1 March 1881 came to Valuev not as a surprise, but as a confirmation of his fears. For the next two years he lived in expectation of a governmental collapse. The old statesman could only think that "above all doors one may write: *'pour le quart d'heure.'* This *quart d'heure*, of course, may prolong itself, but it will not last a historical day."[3]

Valuev's pessimism was doubtless a consequence of his acerbity and tendency to exaggerate, but it was also a response to the objective historical conditions described so faithfully in P. A. Zaionchkovsky's works. The government was beleaguered by a host of problems ranging from virtual diplomatic isolation to social tensions in the countryside, and now the tsar had been threatened and finally killed by terrorists. To Valuev it seemed that the situation was spinning out of control and that the government had lost permanently the statesman's gift for mastering reality. Valuev was not alone in his anxiety: Iu. B. Soloviev has demonstrated that other high officials were just as frightened by terrorism and the government's apparent ineptitude. Given this atmosphere of fear, one should not be surprised that the years from 1878 to 1882 were a time of intense discussion within the government over the proper shape of official administration and the political system.

What has not been sufficiently emphasized by other historians is that the governmental debate over the Russian political system was accompanied by a debate outside of government in which politically active Russian nobles took part. The atmosphere of crisis which Valuev so sensitively recorded could not be confined to government circles: it permeated society and created an imperative for nobles to contribute ideas and plans that might help the state survive terrorism.

The first arena in which the nobility debated the proper response to terrorism was the zemstvo assemblies. Zemstvo activists thought of the zemstvo as the one Russian institution that could defeat the revolutionary movement, mainly by denying revolutionaries popular support and by gradually ameliorating those social ills which gave rise to popular discontent. The zemtsy also argued that county and provincial self-government, untainted by the administrative arbitrariness of the existing central government, might serve as a basis for reconstructing the whole Russian political apparatus. A reform of the central administration was, of course, essential if the triumph of revolutionary terrorism was to be avoided. In the view of many zemstvo liberals, Russian politics was at root a triangular struggle between the central government, the terrorists, and the zemstvos. In this struggle the government was animated by a narrow conservatism and arbitrariness, the terrorists by fanaticism and violence, while the zemstvo represented the path of rational change, true patriotism, and respect for the human personality.

Unfortunately, zemstvo liberalism suffered from several problems. First, the liberals were a small minority of the Russian nobility, too insubstantial a foundation on which to build a reformed political order. The earliest political petitions demanding fundamental reform —those adopted in 1878 and 1879 in Khar'kov, Tver', Chernigov, Samara, and Poltava provincial zemstvos—were engineered by small liberal factions whose enthusiasm for reform seemed to overcome the conservatism of other delegates; and in three cases (Khar'kov, Tver', and Chernigov) zemstvo petitions were inspired by the efforts of a single activist, I. I. Petrunkevich.[4] There was only one national meeting of zemstvo activists in the entire four-year period from 1878 to 1882: the so-called Moscow zemstvo congress, a meeting of about forty activists called in March 1879 by Petrunkevich. After the exile of Petrunkevich in mid-1879 and the government's clear rebuff of liberal constitutionalism, zemstvo leaders found themselves too weak and divided to forge a liberal party that might have forced the government to heed its demands.

The second liability of the zemstvo liberals was that they lacked a coherent ideological and organizational foundation for challenging monarchical absolutism. As noted in Chapter 3, there were several distinct varieties of liberalism which developed out of the Westernizer Weltanschauung. These differences within the already small liberal camp prevented a coalescence of reformists interested in political change between 1878 and 1882. The clearest diagnosis of the effects of liberal ideological disagreement and organizational weakness is a letter from V. Iu. Skalon to the Novgorod zemstvo activist N. N. Nechaev in April 1882: "Now an organization is needed, if one may so express oneself, of a political party, and to work out a definite political program, which our present so-called liberal party lacks. People who are numbered or who number themselves as members of this party have among themselves very little in common; there are vast differences of opinion among them, and as soon as an issue goes beyond the sphere of liberal polemics and 'illusions,' liberals clash with one another cruelly. . . ." Skalon admitted that "on basic concepts—on freedom of speech, of conscience, etc.—all of them [the liberals] agree," but, he added, "as soon as one raises the practical realization of these concepts, among the liberals there flames up a brutal war."[5] Thus, liberals in the zemstvo assemblies could not speak with one voice for a reform program or constitution.

In the months following the assassination of Alexander II, all the weaknesses of provincial liberalism manifested themselves in zemstvo debates over whether to call for the opening of a zemsky sobor. These debates, far from being a new departure for the nation, illustrated all the symptoms of the crisis facing the nation: intellectual confusion, emotional but empty patriotism, lack of direction, and political paralysis. Nowhere was the liberals' impasse so evident as in the deliberations of zemstvo and noble assemblies in Samara province in March 1881.

On 5 March the chairman of the Samara provincial zemstvo introduced a proposed address that would express to Alexander III the zemstvo's commiseration over the recent assassination. Such an address might have been passed through a rational assembly without demur, but now all but three delegates voted against it. The majority apparently agreed with the confused sentiments of delegate Naumov, who said: "There are no words capable of expressing all that is now in our souls. We do not know what awaits us in the future. To what end the empty formality of an address? It is better to be silent." But at the very same session another delegate named Zhdanov stated that while he too was against an expression of sympathy for the new tsar as "untimely," he was not opposed to petitioning the government on other grounds. "If one is to petition about something, then let it not be about trivia. It is time directly to say that it is desirable to broaden the zemstvo's jurisdiction not over some *isolated* matter within its purview, but to broaden the rights of the people and the people's participation, in the persons of their representatives, in the self-government of the whole nation." Zhdanov's plea for broadening popular participation led delegate Nudatov to propose creation of a commission to discuss zemstvo rights, at which point the zemstvo chairman cut off debate. The matter then died on the zemstvo floor.[6]

Three days after the opening of the Samara zemstvo assembly there was a meeting of the Samara nobility. The Nikolaevsky district marshal of the nobility, Tenniakov, told his peers: "It is urgent to begin thinking about the future. Today they [the revolutionaries] killed one Monarch, and tomorrow they will begin plotting to kill another. We must discuss measures that should be enacted to prevent similar terrible tragedies. I propose to the noble assembly that we discuss this important question." Following Tenniakov's proposal, Nudatov agreed that this problem needed to be discussed, but not in a noble assembly. "This, in the highest degree, difficult issue must be resolved only by freely elected representatives from all social Estates, and not from the nobility alone, and these representatives must be called for this purpose." Nudatov's call for an all-Estate assembly was greeted by cries: "True! True!" Nudatov then continued:

> I am already old and in my declining days. I love my motherland and
> wish it happiness and glory. No one can suspect me or say that I am a
> revolutionary. But for the welfare of the fatherland, for the sake of our
> children's happiness, I tell you that the trouble [*smuta*] which has
> lacerated the Russian land already for two years can only be alleviated
> by the common efforts of freely elected representatives of the people.
> Only they, and not merely the nobility, can bring peace and tran-
> quility to our unfortunate motherland.

As Nudatov moved toward his seat, tears ran down his cheeks. His peers began to applaud him thunderously, and there were cries: "Exactly! True! True!"

Before the applause had died out, Count Tolstoy, another delegate, said:

> The road we have indicated is neither new nor revolutionary. In old
> Russia it was followed long ago. Thus, even the most absolute mon-
> archs, such as Ivan Grozny and Alexei Mikhailovich, summoned
> zemskie sobory. Who should defend their tsar, if not representatives
> of the people? If not those who deceived the deceased tsar?

The provincial marshal interrupted Tolstoy before the latter finished his speech. "Such criticism cannot be allowed," said the nervous marshal. Nevertheless, the noble assembly was not deterred from voting to establish a committee to draft a petition for a convocation of elected representatives which would "discuss and adopt measures to pacify the fatherland and eradicate evil."[7]

Thus, as I noted earlier, the Samara debates manifested the uncertainty of Russian liberals. Delegates to the zemstvo thought a petition of sympathy to the new tsar "untimely," but convinced themselves that it was timely to openly discuss national representation. Nudatov pleaded emotionally and patriotically for a national assembly, and he even told the Samara nobility that they alone were not competent to discuss, much less to resolve, national issues. Yet the national assembly Nudatov advocated would be called mainly to halt the revolutionary movement. Count Tolstoy defended a zemsky sobor as a hedge against another assassination, yet he admitted that the people had somehow "deceived the deceased" tsar, and he seemed to imply that a zemsky sobor would enable these same deceptive people to atone for their prior dishonesty. In the Samara debates there was anything but a coherent discussion of the tasks facing liberalism in the wake of the assassination. The Samarans did not escape the tripartite vision of politics that had characterized liberalism since the terrorist movement had arisen; they could only repeat that if the central government wished to preserve itself from the revolutionaries, it must "crown" the zemstvo edifice.

In addition to being confused and unoriginal in their responses to the assassination, the liberals were passive. They spoke of a zemsky sobor where Russia's problems might be solved, but it was to be called by the tsar. Once the liberals had recommended summoning a zemsky sobor, they were content to wait for Alexander III to move. Moreover, the liberals were unclear about what concretely would be done at a zemsky sobor. Such an assembly would provide, of course, a symbolic union of tsar and people, and a catharsis after the terrorist triumph of 1 March. But liberals were evidently afraid to imagine anything beyond that. In fact, it is not even certain that most liberals wished for the powers of the autocrat to be restricted. In some liberal publications the zemsky sobor was envisioned as a love feast between tsar and people, nothing more. In the newspaper *Poriadok* only two days after the assassination, the liberal jurist M. M. Stasiulevich wrote the following:

> Your land, Sovereign, has for centuries preserved in itself both reason
> and strength to order and arrange the state. It has supported by its
> love your forebears, it taught them and thought with them in years of
> great misfortune. Ask the land in the person of its beloved representa-
> tives [*v litse izliublennykh liudei*]. What they will answer, we cannot
> determine precisely, but most surely in one spirit, holy and profound,
> they will merge closely with you, Sovereign, [*oni tesno sol'iutsia s
> Vami*]—in a spirit of burning love for Russia.[8]

Needless to say, the lovelorn liberalism of Stasiulevich did not impress Alexander III, who, on instructions from Pobedonostsev, locked himself up in Anichkov Palace and began checking under his bed each night for hidden terrorists.[9]

By the end of 1881 only four provincial and one district zemstvo and two noble assemblies had even debated the problem of a constitution, and none got past the problem of what might be done at a zemsky sobor. As the historian Bogucharsky has noted, "About the limitation of the autocracy. . . . there is not even a hint; such an idea is impossible to find [in zemstvo petitions] even with a microscope."[10] The passivity of Russian liberals after the assassination, combined with their disorganization and confusion, was a fatal political liability. By confining themselves to a poorly formulated plea for a zemsky sobor, the liberals surrendered political initiative to the central government at a time when the central government was populated increasingly by illiberals of the Pobedonostsev stripe. This political blunder, as we shall see, had catastrophic consequences for liberal politics in the next generation.

The second arena in which the nobility debated the proper response to terrorism was an organization created by high members of the imperial court, an organization christened the *Sviashchennaia druzhina*, the Holy Retinue. The avowed purposes of this semiclandestine organization were to preserve the lives of the sovereign and the royal family; to gather information on revolutionary circles; to infiltrate, disrupt, and destroy revolutionary groups; and to draft "not only a principled, but a practical conservative program" that would serve as an ideological basis for the guardians of Russia's social order.[11] Between 12 March 1881, when the Holy Retinue constituted itself, and 26 November 1882, when the police disbanded it, the organization funded a volunteer guard which protected the emperor and his family on outdoor trips; it also funded three newspapers designed to break up the revolutionary movement by provocation, and used its agents abroad to threaten the lives of well-known revolutionaries such as Lev Gartman and Prince Kropotkin.[12]

The official history of the Holy Retinue reported that the organization had 729 members.[13] Although there is no published membership roster of the St. Petersburg area adherents, Bogucharsky and Lukashevich have partially uncovered the composition of the organization's ruling bodies. Among members of the Executive Committee were Prince A. Shcherbatov, Prince P. Demidov San Donato, A. Bezobrazov, and Count Pavel Petrovich Shuvalov. In the Organizational Committee were General P. Durnovo and Count N. Levashov. The Central Committee, which oversaw all the activities of the Retinue, was headed by Count I. I. Vorontsov-Dashkov, and included Count Pavel Shuvalov and Senator Schmidt. There is a published membership roster for the Moscow area which indicated that a majority of the Muscovite members belonged to the titled nobility.[14]

The significance of the membership information cannot be overstated. Of those known participants in the ruling bodies of the Retinue, five individuals—Count Shuvalov, Count Vorontsov-Dashkov, General Durnovo, Prince Shcherbatov, and Prince Demidov—were part of the "hundred families," that is, of that tiny section of the noble magnates who were the richest landowners in Russia.[15] Another activist in the Holy Retinue, though not a member of its ruling bodies, was A. A. Bobrinsky, also a scion of the hundred families. These individuals brought to the Holy Retinue enormous financial resources; one member's diary gives the figure of three million rubles contributed by aristocrats in the first five months of the Retinue's existence.[16] This was the money that made possible the volunteer guard as well as clandestine activity. Moreover, the members from the hundred families brought prestige and political clout to the Retinue. Count Vorontsov-Dashkov was an intimate of Alexander III who, after Alexander's accession, became chief of the imperial security entourage, and then Minister of the Imperial Court. From these two positions Vorontsov commanded the palace police, secret police, and the railroad police. Thus, the Retinue's unofficial voluntary guard carried behind it the weight of Vorontsov-Dashkov's officially constituted police authority. Count Shuvalov was an associate of N. P. Ignatiev, who at one point wished to appoint Shuvalov as governor-general of Moscow; Demidov San Donato was an official in the Ministry of Foreign Affairs, while Durnovo had a high army post. A. A. Bobrinsky was provincial marshal of the St. Petersburg nobility. The political and economic power of the Holy Retinue's leadership gave that organization special status within official circles. The Holy Retinue became, in the words of an opponent, *status in statu*—a state within the state.

Only if one remembers the Holy Retinue's position as state within the state can one understand the Retinue's ideology. The Holy Retinue was a league of the already powerful and privileged, of insiders who believed that they alone had the wisdom to preserve the state from the threat posed by terrorism. Vorontsov-Dashkov, Shuvalov, and Bobrinsky in particular saw themselves not as modern Western-style conservatives, but as *okhraniteli*, as guardians of order in the Greek sense. It was the privilege and duty of true guardians to introduce into the state those changes made necessary by external threats, so long as the changes were consistent with the higher criteria of justice and the popular character. Thus the ideologues of the Holy Retinue contemplated the introduction of representative elements into Russian government, but they did not interest themselves in the classic goals of Russian liberalism, freedom of speech and assembly. What mattered was the preservation of the state.

The Holy Retinue saw the political situation in Russia as essentially bipolar. At one pole there was the Russian government and its Russian supporters from the peasantry, upper nobility, and zemstvo. At the opposite pole were terrorists, revolutionaries, liberals from the zemstvo and intelligentsia, poor nobles, students, and also the non-Russian peoples of the Empire. This bipolar political alignment, the ideologues thought, was a temporary phenomenon, subject to rapid change by vigorous political leadership. Revolutionaries could be isolated from the rest of society by a strong ideological offensive against revolutionary ideas. All the erstwhile allies of the terrorists could be won back to the government's camp or politically neutralized. Once the milieu that fostered terrorism had been eliminated, terrorism itself could be destroyed.

The Holy Retinue's ideology was nowhere elaborated in a single document. The official history spoke of a "principled but practical conservative program" as the goal of the group, but the leadership did not publish such a program. Still, enough is known about the political attitudes of Shuvalov, Vorontsov-Dashkov, and Bobrinsky for historians to gauge the Holy Retinue's politics.

Shuvalov was perhaps the most important of the Retinue's ideologues. Before the assassination of Alexander II, Shuvalov had circulated a memorandum calling for the creation of a two-house consultative agency for advising the government. The upper house would be based on a limited number of well-propertied electors who would vote a list of candidates; the government would then select delegates to the upper house from this list. The lower chamber was to be elected through procedures used in zemstvo elections. Shuvalov justified his bicameral body by mentioning the inevitability of popular representation, but there was nothing "popular" about his scheme, which would have led to the nobility's domination in both houses. Two months after the assassination Shuvalov circulated a second memorandum. This one said nothing of bicameralism; instead it argued for the addition of zemstvo personnel to the State Council. The zemtsy would be elected at the local level as candidates, and the central government would select State Council representatives from among them. This new plan, like its predecessor, Shuvalov saw as a way to put able conservatives into power. Neither proposal referred to personal liberties, and neither proposal would have infringed on the autocrat's prerogatives.[17]

In the second memorandum Shuvalov complained that other members of high society had favored different proposals:

> Some place all their hopes on the preventive and repressive measures of government; others see no salvation other than the adaptation of Western constitutional forms to our society; still others console themselves with various eloquent sayings, lacking in substance. Finally, there are very many, not seeing any trustworthy solution, who respond to the phenomena surrounding them with a sort·of apathetic fatalism.[18]

Shuvalov rejected repression alone as a course that had worked under Nicholas I but could not succeed in the new social conditions of post-emancipation Russia. He dismissed Western constitutionalism as incompatible with autocracy: "The autocracy has been preserved intact. It constitutes even now the sole source of authority and the cornerstone of the entire state structure."[19] Most of all, Shuvalov disagreed with the empty phrase-makers and fatalists. Russia was surely in crisis, but the crisis could be overcome by his legislation.

> This apparent victory of hostile forces is a very superficial phenomenon. It failed to stifle native popular emotions, the force of which recently showed itself so clearly at the new tsar's accession to the throne. And, whatever the temporary waverings in the apparent mood of society, there is every assurance that these emotions remain vital and that in the hearts of the great majority of Russian people are concealed well-tuned native strings [*blagotvornye rodnye struny*] which the Sovereign may easily touch with trusting hand.
>   A sure means to attain this goal would be the Sovereign's call to the active elected elements of the nation to participate in government affairs.[20]

Yet Shuvalov, for all his confidence about Russia's ultimate loyalties to the autocracy, admitted that educated society was then "ill and disturbed," that "our society is a fertile ground for the clever disseminators of dangerous doctrines." Russia suffered from the syndrome later identified by the Vekhi collective: "extreme impressionability, easy susceptibility to every cleverly dressed up novelty and a general lack of steadfastness and independence of judgment." Only by treating the underlying causes of the Russian sickness, by treating terrorism as a disease "rooted in the human soul," could the government survive. Unfortunately, Shuvalov did not tell the government precisely how to fight a moral disease.

A. A. Bobrinsky reacted to the assassination with a plea for a zemsky sobor. He worried lest the government should mistakenly rely on repression alone to stop terrorism:

> To what end have been high commissions? The exalted powers of governors-generals? Military tribunals? Administrative exiles? They [the revolutionaries] murdered the Sovereign, our Sovereign, in Petersburg, in broad daylight. Our enemies dug tunnels under the most heavily traveled streets. No, these extreme measures have led to no good.[21]

Bobrinsky believed that no one in the government was strong enough to wield the "heavy sword" of repression. "We fear that the heavy sword will slip from the incapable hands [*neposil'nikh ruk*], into which it might be placed by the tsar's trust. We are convinced that if this sword merely slips, that all Russia will shudder."[22] Yet Bobrinsky rather inconsistently asked that no concessions be made to terrorists, who should be ruthlessly suppressed.

Bobrinsky believed that the government's interests would best be served by a policy that harnessed the energies of the Russian land against the revolutionary movement. Like Shuvalov, he thought that most Russians were loyal to the autocracy and not to nihilism. Unspoken in his memorandum was the conviction that in the zemsky sobor the government would find strong hands, people like himself, who could lift the sword of state without losing their grip.

Historians know less about the politics of Count Vorontsov-Dashkov than about those of Shuvalov and Bobrinsky because the documents of Vorontsov-Dashkov's archive remain unpublished. However, it is known that in May 1882 Vorontsov expressed an interest in a zemsky sobor. On 4 May D. I. Voeikov, second in command at the Ministry of Internal Affairs, received a certain Fadeev, who reported that "everyone was pressing Vorontsov to oppose the sobor, but yesterday Vorontsov had said he was in favor of the sobor, but only of a real sobor that would meet in the fall."[23] One may assume that Vorontsov's ideas were expressed in the official history of the Holy Retinue. That document noted that repression alone could not destroy the revolutionary movement; such a task required an attack on the ideology of revolution and the organization of "those people, who by their expertise and social position could serve as leaders or as strong activists in the conservative movement." The document specifically referred to the need for native Russian conservatives. "The society had little faith in Polish and Jewish conservatism, since the political interests of these nationalities diverge from native Russian interests."[24]

Thus, the ideology of the Holy Retinue was a variant of aristocratic constitutionalism adapted to the circumstances existing in Russia after the assassination of Alexander II. It emphasized the loyalty to the throne of the Russian propertied elements and of the Russian people and demanded that these loyal elements be given an advisory role in the fight against terrorism. Since the Holy Retinue organized the wealthy nobility behind the throne and advocated political changes that were in no sense liberal, the government allowed it to exist for some time. But the arrogant notion of the Retinue's leaders that they could guide the state, coupled with the commitment of Shuvalov, Bobrinsky, and Vorontsov-Dashkov to a zemsky sobor, or some other form of representation, worried the government and positively alarmed Pobedonostsev and D. A. Tolstoy.

The Holy Retinue's fatal strategic error was to sponsor the publication of three newspapers: *Vol'noe slovo, Moskovsky telegraf,* and *Pravda.* All these papers were to discredit the teaching of The People's Will in revolutionary spheres by casting doubt on the applicability of its doctrines, by "provoking artificial quarrels among members of parties and by trying to produce schisms among their personnel." *Pravda,* published in Geneva by the police spy Klimov, was to exaggerate the revolutionary program in such a way as to make it "obviously absurd even to politically unbalanced [*otumannikh*] persons." *Moskovsky Telegraf* was a moderate organ designed to split the zemstvo liberals into political activist and economic reformist factions. *Vol'noe slovo* was supposed to criticize the revolutionary movement from a liberal constitutionalist perspective, although in fact the overriding concern of *Vol'noe slovo* was the Jewish question, on which it took a violently anti-Semitic stance.[25]

The Holy Retinue's attempted provocations of the left opened the organization to charges that it was actually a revolutionary league within the Russian court. Minister of Internal Affairs Ignatiev complained to Pobedonostsev that the Retinue "compromises us everywhere," and Pobedonostsev himself later denounced a leader of the Retinue as an almost radical constitutionalist. Ultimately, it was from material gathered from the Holy Retinue's newspapers that Pobedonostsev composed two scathing attacks on the organization, thus prompting the tsar to order the Retinue disbanded.

It is sometimes argued by liberal historians that the enduring significance of Alexander II's assassination was that with the accession of Alexander III and the defeat of the Loris-Melikov project, Russia lost its golden opportunity for democratic reforms based upon the zemstvo. For example, in unpublished memoirs written shortly after the Bolshevik revolution, Alexander Kornilov forcefully claimed that had there been no catastrophe on 1 March and the enduring reaction that followed upon it, by which the revolutionaries of that time were, in any case, swept away without having achieved anything, we would have had a broad and solid development of democratic zemstvo self-administration, and moreover, it would have been given the foundation it lacked, in the form of a *small zemstvo unit* of one kind or another. At the same time we would have seen the free development of popular education, so necessary for Russia.[26]

But Kornilov and other liberal historians have greatly oversimplified the impact of the assassination and Alexander III's accession to the throne. The *initial* impact of the assassination was to make possible political debate over Russia's future, a debate in which both zemstvo activists and aristocratic constitutionalists in the Holy Retinue played a part. But the very fashion in which these groups engaged in debate strengthened the government's hand: the liberals surrendered political initiative to the crown; the Holy Retinue, having assumed the risky role of provocateur vis-à-vis radical liberals and revolutionaries, found itself embarrassed and disbanded by the crown. The fumbling attempts of these groups within the nobility to change the autocratic political system failed, and the conservative ministers of Alexander III exploited this failure by virtually banning any future debate within the zemstvo or voluntary organizations that might threaten the structure of the state. Thus, terrorism and the assassination altered noble politics by making structural change of the autocracy a forbidden topic: the agenda of noble politics was thereby sharply delimited, even in comparison with the 1860s and 1870s.

The ministerial delimitation of the legitimate agenda of noble politics was accompanied by a polarization of sentiment dividing the government even further from educated society. The depth of distrust and resentment was evident in a meeting between Pobedonostsev and the liberal B. N. Chicherin in the summer of 1882. Until this meeting Chicherin had been on friendly terms with Pobedonostsev, whom Chicherin thought a capable statesman with an open mind. Chicherin told Pobedonostsev:

You are the only serious man among all those surrounding the tsar; he [the tsar] must trust you more than the rest. Therefore, Russia considers you to be more responsible for what is being done; from you we Russians may rightfully demand an accounting. Where have you led us? After 1 March everyone without exception was ready to gather around the throne and to obey every wave of the tsar's hand. But now what kind of a position have you put us in? You have surrounded the throne with mud, so that it is now bespattered. You have pulled out of the mob all kinds of trash, and entrusted to it the governance of Russia. All decent people are forced to turn away with indignation. You object against a zemsky sobor, but you are driving us by compulsion toward a zemsky sobor.

Pobedonostsev stopped Chicherin and exclaimed: "A zemsky sobor— that is chaos!" Chicherin answered, "I know that it is chaos, but from chaos comes a new world, and out of a rotten tree nothing will come, except decay." "And who will give it [a zemsky sobor] to you?" Pobedonostsev asked. Chicherin then reached up and grabbed the Ober-Procurator of the Synod by the shoulders and said: "We will take it, Konstantin Petrovich, we will take it. And for this we don't even have to move a muscle; it is enough to sit with an open mouth and everything will fall into it. Do you really imagine that you, with your Petersburg rot, can lead Russia onto a proper course?"[27] Chicherin concluded this account of his conversation with Pobedonostsev, by observing that "Pobedonostsev dolefully listened to my indignant reproaches. He considered me an irretrievably fallen man."[28]

Chicherin's story demonstrates that within a year after the assassination serious political discourse, even amongst old friends, had become impossible. If the question demanded that the parties consider limitation of the autocrat's prerogatives or the calling of a zemsky sobor, one side was reduced to bitter reproach, and the other to melancholy reflection on the loss of sanity in political life. And when we remember that the Chicherin-Pobedonostsev encounter was a private conversation, it becomes obvious that public consideration of these matters of state was now utterly out of the question. Liberalism and aristocratic conservatism were pushed firmly out of Petersburg political life and would not return for a generation. Provincial noble politics in the 1880s and 1890s would not be dominated by large questions of state, but by narrower questions of economic self-interest, questions dictated to the nobility by the Great Depression.

THE GREAT DEPRESSION AND NOBLE AGRICULTURE

The second historical development that affected noble provincial politics was the Great Depression of the 1880s and 1890s. The Great Depression was the result of an unfavorable conjuncture of international and national economic trends that drove down grain prices around the world and put enormous market pressures on grain producers in Russia and the West. These market pressures dictated to Russian noble landowners, as to American farmers and Western European agrarian groups, a set of political problems that became the basis for American populism and for agrarian interest politics in Western Europe and Russia.

The Great Depression in agriculture struck Western Europe sometime in the mid-1870s. In England the situation was so bad that between 1876 and 1886 the yearly income of landlords, tenants, and farm laborers had diminished by £42,800,000. The grain-growing area of England and Wales shrank from 8.2 million acres in 1871 to almost 5.9 million acres in 1901, as farmers abandoned their fields to pasture or, in some cases, allowed them to go to seed altogether.[29] In France the depression hit as early as 1873 and, according to Robert Estier, "French agriculture entered a chronic state of crisis that lasted until 1914." In the years between 1872 and 1876 the price of wheat in France averaged 29.4 francs a quintal, but twenty years later in the period from 1892 to 1896 a quintal of wheat brought only 20 francs.[30] In Germany the fall of grain prices began in 1876 and by the mid-1880s a catastrophic situation seemed imminent. German agriculture was so hard pressed that Bismarck was compelled to push protectionist legislation through the Reichstag and to commit his prestige to the cause of needy farmers. In 1885 he told the Reichstag that agriculture had suffered more than other industries in the general commercial depression, and warned of a national disaster if rye prices were allowed to sink any further.[31]

The price depression in Europe was a consequence of rising supplies of grain made possible by greater productivity, and of the rather sudden appearance in the second half of the nineteenth century of a transportation network that facilitated inexpensive long-distance shipments of grain to European and English market centers. In the United States the construction of over 200,000 miles of railroad track between 1860 and 1900 enabled farmers to ship vast quantities of wheat and rye to Chicago and New York, whence these grains could be transferred to Europe.[32] And the introduction of the steamship with its enormous holds and efficient engines led to a radical cut in the cost of American export freights between 1873 and 1897. In the eleven years from 1873 to 1884 the cost of sending one ton of grain from Chicago to Liverpool declined from £3.75 to £1.45.[33]

Simultaneously with the appearance of a world market in grain-stuffs and the building of the trans-American and trans-Atlantic transport systems, Russia completed the development of its own national market system. The evolution of a national grain market within Russia had been a painfully slow process. In the seventeenth century the surplus extracted from agriculture was trifling; according to the respected Soviet economic historian V. K. Iatsunsky, "In the seventeenth century the agricultural population just managed to feed itself."[34] Under these circumstances the formation of a real grain market was clearly impossible. By the end of the eighteenth century there was still no national grain market, but there did exist a series of regional markets. L. V. Milov and I. D. Koval'chenko, the two foremost contemporary Soviet economic historians, have asserted that there were "three gigantic regional rye markets and one enormous regional market for oats" in the period from 1750 to 1820.[35] In the middle of the nineteenth century Russia gradually moved toward the creation of a national commodity market, but this process was retarded by Russia's enormous territorial expanse and by the existence of serfdom, which tended to delay the process of capital formation. By 1861 there was a single national market for only one cereal—oats; the completion of the national commodity market for agricultural goods occurred only in the 1880s.[36]

As in Europe and America, the growth of Russian commerce was facilitated by railroad construction. P. I. Liashchenko noted that "railroads exerted the strongest single influence on the expansion and intensification of the sales of agricultural products."[37] A recent study by a young cliometrician agreed with Liashchenko; according to Jacob Metzer, "The reduction in transportation costs associated with major railroad construction had a decisive impact on the quality of inter-regional trade in European Russia."[38] In 1855 there were less than one thousand versts of railroad track in European Russia. Railroads increased to 10,200 versts in 1870 and reached 41,700 versts in 1900.[39] By 1885 railroads carried shipments of grain equal to 150 million poods, or nearly 29 percent of the harvest. By the turn of the century the railroads hauled 812 million poods, or 33 percent of the total harvest.[40]

Though railroads became the most important single component of the grain commerce system, historians should not overlook the role of water transportation in the grain trade. In 1884, for example, 27.5 percent of the cereals shipped to market were sent by barge.[41] Water transport was cheapest for producers in the Volga region who often used the river system to send grain north and west to market. It is true that water transportation was inconvenient, especially when compared to railroads. One government study in 1892 referred to "complicated routing with loading and unloading, unexpected delays, and a large risk," and asserted that these factors made producers prefer "to sell their goods on the spot to a commercial middleman" rather than arrange water transportation by themselves.[42] There is a wonderful satiric tale, written in 1884 by Nikolai Leskov, about the deliberate sinking of grain barges for the purpose of collecting insurance money—a tale ironically titled "Choice Grain." But whatever could be said in criticism of Russia's water transportation, the system continued to carry cereals until the end of the nineteenth century.

Upon returning from a prolonged stay in Russia, a foreign traveler was reported to have remarked: "In all my days in Russia I never saw anyone building a road. Perhaps that is because the task is so hopeless." Anyone who has attempted to walk or drive along a muddy Russian road in the autumn rainy season or in the spring melting period can well appreciate the aptness of this quip. Yet public institutions like the Ministry of Communications and the zemstvos did succeed in improving the freight roads of rural Russia. By the early 1890s there were 150,000 versts of freight roads under zemstvo or provincial supervision. There were also 8,500 versts of modern highway (*shosse*) of which some 5,000 ran parallel to railroads.[43] These roads usually provided the links between a country estate and a railroad station or river wharf, but sometimes noble landowners and peasants hauled their grain overland the entire distance from field to market. Land freighting occurred as late as 1889 in Khar'kov province, where there were few convenient railroad lines and no navigable streams. The improvement and extension of commercial transport in late nineteenth-century Russia provided a solid, if imperfect infrastructure for the Russian domestic cereal market, as well as for the export trade.

That the elements of a national market system based on the growth of the transportation system had appeared by the 1880s is a crucial historical fact: the Russian national market came into existence precisely when the international grain market was in the throes of a severe price depression. Since agricultural export trade with Europe had existed for some time and grew rapidly in this period, Russia's agrarian system was drawn into the vortex of the Great Depression.

Statistics on Russian export trade show an increasing involvement of Russian producers in the world grain trade during the second half of the nineteenth century. The export of grain grew by a factor of eight between 1861 and 1913. The value of Russian grain exported rose from a mere 56 million rubles in the period from 1861 to 1865, to 298 million rubles in the five years between 1896 and 1900, and 655 million rubles on the eve of World War I. A major share of Russia's wheat, barley, and oats was eventually exported to Western Europe.[44]

By the mid-1880s Russian growers were already enmeshed in the world grain market system and in Russia's own commercial market. Given the rapid rise in Russian grain production and the downward trends in international market prices, one would expect the world price depression to have been reflected in depressed prices at the local level in Russia. So it was. The data on average prices indicate that the depression in Russia had two distinct phases: the first lasting from the early 1880s to the famine of 1891/92 when prices temporarily rose because of food shortages; the second lasting from 1892 to 1897 when price recovery began to occur. Winter wheat fell from one hundred and nine kopecks per pood in 1883 to a low of fifty-one kopecks per pood in 1894. By 1900 the price had only climbed as high as eighty kopecks, indicating a strong, but partial, recovery. Oats dropped from sixty-two kopecks per pood in 1881 to a low of thirty-five kopecks in 1893. Barley fell from sixty-eight kopecks per pood in 1883 to a mere forty-one kopecks in 1894. Neither oats nor barley had reached their earlier price levels by the turn of the century. Rye prices plummeted from ninety-eight kopecks per pood in 1881 to forty-one kopecks in 1894. By 1900 a pood of rye sold for an average of fifty-nine kopecks—less than two-thirds of the price prevailing twenty years before.[45] Because rye was the staple crop in most of northern and central Russia, its lower prices were particularly hard for commercial growers.

How did the rapidly falling cereal prices affect the landed nobility? Two obvious effects of the Great Depression were the acceleration of land sales and a net increase in noble indebtedness. Between 1877 and 1905 the noble land fund declined from roughly 73.1 million desiatins to 53.1 million desiatins—a loss of more than one-fourth of the nobility's land in less than three decades. The economic historian P. Liashchenko has calculated that between 1875 and 1900 noble lands decreased by an average of 1.12 percent a year, with the largest rates of decline occurring between 1887 and 1900 (see Table 4.1).

Falling prices also pushed many nobles to mortgage their lands, either because they were forced by the absence of cash to get bank loans or because they thought it a proper investment, in the wake of financial pressures induced by the Great Depression, to modernize their estates with mortgage money. Between 1885 and 1900 the State Noble Land Bank alone issued mortgages totaling nearly one billion rubles on 28.2 million desiatins of land.[46] One government commission set up to investigate agricultural problems discovered

TABLE 4.1
Annual Rate of Decline
in the Noble Land Fund, 1875–1900

Years	Percent of decline
1875–1877	1.00
1877–1887	0.65
1887–1897	1.27
1897–1900	2.25

SOURCE: P. I. Liashchenko, "Mobilizatsiia zemlevladeniia v Rossii i ego statistika," p. 51.

that among estates mortgaged to the State Noble Land Bank before 1900, between 15 and 19 percent were announced for auctioning every year because owners had not enough money to meet their mortgage payments.[47]

The statistics on the decline of the noble land fund and the rise of noble indebtedness to land banks are frequently cited as hard evidence of the impoverishment of the First Estate. Yet aggregate statistics conceal as much as they reveal. In this case, the national data obscure the effect of the Great Depression on different regions of the country and on different strata within the nobility. These more subtle effects on the depression help to explain the peculiarities of interest politics both during and after the depression.

In what Druzhinin called the first agricultural zone—the nonblack-soil provinces of the central industrial, northwest, and northern regions—the noble land fund declined by 46 percent between 1877 and 1905 (see Table 4.2). The rate of decline in this agricultural zone equaled that in the third agricultural zone as the highest in the Empire. In such provinces as Vologda, Kostroma, Iaroslavl', Smolensk, and Tver' the decline exceeded 50 percent of the total noble land fund.

In addition to the decline in the noble land fund, there was a rise in agricultural indebtedness; yet, the percentages of privately owned land mortgaged here were much lower than the national average. Of the sixty-seven provinces of European Russia, Poland, and Central Asia the most heavily indebted nobility of the first agricultural zone—that in Smolensk province—ranked only 35th in indebtedness for 1899.[48] Noble landowners of this region, when faced by the Great Depression, sold their estates in great numbers but were less likely to continue farming on borrowed money than their counterparts elsewhere in Russia.

TABLE 4.2
Noble Landowning in Nonblacksoil
Provinces, 1877–1905

Province	Noble land in 1877 (1,000s of des.)	Noble land in 1905 (1,000s of des.)	Percent of change
Moscow	737.9	455.6	−38
Kostroma	2,003.1	974.7	−52
Iaroslavl'	786.8	399.1	−50
Tver'	1,255.7	621.6	−50
Kaluga	756.9	420.9	−44
Vladimir	809.7	438.7	−46
Nizhny Novgorod	1,168.8	671.8	−43
Smolensk	1,915.5	961.9	−50
Petersburg	1,418.4	977.5	−31
Novgorod	2,455.3	1,428.1	−42
Pskov	1,217.6	635.7	−48
Vologda	774.2	248.8	−68
TOTAL	15,299.9	8,234.4	−46

SOURCE: N. A. Proskuriakova, "Razmeshchenie i struktura dvorianskogo zemle-vladeniia Evropeiskoi Rossii v kontse XIX–nachale XX veka," p. 73.

How can one account for the high rate of land sales and the comparatively low indebtedness of noble landowners in the first agricultural zone? Probably the main reason for the high rate of land sales was that landowners here grew gray cereals on intrinsically inferior soils. The gray cereals—rye, oats, and barley—yielded at best small profits for the commercial farmer, and at worst these crops could bring heavy losses to their producers. According to a Ministry of Agriculture study of agricultural costs between 1885 and 1888, rye growers in Vladimir province lost an average of nine rubles and seventy-four kopecks per desiatin.[49] Such heavy losses could not long be sustained by growers. The poor soils of the zone meant that landowners could not expect to compete with southern growers without massive investments in fertilizers and complete estate reorganization; it was simply easier for many to sell their lands.

Another problem faced by growers in this area was the presence of a rapidly expanding industrial sector in St. Petersburg and Moscow, and also in smaller cities of the region. To a limited extent, industry forced landowners to pay higher wages than they otherwise might have for peasant laborers, and industry drew thousands of able workers off the land into the cities. Thus, the market situation facing even the most clever entrepreneurs was so discouraging

TABLE 4.3
Noble Landowning
in the Blacksoil Belt, 1877–1905

Province	Noble land in 1877 (1,000s of des.)	Noble land in 1905 (1,000s of des.)	Percent of change
Orel	1,231.0	845.1	−31
Kursk	1,165.4	859.3	−27
Tambov	1,593.4	1,114.0	−30
Voronezh	1,378.9	995.6	−28
Tula	1,026.9	797.9	−22
Riazan'	1,053.5	682.6	−35
Kazan'	590.5	457.9	−22
Simbirsk	1,173.0	632.7	−46
Saratov	2,259.6	1,311.2	−42
Penza	1,077.1	787.1	−37
Poltava	1,726.8	1,080.0	−37
Khar'kov	1,345.0	808.4	−40
Chernigov	1,351.9	789.4	−42
TOTAL	16,973.0	11,162.0	−34

SOURCE: N. A. Proskuriakova, "Razmeshchenie i struktura dvorianskogo zemle-vladeniia Evropeiskoi Rossii v kontse XIX–nachale XX veka," p. 73.

as to have tempted them to leave farming altogether. Those who decided to stay on the land usually rented out their estates to peasants as many landowners had already done before 1877. The prevalence of renting in various forms doubtless helped account for the comparatively low mortgage indebtedness among nobles in this area; rented land required little in the way of operating capital, virtually no organizational changes, and land rents could be raised over time in order to cover a landowner's rising expenses.

In the second agricultural zone—the blacksoil belt provinces of the central agricultural, Mid-Volga, and Left-bank Ukraine regions—the decline in the noble land fund was less severe than in the non-blacksoil region. The most severe problems for the nobility seem to have been experienced in the Mid-Volga region (Saratov, Simbirsk, Penza) and in the Left-bank Ukraine (Poltava, Khar'kov, Chernigov) (see Table 4.3).

While greater numbers of noble landowners in the blacksoil belt stayed on their land, they did so only by borrowing heavily from land banks. In 1899 only three provinces in the second zone (Kursk, Riazan', Chernigov) had indebtedness rates of less than 50 percent for privately owned land. And in six provinces (Orel, Tula, Kazan',

Saratov, Penza, Khar'kov) over 60 percent of all privately owned land was mortgaged.[50]

The blacksoil zone was also severely affected by low prices for gray cereals. In Kursk, Chernigov, Orel, and Tula rye producers lost from one to fifteen rubles per desiatin in the 1880s.[51] In Kashkirsky district, Tula province, one landowner wrote: "Farming is a losing proposition for everyone. If we have a few more years like this, we will all be ruined. One can now run an estate only by cutting back expenses, denying oneself even the essential goods, and by relying on other sources of income."[52] In the Volga region rye producers also lost money—from three to eleven rubles per desiatin. Worried observers complained in 1888 that "estates whose owners lack supplementary sources of income to cover annual expenses will inevitably be sold at auction for failure to meet interest payments on bank loans, if cereal prices do not rise."[53]

Another difficulty facing commercial growers in the blacksoil provinces was the need to rely on cumbersome transportation links to get their grain to market. Volga producers depended on slow river barges to get their grain to Moscow and by the time the grain arrived in the autumn, prices were generally at their lowest point of the year. Other producers relied on railroads that provided what were considered very costly services. Producers in the eastern area of the blacksoil zone had to send their grain over long distances to central marketing areas such as Moscow, or to ports in the north and south; the expense of shipping their grain meant that these growers could not easily compete with others who might be located nearer to main markets. In addition, the high price of draft animals and agricultural laborers in the central agricultural and Mid-Volga regions meant another competitive disadvantage.

Nobles in the blacksoil provinces, however, had two advantages not shared by those in the nonblacksoil zone. First, in most blacksoil provinces in the southern sector of the zone red cereals (winter and spring wheats) could be grown, and throughout the 1880s wheat remained a profitable crop; thus, producers who were intelligent enough to diversify their crops might offset losses from gray cereals. Second, growers sat atop the best soils in Russia in much of this zone; if they fertilized their land properly, they could achieve relatively high yields. Unfortunately, many landowners neglected proper fertilization with the consequence that near the turn of the century, some estates were unproductive or even utterly exhausted. Nevertheless, wheat cultivation and generally good soils made it possible for blacksoil nobles to avoid selling their estates as rapidly as nobles in the nonblacksoil zone had done, and the brighter long-run pros-

TABLE 4.4

Noble Landowning
in the Southern Steppes, 1877–1905[a]

Province	Noble land in 1877 (1,000s of des.)	Noble land in 1905 (1,000s of des.)	Percent of change
Kherson	2,549.1	1240.9	−51
Tauride	1,585.8	869.6	−45
Ekaterinoslav	2,377.8	1185.0	−50
Samara	2,033.1	926.0	−54
Ufa	1,851.1	1381.8	−25
TOTAL	10,396.9	5603.3	−46

SOURCE: N. A. Proskuriakova, "Razmeshchenie i struktura dvorianskogo zemle-vladeniia Evropeiskoi Rossii v kontse XIX–nachale XX veka," p. 73.

[a]There were no data on the Don oblast' in the land survey of 1877.

pects for agriculture here made them desire to hold on to land, even at the price of heavy mortgage indebtedness.

In the third agricultural zone—the southern steppes provinces of New Russia, the Don oblast', and the Lower Volga Basin—the decline of the noble land fund equaled that in the nonblacksoil zone (see Table 4.4). With the exception of Ufa province, the southern steppes was an area of unbroken retreat for the nobility.

The problem of indebtedness in the southern steppes ranged from severe in New Russia and Ufa province to manageable in Samara and the Don oblast'. In both Kherson and Ekaterinoslav provinces over two-thirds of privately owned land was mortgaged to land banks in 1899.[54] In general, the statistical evidence suggests that noble agriculture throughout this zone was beset by serious difficulties, and that the problems faced in New Russia were the gravest in the empire.

That the nobility in the southern steppes should have experienced both high rates of land sales and high indebtedness is a paradox, because throughout the first stage of the Great Depression, profit margins for commercial growers were greater here than elsewhere in Russia. The cash crop in most of the southern steppes was wheat, and over the four-year period from 1885 to 1888 the average profit per desiatin of wheat ranged between seven rubles and twenty-seven rubles for spring wheat, and between eleven rubles and forty-two rubles for winter wheat.[55] Thus, during a period when many cereal growers were losing money, nobles in the southern steppes were making substantial profits. Yet there were several long-term problems that the nobility failed to solve which proved ultimately damaging to noble agriculture. First, commercial agriculture on the southern steppes was to a considerable extent capital intensive. A government report on shipments of agricultural machinery showed that in the decade from 1891 to 1900 more agricultural machines and tools were sent by railroad to New Russia than to any other region of the Empire.[56] Agricultural machines were very expensive, and their purchase would require debt financing in most cases. Thus, even in years with good harvests and favorable prices, nobles were compelled to borrow capital to continue their farming operations. Second, certain provinces in the southern steppes, such as Kherson and Tauride, required thousands of agricultural laborers to work alongside the harvesting machines. This was the phenomenon so well described by Lenin mentioned above in Chapter 2. Wages for agricultural workers in the southern steppes became very dear in the 1880s and 1890s. In the rest of European Russia the average daily wage for an agricultural worker during the spring sowing fluctuated between 39 and 49 kopecks, and during the fall hearvest it fluctuated between 53 and 74 kopecks. But in the southern steppes wages were twice or even three times as high; in 1883 daily wages in Kherson were 117 kopecks, in Ekaterinoslav 120 kopecks, and in Tauride 141 kopecks.[57] For as long as the favorable wheat market held out, high expenses on machines and labor could continue, but as soon as the bottom dropped out of the wheat market as it did in the 1890s, the nobility in the southern steppes found themselves in **desperate straits.**

The final problem in the southern steppes was that the soils here, many farmed for the first time after the emancipation, were quickly exhausted without fertilizers, and the climate, always fickle, was so unstable in the 1880s and 1890s that many areas suffered complete crop failures. The southern steppes had much land of marginal quality for long-term agriculture which was nevertheless capable of giving a few highly productive years before fertility dropped radically; the southern steppes were, in a sense, the "virgin lands" of the 1880s and 1890s.

While nobles in the first three agricultural zones were forced to sell and/or mortgage their lands at a dizzying rate, nobles in the fourth zone found themselves in a more favorable position (see Table 4.5). The western periphery provinces—including the Baltic area, Belorussia and Lithuania, the Right-bank Ukraine, and Bessarabia—showed only a small decrease in the noble land fund. Nobles in the Baltic provinces of Estland and Courland and in the

TABLE 4.5

Noble Landowning
in the Western Periphery, 1877–1905

Province	Noble land in 1877 (1,000s of des.)	Noble land in 1905 (1,000s of des.)	Percent of change
Estland	852.1	1,105.6	+30
Lifland	1,677.5	1,355.9	−19
Courland	917.7	939.4	+ 2
Mogilev	1,976.3	1,401.8	−29
Minsk	3,983.7	4,041.8	+ 1
Vitebsk	1,606.4	1,294.7	−19
Kov'no	1,490.0	1,451.1	− 3
Grodno	1,043.8	790.6	−24
Vil'no	1,440.9	1,241.5	−14
Kiev	1,833.9	1,528.0	−17
Podolia	1,565.5	1,309.5	−16
Volynia	2,424.1	2,044.1	−16
Bessarabia	945.0	860.2	− 9
TOTAL	21,756.9	19,364.3	−11

SOURCE: N. A. Proskuriakova, "Razmeshchenie i struktura dvorianskogo zemle-vladeniia Evropeiskoi Rossii v kontse XIX–nachale XX veka," p. 73.

Belorussian province of Minsk actually acquired more land in the Great Depression than they sold. The noble land fund in other provinces was relatively stable. The only areas where land sales approached the level found in other zones were Mogilev and Grodno, but even here the noble land fund fell less than 30 percent.

In the western periphery the rate of indebtedness was relatively high, particularly in the Baltic provinces, Podolia, and Minsk, which ranked among the ten most indebted provinces in 1899. In fact, in Estland over 85 percent of privately owned land was mortgaged to land banks, and in Lifland 79 percent was so mortgaged.[58]

The western periphery provinces had a number of economic advantages that insulated the nobility from the necessity to sell their lands. First, in most provinces during the first stage of the Great Depression both red and gray cereals were grown profitably. In only five provinces were oats unprofitable between 1885 and 1888, and in only four provinces was rye unprofitable—and in all but one instance the average losses were less than four rubles per desiatin. Elsewhere gray cereals brought profits as high as thirteen rubles per desiatin, and red cereals (grown in the west and the Right-bank Ukraine) did even better.[59] Second, in the late 1880s and throughout the 1890s growers in the western periphery shifted land from grain production to potatoes. The average potato production more than doubled throughout this zone, and in the 1890s in the Baltic provinces and in Minsk, Vitebsk, Grodno, Vil'no, Kov'no, and Mogilev, potato production accounted for roughly 40 percent of the total harvest.[60] Because of this shift to potatoes in the 1890s, the western periphery was not as severely affected as other regions in the second wave of the Great Depression. Third, transportation costs for commercial growers were relatively low in the western periphery because of the proximity of ports in the north and south, and because grains could easily be shipped from the west overland into Western European market centers, especially in Germany. Of course, in much of the fourth zone agriculture was capital intensive; consequently, growers here did borrow heavily from land banks.

Thus, the Great Depression had a far from uniform impact on the Russian landed nobility. In its first phase the Depression severely affected producers of gray cereals, especially in the nonblacksoil and blacksoil zones where rye culture predominated. In its second phase the hardest hit areas were the first two agricultural zones and the southern steppes provinces where agriculture was capital intensive and labor expensive. The western periphery largely escaped the effects of the Depression, except that indebtedness grew rapidly in the Baltic states and the Right-bank Ukraine.

While the Depression affected various agricultural zones in different ways, it also affected differently the three economic strata within the nobility. Yet precisely which stratum suffered most before 1905 has been a matter of debate among historians. The most influential interpretation has been that of P. Liashchenko, who insisted in a 1905 article that Russian land mobilization after 1875 led to the concentration of land holdings among all social groups, including the nobility. Liashchenko demonstrated that the nobility were great buyers of land as well as sellers after 1875, and that land purchased by the nobility came in larger parcels on the average than land sold. The only stratum within the nobility to suffer, Liashchenko believed, was the gentry, "who rarely knew how to acquire land, or even how to hold onto their existing capital for productive purposes."[61] Recently the Soviet historian N. A. Proskuriakova disagreed with Liashchenko by asserting that the magnates were the biggest losers of land between 1877 and 1905. During that period land owned by the petty nobility decreased by 13.7 percent and that owned by the gentry decreased 18.8 percent; at the same time the magnates lost 30.4 percent of their lands (see Table 4.6).

In his recent book on the nobility, A. P. Korelin has agreed with Proskuriakova that the group who lost the most land was the mag-

TABLE 4.6
Noble Landownership by Strata, 1877–1905

Stratum	Number of owners, 1877	Number of owners, 1905	Percent of change	Land owned, 1877 (1,000s of des.)	Land owned, 1905 (1,000s of des.)	Percent of change
Petty (1–100 des.)	56,551	60,910	+7.7	1,924.4	1,662.6	−13.7
Gentry 101–1,000 des.)	44,827	37,003	−17.5	16,264.7	13,218.8	−18.8
Magnate (1,000+ des.)	13,388	9,324	−30.4	54,976.4	38,290.0	−30.4
TOTAL	114,716	107,237	− 6.6	73,163.5	53,169.3	−27.4

SOURCE: N. A. Proskuriakova, "Razmeshchenie i struktura dvorianskogo zemle-vladeniia Evropeiskoi Rossii v kontse XIX–nachale XX veka," pp. 66–68.

nates. The number of estates between 1,000 and 5,000 desiatins, according to Korelin, fell 33.8 percent, and the acreage of this group of owners fell 35.6 percent. The number of estates larger than 5,000 desiatins fell 37.7 percent and their acreage declined 30.7 percent.[62]

My own calculations show that throughout the Empire, the largest declines in land ownership occurred among the magnates (see Table 4.7). Those in the southern steppes and nonblacksoil zones were the worst affected by the Great Depression, while those in the western periphery were comparatively little affected. Interestingly enough, the gentry, whom Liashchenko had seen as the main victims of land sales, actually gained land in the western periphery, though their lands decreased elsewhere in the Empire. Thus, to a considerable extent, the Great Depression was a disaster for large landowners as a group, though one would not wish to claim that they suffered more as individuals than did members of other strata. The two primary reasons that large owners lost more land than other strata were probably the great impact of testamentary divisions on larger non-*maiorat* estates and the intense involvement of many magnates with the commercial grain market.

Indebtedness and Political Leadership

Given the deleterious effects of the Great Depression on noble land-ownership, particularly on the magnates, one would expect the de-

TABLE 4.7
Noble Landownership by Strata
and by Agricultural Zone, 1877–1905[a]

Stratum	Land owned in 1877 (1,000s of des.)	Percent of total	Land owned in 1905 (1,000s of des.)	Percent of total	Percent of change
Nonblacksoil					
Petty	498.2	3.3	294.9	3.6	−40.9
Gentry	4,644.8	30.4	2,689.0	32.6	−42.2
Magnate	10,115.7	66.3	5,250.2	63.8	−48.1
Blacksoil					
Petty	880.8	5.3	612.6	5.5	−30.5
Gentry	5,420.0	32.5	4,056.7	36.4	−25.2
Magnate	10,372.7	62.2	6,479.8	58.1	−37.6
Southern Steppes					
Petty	88.1	0.9	77.1	1.4	−12.5
Gentry	1,587.4	15.1	1,136.9	20.4	−38.4
Magnate	8,808.6	84.0	4,367.5	78.2	−50.5
Western Periphery					
Petty	646.6	3.0	586.4	3.0	− 9.4
Gentry	4,079.4	18.7	4,569.8	23.6	+12.0
Magnate	17,081.9	78.3	14,235.9	73.4	−16.7

SOURCE: N. A. Proskuriakova, "Razmeshchenie i struktura dvorianskogo zemle-vladeniia Evropeiskoi Rossii v kontse XIX–nachale XX veka," p. 74.

[a]Total data on land owned in each zone would, if added up, differ slightly from data cited above because of rounding off of provincial data for various strata.

pression to have had a direct impact on the noble political leadership which was recruited in large part from this stratum and from the upper reaches of the gentry. It is unfortunately impossible to determine how many marshals of the nobility and zemstvo chairmen were compelled to sell land after the depression began, but there do exist records in the State Noble Land Bank archives that enable one to assess the approximate level of mortgage indebtedness experienced by the noble leadership after the founding of that bank in 1885.

I have collected data on 60 provincial marshals, 728 district marshals, 53 provincial zemstvo board chairmen, and 403 district board chairmen who served in the period from 1885 to 1917 (see Table 4.8). The data measure the number of officials who mortgaged their estates with the State Noble Land Bank, the number who took second mortgages from that bank, and the number who were free of any indebtedness. I have also included the number of officials whose families mortgaged estates to the bank because the indebtedness of an individual's family may have influenced, at least indirectly, both the individual's economic welfare and his perception of the seriousness of the economic problems facing the nobility.

TABLE 4.8

Officials' Indebtedness by Office, 1885–1917[a]

(Mortgage Holders Indebted to the Noble Land Bank)

Provincial Marshals	= 60 (100%)
With mortgage	= 38 (63%)
With remortgage	= 12 (20%)
With family mortgage	= 39 (65%)
Not indebted	= 12 (20%)
Provincial Zemstvo Chairmen	= 53 (100%)
With mortgage	= 29 (55%)
With remortgage	= 18 (34%)
With family mortgage	= 29 (55%)
Not indebted	= 15 (28%)
District Marshals	= 728 (100%)
With mortgage	= 335 (46%)
With remortgage	= 125 (17%)
With family mortgage	= 361 (50%)
Not indebted	= 230 (32%)
District Zemstvo Chairmen	= 403 (100%)
With mortgage	= 182 (45%)
With remortgage	= 77 (19%)
With family mortgage	= 194 (48%)
Not indebted	= 122 (30%)

SOURCE: TsGIA, fond 593, opisi 3–26, *raznye dela.*

[a]Each official may have had a mortgage, remortgage, and family mortgage; figures in the subcategories reflect this double counting.

The data indicate that almost half of all these officials had mortgaged estates with the land bank, and roughly 20 percent had second mortgages on their lands. In addition, more than half the families of provincial officials studied had estates mortgaged to the land bank. Only 379, or 30 percent, of the officials were not burdened in any way by debts to the State Noble Land Bank. When broken down by region (see Table 4.9), the data also show that indebtedness rates were highest in the southern steppes and blacksoil belt, where over 50 percent of noble officials had incurred personal mortgages to the bank; these two zones also showed the highest percentage of second mortgages.

Thus, in the last decades of the old regime, Russian provincial officials were typical representatives of the upper strata of the landed nobility: their lives and agricultural activity often led to the assumption of large debts, the extent of which would become a subject of grave political concern.

As mansion after mansion was forsaken, as window panes took their veil of chalk, the fate of the Russian nobility was discussed endlessly. Noble producers of grain could do nothing individually to arrest the slide in world market prices, and try as they might,

TABLE 4.9
Officials' Indebtedness by Region, 1885–1917[a]
(Mortgage Holders Indebted to the Noble Land Bank)

Region	Total number of officeholders	With mortgages	With remortgages	With family mortgages	Not indebted
Nonblacksoil (Tver', Moscow, Pskov, Vladimir)	360	124 (34%)	41 (11%)	124 (34%)	165 (46%)
Blacksoil (Riazan', Kursk, Penza, Voronezh, Kazan' Poltava, Simbirsk, Saratov)	702	395 (56%)	156 (22%)	415 (59%)	136 (19%)
Southern steppes (Ekaterinoslav)	38	25 (66%)	14 (37%)	23 (60%)	9 (24%)
Western periphery (Vil'no, Kiev, Bessarabia)	142	40 (28%)	21 (15%)	61 (43%)	69 (49%)
TOTAL	1,242	584 (47%)	232 (19%)	623 (50%)	377 (30%)

SOURCE: TsGIA, fond 593, opisi 3–26, *raznye dela.*

[a]Each official may have had a mortgage, remortgage, and family mortgage; figures in the subcategories reflect this double counting.

not all could find better and more profitable ways to organize their estates. Therefore, many nobles turned to their political leadership, a leadership itself seriously affected by the Great Depression, to alleviate the problems confronting individual districts and provinces.

Throughout the 1880s and the 1890s marshals of the nobility worked to secure the cooperation of the Russian central government in improving local prospects for the landed nobility. As we shall see, the marshals pressed the central government to assist the nobility by offering cheap credit to noble grain producers, by reorganizing the inheritance system to prevent testamentary divisions from destroying viable estates, by reducing railroad transportation costs, and by assisting the whole rural sector—including the peasantry—to survive at a time when industry seemed the favorite of the central government. These proposals, inspired by what many took as impending economic disaster, became the agenda of noble politics in the reign of Alexander III and in the first part of Nicholas II's reign.

Thus a conjunction of circumstances in the early 1880s resulted in the displacement of a politics of structural change by a politics of economic interest. The defeat of liberalism and aristocratic constitutionalism meant that the survival of the First Estate could not be guaranteed by changes of the state structure, but would have to be won on the economic front—slowly and painfully—through petitions written by marshals of the nobility. It is to these petitions and their ultimate failure, a failure conditioned by the very diversity of the First Estate they were designed to save, that we now turn.

CHAPTER 5

Founding the Noble Land Bank

Befor the emancipation there was an almost casual element in loan transactions. As one observer put it, there was "a simplicity and human warmth" between borrower and lender which stemmed from personal acquaintance and an understanding "that they were not conducting a business transaction, but playing a childish game."[1] "The devil only knows why a gentleman came to mortgage his estate; he certainly had no idea what he would do with the money. He came because everyone else was coming, or had already come: they had got money—why shouldn't he go and get some too? The banker knew all this perfectly well. . . . They both took account of this frivolous element in their calculations."[2]

After the emancipation the need for credit became a weightier matter for landowners. The government had closed the Trustee Council [*Opekunsky sovet*] and the Reserve Treasury [*Sokhrannaia kazna*] which had supplied the nobility with low interest loans for nearly a century. In the 1870s various private land banks opened to provide credit to landowners, but these banks commanded anywhere from 8 to 11 percent interest on mortgage loans. With money supplies short and interest rates high, nobles already had ample reason to be dissatisfied with the post-emancipation credit system. With the first wave of the Great Depression their dissatisfaction intensified, and "simplicity and human warmth" left the relationship between borrower and lender for good.

Given the increasingly disturbing trends in the market, certain nobles began to argue what was an essentially novel proposition: it was the duty of government to save Russian landowners from the effects of high grain prices and iniquitous private lenders. One of the first marshals to plead for government intervention in the marketplace was Khar'kov provincial marshal A. R. Shidlovsky, who was concerned about the tendency of Khar'kov nobles to fall further and further into debt to private banks. In a series of memoranda sent to the Ministry of Internal Affairs in 1881 and 1882, Shidlovsky complained that none of the existing lending agencies in Khar'kov was adequate to the needs of the local nobility: all charged high interest, especially on long-term loans; and all acted not to help the nobility, but to make a profit. Shidlovsky grew exceedingly alarmed in 1881 and 1882 at rumors that the central government was considering creating a land bank to help peasants purchase land. For the Khar'kov nobility a peasant bank would be the coup de grâce, accelerating land transfers from the nobility to other social groups. Shidlovsky demanded that the government drop its consideration of a peasant bank and that it reestablish the pre-emancipation credit institutions to serve the nobility.

Of course, it might have been objected that the Russian nobility did not deserve special consideration; that if nobles now had to sell off their lands, they had only themselves to blame. Shidlovsky anticipated this objection by making two additional claims. First, he contended that the nobility must necessarily be the foundation for a monarchial state: "It is essential that in the building being completed by the monarchical authority, the local hereditary nobility be a fundamental part." Second, he argued that the economic mistakes of the nobility, however serious, were irrelevant to the question of government support for the nobility, because the government's responsibility requires it to save the nobility, no matter what. "Even if this class of property owners caused the sorry state of their own affairs, even in this case the government would have to come to their aid, for the business of government is to avert the ruin both of him who comes to ruin by carelessness, by lack of caution, and especially of him who is an essential factor in supporting the foundations of the governmental system."[3]

Shidlovsky's memoranda were rejected by the Ministry of Finance, which in 1881–82 was more worried about conditions of peasant agriculture than about the nobility. But Shidlovsky did not give up hope. In 1883, after the government had promulgated the institution of the State Peasant Land Bank, Shidlovsky sent copies of his memoranda to other marshals of the nobility and called upon them to support his plan to reestablish the old credit institutions.[4] Between December 1883 and May 1885 thirteen provincial marshals and noble assemblies plus six provincial zemstvo assemblies petitioned the government to alter the existing credit system for the nobility's benefit. Most of these proposals went beyond Shidlovsky's plan by calling not for the old credit agencies, but for an entirely new one—a central land bank for the nobility.[5]

Several characteristics of the nobility's pro-bank petitions deserve close attention. The most striking feature of the petitions was sharp criticisms of private banks. The marshals followed Shidlovsky's argument that private banks were irreconcilable with the material interests of the nobility. In the words of Ufa provincial marshal A. I. Kugushev, "although newly created private banks were to lend assistance [to the nobility], their operations were not based on the interests of debtors nor were they intended to support agriculture; these banks pursued exclusively their own interests. Therefore, most estates fell into decline and were often sold at auctions."[6] Private banks set interest rates high in order to maximize profit for stockholders, and they issued loans in the form of commercial paper [*zakladnye listki*] that depreciated in value. According to the Kaluga noble assembly, "Such loans are of little help to noble landowners, and in cases where harvests are slightly below average or in other unfavorable conditions, these loans create an impossible burden for farmers who are unable to keep up their yearly payments. In this way the plans of many landowners have been upset and many estates have been sold to other Estates."[7]

Bessarabia's provincial marshal, I. E. Katarzhi, went to the trouble of comparing local agricultural income with loan interest payments. He noted that the net income of an average estate "could not be more than four percent, or in the most exceptional cases six percent, of estate value." Annual interest charged by the Kherson Land Bank was 7.9 percent and at the Bessarabia-Tauride Bank 8.1 percent of the principal. "Since mortgages were based on fifty to sixty percent and on even higher percentages of estate value, the first result of estate mortgages was to consume completely the income of these estates, and that under normal circumstances."[8]

In addition to their conviction that private banks were ruinous, the noble petitioners complained about advantages allegedly enjoyed by other borrowers. The Orel provincial assembly gave this problem much prominence in its petition of December 1883, a petition which asserted that agriculture was, in effect, the stepchild to Russian industry:

> One consequence of the regnant economic and financial theory was
> that commerce, factories, and manufacturing industry, railroads and
> private banks used and still use cheap state credit to the detriment
> of local agriculture. Land taxes have increased and so has protection
> for these [industrial] concerns of the national economy. We note with
> distress that long-term credit, the form most suitable to farmers,
> remains to this day a monopoly of capitalist companies, and that
> the nobility are being ruined as they fall under the yoke of private
> land banks.[9]

The Voronezh provincial noble assembly made the same argument, but added a pointed reference to the peasant bank:

> Since 1868 in Voronezh 191,663 desiatins of the 1,315,624 desiatins
> belonging to the nobility have gone to other Estates. . . . The basic rea-
> son for this land transfer, which is neither in the interest of the nobility
> nor of the state, is the inequality of access to easy credit which has
> long been enjoyed by the merchantry and which now even the peasant
> classes use to purchase land.[10]

In a sense, the noble complaints about favoritism had justification: the government had given long-term loans to railroad builders at 5 percent interest, and similarly low interest to borrowers at the Peasant Land Bank. But what was important historically was the growing suspicion that other social groups, particularly the merchantry, might now prosper more than the nobility. (And God forbid that the peasants have any advantage in buying noble land!)

Yet certain nobles were becoming aware that the agency responsible for their economic difficulties was neither the private bank nor industry, but rather the market economy itself. In a report on the credit problem written in 1884, Bessarabian provincial marshal Katarzhi made adaptation to a money economy and foreign competition the central problems facing the nobility after the emancipation:

> We had to adapt immediately to a money economy, but given the
> unfortunate state of our grain trade, which more and more often com-
> pels the producer to expect losses on his product, all the free capital
> still in circulation was swallowed up.
>   At that juncture the economic growth of the nation, following the
> natural law of its development, in connection with the increasing com-

petition on the world grain market from other nations, and especially from America, forced noble landowners into a dilemma: either get rid of their estates, or meet the demands of the new economic order by making gradual improvements in their farms.

But to accomplish all this landowners . . . needed new and very significant sources of capital, which could only be provided through long-term credit.[11]

Thus, the impulse behind the bank petition campaign from 1883 to 1885 was one of resistance to the market. Nobles complained about the activity of banks, merchants, industry, about the new money economy and foreign competition. This noble anti-capitalism became a leitmotiv of other petitions in the 1880s and 1890s.

Yet it should be recognized that there were certain limits on noble hostility to the market. First, this hostility was not ideological, if one means by ideology a coherent political-philosophical system suggesting a concrete program of activity in the world. Noble hostility to the market was of an empirical nature: to be sure there were certain unpleasant consequences of living in the new, market-dominated order that required corrective action by government; but this corrective activity was not motivated by ideological a priori considerations, but rather by difficulties experienced in everyday life by members of the First Estate. Second, noble hostility to the market did not extend to a demand that serfdom be reinstituted or that market relations be abolished by government decree. There was no retrospective utopianism in the noble petitions—that is, no desire, explicit or implicit, to return to the old serf order. Instead there was an assertion that nobles deserved to be protected against the effects of the market, at least to the extent that they had been protected before the emancipation by cheap credit, and at least to the extent that the government currently protected merchants and peasants. Fair was fair.

Another feature of the bank petitions was their deferential tone. While sharp words were addressed to the alleged villains in the marketplace, there were no overt criticisms of government policy, and none of the crown. In the view of noble petitioners, government was, if not wholly beneficent toward the nobility, at least well-disposed toward them: any untoward consequences of the abolition of old credit agencies or the chartering of private banks would be rectified in due course by the government. What was threatened in the meantime was the collapse of the nobility's strength, a collapse that would indirectly threaten the government. In his 1884 petition, the

Bessarabian Katarzhi depicted a helpless nobility that could only be saved by the government:

> The decline in the importance of the noble element is a universal phenomenon in Russia. Bessarabia has fallen under the influence of factors that affect the nation at large.
>
> Although the local nobility have been less distracted by state service than native Russian nobles and have lived more on income from their estates and have taken care of their own interests, nevertheless the local nobility have not possessed the strength to stand up against the general current. Now we must watch as helpless spectators the increasingly rapid transfer of family estates to other Estates.
>
> It is in the national interest of Russia, as an agricultural country, to assure that the products of popular labor hold their shaky place on the world market. Otherwise, there will be complete regression and mass impoverishment.

According to Katarzhi, only a government-funded lending agency dispensing loans at 4 percent interest could rescue the nobility from doom.[12] The Orel nobility argued the case much more succinctly: "If your Majesty's imperial will does not assist us, then the time is not far away when the nobility will cease to be the leading Estate, and to lead the people on the road to social welfare and agronomic perfection."[13]

A third feature of the bank petitions is that they came from a minority of provinces—only sixteen provinces of the forty-four in European Russia asked the government to create better credit agencies for the nobility. Of these provinces some three (Kostroma, Kaluga, Smolensk) were in the nonblacksoil area, nine (Orel, Voronezh, Khar'kov, Chernigov, Penza, Kazan', Tambov, Poltava, Saratov) were in the blacksoil belt, two (Samara, Ufa) were in the southern steppes, one (Bessarabia) was in the west, and one (Orenburg) was to the east of the four main agricultural zones. The incidence of petitions suggests that desire for improvement of agricultural credit was most widely shared in the blacksoil belt and the southern steppes where high indebtedness to private land banks was a problem. The low incidence of petitions in the nonblacksoil zone and the western periphery reflected the differential impact of the Great Depression: in the nonblacksoil zone landowners preferred selling their estates to mortgaging them because the rate of return from farming was too low to pay off mortgages; in the west the depression was not yet such a serious problem.

DEBATE OVER THE FOUNDATION
OF THE NOBLE LAND BANK, 1883–1885

As early as December 1883 when he first read the petition of the Orel provincial noble assembly, Alexander III indicated his tentative support for a bank loan system to help noble landowners. At the end of the petition he scrawled: "Talk with the Minister of Finance about this. It is really time to do something to help the nobility."[14] Later that month, on the 24th, Alexander read two more petitions on bank credit from the Kaluga and Voronezh noble assemblies. On these he noted: "All about the same thing! I spoke today with the Minister of Finance; I hope that one may be able to help."[15]

Alexander III's decision to consider a noble bank made serious legislative discussion within the government inevitable, but it did not mean that the government would act to create a bank. There was no guarantee that the Ministry of Finance would support the foundation of another state-run bank; after all, such an undertaking would require an enormous capital sum and demand the organization of a bureau to administer the loans. Moreover, Alexander III, though he may have thought a bank desirable, did not know precisely what kind of bank was best, or even which nobles it should help.

There is a wonderful anecdote in the diary of State Secretary A. A. Polovtsov about a conversation between Alexander and A. A. Abaza, then the chairman-designate of the Department of Economy in the State Council.

> The tsar spoke about the necessity to found a bank which would serve as an aid to gentry landowners [*srednemu zemlevladeniiu*]. Abaza expressed the idea that it was necessary to help all landowners, including peasants, and both gentry and magnates. Pointing through the window toward the trees surrounding the Gatchina Palace, Abaza said: "In your Majesty's park grow small, middle-size and large trees—all of them equally need to be looked after; the same may be said for land-ownership which without any exception is beneficial to the state, regardless of the differences in its dimensions."[16]

This anecdote shows, by the vagueness of Alexander's desires and the crudity and condescension of Abaza's remarks, just how unsettled the bank question was in October 1884, nearly a year after Alexander's initial positive reaction to the Orel petition.

Alexander's irresoluteness on the bank was not without effect, because it opened up the field of maneuver to friends of the nobility both inside and outside the central government. At the provincial level there was some attempt to specify the sort of bank that would be most helpful to nobility. For example, in 1884 several noble landowners in Gdovsky district, St. Petersburg province, wrote the government suggesting an organizational and procedural framework that would serve to control the commercial activity of the projected bank. A special oversight committee consisting of the marshal and six local nobles would be created in each district in order to supervise bank loans. A landowner who wished to take out a loan would have to submit a detailed plan of his estate to the oversight committee. The plan would spell out basic information on the location, type of land tenure, and costs of proposed estate improvements. The plan would be registered with a senior notary and official copies would be sent to the bank, the landowner, and the oversight committee. After receipt of a loan the landowner would be obliged to demonstrate to the oversight committee that the money had been used for the purpose originally projected.[17]

The Gdovsky bank organization scheme was designed to permit the maximum possible participation of noble landowners in the loan procurement process. The role of the central government was reduced to financial support for a noble-initiated, noble-run bank, and the real powers of approval and enforcement were rested at the local level with the district oversight committee rather than at St. Petersburg. Several details of the Gdovsky scheme were eventually incorporated into the bank statute in 1885; for instance, the detailed estate plan was made a prerequisite for loans. However, in the actual statute the central government took over supervisory and administrative tasks that the Gdovsky landowners had wanted to reserve for the oversight committee.

Another attempt to influence the bank statue was made by the archreactionary journalist, V. P. Meshchersky, editor of *Grazhdanin*. On 11 June 1884 Meshchersky sent the tsar a letter in which he discussed ways to strengthen the local nobility: the first desideratum Meshshersky mentioned was long-term and cheap credit for the landed nobility. Meshchersky also advocated a plan whereby provincial noble assemblies could borrow from the treasury to buy estates that local nobles were considering for sale to non-nobles.[18] The obvious intention of Meshchersky's plan was to circumvent the land market by making the sale of noble lands to peasants and merchants virtually impossible. If adopted, Meshchersky's proposal would have undercut the State Peasant Land Bank, rendering it all but a dead letter. Meshchersky acted from a deep aversion to liberalism, a disease he saw lurking everywhere, a disease that would destroy the nobility and the aristocracy in the name of peasant happiness:

Imperceptibly succumbing to theory, it is very easy from the theory
of peasant happiness, from an all-Estate or zemstvo managed economy, to arrive at the theory of the nobility's destruction: and from it to
the equalization of all Estates with the franchise determined by
education, from this theory to the theory of the uselessness of autocracy is only one step. This step has almost been taken.[19]

Meshchersky had the opportunity to follow up his letter with a
personal audience granted by Alexander III on 22 October 1884.
Meshchersky raised the problem of the bank again and "found it
gratifying to learn that His Majesty shared my ideas about noble
landowners." Meshchersky was most concerned that Alexander
press the Minister of Finance to finish drafting a bank project as
quickly as possible. "It is essential that His Majesty hurry the Minister of Finance—that is, he should express impatience and his close
participation in this affair." What worried Meshchersky, he told
Alexander, was his conviction that Bunge was subject to pressure
from private land banks:

They hate the notion of strengthening the nobility, for they sense that
as the nobility become stronger, so too will the autocracy, and the
scheme of the constitution—that is of a Yid dictatorship [*zhidovskoe pol-
novlastie*]—will become less likely. It is most essential also that credit
for the nobility be as long-term and as inexpensive as possible.

Meshchersky concluded his visit by asking the tsar to set up a special commission that would include noble landowners to work out
measures that would "improve the condition of noble landowners."[20]

Meshchersky's intervention in the bank debate demonstrated the
difference between provincial politics and court politics of the nobility. Provincial assemblies were obviously concerned most about
the economic difficulties they faced in the Great Depression: their
petitions, based on hostility to the market, were not ideologically
motivated. But Meshchersky, who owned very little land and whose
living came from journalism, was motivated mainly by ideology. He
too was hostile to the market and wished to circumvent it, but what
Meshchersky feared were liberalism and constitutionalism, which for
him meant Jewish control. He saw the bank primarily as a political
instrument to shore up the nobility and thus the autocracy, and not
as a reform desirable for economic reasons.

It is doubtful that Meshchersky's intervention made Alexander
any more certain about the type of bank needed to save the nobility.
But, as Soloviev has suggested, Meshchersky probably did push the
tsar toward appointment of a special commission of nobles to discuss

the bank question. This agency provided still another forum for nobles to influence the shape of bank legislation. The Special Commission for Discussion of the State Land Bank met three times in early 1885—on 31 January, 4 and 8 February. The committee was chaired by Minister of Finance Bunge and included among its participants: Khar'kov provincial marshal A. R. Shidlovsky, the originator of the bank campaign; Penza provincial marshal Prince A. D. Obolensky; Eletsky district marshal S. S. Bekhteev; St. Petersburg provincial zemstvo chairman I. A. Gorchakov; Moscow provincial zemstvo chairman D. A. Naumov; and Riazan' provincial zemstvo chairman Prince A. I. Gagarin.

One bitterly debated issue was whether loans to noble landowners should be given by the same institution that lent money to peasants. Prince Obolensky and S. S. Bekhteev argued that it would be awkward to unite these two operations in a single agency. They admitted that from a formal point of view these loans served a similar purpose, but from a practical point of view the loans were contradictory in purpose. Loans to nobles were supposed to help the nobility hold on to their property, while loans given to peasants facilitated the transfer of property from the nobility to the peasantry. Obolensky and Bekhteev also argued that peasant loans represented a net financial loss to the government which would be compensated out of profits from noble loans. Upset by the prospect of a hidden noble subsidy to peasant agriculture, the two outspoken nobles advocated that the projected State Land Bank be affiliated with the existing State Bank, not with the Peasant Land Bank. If that solution were to prove unfeasible, Obolensky and Bekhteev would not object to an independent land bank that could disperse long-term loans.

Minister of Finance Bunge explained that he had never intended to merge noble loan operations with peasant loans in the Land Bank. Bunge would have two separate departments within the same bank, and each department would keep a separate account; the profits from one department would not be used to make up for losses in the other. Having heard Bunge's explanation, four committee members—Prince Gagarin, Gorchakov, Naumov, and Shidlovsky—announced that they did not object to the housing of noble operations and peasant loan operations under one roof; on the contrary, they thought a single institution expedient.[21]

The majority vote for a single bank agency did not silence Obolensky and Bekhteev. They decided to write a special minority opinion on the bank merger issue. Their arguments against the merger were substantially the same in the minority opinion as formerly, but the language of the special opinion was crisper.

The bank's goal in noble loans is to provide cheap credit so that noble landowners can escape the onerous conditions into which they were forced by private credit institutions and preserve their landed property. The task of the Peasant Bank is to provide loans that will hasten the transfer of that property to the peasantry. One cannot help but fear that the pursuit of two completely contradictory goals by a single institution may have a deleterious effect on bank operations by depriving its administration, especially in local branches, of the proper unity of action. . . . Doubtless the bankers, especially those from provincial areas, will introduce their own subjective views on the agrarian question into bank operations, since the [agrarian] question is such a burning issue that a completely dispassionate and disinterested approach to it by provincial figures is inconceivable.

Obolensky and Bekhteev concluded that a merger of bank operations might very well increase the sale of noble land to other classes, rather than help preserve noble estates.[22]

A second issue that provoked disagreements within the Special Commission was the transfer of debts from private banks to the projected State Land Bank. The majority evidently believed that there need be no special arrangements to facilitate such debt transfers. However, Shidlovsky thought differently and filed a special minority report on this issue.

I assert that, independent of the publication of the State Land Bank Statute, it is essential to publish special rules concerning repayment by this bank of debts held by existing land banks in the form of mortgages on landed property. The best way to accomplish this, in my opinion, would be a directive to issue credit vouchers [*kreditnye bilety*] in the amount of mortgages held by existing banks and to pay off the mortgages with these vouchers; this would cost approximately five hundred million rubles.[23]

In other words, Shidlovsky argued that the purpose of a new bank should be to eliminate entirely the influence of private banks on the noble land market. What was at stake was more than future benefits to new noble borrowers; it was the elimination of past damage done by the market. Thus, Shidlovsky unblushingly recommended a program costing a half-billion rubles. Since the income of the Russian treasury was 833 million rubles in 1885 and the budgetary expenditures 913 million rubles, one should hardly be surprised that Minister of Finance Bunge turned a deaf ear to Shidlovsky's proposal.[24]

Out of the Special Commission and out of deliberations in the Ministry of Finance there came a working proposal for a centralized

State Land Bank that would house both a noble loan operation and the existing peasant bank. However, this project was leaked to Meshchersky and to the reactionary Muscovite journalist M. N. Katkov, editor of *Moskovskie vedomosti*. Both Meshchersky and Katkov attacked the joint bank plan. To Meshchersky the plan was the result of a "terrible conspiracy" against noble landowners. For Katkov the plan was a disaster. It would make noble estates more rather than less likely to be sold; and because the bank would be run according to specified business principles, Katkov thought it would prove heartless to landowners truly in need.[25] Since the joint bank project was under heavy pressure from the reactionary press, the Ministry of Finance abandoned the proposal on 5 April and adopted a new plan for a separate State Noble Land Bank. Obolensky and Bekhteev were victorious after all.

Rescript on the Nobility and Foundation of the State Noble Land Bank

In April 1885 political maneuvering on the bank question was interrupted by, or rather encompassed by, discussion of a larger issue: what would be the attitude of Alexander III and his government toward the nobility as a whole? This larger discussion was stimulated by the approaching centennial of the Noble Charter to be celebrated on 21 April 1885, for on such an occasion the tsar was expected to make public his sentiments concerning the nobility's place in Russian society. In order to prepare a suitable rescript, Alexander established at the end of March a special committee to consider measures to be taken in connection with the approaching centennial and to draft his statement to be read that day.

The special committee consisted of K. P. Pobedonostsev, Ober-Procurator of the Synod; A. A. Abaza, chairman of the Department of State Economy in the State Council; M. N. Ostrovsky, Minister of State Domains; D. N. Nabokov, Minister of Justice; Minister of Finance N. Kh. Bunge; and A. A. Polovtsov, State Secretary of His Majesty. The committee had to decide three concrete questions: first, whether to draft new rules limiting access to noble status—an issue raised in the report of the so-called Taneev Commission; second, whether to draft a new bank statute; third, whether to include these two matters in the general text of the imperial rescript on 21 April. The first issue was quickly resolved: after a brief debate on 2 April between Ostrovsky and Abaza over the Taneev Commission, Alexander removed the issue of access to noble status from the special committee's agenda.[26] On the second and third issues there emerged a consensus that the establishment of the new bank should be mentioned explicitly in the imperial rescript. By 9 April, Pobedonostsev had written a first draft of the rescript and submitted it to the committee for discussion and by 13 April, the finished rescript was in the tsar's hands.[27]

On 21 April, the St. Petersburg nobility assembled in their meetinghall to hear the imperial rescript. For this special occasion all the grand dukes were in attendance, as were high ranking courtiers— Vorontsov-Dashkov, Cherevin, Trubetskoi, and Dolgoruky. The St. Petersburg provincial marshal was designated to read to the dignitaries the following statement from Alexander III:

> On this significant day, pondering gratefully the history of the noble Estate, which is inseparable from the history of the state and Russian people, WE firmly hope that sons of valorous fathers, who have served the state, will show themselves worthy members of this Estate in service to the fatherland. OUR charge is to facilitate their ways of fulfilling with honor such a high calling in the future. In view of the **needs of noble landownership, in many places shattered by the im**-poverishment of economic resources and the tightening of credit, WE have ordered the Minister of Finance to approach, according to principles indicated by US, the foundation of a special Noble Land Bank, in order that nobles may be more attracted to constant residence on their estates, where henceforth they may apply all their efforts to the activity required them by their duty and calling. Not doubting that with the continuation of this activity will correspond brilliant successes in other fields, long ago indicated to the nobility by history and the Will of Monarchs, WE, for the good of the state, deem as a blessing that the Russian nobility both now, as in past times, retain the **preeminent place in military leadership, in the affairs of local ad**-ministration and the courts, in disinterested guardianship of the needs of the people, in spreading by their example the rules of faith and faithfulness and healthy principles of popular education.[28]

The imperial rescript of 21 April had a tremendous impact on those assembled and on those interested in the fate of the nobility. State Secretary Polovtsov, who had been involved in drafting the rescript, came home from the noble assembly and wrote in his diary: "Throughout the entire ceremony is heard a turning [*povorot*] in government policy. In contradiction to Grand Duke Konstantin Nikolaevich and Miliutin there is announced support for the upper class as leader [*rukovoditeliu*] of the populace." Polovtsov added: "That is wonderful, but one shouldn't go too far in that direction either."[29] In his editorial on the rescript, Katkov gloated about the crushing defeat Alexander had handed the liberal zealots who had expected a law to finish off the nobility. And Katkov exulted that "the strength of the nobility is living, like Russia itself."

The imperial rescript also had an effect on the bank statute, though perhaps this effect was hidden in Pobedonostsev's pompous and florid language. The rescript had emphasized noble tradition, the continuity of leadership in war, and state service. But how, having devoted such attention to tradition, could the government give mortgage money to nonhereditary noble landowners? These latter were not, after all, "sons of valorous fathers"; they were parvenus, Vanias-come-lately, and they did not deserve equal treatment with those whose history was "inseparable from the history of the state."

And so once the State Council did get around to deliberating on the bank statute in meetings on 18 and 23 April and 20 May, the prevailing disposition was that the bank should serve only the hereditary nobility. State Secretary Polovtsov found himself fighting a rearguard action against the the exclusion of personal nobles from the bank:

> I find it irrational to set up the property rights on the basis of Estate membership [*na soslovnuiu pochvu*]. What is to be done with an estate mortgaged to the Noble Bank and being transferred to a non-noble, and so on? Help and protect an educated landowner, but do not demand from him his genealogical table. In 1861, it was not necessary to bury the *pomeshchik*, but to resurrect him now is impossible; what must be done is to make the new landowners as useful, as educated and as influential as possible.[30]

Polovtsov was probably sensitive to the matter of genealogy because his wife was an illegitimate child; unfortunately for personal nobles, others on the State Council did not share his sensitivity and on 20 May the Council restricted loans to the hereditary nobility.

The bank statute finally approved by the State Council and confirmed by Alexander III on 3 June 1885 provided for the establishment of a State Noble Land Bank to provide mortgage money to hereditary nobles at 6.5 percent annual interest for long-term loans, and short-term loan money at 10 percent interest. The statute permitted mortgages of up to 75 percent of an estate's value with a payback period of forty-eight years. The statute also set strict rules for application procedures with final approval of all loans to be given in St. Petersburg, and it explicitly ruled out loans in cases of crop failure and natural disaster, unless all the specified application procedures were followed. The statute noted that in the case of failure to service a debt, the bank could charge high-interest penalty fees to a debtor or auction off the estate to the highest bidder.

REACTION TO THE FOUNDATION
OF THE NOBLE LAND BANK

One might think that the establishment of the Noble Land Bank was a signal victory for the provincial nobility, and so it was thought to be in most provinces. B. N. Chicherin remembered that "newspaper columns were filled to overflowing by servile addresses. In lyrical effusions they expressed how the nobility rejoiced over worthless crumbs [*groshovye podachki*] and saw before themselves the dawn of a new era."[31]

And yet the leaders of the reactionary press were very disappointed in the new bank. On May 10 Meshchersky wrote: "Even the most impartial persons such as Isakov, even Bunge's admirers such as Abaza, speak loudly about the tendentious and anti-noble character of the Noble Bank project which was initiated by His Majesty, who wanted the bank to provide a means to save noble landowners from a hopeless situation." According to Meshchersky, "the whole Noble Bank project was based on a single unspoken idea which its drafters did not hide—namely, how to help the nobility as little as possible."[32] Katkov was also unimpressed with the final version of the statute "which had gone through the laboratory of commissions, ministries, departments and joint meetings" and had lost much of its original substance. Katkov even suspected that the project might reduce to nothing the whole impact of state-supported credit to the nobility.[33]

Meshchersky and Katkov were upset by the commercial nature of the Noble Bank's operations. Although long-term interest rates were lower than in private banks, they were, nevertheless, higher than the government had charged before emancipation. Moreover, the bank statute provided for centralized loan distribution under strict rules. Meshchersky and Katkov worried that a formalized and centralized loan operation would not be "compassionate" to needy nobles. In addition, the provisions for interest penalties and estate auctioning seemed to the reactionaries to cut against the very purpose for which the bank was being founded—preservation of the noble land fund.

On balance, it seems fair to say that the Noble Bank Statute of 1885 was a mixed blessing for the nobility. After 1885 thousands of desiatins were mortgaged to the bank and many estates were saved temporarily from the auction block. If grain prices had been somewhat higher in the 1880s, if local crop failures had occurred less often, perhaps the provisions of the statute would not have been criticized much by spokesmen for the nobility. But the Great Depression intensified and the initial dissatisfaction of the ultras did not dissipate. Resentment festered and there was soon a second round of noble petitions on the credit question.

The history of the Noble Land Bank demonstrates the difficulties of any strict class interpretation of Russian noble politics. The bank question was first raised by noble and zemstvo assemblies from a minority of provinces—principally those in the blacksoil belt and southern steppes, where indebtedness to private banks was a serious concern. Nobles from other provinces where agriculture had a different character did not join the petition campaign. Thus, initiative for the Noble Land Bank was not the result of an effort by the entire landed nobility to impose their will on the central government.

The legislative debate over the bank statute was marked by sharp disagreements over the nature of the bank and its ultimate intentions. Would the bank be an institution with the limited aim of aiding the middle nobility, as Alexander III wanted? Would it be a part of a broader strategy of assistance to all landowners—large and small, peasant and noble—as Abaza insisted? Would it rather be an institution that would circumvent the land market by freezing noble lands in noble hands—a program recommended by Meshchersky, Katkov, and Shidlovsky? Should all nobles be eligible to borrow from the bank, or should funds be limited to the hereditary nobility? The fact that all these questions were posed indicates that there was little "class consciousness" in noble political thinking, despite the pompous phraseology of the 1885 rescript. Noble politics in practice reflected the major characteristics and constituent elements of the First Estate: its various status groups (hereditary and personal nobles; landowners vs. landless); its economic strata; its regional distinctions; its different traditions of political thought and modes of political activity (nonideological provincial interest politics; patronage politics of the crown; ideological ultraconservatism, and so on). Only in terms of these characteristics and elements of the First Estate rather than in terms of class analysis can the establishment of the Noble Land Bank be understood. Only by reference to these factors can one appreciate why so many provincial nobles initially hailed the bank statute "in servile petitions," while Meshchersky and Katkov ungraciously dismissed it as anti-noble.

His father died; and (as expected)
before Onegin there collected
the usurers' voracious tribe.
To private tastes we each subscribe:
Evgeny, hating litigation,
and satisfied with what he'd got,
made over to them his whole lot. . . .
—*A. S. Pushkin*
Eugene Onegin, Canto I

CHAPTER 6
The Politics of Entail

In the early 1880s it was easy for some landowners to believe that the sole answer to the Great Depression was a state land bank that could provide the nobility with cheap credit. By 1887 it was clear that the new Noble Land Bank was no panacea. The bank had failed to arrest the sale of noble estates to peasants and merchants; in fact, the erosion of the nobility's economic position seemed to be accelerating. Nobles now began to explore other possible solutions to their economic problems, in particular various legal mechanisms that would slow down the transfer of noble estates to other social groups. One device that received attention was the entailment of estates.

Entail is, of course, the settlement of the succession of a landed estate so that the estate cannot be bequeathed at the pleasure of any one possessor. One common form of entail encountered in Europe under the old regime was primogeniture, which prescribed the inheritance of landed property by the firstborn male heir. A more encompassing form of entail was the so-called strict settlement that developed in England in the seventeenth century. Strict settlement demanded that landed property be settled on a single heir who was, in effect, a tenant for life: he could enjoy the income of an estate, but he could neither sell it nor raise loans on the security of his lands.[1] Both primogeniture and strict settlement were intended to keep large landed property in the hands of a small privileged elite, and at this task strict settlement was most successful. At the same time, entail had certain significant drawbacks: it retarded the formation and development of land markets; it reduced the liquidity of a landowner's assets and may have hindered capital formation in general; and it created enormous social tensions both within and without a noble family. What, after all, was to become of dispossessed children from a landed family?

Before the emancipation Russians had had two experiences with entail legislation. The first was the law on single inheritance promulgated under Peter the Great in 1714. Under this statute immovable property was to remain with a family and be settled upon one son of the parents' choosing (or in the absence of sons, on one of the daughters). Movable property could be divided among the other children if the parents wished. This law, which adapted strict settlement to Russian conditions, was part of Peter's plan to create a group of military and civilian officials who could serve the state without at the same time ruining their peasants. It was also intended to save noble property from fragmentation and impoverishment. The statute was a failure in practice: some nobles had continued to sell their estates to those outside their families; others had given land to one son and farm equipment to the remaining children, thus insuring the failure of agriculture on their estate. There were also what Kliuchevsky called "terrible fights" among children over prospective inheritances. This unfortunate statute was abolished in 1731 by the Empress Anna, who ordered immovable property to be divided equally among children.[2] The second experience with entail was the creation of *maioraty*—indivisible estates for the largest landowners in the Empire. The law on *maioraty* had been promulgated under Nicholas I and it remained in force after the emancipation, evidently without causing serious social or economic problems.

THE CAMPAIGN
FOR ENTAILED ESTATES, 1887–1892

In 1887 the Poltava provincial marshal, Prince Alexander Vasilievich Meshchersky began to argue for the wider application of entail in the Russian Empire. Meshchersky (a distant relative of the St. Petersburg journalist) told Poltava's nobility that Peter the Great had tried to forestall the fragmentation of the noble land fund, but the First Estate had not listened to Peter's advice: "It is undoubtedly a misfortune, even a great misfortune for society and the state, that the fragmentation of estates so detested by Peter attained such grandiose and disgusting proportions before the emancipation; the bulk of free nobles lived in wretched manors, in idleness and ignorance, and survived because of the work of three or four souls, three or four slaves." Meshchersky also referred to the law on *maioraty* "which created a small class of people who have a very substantial guaranteed income, who can live free from worry, who can spend their money at will." Meshchersky recommended that the principles of Peter's legislation and of the *maioraty* be extended to smaller estates so that landowners meeting certain minimum standards might create entailed estates and "live free from worry" too.[3]

Meshchersky's recommendation led the Poltava noble assembly to petition the government to change inheritance laws. By early 1892, sixteen other noble assemblies had debated entail and sent petitions to the central government demanding new legislation in this field.[4]

No one who reads the petitions on entail can fail to be struck by their aggressive, their almost belligerent attitude toward the nobility's competitors on the land market. It is true that entail petitions make some of the same arguments for alterations in inheritance law that had been made earlier in the bank campaign: land resources were slipping away because of foreign competition, because of excessive indebtedness to banks, because it was objectively difficult to adapt to a rapidly changing market. But there is an unmistakable change in the tone of the petitions, a bitterness and fear that transcend the well-modulated antipathies and anxieties of the bank petitions.

One interesting example of the new belligerence of the provincial nobility was Meshchersky's 1887 petition, mentioned earlier. Meshchersky was clearly possessed, not of dispassionate desire to discover the reasons for the Poltava nobility's predicament, but of the need to discover *"kto vinovat"*—who is to blame for the nobility's distress. In the initial passages of his report Meshchersky wrote:

> Preoccupied with the unprofitability of our estates, we are straining to increase their income, to resuscitate our estates by increasing our operating capital, by running to banks. But in the great majority of cases our hopes have proved fruitless; they have not been realized. Who is guilty? Naturally, we ourselves are partly to blame, but we are not to blame for everything. We are certainly not responsible for the general economic and financial crisis, from which everyone suffers, and which has affected us more than anyone else for many years.

In Meshchersky's view, one of the paradoxes of the "general crisis" was that the most capable landowners suffered more than any other group:

One cay even say that the most intelligent, the most obviously rational
people have suffered more than anyone else; they have been found
guilty, yet are blameless [*oni bez viny vinovatymi*]. Given the general mo-
bility of land and the private transfer of it from person to person,
they have acquired land at a cheap price using bank credits for payments. But when the crisis came, when everything produced on an
estate had to be sold at a loss, when estate income became inadequate
to pay interest on bank loans, then even these rational people were
made to seem irrational; experience, cleverness, and knowledge were
useless. New additional loans, contracted in the hope that the situation
would finally improve, became merely new sources of final ruin;
they merely delayed the "crash," the sale of the estate at auction.

Having established that the nobility were not ultimately to blame
for the sale of their lands, Meshchersky pointed an accusing finger
at the "new people," the various non-nobles who appeared in Poltava as if to take advantage of the blameless nobles:

It is clear that before us lies the further economic disintegration of our
estates, and an even more rapid sale to merchants, to the so-called
"new people," who, if everything else remains unchanged, will some-
day replace us in the social and governmental structure of Russia.
So far these new people have not enjoyed a good reputation.
They are called Kolupaevs and Razuvaevs because they generally try to
squeeze the last drop from the muzhik and from the land; they try
to obtain a return on their investment in the shortest possible time.[5]

From first to last Meshchersky's report on entail was an effort to
fix blame for the sales of noble land in Poltava. In psychological
terms, Meshchersky was engaged in guilt displacement. He first
admitted the nobility were partly responsible for their plight, then
he proceeded to deny that responsibility ("they have been found
guilty, yet are blameless"). Finally, he asserted that the "new
people" were behind the nobility's difficulties. In political terms,
Meshchersky was appealing to the government to understand that
founding a new land bank could not solve the nobility's problems:
the government must insulate the nobility completely from competitors on the land market, otherwise the "new people" would squeeze
the innocent nobles dry. It is true that in the bank campaign certain
noble petitions had complained about the market and its agents
(banks, merchants), but these complaints had lacked the emotional
connotations, the psychological dimensions of Meshchersky's report.
A second example of noble hostility toward the "new people" was

a speech in December 1888 by Karsunsky district marshal Iu. D. Rodionov to the Simbirsk nobility. Rodionov told his peers:

> Money is faceless, and it makes no difference who has it; it is quite the opposite with land which carries the stamp of its owner and is, in fact, an integrated whole with the owner. Therefore, who owns land is far from a matter of indifference to the state: whether the land is owned by persons who have traditionally worked with the land and lived from it—persons who love it and show their love in the way they exploit it and cultivate it, and who hope to pass it along to their heirs; or whether the land is owned by people who have nothing in common with it, people who strive only to obtain the fastest possible return on their investment and then abandon the land, or if possible, sell it. Predators of this kind serve only to impoverish a region, to destroy the productivity of the country, which in the end will be transformed into a desert.[6]

Here was a direct warning to the state that failure to support the nobility would hand the Russian countryside over to predators who would transform it into a desert. What government could stand idle in the face of such a prospect?

A third example of belligerence in noble petitions was the speech of Vladimir Vasilievich Khvoshchinsky, Makarievsky district marshal, to the Nizhny-Novgorod noble assembly in 1887. Khvoshchinsky explained the historical role of the nobility in the Russian countryside, and why this role could no longer be performed:

> . . . the landed nobility are necessary to our state as a link between tsar and people. The nobility stand as a sentinel over conservative values and they guide and direct to the good the masses of our unenlightened peasantry. In order to carry out their assigned task, the nobility must live on their estates, and that is becoming harder every day. Under the existing arrangement the village assembly and village court and, in part, the zemstvo are dominated by the kulak, a drunken brawler, or by the tavern owner with the help of the volost clerk. With such leaders the people are developing more and more disrespect for property rights, for family rights, and for governmental authority, since any decision or directive can be cancelled if one hires a clever lawyer. . . .
>
> The peasants, who have been liberated from serfdom and made legally equal to their former owners, do not recognize their equality; they are prepared to obey the local nobility, understanding their own ignorance [*temnota*] and supposing that the nobles stand closer to the tsar. This arrangement has been disturbed by the new self-appointed leaders of the people—the kulak, tavern owner, and clerk, whose cabal oppresses the peasants more than serfdom did. These

leaders easily destroy the authority of the nobility, since they have the same rights as the nobility, but they also have certain means of which nobles have been deprived.

Under the pressure of the vulgar strength [*grubaia sila*] of the current popular leaders, of the general economic crisis that increasingly affects landlords, the local nobility are abandoning their land, leaving their estates and the peasant populace to be devoured by the insolent cupidity of the kulaks and tavern owners.[7]

Khvoshchinsky's speech was noteworthy for its slanderous insinuations: all peasants were ignorant; all rich peasants were drunken brawlers; literate peasants (the clerks) taught disrespect for authority; clever lawyers were enemies of justice and order; popular leaders were "self-appointed" (hence arrogant), vulgar, insolent, avaricious and, above all, they aimed to destroy noble landowners. There was no evidence offered in support of these propositions, if one may dignify Khvoshchinsky's invective by that term. Slander needs no evidence, only a credulous and malicious auditor. Khvoshchinsky added to his ad hominem attacks the implication that things were better under serfdom, an unusual departure in noble petitions which almost universally accepted the 1861 reforms as irreversible.

In retrospect, the oddest feature of Khvoshchinsky's speech was not that he leveled his reproach at the new order and at certain actors in the countryside, but that he should have picked on members of the peasant community. One might have understood a petition that attacked, however unjustifiably, bankers and merchants, for they did buy larger parcels of land. But peasants bought only small tracts. Apparently Khvoshchinsky, like his counterpart Meshchersky, felt compelled to blame someone for the nobility's problems; Khvoshchinsky decided to make the peasants the scapegoat.

The three noble memoranda cited above show that earlier hostilities toward the market had now become more intense and had been extended to include parts of the peasant community. This subjective change was one indication of the deepening agricultural depression.

What attitude did noble petitioners express toward the government in the late 1880s and early 1890s? As in the bank campaign, there were no frontal attacks on government policies. After all, there was no reason to assume the government's ill will toward the nobility, especially since the imperial rescript of 1885 and the funding of the Noble Bank. And if one could command His Majesty's attention by the time-honored method of servile petitions, why take the risk of criticizing the government directly? Yet if the nobility generally avoided attacking government policies, it was nevertheless obvious that they were growing restless under the effects of the Great Depression. It could not be but a matter of grave concern to the government that twenty-five years after the emancipation some nobles openly suggested that life had been better under serfdom. And the open contempt with which certain nobles viewed the "new people" was evidence that tempers in the countryside would not long tolerate a continuation of the economic status quo.

There were also disturbing signs that the nobility might soon openly challenge the government. In October 1888 Sudzha district marshal S. Zhekulin presented a long defense of entail to the Kursk provincial noble assembly. At one point in his speech Zhekulin mentioned the threat posed to the hereditary nobility by civil servants who were promoted into the nobility by the imperial bureaucracy:

> Since the time of Peter the Great, access to the nobility has been open
> to the best people in the state. The reformer of Russia desired that
> the nobility be constantly renewed and that it assimilate all the best in
> the state. This idea has had lamentable results: there has appeared
> a special contingent of personal nobles, who have harmed the noble Es-
> tate. It is time to correct this past error and to petition that hered-
> itary nobility be granted to non-nobles only by imperial decree or by a
> two-thirds majority of the nobility. No office ranks or awards should
> bestow hereditary or personal nobility on commoners.[8]

Superficially Zhekulin's remark seems to be a reasonable request to restrict access to the hereditary nobility. But at a deeper level it had many almost subversive implications. First, Zhekulin was criticizing the very foundation of the Petrine political system which connected rank with promotion into the personal and hereditary nobility. To divorce the bureaucratic apparatus from the nobility would be to create a bureaucracy without firm social foundations. Second, Zhekulin's criticism was based on the assumption that there was no common interest between hereditary landed nobles and commoners ennobled by the state, and that their interests were contradictory. Was it not a very small step to the assertion that the bureaucracy itself was hostile to the nobility? Third, Zhekulin's solution to this problem (aside from entailment of landed estates) was to make the nobility rather than the government responsible for *ennoblissements*. Was this not a naked demand for power at the expense of the government?

Thus, in the late 1880s and early 1890s there was no formal noble opposition to the state. But noble resentment against the market, against the so-called new people, threatened to spill over into an attack on the government. Zhekulin's attack on the personal nobility was a veiled thrust against the bureaucracy. Unless grain prices recovered their former levels, the future did not promise pacific relations between the nobility and the state.

DISAGREEMENTS OVER ENTAIL, 1887–1892

The categorical language of the entail petitions, the sweeping attacks against those who did not belong to the hereditary landed nobility might lead one to believe that class consciousness was growing in the First Estate. However, the actual social basis of the entail campaign was narrower than its rhetoric would suggest and, in fact, there were substantial disagreements amongst nobles over the kind of entail that should be adopted.

It was noted above that between 1887 and 1892, seventeen provincial assemblies asked the government to change inheritance laws. These included five provinces (Petersburg, Pskov, Smolensk, Kaluga, Nizhny-Novgorod) from the nonblacksoil zone, eight provinces (Tula, Riazan', Kursk, Penza, Kazan', Simbirsk, Poltava, Khar'kov) from the blacksoil belt, and four of the five southern steppe provinces (Ufa, Ekaterinoslav, Kherson, Tauride). As in the bank campaign, the blacksoil belt and southern steppes were centers of agitation, but now the nonblacksoil zone was also involved. This modest increase in political activity was the logical result of mounting economic pressure against noble lands in all three agricultural zones outside the western periphery. Yet seventeen provinces were still a minority of provinces in European Russia, and it is worth remarking that politically significant assemblies such as those in Moscow and Tver' remained silent on the question of entail.

Amongst the provinces that adopted petitions on entail, there was little harmony on the rules of entailment. The Kursk nobility wanted the minimum size of entailed estates set at 200 desiatins; Poltava and Nizhny-Novgorod desired a 400-desiatin miminum, while Kherson and Smolensk urged a 500-desiatin standard. Ufa, Tauride, Kaluga, Simbirsk, Khar'kov, Kazan', and Tula provincial assemblies did not specify any minimum standard size for entailed estates, but confined themselves to affirmation of entail in principle. And two assemblies (Pskov and Penza) could not agree among their own membership what kind of property standards to establish. In Pskov, for example, the noble assembly argued for days over whether the property qualification [*tsenz*] for justices of the peace or the lesser qualification for zemstvo deputies should be the standard written into their petition. Finally, it was decided to appeal for the larger standard in five districts of Pskov and for the lesser standard in the remaining three districts.[9]

The failure to agree on a national standard for entail or, in some cases, on a provincial standard indicated a deep ambivalence among the landed nobility over who was worthy to be saved from estate auctions. Those assemblies whose proposed standards fell in the 200- to 500-desiatin range were arguing tacitly that the gentry needed and deserved help, but the petty nobility did not. Other assemblies that did not specify minimum standards were urging assistance to all landed nobles, regardless of strata. From a social standpoint then, the movement for entail was one restricted to the middle nobility in certain provinces, but in other provinces was not thus restricted. From a political standpoint, the disagreement over entail standards would enable the government to drive a wedge between the gentry and other strata and to adopt a program which saved not the entire First Estate but only part of it.

In addition to disagreements over the kind of entail desired, there were many nobles within the provinces petitioning for entail who doubted that entail would work at all.[10] For example, in Poltava province Romensky district marshal Grigory Navritsky argued that a proposal to create the possibility of indivisible and inalienable estates would not be enough to rescue the gentry from selling their estates:

> The publication of a law on the system of instituting inalienable and indivisible noble allotments will be advantageous to those landowners who already feel secure and completely independent as farmers.
> The landowners who are now squandering their last resources and strength in struggling against indebtedness will remain in their former state—that is, as sure bets to lose their estates in the near future. Since this latter group owns about half of all noble land, it is obvious that the new law, despite its theoretical benefits, will not meet the unavoidable need of the present—it will not avert the further massive reduction of noble landowning and the diminution of the number of local noble farmers.

Navritsky reasoned that entail would do nothing to eliminate existing mortgage indebtedness. Therefore, a struggling landowner would find it unhelpful to create an entailed estate because the mere act of entailment would do nothing to solve the problem of how to pay one's debts; it would be more rational for the owner to sell his estate to get out of debt. Navritsky's solution to the problem facing nobles was novel: the state should "liquidate noble indebtedness by applying the basic principles of the Statute of 19 February 1861—

i.e., by giving each landowner the right granted in the statute to peasants' village societies, the right to an inalienable land title for every estate subject to a redemption operation."[11] In short, Navritsky advocated the emancipation of the landed nobility from the servile state of indebtedness! Noble indebtedness would be assumed by the state, and nobles would redeem their property in the way that peasants were doing.

Other nobles objected against entail on the grounds that it would not work as well as their own economic cooperation. In Smolensk province M. A. Liagotino told his peers that the gentry had suffered more in the Great Depression than other strata of the nobility: "The magnates still possess money that cushions them from the worst effects of temporary adversities; middle and petty proprietors, after payment of their bank and credit obligations, find themselves every spring in a hopeless situation, without means to run their farms." Liagotino thought that the necessary operating capital might be collected from the nobility themselves through a monthly tax; money gathered from the monthly payments would be lent at low interest rates by an economic corporation of all noble landowners. The idea behind the Liagotino plan was a scheme of capital redistribution that would take the surplus capital of the magnates and lend it to less wealthy nobles.[12]

A similar plan was defended by Senator Prints, who decried the tendency of nobles to run to the government for financial assistance. Prints believed that self-help in cases of bad harvests, deaths of family heads, and other disasters should be encouraged. Both Liagotino and Prints appealed to the nobility for greater corporate solidarity in the belief that it was demeaning to depend on the government and legal devices to preserve the First Estate.[13]

The nobility's lack of clarity about standards for entailment and doubts about the efficacy of entail substantially diminished the impact of the petition campaign on the government. Officials viewed the matter of entail with their usual skepticism and studied its alleged advantages with all deliberate speed.

THE CENTRAL GOVERNMENT AND THE ENTAIL QUESTION, 1891–1899

On 20 November 1891 Alexander III set the wheels of the bureaucratic machine on their slow grind forward. Alexander appointed a conservative member of the State Council, N. S. Abaza, head of a Special Commission to Draft Measures to Fortify Noble Landowning.

The Abaza Commission counted among its members thirteen high officals from the Ministries of Internal Affairs, Justice, Finance, and State Domains, plus several provincial marshals from provinces that had petitioned for change in inheritance laws. The Abaza Commission held its working sessions from 4 February 1892 to 16 November 1892; however, Abaza did not submit his preliminary recommendations to the State Council until December 1893, and his final recommendations were not drafted until November 1895. Only in January 1896 did the Joint Departments of the State Council formally debate the Abaza proposals. When the statute on temporary entail was actually published in May 1899, more than a decade had passed since the first petition from Poltava province.[14]

As Soloviev has demonstrated, the Abaza Commission began its deliberations by accepting as valid two assertions made in entail petitions. First, the commission agreed that merchants were dangerous competitors of the nobility on the land market and were inimical to provincial life. "Lacking any intellectual or ethical development, the majority of these people [merchants] have only one goal—profit, and therefore they usually have a corrupting influence on public affairs; they are a scourge to the local populace and they act as predators toward their own estates." Second, the commission judged the decline of noble landownership to be dangerous for the government. "The government can scarcely feel indifferent about the diminution of noble landowning since this diminution signifies the strengthening of those local elements which may be justly called anti-social and anti-governmental."[15] Thus, the Abaza Commission manifested a hostility toward "the new people" in the countryside that would have been gratifying to Meshchersky and Rodionov.

But words come more easily than deeds. As soon as the Abaza Commission turned to its real task, the elaboration of concrete proposals on entail, it found itself facing two virtually insuperable problems. The first was how to reconcile the principle of entail with existing institutional credit operations. The state had created the Noble Land Bank partly to lend operating capital to growers needing it, but the bank's rules provided that in cases of serious arrears or default on mortgage payments, estates could be sold at auction to the highest bidder. This was nothing but a legal way to protect the integrity of the bank's assets. If an estate were legally entailed, however, if it could not be sold or even divided for mortgage arrears, then the bank would have no collateral protecting its capital. Moreover, if the idea of entail was to pass on estates unencumbered from generation to generation, how could mortgages be accepted? Were mortgages not monetary encumbrances? In England, after all, one could not raise loans against the security of strictly settled estates. Finally, if the commission were to decide that entailed estates could not be encumbered by debts, how many nobles would entail their lands? Was not operating capital more important in the end than the security of knowing one could pass on a piece of property that one's heir would find impossible to farm for want of capital?

The second problem was how entailment could be reconciled with the principles of multiple inheritance and testamentary division. What good would it do five children to inherit a 200-desiatin entailed estate? And their children? Obviously the government would have to adopt the principle of single inheritance, but such a plan would open the way to the "terrible fights" among children experienced in noble families under Peter the Great. Moreover, the government would risk creating a new alienated caste of propertyless noble children. Peter the Great had required that all nobles do government service, but such a requirement was no longer practical nor desirable. Thus, the autocracy would end up turning countless nobles out into the courtyard.

The Abaza Commission attempted to solve these problems by adopting two expedients. First, the commission decided that entail should be applied only to the gentry, not to petty nobles and magnates. The Commission defined the gentry as those whose estates yielded an annual income of 1,500 to 7,500 rubles and had a capital value of 30,000 to 150,000 rubles.[16] According to the commission's journal, the members believed that preservation of larger and smaller estates was not a matter of "governmental necessity." In fact, of course, the Abaza Commission merely followed the suggestions of provincial assemblies in Kursk, Poltava, Nizhny-Novgorod, Kherson, and Smolensk, all of which were interested primarily in saving the gentry's estates from the auction block. Under the commission's logic, larger and smaller estates would continue to be bought, sold, and mortgaged as before; thus, the Noble Land Bank could continue to operate with land as loan collateral in most cases. However, the commission would also permit gentry owners of entailed estates to mortgage their estates, and in these cases the Noble Land Bank would have no security on the mortgage loans. The commission admitted that this might pose "certain dangers" to the bank's integrity, but argued that such risks were necessary if the middle nobility were to be preserved.[17] Second, the commission decided that entailment would be legally binding on one generation only. Thus, the son of someone who had entailed an estate could neither sell nor divide the entailed property; however, the grandson could choose to do either. The temporal restriction on entail was designed to partially alleviate the family quarrels attendant on single inheritance.

In reality, neither expedient avoided the contradictions discussed earlier, and both expedients so weakened the attractions of entail as a legislative solution to the nobility's problems that the most elementary objections blocked its adoption for years. On 30 January 1893 State Secretary L. Frisch sent Abaza a letter attacking the idea of single inheritance, even on a limited basis. And on 21 May 1893 Minister of Justice Manasein complained that permitting temporary entailed estates to carry large mortgage debts was "pointless and by no means desirable."[18] Abaza had no real answer to either objection, and although he continued to work on details of his plans, he never changed his basic proposals. When, after much delay, Abaza finally forwarded his recommendations to the Joint Departments in January 1896, the Departments raised the question of whether Abaza's plan was in the interests of the nobility at all. The Departments demanded a further study of the issues by the Ministry of Internal Affairs, thus blocking entailment on the pawn file of the bureaucratic chessboard.

Not until February 1898 did the bureaucracy permit the Abaza project movement: in that month entail was discussed by the Special Commission on the Nobility, an ad hoc agency appointed by Nicholas II to study the needs of the nobility. The dominant figure on the Special Commission was then Minister of Finance Sergei Iulievich Witte, who looked on entail as an innocuous measure that one must support because the tsar was favorably inclined to it: "On the principle of entailment one can argue long and hard, and, probably from a theoretical standpoint one can say more against it than for it. Strictly speaking, I am for the project on temporary entailed estates because there is at hand a directly expressed command by His Majesty, the Emperor, to maintain the economic strength of the noble Estate."[19] Witte's sentiment was widely shared by other commission members, even Witte's archenemy V. K. Plehve, who observed: "I think that one must not expect real benefits for noble landowning from the measures being discussed; there will be few enthusiasts to set up entailed or indivisible estates."[20]

From 7 February to 2 May the Special Commission worked out its recommendations on entail. Following the lead of the Abaza Commission, the Special Commission designed a proposal to assist the middling nobility. However, the Special Commission gave a much clearer rationale for assisting the gentry than had Abaza. The Special Commission argued that large landowners did not live on their estates and were not involved in provincial government, while the gentry were "more tied to the land by their traditions and inclinations, and also more active members of their Estate. . . ." The gentry "almost alone carry the burden of local service, both governmental and corporative."[21] The Special Commission also recognized explicitly the conflicts between credit and entail. The commission was willing to permit the entailment of estates that were already 60 percent mortgaged and would allow new debts to be contracted up to 33 percent of estate value. Witte admitted that this plan was at "cross-purposes with strict principles of economic politics," but he winked at the proposal because he suspected there would be few takers. On the question of single inheritance there was much discussion over the problems to be faced by disinherited children, but the commission swallowed hard and accepted single inheritance as a necessary evil.

The proposals of the Special Commission were reviewed in February and March of 1899 by the Joint Departments of the State Council, and in May 1899 by the State Council itself. The latter institutions made no substantive changes in the Special Commission's recommendations, except to soften the principle of single inheritance. The State Council demanded that the widow of an estate owner be provided with means of sustenance in her lifetime, and that the brothers and sisters of an estate legatee be taken care of if the entailed estate were not mortgaged up to 33 percent of its value. On 25 May 1899 the Statute on Temporary Entailed Estates was affirmed by Nicholas II and became law.

Witte's belief that few members of the nobility would voluntarily create entailed estates under the new statute proved correct. In the first year of the law's existence only one noble established such an estate. Soloviev was correct to argue that in the twelve years following the Poltava petition of 1887, the Russian nobility had moved beyond entail.[22] In those twelve years roughly ten million desiatins had been sold from the noble land fund, and bank indebtedness had grown catastrophically. There were now fewer members of the gentry who could take advantage of the entail law, and virtually no one had the desire to do so. By 1899 the government was like a player in a deserted shadow theater whose dramatic gestures were meant to impress an audience that had long ago slipped away.

He who has lived and thought is certain
to scorn the men with whom he deals.
—A. S. Pushkin,
Eugene Onegin, Canto I

C H A P T E R   7
Remaking
the Noble Land Bank

The politics of provincial nobles in the 1880s was animated by a spirit of resistance to the free market. Yet this resistance was not a direct threat to the state. In the petition campaigns for the State Noble Land Bank and entail, nobles asked the government to establish new institutions and legal procedures, but these requests were made largely without explicit criticism of existing bureaucratic agencies. Only in isolated instances such as the 1888 speech of Zhekulin to the Kursk provincial assembly did nobles explicitly criticize the state.

During the second phase of the Great Depression, in the 1890s, provincial assemblies engaged more frequently in direct struggle with the bureaucracy over agrarian politics. The reason for this struggle was not an inherent predilection for criticizing the government, nor was it a desire to transform the state according to a predetermined ideological agenda. On the contrary, provincial noble assemblies continued to be concerned about the economic pressures exerted by the Great Depression, just as they had been in the 1880s. Yet in the 1890s some provincial nobles became convinced that these economic pressures could not be alleviated without changes in existing government programs and agencies. And to justify appropriate economic changes nobles had to level direct criticisms against the bureaucracy.

There were three issues that provoked intense struggle between provincial nobles and the bureaucracy: the nature of the State Noble Land Bank and its operations; governmental regulation of railroads; and governmental policies toward the post-emancipation peasantry. All three political issues involved the Ministry of Finance, which supervised the Noble Land Bank, set railroad tariffs, and determined to a considerable extent fiscal and social policies toward the peasantry. And, thus, all three issues led to clashes between dissatisfied provincial nobles and Russia's most brilliant statesman, Minister of Finance Sergei Iulievich Witte.

THE PROBLEM OF BANK CENTRALIZATION, 1891–1895

After the Noble Land Bank began to function in 1885, landowners conducted thousands of business transactions with bank agents. Some nobles merely investigated the terms for borrowing money, others mortgaged small parcels of land in order to secure ready capital, and hundreds each year went through the laborious process of mortgaging their entire estates. The bank became a major part of landowners' lives, but like every other important institution, it was imperfect and its imperfections gave rise to dissatisfaction.

One source of discontent with the bank was the institutional structure which thwarted local initiative. The bank was a highly centralized agency. Although it had branch offices in more than thirty provincial capitals, every loan had to be approved in St. Petersburg. Centralization meant lengthy correspondence with faceless bank officials in distant Petersburg, and it meant that weighty decisions governing the financial solvency of an individual landowner were made by persons whom the landowner had probably never met. In a society that prized reputation, individual probity, and personal associations so highly, a centralized bank was bound to frustrate its patrons. Another problem with bank regulations was the paperwork required to complete loan applications. The need to notarize a myriad of documents, to arrange for an official appraisal of estate value by a licensed bank appraiser, to secure the signature of the district or provincial marshal—these steps were time consuming and irritating to financially pressed landlords. While no nineteenth-century bureaucracy functioned without mountains of paper grist for its mill, the tsarist government, with its celebrated appetite for control of the most minute questions of local life, seemed an especial abomination to many provincial nobles.

Curiously enough, the provincial campaign to reorganize the Noble Land Bank began within the bank, when two bank officials in Khar'kov urged the government to take greater account of local needs. I. I. Karazin and I. P. Sarandinaki, landowners and members of the Khar'kov office of the bank, reported in October 1891 that they "could not avoid study of those peculiarities of the Bank Statute that hinder the development of local estates by forcing useless, and sometimes significant expenses, and the loss of time . . . on formalities." Karazin and Sarandinaki thought that too many mortgage transactions involved formal appraisals of estate value, and that the nobility should be able to borrow money based on the average value of land in their districts. This new plan would save the bank time and the expense of estate appraisals, and it would save nobles "time and many thousands of rubles since money is needed quickly in a fixed period, and land mortgages through Petersburg drag on for months." Because the current loan process was so slow and painful, many nobles were inclined to take out mortgages at private land banks, even though interest rates were frequently higher than at the Noble Land Bank. Karazin and Sarandinaki also recommended that local branches be permittted to make cash loans to landlords, since the branches were "doubtless more aware of the economic circumstances of estates and landowners." Cash loans would be set at the proper amount by local branches, not by the Petersburg Bank Council, which often determined the amount of loans "on the basis of very questionable and dubious reasoning."

Karazin and Sarandinaki called in addition for the abolition of the installment payment system. Current rules required that a borrower pay a predetermined sum of money each installment period. The Khar'kov landowners said that the existing system was ill suited to the nature of farming operations, since income from an estate arrived at various times and in unequal amounts. The solution was to make a "running balance" of payments: the size of payments would be subject to change at the discretion of the landowner, who would be obliged only to inform a responsible committee of his proposed payment schedule. This plan would introduce flexibility into credit arrangements, thus giving borrowers greater leeway in lean years.

Another reform that Karazin and Sarandinaki wanted adopted was local auctions of noble estates. Under the current law when owners failed to meet their bank obligations, their estates were auctioned to the highest bidder in Petersburg: these Petersburg auctions were dominated by speculators many of whom were not nobles. The plan for local auctions would enable local buyers, who were familiar with land in their areas of a province, to make bids on noble properties.[1]

Having composed their report on the problems of bank centralization, Karazin and Sarandinaki sent one copy to the head of the Noble Land Bank in Petersburg and a second copy to the Khar'kov provincial marshal, Count Kapnist. In the hands of Kapnist, Karazin and Sarandinaki's dry, bureaucratic report became the basis of a furious attack on governmental centralization. Kapnist depicted the board of directors of the Noble Land Bank as a willful group of men "bent on arrogating to themselves the impossible burden of con-ducting an operation that is too expensive and complex." The direc-tors, in Kapnist's view, deliberately concentrated in their own hands "the right to decide all issues large and small bearing any relation to borrowers' interests." In the process, the importance of local bank offices was destroyed and the interests of borrowers "sacrificed to unwonted centralization."[2]

Within three years after Kapnist's protest against bank centrali-zation, noble assemblies in ten other provinces expressed their dis-satisfaction with the bank's organization and loan disbursement pro-cedures. The petitioners included two provinces in the nonblacksoil zone (Moscow, Nizhny-Novgorod), six provinces from the blacksoil zone (Riazan', Orel, Voronezh, Chernigov, Poltava, Khar'kov), two southern steppes provinces (Samara, Ekaterinoslav), plus Bessarabia. The pattern of petitions was geographically amorphous, but there was some positive correlation with distance from St. Petersburg; delays in communications with the bank may have become more prolonged as distance from the capital increased. The discontent in the blacksoil and southern steppe regions was also related to a generally higher level of estate indebtedness and of noble economic difficulties in these areas.

Like the Khar'kov petition, other petitions argued for a stronger local voice in decision making and for reduced paperwork. To a certain extent, the attack against bank centralization and red tape paralleled growing contemporary criticism of bureaucratic absolutism as a serious problem of Russian society. In both instances there was anger over the central government's distrust of provincial society, over governmental "formalism," over the waste, inefficiency, and perceived injustice of operations run in Petersburg.[3] Thus, interest politics on such a narrow issue as the powers of a local bank office began to dovetail with wider provincial concerns of certain zemstvo and noble activists who quietly wished for some form of local self-government or bureaucratic decentralization.

THE BANK AND LOCAL AGRICULTURAL PROBLEMS

A second source of disenchantment with the bank was the disparity between expectations of economic assistance and the reluctance of the bank to relieve economically hard-hit nobles. From the beginning the bank had functioned as a commercial enterprise in the sense that it demanded regular payments and a fairly high rate of interest. The bank was to be a source of capital for agricultural investment and development, not a device to subsidize every needy landowner. Yet many nobles had anticipated much more favorable treatment, especially in the wake of the great famine in 1891/92 and the commercial grain price depression of the mid-1890s. In the steadily deepening crisis of agriculture, nobles' expectations of government assistance rose faster than the government's capacity and will to help.

These expectations were first manifested in petitions from provincial assemblies requesting government concessions in response to local agricultural problems. A good example of a petition justified by reference to bad local conditions was the Khar'kov petition of September 1893. Eighteen months after his plea for bank decentralization, Khar'kov provincial marshal Count Kapnist wrote to A. A. Golenishchev-Kutuzov, director of the Noble Land Bank, about the unusual problems facing Khar'kov landowners. Kapnist began by mentioning that the district marshals and various other parties were concerned about the "stagnation in demand for agricultural goods that is having such a dreadful impact, mainly on noble landowners in this province." He then discussed weather conditions in July which had delayed reaping for a month, and the very good harvest that caused landowners to hire extra hands to gather the crop. The lateness of the harvest, the poor quality of the rye crop, and the unusual expenditures on peasant workers "deprived landowners of the chance to make ends meet, given the absence of demand and the low prices of grain on the market." Kapnist noted that "while this year's harvest may have been profitable for the working population, it has been a disaster for the nobility—especially for those who are already in debt because of previous expenses." As evidence Count Kapnist cited the unprecedented number of estates slated for sale by the Noble Land Bank due to failure to meet mortgage payments.

In his observations, Kapnist remarked on the absence of well-designed grain storage centers that might aid producers by sorting and cleaning grain. He also discussed the nobility's difficulties in selling grain to the army. He concluded ruefully by saying that the situation for indebted landowners was "almost more grim than in years of complete crop failure, when at least expenses are insignificant and even the most modest harvests can be marketed at a high price."[4] Kapnist and the Khar'kov nobility sought a delay in their periodic mortgage installment payments and a rescheduling of payments under the same rules that had been followed during the famine of 1891/92.

Within a month Count Golenishchev-Kutuzov answered Kapnist's letter with a flat rejection of the Khar'kov petition. On 22 October 1893 Kapnist acknowledged the rejection, but repeated his earlier demands:

Under . . . normal circumstances . . . such petitions would, of course, lack justification. Yet now, when the government itself is searching earnestly for extreme measures to help landowners of all Estates and thus admits that the situation this year represents danger and in any case cannot be considered normal, such petitions cannot be without significance and they deserve serious attention.[5]

Kapnist asserted that the depressed condition of the Khar'kov grain market "can surely be called unprecedented. Demand is non-existent, and if sales are made, they are . . . merely fortunate exceptions." "No one knows," continued Kapnist, "how long this may continue and the uncertainty frightens both producers and buyers. In the meantime, most debtors of the Noble Bank, having exhausted their resources and credit in the harvest, . . . are forced to look on the sale of their estates as the only practical alternative." Kapnist emphasized that delay of mortgage installments was the only realistic step that the government could take to avoid estate sales. Golenishchev-Kutuzov did not respond to Kapnist's repeated entreaty for aid.

Another example of a petition justified by reference to bad local conditions was the Bessarabian petition of October 1896. On 9 October the Bessarabia provincial noble assembly met in extraordinary session to discuss the harvest and possible governmental assistance. The provincial zemstvo board supplied statistics that showed a complete failure of all varieties of grain and grasses in all but two districts. The majority of landowners could not recoup their expenses on the spring sowing. They were "forced to sell many of their cattle and horses or to run to the ruinous services of private creditors." The position of landowners with mortgaged estates "became truly critical."[6]

According to the record of the extraordinary session, there was an "animated debate [*ozhivlennaia preniia*]" about possible solutions to Bessarabia's crisis. One landowner, M. K. Buzni, said that the first priority was to provide relief for those nobles whose estates were slated for sale in early December because of failure to pay their debts to the Noble Land Bank. K. V. Leonard who thought that Buzni was correct, proposed a petition for the removal of these estates from the auction block; the arrears on past payments would merely be added to the total capital debt on the estates. In effect, this would have meant temporary forgiveness of many outstanding debts. Other members of the assembly, including I. V. Kristi and M. L. Derozhinsky, advocated a second petition that proposed delaying the 1896 mortgage installments of all Bessarabian noble debtors. The chairman of the assembly thought that even this would not be enough to satisfy the current needs of the province. He urged the government to make financial concessions to Bessarabia's wine producers. In the last year, due to new governmental regulation of the liquor industry, the price of wine had dropped 20 to 30 percent. Vineyards were very important to Bessarabia's economy, "a vital supplementary source of income, especially since grain production had become so little profitable." The wine trade in Bessarabia deserved government assistance.[7]

In the end the Bessarabian nobility petitioned that the government place a moratorium on estate auctions for 1896, that the semiannual mortgage installments be delayed, and that payments in arrears be added to the capital balance of mortgage debts. This petition was submitted with a cover letter from the provincial marshal, I. E. Katarzhi, who complained about the "unprecedented low prices of grain that deprive us of income," and about the good harvests before 1896 "which deepened and intensified the burden of the economic crisis."[8]

In spite of these just complaints, the directorship of the bank and the Ministry of Finance denied the Bessarabian requests. Not all petitions for local aid were rejected, of course,[9] but when such apparently reasonable requests for assistance were turned down, there was understandable disappointment with the central government and, in the Khar'kov case, mild criticism of the government's policies. Yet as long as the issues were confined to a single province, or to several districts in a province, pressure on the government rarely had the desired results. The central government had no good political reason to undertake substantive review of financial practice.

The Campaign to Reform the Noble Land Bank, 1893–1895

Unfortunately for the government, nobles in certain provinces began to treat conditions in their respective areas as symptoms of broader problems, and to criticize the government's agrarian policies as one cause of the agrarian crisis in Russia. This merging of local problems with national concerns was a source of anxiety for the government in the mid-1890s.

The Poltava petitions of 1893/94 admirably illustrate how grievances could be transformed into complaints about national financial policy. On 14 October 1893 the Poltava provincial marshal, S. Brazol, described to Count Golenishchev-Kutuzov how stagnation in market demand for agricultural products and low grain prices had "placed Poltava landowners in a difficult position."[10] The plight of the growers was complicated still further by wage payments to farm workers that were "two or three times greater than normal," and by the late arrival of these workers which resulted in much of the crop being ruined by fall rains.[11] Brazol argued that the combination of unfavorable circumstances had created a situation "worse than in the preceding lean years [i.e., the famine years of 1891/92]." Therefore, Brazol averred, the Noble Land Bank would be wise to grant concessions [*l'goty*] to its debtors—and in particular to delay the May 1893 debt collection and to postpone auctions until May or June of 1894.[12]

By March 1894 the Poltava nobility had begun to consider more-sweeping remedies than temporary debt forgiveness. A special Poltava commission on the bank and its debtors urged a series of changes in the Bank Statute itself.[13] The commission asked that only those estates on which mortgage arrears equaled more than half the annual mortgage installment be subject to auction. It proposed that in the event of nonpayment of arrears for more than six months, the bank warn a landowner officially that payment must be completed in another three months. If after this three-month period the arrears were still unpaid, then the bank could propose that a noble trust [*dvorianskaia opeka*] administer the mortgaged estate. The trust would have a month to decide whether to take over administration of an estate. If the trust decided to run the estate, then the accumulated arrears would be paid back to the bank over three years. If this proved impossible, then the bank would auction the estate under the rules laid down in 1889. The commission also requested that in cases of local crop failures or other unforeseen misfortunes, the landowner should be granted the right to delay installment payments. The landowner would have to present documents from the local zemstvo board or police to certify that his estate had suffered misfortune.

Even though the commission's recommendations for better financial terms on loans and what might be called indirect subsidy to noble agriculture implied a change in the bank's attitude toward noble needs, the actual recommendations of the Poltava provincial assembly went much further. The assembly asked a reduction of installment payments to the bank and an increase in the debt limit to 85 percent of nominal estate value. Old debts to the Mutual Land

Credit Society would also be reduced in certain cases. All of these provisions would apply to mortgages held by other land banks if the mortgages were transferred to the Noble Land Bank. The assembly also demanded that public estate auctions be replaced by trusteeships until arrears were covered. In addition confiscation of livestock and farm machinery to pay private debts was to be prohibited.[14]

In a letter to the tsar justifying the Poltava petition, S. Brazol argued that over the past seven years agriculture had returned only 3 percent profit; this made it nearly impossible to meet mortgage installment payments with their 5 percent annual interest. The low income of noble landowners and the comparatively high interest demanded by the bank had led to a ten million ruble increase in noble debts over the past five years. Brazol then stated that the burden of mortgage payments "brings about the transfer of landed property to other Estates, and forces its former owners to abandon the countryside to search for nonagricultural occupations." For thirty years, contended Brazol, ever-increasing indebtedness had been "a factor in the loss of one-fourth of the noble land fund and in reducing the number of nobles." The continued rapid and significant growth of indebtedness would "doubtless reduce both [the land fund and noble population] still further."[15]

Brazol's criticisms of the bank implied censure of government financial policy, especially since Brazol spoke about indebtedness in a thirty-year period. What was implicit in the marshal's letter was made explicit in an unsigned "explanatory document" submitted with the Poltava petitions. This extraordinary document indicted the whole course of government policy since 1861:

> The reform of 19 February 1861, prompted by the requirements of
> national growth and the civil development of Russia, radically changed
> the existing conditions of agricultural organization in Poltava prov-
> ince, but the subsequent economic policy of the government made the
> further development and existence [of agriculture] impossible.[16]

According to the Poltava assembly, the emancipation had destroyed serfdom and the benefits of serf labor in order to make way for capitalist production, whose chief ingredients were "capital and a contingent of landless unbonded workers." Unfortunately liberated peasants preferred to till their own lands rather than sell their labor cheaply to the nobility. In order to cultivate estates, nobles were compelled to pay high wages to laborers; yet the payment of these wages was made difficult by the absence of operating capital. "Under such circumstances, a money economy was impossible." The failure of the emancipation to provide an alternative source of cheap labor drove the nobility to seek bank loans, but the government had closed its lending operations to nobles and "private sources of credit were virtually nonexistent." Doubly frustrated by government policy, nobles got along as best they could by reducing farming operations to the most profitable single activity of the sixties and seventies —grain production. The tendency to convert to grain production was also reinforced by government policy which destroyed saltpeter manufacturing, taxed wine and tobacco, and allowed sheep raising to decline as an industry:

> The landed nobility concentrated their agricultural activity exclusively on the production of grain, and disregarded completely the organization of other agricultural enterprises. Thanks to the railroads, which facilitated export of grain to foreign markets, and to high prices for grain determined by foreign demand . . . the landed nobility ignored the proper exploitation of the natural fertility of the soil in order to make a quick profit on cereal production. Once having set out on this path and having fallen into debt, the landed nobility could not save themselves from ruin.[17]

Here the Poltava assembly had the advantage of hindsight. In responding to market conditions in the good years of the sixties and seventies, nobles had stumbled into the fatal trap of the eighties and nineties—a monocultural economy dependent on cereals when grain prices were moving steadily lower. The complete destruction of noble prosperity required only one factor: an encounter with "a dangerous competitor, the North American grain farmer, who is the same sort of predator [as the Russian farmer], but is armed with capital, universal technical knowledge, and experience of the old world." Once the battle with American farmers had begun, the fate of the Russian nobility was sealed. Russian grain could compete with American grain only if Russian farmers would sell at a loss. Noble producers accepted these losses and survived only by going further and further into debt until payments exceeded farm income.

In 1859 noble debts in Poltava province amounted to 7.6 million rubles; by January 1888 debts had risen to 49.9 million rubles, and by the end of 1893 they had grown another 13 million rubles. Meanwhile income from farming declined from 4.3 percent of estate value between 1881 and 1885, to 3.3 percent in 1891/92.[18]

Having traced the history of Poltava agriculture since the emancipation, the assembly went on to assert that "economic circumstances threaten farmers with complete ruin." The noblity now faced a dilemma:

either to cease their ancient agricultural activity, to sell their land, and,
breaking age-old ties with the populace and their native regions,
to sell their estates to the first opportunist; or, maintaining their moral
connection with the populace by continuing to farm and by a com-
munality of interests, to perish at their post.[19]

In this dramatic passage the Poltava assembly confessed a profound
pessimism, a belief that the future would pronounce the nobility to
be entirely irrelevant or merely superfluous. In this pessimistic spirit
there was also a clear condemnation of the government which had
allowed nobles to come to the terrible crossroads. The Poltava document dealt with a thirty-year history of errors, misjudgments, and
unsound financial policy. It echoed the themes of petitions from
the 1883–1885 period, but included criticism of the next decade of
government activity. In the Poltava petition noble politics on credit
came full circle, for despite the foundation of the Noble Land Bank
and the promulgation of the counterreforms, the provincial nobility
now spoke of the bankruptcy of government financial policies.

The Poltava petition had an influence on politics in other provinces. For example, in July 1894 the Bugul'insky district marshal
in Samara province, M. D. Mordvinov, attempted to discuss the
Poltava petition at an extraordinary session of the Samara provincial
noble assembly. The provincial marshal, A. N. Bulgakov, thought
the issue so politically explosive that he forbade debate on it during
the assembly. Undeterred by Bulgakov's reluctance, Mordvinov submitted his special opinion on the Poltava petition in writing to the
central government. According to Mordvinov,

the economic strangulation threatening the nobility, described by the
Poltava noble petition, also threatens the Samara nobility in general, and presents an even greater danger to my own Bugul'insky district, where the sale price on grain, given the lack of railroads in
this peripheral region, is more unstable and much lower than in other
areas. No one doubts that the situation of Samara noble landowners is critical; this is proven by a glance at the loss of noble lands since
1861—a loss that unfortunately concedes nothing [in its severity]
to that in Poltava province—and by the increasing difficulty in paying
interest to the Noble Land Bank.[20]

The Samara assembly did adopt a petition on the credit question,
but this petition was moderate in its approach and dealt chiefly with
organizational matters. It should be mentioned that the Samara
nobles asked that estates be subjected to auction only if arrears became greater than 50 percent of the semiannual payment; the Samara

petition also requested that, where feasible, indebted estates be administered by a trust rather than sold.

The Poltava petition also had an impact on the government, because Minister of Finance Witte decided to delay a scheduled auction of noble estates in December 1894.[21] If Witte hoped by his action to forestall further petitions on the credit question, his hopes were unrealistic; the delayed estate auction seemed to stimulate petition activity, not reduce it. On 24 January 1895 the government received a report signed by eleven marshals and three private landowners from eight provinces.[22] The report dealt with bank policy, and it was significant not only because it perceived the credit question as a national problem, but because it was an attempt at concerted action.

The memorandum began by thanking Witte for the estate auction delay, but it went on to claim that in the absence of further assistance, "the fate of these estates is nevertheless hopeless." Then the memorandum complained about the two devastating aspects of the Russian agrarian crisis: "the unprecedented price depression" and "the absence of adequate bread reserves in areas where harvests have failed." These two factors prevented the nobility from covering arrears and installment payments to the Noble Land Bank so that their "estates will be put up for auction in the next six months." The bank had agreed to reduce interest rates from 5 percent to 4.5 percent on new loans, but this measure would have no effect on the owners who would soon see their estates sold. The memorandum urged the government to give a "discount" on these old debts; in other words, the petition signatories meant that the government should discount the extra half-percent paid on old loans against any arrears that had mounted up against mortgaged estates. This plan would have simply wiped out a portion of the existing bank debt and would have "given many nobles the chance to save their estates from sale."

The assumptions of the January memorandum were not spelled out fully in the document itself, but one of the memo's signatories—Valkovsky district marshal Valerian Shirkov—later submitted another report which was more specific than the original.[23] Shirkov wrote his report in February 1895, and his view of the noble question recalled that in the Poltava "explanatory document." Shirkov began with an appeal about the ethical milieu in which the nobility lived; this appeal was at root a plea not to disrupt the ancient tradition of family ties to the land:

> On the estate of a noble lived his ancestors, who had passed away, having transferred the estate from one to another. The poignant

fact that the estate came to him from them, because they have died, reminds the noble every minute that he too will die, and this compels him to think of posterity. The thought of providing for one's descendants, a thought that centers on land which is more stable and long-lived than man, is passed on with the land, blessing those who live on it. That is why the landowner's concern grows and finally encompasses [his] descendants and this concern of his—the essence of noble thought—insistently demands . . . that in 150 or 500 years no one will be able to do harm to his descendants or . . . take away from them the right to render faithful service to the fatherland. This service will not be affected by the incidental fashions of today or tomorrow; it will not pay heed to the opinions and words of an age; rather it will be genuine service in the spirit of faith and justice, which the sovereign will never allow to disappear from his state.[24]

After this paean to the noble traditions, Shirkov turned to the discouraging contemporary situation: "The position of the nobility at present is almost hopeless. In the last three years, characterized by crop failures, by falling prices on produce, and by the swiftly rising cost of production in the wake of the workers' crisis, thousands of estates have been advertised for sale, and will not be able to provide even minimal debt service payments." The bad farming conditions of the early 1890s were not solely responsible for the present crisis; they were only the culmination of a situation long in the making:

The absence of cheap credit during a quarter century of the hired labor system and the need for an almost commercial direction of agriculture had necessitated recourse to expensive joint-stock banks, whose interest rates could not be covered by land rent. Late-arriving cheap credit offered neither operating nor accessory capital. . . . When noble estates were finally mortgaged to the Noble Bank, the debts exceeded half the estate value. In addition, most bank loans were not used to increase productivity, . . . but only to liquidate existing debts [to other banks].

Shirkov's memorandum presented basically the same argument heard earlier in the Poltava petitions. If it is reasonable to see Shirkov as representative of the group that composed the January 1895 memorandum, then it can be argued that there was a fundamental continuity between the Poltava petition and noble activism in 1895. Judging by these petitions, nobles were no longer grateful for previous attempts by the state to support them. Indeed, there was a growing conviction that the government had been blind to provincial needs all along. Even though this belief was expressed openly by only a small minority of marshals, mostly from the blacksoil zone, it was a belief that the government could ill afford to ignore.

THE 1896 CONVOCATION
OF PROVINCIAL MARSHALS

By January 1896 the problem of the nobility had become the question of the day. On 25 January the archreactionary Meshchersky wrote: "In Moscow in recent years there has not been such a gathering of nobles, such excitement, such heated conversations on the 'noble theme.'"[25] If, in this politically charged atmosphere, the government sought a pretext to reexamine the role of the nobility, that pretext was provided by Orel provincial marshal Stakhovich, who spoke to Nicholas II about the economic crisis in the countryside. According to A. A. Kireev, Stakhovich met with the tsar on 28 January and told Nicholas that the annual return from agriculture was only 3 percent, while the interest due on bank payments was 6 percent. (Stakhovich spoke primarily about interest rates on short-term loans from the State Bank rather than about long-term rates charged by the Noble Land Bank.) Stakhovich asked that a commission be created to study the problem of the nobility. Three days later Stakhovich saw Nicholas again. "He did not repeat the request for support. St[akhovich] told the Tsar in the name of the nobility that if the Tsar did not help out, the nobility would lose its capacity to serve Russia and the Tsar and would be replaced by less reliable elements. Generally he was *completely* candid. His Majesty repeated twice that He desired the nobility to maintain their position, that He was concerned about them."[26]

In early February 1896 Minister of Internal Affairs Goremykin summoned the provincial marshals to Petersburg to discuss the question. For more than a month, between 10 February and the middle of March, the marshals deliberated about problems in the countryside and the needs of the landed nobility. This was an extraordinary meeting, unprecedented in Russia since the emancipation of 1861: the government in its eagerness to solve the noble question and to head off potential opposition from the landowning elite, provided an opportunity for joint consultation between the marshals and the Ministry of Internal Affairs. The main outcome of the St. Petersburg convocation was a seventy-page memorandum on the needs of the nobility signed by the participating marshals. One section of the memorandum was devoted to the issue of noble credit, to the Noble Bank, and to the State Bank.

The marshals noted that the nobility's problem had its roots in the 1860s. Its causes were "the absence of rational credit, the abolition of serf labor and its replacement by hired labor, plus the simultaneous purchase of agricultural machinery [*inventar'*]. In the presence of this great need for operating capital, there were no government lending institutions, since these had been abolished in 1859. There was an artificially-created need to turn to ruinous credit from private individuals."[27]

The marshals contended that the government indemnification for abolishing serfdom was given out "much later than the actual emancipation and was much reduced by a series of unjust measures." There followed the complaint that the government had paid nobles not with specie, "but with redemption bonds which fell to seventy percent of their nominal value on the currency exchange." Moreover, when nobles paid off their pre-emancipation mortgages to the Mutual Land Credit Society, they had to pay the interest in gold rubles; given the prevailing rate of exchange, this meant a rate of more than ten percent a year."[28]

These contentions had been the familiar stock of noble spokesmen since the mid-1880s, when they were used in the agitation for a noble land bank. Having been revived by the 1894 Poltava petition, these charges were again hurled at the government.

The marshals also turned to the contemporary price depression that had precipitated the criticism of government policy. "In many areas of Russia grain prices in recent years have been established and held at levels insufficient to cover the cost of production." The marshals were anxious to demonstrate that everyone suffered from depressed prices. "Low prices affect adversely not only large landowners, as the Minister of Finance asserted, but everyone who sells the harvest, whether [they] farm an allotment, or purchased or rented land. . . . Given the ever more serious land shortage of the last thirty years, given allotments which hardly suffice to feed a peasant and his family, peasants can meet their tax and fiscal obligations only by purchasing and renting extra land and selling the grain produced on it. Therefore, low prices are damaging to all still financially-solvent peasants."

The marshals concluded unanimously that the economic situation in rural Russia was "becoming worse instead of better." "The rural population—people connected with the land and agriculture—noble landowners, peasants, grain traders, are growing poorer . . . are falling further into a web of debts and arrears, and they see no relief since there is insufficient attention to their needs and burdens.[29]

According to the marshals, credit was "the most powerful factor not only in the development, but in the whole operation of economic life. Without it, it is impossible to farm properly. Agricultural loans should be very inexpensive . . . and their repayment should be spread out over no less than fifteen months."[30] One problem with short-term loans in the 1893–1895 period was the "instability" of the lending rate. In late July 1894 the going interest rate was 4.5 percent, in July 1895 it was 5 percent, in August 1895 it rose to 5.5 percent, and in late September it peaked at 6.5 percent. The upward swing in the lending rate "twice exceeded the normal return from the land," and in the marshals' opinion "completely contradicted the tenets and purpose of agricultural credit enunciated by Alexander III."[31] Another unseemly feature of the existing credit system was that industry borrowed at a lower rate of interest than did nobles. While the State Bank lent 27 million rubles to the nobility at rates as high as 6.5 percent, it also distributed 130 million rubles in commercial loans at 4.5 percent. This occurred even though "the Minister of Finance knew full well how much harder and more oppressive was the situation facing agriculture than that facing industry."

The marshals outlined a series of proposals to improve the commercial conditions in the countryside. These proposals included generally lower interest rates, the transfer of heavily indebted estates from the special section of the bank (where interest rates were 6.15 percent for personal nobles and 5.9 percent for hereditary nobles) to the ordinary loans section, and the reduction of the fine levied on late payments to 6 percent a year. Borrowing rules should be liberalized to permit mortgages up to 75 percent of nominal value, instead of the current 60 percent limit. In case arrears on payments mounted, these could be added to the outstanding balance on a loan by the bank. Penalty fees on late payments might also be reduced from 12 percent of the unpaid installment to 6 percent.

The marshals also urged the government to change its policy of auctioning insolvent estates to the highest bidder. The bank should undertake temporary administration of indebted estates in cases where estates suffered from bad management. The estates of hereditary nobles should not be sold, according to the marshals. Instead, the bank should buy these estates so that they did not fall into the hands of other Estates.[32]

The marshals' plan stressed improved economic arrangements rather than changes in bank organization. This was understandable, because by early 1896 the economic pressure on the nobility had reached its maximum. Yet the marshals' grievances were not limited to the immediate financial crisis, as their broad attacks against long-term governmental financial policy illustrated. By returning to the mistakes of the early sixties, the marshals questioned the whole course of government decision making that they believed had seriously injured the nobility.

THE GOVERNMENT AND
THE BANK QUESTION, 1896–1898

Once the marshals had indicted Russia's national credit policy following the emancipation, the government was politically compelled to respond. The choices before the ministers were clear: either to defend past and current policy by refuting the marshals' charges, or to make concessions by adopting parts of the marshals' program. This latter course had the advantage that it might reduce dissatisfaction, but it involved an implicit admission that financial policy since 1861 had been bankrupt. By early 1897 the government was sharply divided over its political options. Witte and his assistants in the Ministry of Finance decided to defend existing credit institutions and credit policy, while officials in the Ministry of Internal Affairs preferred to make concessions to the nobility.

Witte spelled out his position in a formidable commentary on the marshals' memorandum.[33] He began by refuting the argument that the emancipation had been ruinous to the nobility. He noted that peasant allotments had been reduced substantially by the emancipation, much to the advantage of noble landowners. He observed that the nobility, not the peasants, set the timetable for cessation of peasant duties and determined the context of future peasant redemption payments (redemption of peasant garden plots or of field strips as well).[34] Witte reminded the marshals that the treasury had reimbursed the nobility for lost land and peasant service, and that these payments had often been based on inflated land values. He went on to note that the government's economic policy had led to enormous increases in the value of noble land. "Despite the net decline in the total of noble land from 79 to 55½ million desiatins, the value of noble land has increased from 1¼ to 2½ billion rubles since the emancipation."[35]

Witte found no justification for the marshals' criticism of the credit system. He asserted that there had been no need for extensive government lending in the 1860s and 1870s, since the emancipation had wiped out previous debts and the nobility had a large fund of ready capital in the form of government bonds. Witte remarked that noble landowners had only themselves to blame for cashing these bonds at once and thereby cutting the actual value of the bonds on the market.[36] He also pointed to private land banks and merchants as alternate sources of capital for the nobility in the 1870s.

Witte was less concerned about growing noble indebtedness than the marshals had been. He emphasized: "At this time approximately ⅗ (58 percent) of all noble land in European Russia is free from debt to mortgage institutions whereas in 1861 70 percent of the serfs had been mortgaged."[37] Furthermore, Witte stated that not all estates had been mortgaged to the statutory limit. On 1 November 1896, 4,532 estates (out of 12,865 mortgages to the Noble Land Bank) were mortgaged at 60 percent of their nominal value; 8,333 estates were mortgaged at a higher percentage of their value; while only 373 estates (2.8 percent) were mortgaged at more than 75 percent of their nominal value. Witte believed that estates mortgaged at 60 percent of their value "can hardly be considered burdensome for their owners in most cases." Witte acknowledged that many nobles had left the land, but he thought that these individuals would have quit farming no matter what policy the regime had pursued.[38]

Witte devoted a special section of his commentary to the issue of cheap, short-term credit from the State Bank. The premise of his argument was that "a credit institution cannot organize its loan operations on the sole criterion of the demand for credit by a certain group of borrowers, but it must operate according to its supply of available capital."[39] The marshals had argued that credit should be cheaper, that it should be made available on flexible terms, and that other extensive debts should not harm a landowner's credit rating when borrowing in the short term. Witte steadfastly refused to countenance such changes because he believed that the State Bank must necessarily run on a commercial, businesslike basis.[40]

Witte's commentary, as Soloviev has noted, was a devastating rebuttal to the marshals' memorandum. The Minister of Finance "left not a stone upon a stone in his critics' conclusions and arguments."[41] For a time, it appeared that Witte's defense of financial policy would carry the day and that there would be no substantive changes in government credit practice. However, Witte began almost immediately to soften his line.

On 14 March 1897 Witte delivered a Ministry of Finance proposal to the tsar. There would be a slight decrease in interest rates for borrowers at the Noble Land Bank—from 4 percent to 3.5 percent on long-term loans. In exchange for this concession Witte demanded a quid pro quo: nobles would face more stringent enforcement of the rules on loan payment defaults.[42] Nicholas II ordered that the project be considered by the Committee on Finance; the chairman of the Committee of Ministers; the Ministers of Internal Affairs, Finance, and Agriculture. He expressed hope that a final version of the project would be ready by April. On 7 April Witte and Noble Land Bank Director Prince A. D. Obolensky submitted to the Committee on Finance a long memorandum on measures to assist bank customers. This memorandum was rather more sympathetic to noble problems than Witte's earlier commentary, although it did contain some pointed warnings about speculation at the bank's expense. The memorandum discussed payment defaults.

> High interest rates, combined with the effect of the 1891–1892 crop failure on mortgaged estates, the current low prices for cereals, and difficulties in securing loans have created significant arrears in payments to the bank so that many debtors . . . doubtless find it difficult, and in other cases impossible, to discharge their debts.
>
> Yet despite the importance of this significant backlog in payments by a rather large group of landowners, it would scarcely be proper to make this the basis of a new set of regulations to improve customers' positions. These improvements should be constructed on a broader basis, and should not only reach the bank's present clientele, but all noble landowners who may deal with [the bank] in the future.
>
> The most logical and desirable improvement in credit is a reduction in the rate of interest charged on loans.[43]

Thus, Witte and Obolensky attempted to satisfy not only the bank's besieged clients, but all other landowners who might have recourse to the bank. The memorandum then dealt with regulations on swift payment of loans, and with the problem of land speculators. The final section discussed Austrian legislation of 1893 which made it possible for landowners to form economic cooperatives that would cut down on farm costs, and administer mortgaged estates rather than sell them. Witte and Obolensky recommended that the Russian nobility organize such institutions to help themselves.[44] This was a subtle attempt to wean landowners from sustenance by the state.

The Witte-Obolensky memorandum, submitted to the Committee on Finance on 11 April 1897, fell under immediate attack from two directions: from the Ministry of Internal Affairs and from the provincial marshals who had been invited to offer their views on bank legislation. As Iu. B. Soloviev has demonstrated, the attack from the Ministry of Internal Affairs was initiated by the former Minister of Internal Affairs and current chairman of the Committee of Ministers,

I. N. Durnovo, but the campaign against Witte was inspired and orchestrated by State Secretary V. K. Plehve.[45]

In Plehve, Witte met his match in bureaucratic intriguing. The Minister of Finance would later describe Plehve as "a spiteful and vengeful man" who "had no political convictions or principles." Witte wished Nicholas "to govern by relying on the people," but Witte understood that Plehve wanted "to depend solely on the nobility."[46] In choosing April 1897 and the issue of the Noble Land Bank, Plehve found the perfect time and pretext to battle the powerful Minister of Finance.

On 27 April I. N. Durnovo sent Witte a memorandum which agreed with the proposal to lower interest rates from 4.0 to 3.5 percent, but rejected all the other points made by Witte and Obolensky. Durnovo was especially unhappy with Witte's plan to assure payment of arrears. The most important departure in Durnovo's memorandum was a suggestion that the treasury make up deficits incurred by the bank.[47] In effect, Durnovo argued that the bank should no longer be a self-sufficient commercial institution, but a tool through which the state could subsidize even the most irresponsible of noble landowners. Here politics achieved primacy over economics. Durnovo would save the nobility, no matter what the cost.[48]

Witte's reaction to the Durnovo plan was instantaneous and hostile.

Its basic ideas: 1) take money from the treasury, 2) part of this money one expects to be returned, 3) and *après nous le déluge*. Our project is a concession [to the nobility] within the powers of the bank. This project is a bank with its hand in the treasury's pocket.
This latter principle is dangerous, the path is slippery.

Witte added that he could "not believe that the nobility can desire such a project [as Durnovo's]."[49]

The marshals of the nobility were the second group to criticize the Witte-Obolensky plan. The marshals had been invited to study the Ministry of Finance's proposals, and in late April they presented a memorandum analyzing the Witte plan of 7 April. The marshals welcomed a reduction in interest rates, but argued that a half-percent cut was not sufficient to save mortgaged estates.

The current state of the economy forces them [the marshals] to agree with the suggestion of the memorandum endorsing the [reduction in interest rates], and to add that the proposed magnitude (½ percent) will not be large enough to change the position of indebted landowners. Any further reduction in interest would have a salutary effect. . . ."[50]

The marshals then suggested that interest rate reductions apply only to noble landowners, not to members of other Estates who borrowed money from state-supported banks. These merchants and land speculators "would lose nothing thereby, since they still pay less [to such banks] than to private joint-stock banks." The marshals' suggestion would also mean "a stimulus for the nobility to buy land, and to keep land within the noble Estate."[51]

Finally, the marshals warned that the political desiderata of the nobility were more numerous than the 7 April plan acknowledged. The marshals described the interest rate reduction as an "unoriginal and insignificant" measure on behalf of the Noble Land Bank borrowers, who were far from representative of the entire (noble) Estate. To restrict action on the noble question to this "insignificant measure" would

> create a prejudiced attitude among those not affected and a certain disappointment among the landowners most hard-pressed by the problems of contemporary agriculture.
>
> Moreover, the provincial marshals must remind [the government] that . . . from the perspective of the needs of the landed nobility, improved agricultural credit is far less important than an improvement in the economic life of all rural Russia. They are convinced that no measures affecting the Noble Land Bank, however desirable they might be, can be compared to the potential consequences of such changes as the reform of our grain trade, a guarantee of high quality in our exported grain, the equipment of our railroads and ports, the correction of tariffs, the reduction of customs duties, and so on. The advantage to be accrued in this sphere would be not only immeasurably great for the nobility, but would benefit the whole state, since it would alter those facets of recent financial policy that have been burdensome for an agricultural country.[52]

The marshals thus reiterated their conclusions of 1896 calling for sweeping changes in state policy.

The Durnovo memorandum and the marshals' strictures prompted Witte to retreat further from his original position. Now he removed from his plan all reference to the responsibilities of debtors to pay back their debts. However, Witte did not abandon the field completely; he merely changed tactics. He inserted a new proviso in the Ministry of Finance plan that would forbid any further amendments to regulations on payments until the conversion of 4.0 percent and

4.5 percent mortgages had been accomplished.[53] This proviso would freeze the bank's interest rates and rules for a considerable time.

When Witte submitted his revised plan to the Finance Committee on 5 May, he encountered further opposition from a small group of provincial marshals. The leader of the critics was A. Durnovo, Kursk provincial marshal, who presented a written commentary co-signed by Saratov provincial marshal P. Krivsky. Durnovo asserted that

> it is now crucial to declare that estates mortgaged to the Noble
> Bank will not be subject to sale for back debts to the bank: if the owner
> of an estate cannot make the necessary payments, then place it [the
> estate] under the Economic Administration of the bank or in trust
> and deprive the owner of the right to enjoy the income from his es-
> tate. . . . Preserve [in this way] a family estate for the children of the
> erring debtor and bad estate manager.[54]

Durnovo did not want the sins of the father visited upon his children.

Durnovo also wanted to create a special category for those estates that had suffered in the famine of 1891/92. If a landowner's arrears exceeded 12 percent of his total debt because of losses during the famine, the government should wipe out all these arrears. Yet the famine years had not been the only hard times for the nobility. Durnovo believed the price depression to have had a terrible impact on many noble grain producers. He recommended a three-year payment moratorium for these debtors:

> It must be noted that landowners, who suffered in the famine years
> from complete crop failures, and then suffered from the unprece-
> dented fall in grain prices in recent years, have been compelled to rush
> to private and very expensive sources of credit to cover their ex-
> penses, and this has complicated their monetary calculations. Give
> them the chance to pay off their private creditors, suspend all interest
> payments to the Noble Bank for three years, add three years to the
> term of their loans and you will actually save the faltering [*pogibaiu-
> shchee*] landed nobility.[55]

Durnovo believed that, after the three-year moratorium, the nobility would be able to resume payments and enter "a new period in their history."

As for the Witte plan, Durnovo had nothing but scorn. He said that it contained "no elements upon which hard-pressed nobles might rely." Certain aspects of Witte's plan, according to Durnovo, would "hasten the transfer of noble estates to other owners, in all likelihood to merchants."[56]

Durnovo's ideas were based on the assumption that a strong nobility was essential to the welfare of the state. If the continuation of noble landownership required state subsidy, then Durnovo thought the state should pay the price. Iu. B. Soloviev has justly quipped that the Durnovo plan was "open, unveiled parasitism."[57]

Tula provincial marshal A. Arseniev also presented a commentary on the Witte plan. Arseniev began by declaring: "I find the Minister of Finance's project absolutely inadequate not only as support to noble landowning, but as a tool to bolster the material welfare of bank debtors." Arseniev then declared his preference for the plan of former minister I. N. Durnovo, which Arseniev found less stringent in its treatment of debtors with substantial arrears. Arseniev also endorsed the suggestion of Krivsky and A. Durnovo for a three-year debt moratorium applying to landowners with substantial debts to private banks.[58]

Count V. A. Kapnist, Khar'kov provincial marshal, submitted a softly worded memorandum that emphasized key positions of the April 1897 marshals' statement and of the A. Durnovo commentary. Kapnist praised the government for its concern with noble affairs:

> Now in this terrible epoch for noble landowners, one must not fail to recognize the great and salutary effect of government steps to make land credit cheaper and less onerous by lowering interest rates.

Yet lower interest rates, Kapnist wrote, "would improve the difficult position of landowners only slightly." Far more important were efforts

> to reduce tariffs, increase the capacity of railroads, reduce customs duties. Only steps taken in this direction can improve the situation for all landowners in Russia and simultaneously provide genuine support for the nobility which before our time constituted the most cultured and influential group of landowners.[59]

Kapnist recognized that this broad program would take time to exert an influence, so he argued for a three-year debt moratorium as the best stopgap solution available to the government.

The latest memoranda from the marshals changed the entire situation facing Witte. In addition to reiterating the old demands of 1896, the marshals had made entirely new claims on government resources. In Soloviev's words, the marshals "intended to take the state treasury by storm."[60]

The whole political constellation seemed ranged against Witte. As he tried to defend himself against the marshals' frontal attack, Durnovo and Plehve intrigued against him, cutting off his retreat. On 13 April Nicholas II published a rescript on the nobility. The tsar declared that the preservation of noble landowning was "a crucial concern of the state."[61] On 6 May rumors of another rescript reached Witte. He wrote to Pobedonostsev: "It would be just a shame. Already the rescript has created a turbulent sea of desires [*more vsiakikh vozhdelenii*]—what next? Durnovo and company . . . are too shortsighted to see what a tempest [*smutu*] they have stirred up."[62] Yet just as Witte despaired of success, just as the assault on the treasury approached victory, the marshals began to quarrel among themselves. On 9 May the Finance Committee heard sharp exchanges between L. M. Muromtsov and other marshals.

Muromtsov said that he attributed "special significance to the middle nobility, to whose ranks in Riazan' province must be assigned owners of 400 to 500 desiatins." Muromtsov believed that the gentry were particularly loyal to the tsar, and influential in the countryside:

> This category of landowners has preserved those convictions, those traditions which have long made the nobility the support [*opora*] of the throne and made them the First Estate in the social order. . . . This category of landowners has always been, and is now, the most reliable means for introducing these convictions into the consciousness of the enormous mass of the peasantry, with which the nobility is in continuous contact, and upon which the nobility exerts . . . a profound influence in all aspects of popular moral life.[63]

In summary, Muromtsov said that "the gentry constitute that conservative ballast against which the waves of every sort of seditious doctrine beat in vain."[64]

Because of the political importance of the gentry, this group should be protected by the state. Yet Muromtsov noted that reduction in interest rates would do little for the gentry. He observed that on a large farm mortgaged for 300,000 rubles, a half-percent drop in annual payments would mean a savings of 1,500 rubles—a sizable sum. However, on a moderate estate of 450 desiatins, mortgaged for 12,000 rubles, the half-percent concession would yield only 60 rubles a year to the landowner:

> In order to imagine what this 60 rubles means to a landowner, one need only remember that a landowner can lose this amount or more in

a single day, if he is late in hauling his crops to the market [*iarmarka*]
for sale. Such a trifling and unavoidable incident would cancel out
completely the effects of the Ministry of Finance's plan.

Muromtsov asked that the Ministry make a special effort to help the
gentry by declaring an eighteen-month moratorium on their bank
payments.

Perceiving the differences between earlier remarks by the marshals
and Muromtsov's suggestions, Witte saw an opportunity to drive a
wedge between his opponents. Witte said, "This issue becomes the
more important, since as a result of the distinctions in the various
memoranda, one involuntarily begins to doubt whether their authors
are in complete agreement; otherwise, they probably would have
presented a joint statement."[65] P. N. Trubetskoi, Moscow marshal,
and A. D. Zinoviev, Petersburg marshal, followed Witte by attacking Muromtsov:

> We may add that we do not support the payment moratorium because
> charity of this sort completely perverts the very basis of assistance
> and aid; it should be given not to the poor and incompetent, but rather
> to the competent and self-sufficient. It should be greater if the re-
> cipient is more self-sufficient.[66]

A. D. Zinoviev later said that he would support a debt moratorium
only for the really needy nobility, regardless of the size of their
estates.[67]

N. F. Sukhomlinov, the Kherson provincial marshal, was even
harsher in his condemnation of Muromtsov's plan: "Either philanthropy or credit. The two must not be confused. What is too par-
simonious to be philanthropy is too extravagant to be credit."[68]

By cleverly exploiting the disagreements among the marshals at
the 9 May meeting, Witte was able to limit his financial concessions
to the small reduction in interest rates projected in mid-April. On
29 May Nicholas II signed an ukase reducing interest rates one-half
percent. As Soloviev has written, "Publication of the ukase would
normally have received a positive response, but now expectations
had been excited to the extreme, and the announced ½ percent
interest reduction did not satisfy at all the appetite of those who
had organized the Special Commission on the Nobility."[69] Once again
the government had acted to assist the nobility, and had failed
to garner much political credit for its assistance. Once again the
diversity of the nobility had proven to be the Achilles' heel of the
First Estate: having forced Witte to give up much ground, the mar-

shals failed to capitalize on their positional advantage, and an untimely quarrel within their ranks allowed Witte to escape and outflank them.

The marshals had let slip a golden opportunity in May 1897, but they still could hope that the Special Commission on the Nobility would eventually draft legislation that would satisfy them. Unfortunately, the commission's mandate was very broad, so that it was difficult for concerned parties to focus sufficient attention on the issue of agricultural credit. Moreover, the divisions in the noble leadership did not disappear after May 1897; in fact, the procedure of the commission tended to compound them.

Nevertheless, a sizable group of marshals continued to press for changes in national credit policy. There were still several individuals who urged that the Noble Land Bank be made more accommodating to noble interests. Most frequently, it was proposed that a ban be placed on the sale of estates for arrears. It was also suggested that the Noble Land Bank make loans to individuals who wanted to acquire noble-owned land that might otherwise have been sold to other estates. However, the Noble Land Bank's long-term credit was no longer the chief source of attention. Many marshals concentrated on gaining better conditions on short-term credit, either through the Noble Bank or through the State Bank. The effort to acquire cheaper short-term credit may be seen as a continuation of the marshals' 1896 campaign to drop State Bank interest rates. Witte had frustrated this campaign entirely by dealing with the question of long-term interest rates. There was also some desire to give local authorities more effective control over all forms of credit by restructuring bank organization.

Between 1897 and 1899 marshals from at least ten provinces suggested change in Russia's short-term credit policy.[70] Sudzha district (Kursk province) marshal A. V. Evreinov emphasized that short-term credit was a high priority when he wrote in April 1898: "Noble landowning does not need more development of long-term credit; the absence of accessible meliorative short-term credit is the bane of Russian agriculture."[71] Eleven Sudzha district landholders agreed with Evreinov, and on 28 April they appealed to the national government for a better system of short-term credit.[72] D. K. Gevlich, the provincial marshal in Penza province, also stressed that short-term credit was more crucial than improved long-term credit:

It is much more useful to allow farmers to extricate themselves from their difficult financial position, by turning their efforts to increasing the income from their estates through broad and easily accessible meliorative credit. The productive use of short-term credit can always be supervised, whereas long-term loans sometimes disappear without a trace, perhaps saving debtors temporarily but not improving their estates.[73]

Vladimir provincial marshal M. Leontiev called for short-term credit for noble estates "still capable of self-sufficient economic life, and not too burdened by mortgages and other debts."[74] A. M. Dolgorukov, Chernigov provincial marshal, proposed that nobles be allowed to borrow sums from the State Bank and pay them back over a one-year period instead of six months. He also wanted to reduce the interest rate on these loans to 4 percent.[75] A. P. Strukhov, the Ekaterinoslav provincial marshal, asked the government to write a law regulating interest rates for short-term loans just as it had for long-term loans.[76]

A. B. Neidgart, the Nizhny-Novgorod provincial marshal, offered a list of ten desirable changes in the credit system in his April 1898 report to the Special Commission. The first recommendation was for emergency short-term credit to provincial noble organizations that might use the money to save estates from foreclosure. The second recommendation was for short-term loans to individuals who merely wanted to improve already viable estates without incurring a long-term obligation.[77]

There was also some feeling among the marshals that the existing system of bank operations was too cumbersome. Vladimir marshal Leontiev argued that branch banks should be "close to their clients, should operate over a comparatively small territory, should have many clients and large capital resources."[78] Bank reorganization might have removed many obstacles to effective debt financing. Marshal Ianovsky of Kaluga province agreed with Leontiev's diagnosis. He also complained about unnecessary estate appraisals for short-term loans, which were "inconvenient" and often done by "inexperienced officials."[79] These grievances were reminiscent of complaints about Noble Land Bank organization in the 1891–1896 period.

The marshals suggested a number of expedients to keep estates under noble ownership. These proposals ranged from Neidgart's short-term loan plan, mentioned above, to new rules for the bank. For instance, Ianovsky claimed that the Noble Bank should make capital available for estate purchases just as the Peasant Bank had done for peasants.[80] This proposal received support from Sergei Mikhailov of Iaroslavl' province.[81] Another proposal, coming from Ufa marshal A. S. Listovsky, was to legislate against sale of noble estates for arrears. Listovsky would have placed insolvent estates in trusteeships for administration.[82] The marshals of Kherson province would have created a special trust society with the power to purchase insolvent estates.[83]

As usual, the marshal's statements were argued forcibly, but there was not enough unity to forge a consistent program. In fact, no really new or important legislation on the credit problem was promulgated between 1898 and the 1905 revolution.

Surveying the political scene in 1898, Riazan' provincial marshal L. M. Muromtsov was pessimistic. Muromtsov had spent his adult life working against what he regarded as the unsavory aspects of post-emancipation Russia: against the encroachments of the free land market, against the alleged pretensions of the merchantry and peasantry. The positive vision that animated Muromtsov was that of an economically strong nobility, and particularly a strong gentry, who, in partnership with the government, would uphold family values, the social order, and the Russian land itself. Yet in May 1897 Muromtsov had made "a few insignificant proposals" to the Finance Committee and had watched them scuttled. "Everything was rejected," Muromtsov lamented in February 1898, "even though all of it was excessively moderate. In view of this attempt, which ended in complete disaster, I have reason to think that the economic position of the nobility is doomed to chronic exhaustion and ruin."[84]

Muromtsov was perspicacious enough to recognize that not everyone in the First Estate had shared his hopes for patriarchal alliance between landed nobles and the state. His instinct was to blame nobles in the zemstvo assemblies for not having supported a sweeping program to save the nobility. "It cannot be doubted," he wrote, "that a noble in a zemstvo assembly and a noble in a noble assembly view the same issue completely differently. They think in a different way and speak a different language. This phenomenon is psychological, complex, and yet it constantly recurs."[85] Muromtsov was perhaps correct to attribute to zemstvo nobles a different ethos, but the painful truth was that his program had not been supported by other provincial marshals on the Finance Committee. To a large degree, the vision of a financially healthy nobility subsidized by the state had been killed by those who dreamed it: death by self-inflicted wounds was not a diagnosis that Muromtsov had the courage to make.

Yet Muromtsov understood clearly enough Witte's opposition to the noble program, and he saw that as long as Witte was Minister of Finance there could be no partnership between state and nobility. Thus the struggle against bureaucratic mismanagement that had begun in the 1892 Khar'kov petition had ended with the defeat of the nobility. "All that remains," said Muromtsov, "is to care for our spiritual heritage, for the enrichment of the intellectual and moral forces of the noble Estate."[86] Muromtsov might have echoed Voltaire's injunction to "cultivez vôtre jardin," but the garden was being destroyed.

An iron guest will soon appear
Along the track of azure steppes.
His swarthy hand will gather the crops
Spilt all around like the golden dawn.
O lifeless cold and alien hands!
—*Sergei Esenin,*
"The Last Peasant Poet"

CHAPTER 8
The Railroad Question

In a letter to a friend in 1861, the young Vasily Osipovich Kliuchevsky described his first trip by train: "A shiver ran down my
body when I climbed into the train car and the engine, obeying
the bell, started forward—slowly at first, then accelerated, and
finally carried itself along so that it was hard to see the objects
that flashed past. . . . The engine easily pulled behind a whole
country village of cars, and only now and then snorted like a horse,
or deafened us by a prolonged whistle, very much like the neighing
of a healthy horse: this lets steam escape from it. And all the while
one is captivated by the incessant sounds of its mechanical labor: the
levers turn and the wheels click against the iron rails—well, in a
word, a shiver runs down one's body, not from fear . . . but simply
from delight."[1] Kliuchevsky's naive fascination with technology and
utter delight in the new mechanism of travel were typical of positive
responses to the introduction of railroads in the nineteenth century.
But the novelty of the iron roads wore off quickly, and the delight of
the young gave way to serious second thoughts about the impact of
railroads on rural society. For the railroads were not only, and not
even preeminently, a means of travel: they were the channels of
trade, the vehicles by which the Russian and international markets
exerted their hold on the countryside, the nexus between the urban
industrializing world and the gradually changing rural one. No other
invention had the railroad's power to disturb and change the rural
economy and social order.

To minimize the railroads' potential for social disruption, the government strictly controlled the licensing of private railroad companies and itself constructed lines vital to the national economy and

security. In the late 1880s the government also began to consider a comprehensive national schedule for shipping charges. Grain producers from the blacksoil areas, where agricultural income depended heavily on rye and oats, were particularly concerned about the instability of shipping prices which made it "impossible for commerce and industry to operate on the basis of rational economic calculations."[2] The government responded to this concern in 1889 by entering the marketplace as supreme regulator of railroad tariff rates.

The 1889 tariff system held major implications for Russian grain producers and for the government itself. On the one hand, the new tariffs offered certain advantages over the previous system. The 1889 tariff rates were comparatively stable and easily understood. They also generally reduced the price of grain shipments. Net annual shipping costs fell by almost 1.7 million rubles (1,104,000 rubles on grain exports and 579,000 rubles on domestic shipments) in the first year of operation.[3] This net reduction in tariff rates made possible an increase in agricultural exports, and therefore improved Russia's balance of trade. On the other hand, in assuming a regulatory role in setting tariffs, the government made itself a target of growers' resentments over transportation costs. Furthermore, by adjusting railroad tariffs in order to benefit rye and oats producers in the blacksoil zone, the government opened the door to other producers who wished to petition for special tariff rates in their home province or region. The work of regulation would soon prove both thankless and endless.

In 1893 the government made another major adjustment in tariff policy by adopting a so-called differential tariff. The Ministry of Finance created a dual tariff schedule in which one set of rates applied to export grain and another to shipments on the internal market. Long-distance export shipments were made relatively cheaper than short domestic ones. The object of the new export rates, according to the Ministry of Finance, was "to facilitate and make practical the export of grain from all agricultural regions of the country."[4] Such differential rates made it possible for grain from the eastern Volga provinces and from new grain-producing areas in Siberia to compete on the foreign market with grain from traditional exporting regions. At the same time, the Ministry attempted to protect the position of local growers in the domestic grain market by making it comparatively expensive to ship grain long distances to domestic market centers. Theoretically, grain from the east could not now compete on the Moscow market with grain from provinces near Moscow.

The differential tariff scheme succeeded in promoting the growth of Russian grain exports, thus fulfilling the Ministry of Finance's main goal. However, the scheme had several unfortunate side effects. First, differential tariffs in Russia, in combination with bumper harvests from 1894 to 1896, tended to depress the price of grain on the world market, thus delaying the economic recovery of individual noble landowners from the Great Depression. Second, the 1893 differential tariffs discriminated against provinces in the central agricultural area and in the Volga Basin to the west of the river. The adjusted internal market rates were not set high enough to deter Siberian or southern steppe producers from selling grain in central Russia.

The Ministry of Finance studied the results of the differential tariffs and nearly abandoned the policy in 1894 when cereal prices reached an all-time low. Minister of Finance Witte formed a special committee to consider reducing tariffs in response to the price depression. According to a summary of the committee's deliberations prepared by the Department of Railroad Tariffs, some members of the committee endorsed tariff reduction as essential; others "thought the measure would be ineffective in increasing [grain] prices, and even dangerous since it might be counterproductive."[5] In the face of this split within the committee, Witte decided to do nothing for the time being. By 1896, however, Witte was worried enough about growers in central Russia to levy a surcharge on grain shipments from eastern Siberia.[6] Witte's plan, "to protect the agriculture of European Russia from a possible flood of Siberian grain," did make it more expensive for eastern Siberian producers to send grain to internal Russian markets, but because of the international depression in grain prices, the economic situation for central Russian growers still did not substantially improve.

Thus, the Ministry of Finance found itself in an embarrassing situation. It had engaged in the business of railroad regulation in order to protect growers and to facilitate export trade. But objectives that had originally appeared to the Ministry as complementary were now seen to be contradictory: the Ministry discovered that increasing exports from the east was incompatible with the interests of growers from central Russia. As a result, the government was compelled to constantly reconsider and readjust tariff rates in order to ameliorate difficulties created by its own rate system. By 1896 the government's problems with tariff regulations were compounded by a formidable political consideration: spokesmen for the nobility denounced the Ministry of Finance's policies as a major obstacle to the survival of the First Estate.

The Nobility and the
Tariff Question in 1896

At the 1896 convocation in St. Petersburg, twenty-seven provincial marshals challenged the government to change its policies concerning agricultural trade. According to the marshals, there were three problems with the government's existing approach to grain commerce. First, the government permitted the creation and maintenance of railroad tariffs that were both too expensive and discriminatory against certain growers. In the preface of their long memorandum about the problems facing the nobility, the marshals wrote:

> Early construction of railroads was done . . . on a concession basis, perhaps the only possible way at that time. The construction was expensive, and so tariffs from the very beginning of the railroad system were high. [The high tariffs] were harmful to agriculture. The Ministry of Finance's interference in the tariff matter was not beneficial to agriculture. In fact, the differential tariffs of 1893 did direct and significant harm to all of central Russia, exacting from it a new tax.[7]

In the body of the memorandum the marshals devoted a special section to analysis of tariff policy. Here it became clear that the marshals did not object to the differential tariffs on theoretical grounds; they even admitted that, in principle, differential tariffs were "beneficial and just." However, in practice, "by creating through a sharp reduction in distance rates a sudden advantage for far-away localities, the same principle becomes a terrible injustice. It causes overproduction, creates new enterprises where before there were none, and ruins long-existing enterprises by competition." "Unfortunately, it enriches one and impoverishes others, generates uncertainty and vacillation in the national entrepreneurial spirit." The deleterious effects of the high and discriminatory differential tariffs could no longer be tolerated.

A second complaint against the government was that the government had not done enough to improve the efficiency of the Russian railroads. The memorandum referred to "a whole series of inadequacies, shortcomings, and abuses that are liable to cause economic losses, and to harm . . . Russian agriculture." Many railroad stations had no equipment to store grain that was awaiting shipment, so grain was exposed to the elements for days, weeks, or even months. In the winter of 1895/96, grain shipments in some areas were delayed for fifty-three days. These delays were themselves an economic problem because they made it hard for growers to react to price shifts

TABLE 8.1

Comparison of Sale Prices for Agricultural Products[a] and
Manufactured Goods in Western Europe and Russia

	Western Europe	Russia
Agricultural Products		
One pood wheat	90 kopecks	40 kopecks
One pood oats	78 kopecks	27 kopecks
One pood wild straw	25 kopecks	3 kopecks
One pood hay	40 kopecks	6 kopecks
One pood meat	8 rubles, 49 kopecks	2 rubles
Manufactured Goods		
One pood cast iron	30–35 kopecks	90–120 kopecks
One pood iron	65–80 kopecks	180–340 kopecks
One pood steel	75–100 kopecks	220–380 kopecks

SOURCE: TsGIA, fond 593, opis' 1, delo 351, 11. 9–10.

[a]Agricultural prices are averages, with years unspecified, for Europe (London, Marseilles, Danzig) and for Russia (Poltava, Orel, Tambov).

on the international market; moreover, shipping delays also reduced the availability of credit since harvested grain in transit to ports was often used as loan collateral.[8] In the memorandum the marshals also expressed annoyance at the port area merchants' practice of adulterating export grain by mixing in nonfood additives; at the lack of careful supervision in port areas; and at the "unscrupulous" activities of grain speculators and their agents who might deliberately delay the shipment of grain abroad for selfish commercial reasons. The marshals advocated strict governmental grain inspection in port areas and governmental funding of grain elevators throughout Russia.[9]

A third complaint against government trade policy went beyond the issues of Russian railroad tariffs and trade organization to the general problem of the terms of trade for Russian grain producers. The marshals argued that the government's protectionist import tariffs on iron equipment, especially on agricultural machinery like German ploughs and harvesting machines, raised the price of agricultural operations. When the marshals compared the sale prices for agricultural products and manufactured goods in Western Europe and Russia, they discovered that most agricultural products brought a higher sale price in Western Europe while industrial goods were more expensive in Russia (see Table 8.1).

This comparison was intended to establish that Western Europeans got greater returns per pood on their agricultural produce, and at the same time paid less per pood for industrial goods than did Russian farmers. Therefore, in the marshals' opinion, Russian grain producers were at a double disadvantage relative to their Western European counterparts.[10] If this alleged double disadvantage were to be eliminated, then the Ministry of Finance would have to abandon its protectionist import tariffs on iron goods. The marshals believed that abandonment of protectionist tariffs was the more imperative because there was as yet no indigenous Russian iron industry worth protecting. Russian factories were not yet concentrating on heavy iron production, especially for the agricultural sector. Thus, protectionist tariffs were not only harmful to agriculture, but unhelpful to industry and economically unnecessary.

The marshals concluded their discussion of agricultural trade with an urgent plea for "an immediate review of tariffs with a view to reducing them." The marshals insisted that this review should be concluded before the end of the 1896 grain harvest, and they claimed that "spokesmen for agriculture should play an important role in this review." As a guiding principle for the review, the marshals urged nondiscrimination against the old Russian provinces of European Russia: "The government should not use the development of the railroad net in the Far East to justify introduction of cheaper tariff rates for the products of these regions."[11]

The marshals' three complaints about government trade policy were a frontal challenge to Minister of Finance Witte's economic program that used the railroads to promote exports and national market integration, and used government investment in heavy industry and protectionist tariffs to develop native Russian industrial capacity. The marshals protested, in effect, that the First Estate could not survive unless this program was abandoned. In their opinion, the government would have to choose between industry and agriculture, between existing trade policy and the survival of the First Estate. Morover, by demanding formal representation in the tariff review for agriculture's "spokesmen," the marshals were not so subtly expressing their lack of faith in the existing political process. The government in general, and the Ministry of Finance in particular, were judged incompetent to protect the nobility's interests unless decision-making procedures were changed to include elements representative of the landed nobility. Thus, viewed from the perspective of the Minister of Finance, the 1896 memorandum was economic and political dynamite placed at the cornerstone of the existing order.

The Tariff Review of 1896/97

The tariff review of 1896/97 was an excellent example of the tsarist government's response to political criticism from the nobility and a good illustration of the limits of the marshals' power in the bureau-cratic-absolutist order. Four separate government committees studied the tariff laws from mid-1896 until summer 1897. Preliminary analysis was done by a Special Committee which reported to the Tariff Com-mittee of the Ministry of Finance. The interdepartmental Council on Tariffs dealt with unresolved issues in February 1897, and final con-sideration fell to the so-called Joint Bureau of the Committee of Ministers and the Department of State Economy of the State Council. While the government ultimately made only minor alterations in the tariff system and reaffirmed the policy of 1893, there was deep am-bivalence toward that policy at every stage of bureaucratic review.

The initial policy review was carried out in October 1896 by the Special Committee on Tariffs under the aegis of the Ministry of Fi-nance. The nobility were well represented in the Special Committee. All provincial marshals were invited to attend, and they were dele-gated to select four grain producers from each of their respective provinces to participate in the committee meeting. In all there were 169 participants on the Special Committee, of whom 84 were repre-sentatives of agriculture. Most representatives of agriculture came from the central and western provinces—the traditional grain-ex-porting regions. The eastern peripheral provinces, where the new ex-porters lived, were not as well represented in the Special Committee, perhaps because travel from the east to St. Petersburg was difficult and relatively expensive.[12]

After considerable study, the committee rejected the existing dif-ferential tariff—the key element in current government policy:

> The system of differential tariff duties calculated according to dis-tance—the basis of existing grain tariffs—has completely transformed old commercial ties and the relations between various regions, destroyed many of the old secondary commercial centers and under-mined our domestic grain trade. This system has pushed solid commercial firms out of the grain business, and has put it in the hands of petty merchants and agents. Consequently, local grain trade has lost its independent strength and the ability to hold grain reserves with-in the country, the demand for agricultural produce has lost its sta-bility and is now irregular and given to rapid fluctuations, being sub-ject to the arbitrary power of foreign grain exchanges. Given the conditions of our grain trade, [the differential tariff] represents one of the main causes of the sharp fall in grain prices and of the depressed state of our grain market.[13]

After having criticized the existing tariff system, the committee did not propose to abandon the principle of differential rate setting, but rather to moderate it. The committee agreed that there should be a distinction between domestic and export tariffs; however, existing long- and short-distance export rates should be reduced in order to facilitate cheap exports from the central and western provinces. Meanwhile, tariffs on long-distance domestic shipments should be increased in order to eliminate Siberian competition on the domestic grain market and to prop up the domestic price of grain.[14] Both proposed moderations in the differential tariff would have improved the relative positions of the central and western provinces in the grain trade. Clearly, the fact that fewer representatives from peripheral areas attended the Special Committee meant that the political scales in the committee deliberations tilted toward the central provinces.

In late 1896 and early 1897 the Special Committee's conclusions were analyzed by the Tariff Committee of the Ministry of Finance. The Tariff Committee was a permanent agency responsible to the Minister of Finance and, therefore, less susceptible to the marshals' will than the ad hoc Special Committee had been. In its study of price data during the period from 1893 to 1896, the Tariff Committee found an uneven record for red and gray cereals. In areas where gray cereals (rye, oats) predominated, income was lower in 1896 than it had been three years earlier. In central Russia, for example, 1896 income after tariffs was 30 to 40 percent less than it had been in 1893.[15] However, in areas where red cereals were grown, 1896 prices were generally higher than they had been in 1893, though the committee did admit that prices had fallen in a few instances.

While the Tariff Committee's statistics showed that price differentials on gray and red cereals did not favor the central Russian provinces, committee members could not agree amongst themselves whether the tariff law should be used to assist the central provinces. A minority in the committee wanted to reduce tariffs on export shipments over one thousand versts: "A reduction of export tariffs would enable all farmers, particularly those in central Russia, to cope better with competition from overseas nations, and it would protect domestic wheat prices from dropping to the very low level toward which international competition now pushes them."

The minority treated the issue of price determination and protection almost as a matter of ethical concern: "It would be just to allow agricultural industry the chance to set its own domestic prices, which would correspond to national supply and demand and not leave this important field completely to the arbitrary force of international competition." The minority noted that grain-purchasing European states set customs barriers so high that grain-selling nations like Russia made precious little profit on grain sales. In fact, Russian farmers sold their cereals at "ruinously low prices." As an exporting nation, Russia could not very well protect its agriculture by high customs duties. It might, however, manipulate railroad tariff rates so as to "free domestic grain prices from the dictates of world conditions of bread production and commerce."

Like the Special Committee, the minority group pressed for a dual system of tariffs. Export tariffs would be lower than internal rates so that producers could sell surpluses abroad and better compete with foreign producers. Higher domestic tariffs would mean higher domestic bread prices, but these price increases would be passed on to the consumers. Under the minority plan farmers would have two advantages: lower export costs and higher profit margins on domestic sales. Not surprisingly, the minority believed that the central agricultural region and others would benefit from its proposals.[16]

The committee majority rejected the minority brief. The majority thought that reduced export tariffs would not be beneficial to Russian agriculture. Reductions would be unfair to domestic consumers and to grain producers who did not use railroads for shipment.[17] The majority was less worried about these consequences, however, than about others. Railroad tariff reductions on cereal exports would "subject the treasury and private railroads to serious deficits."[18]

The majority analysis of the economic impact of reduced railroad tariffs was economically more sophisticated than that of the minority. The majority saw clearly that reduced transport costs in Russia would not necessarily increase agricultural income in Russia, but they would tend to drive prices lower on the international market. Reduced prices in Western Europe would harm European agriculture, and in the end European states would be forced to counteract the Russian competition. "One would expect from European governments the adoption of countervailing measures . . . which could wipe out all the possible advantages of lower railroad tariffs."[19] The committee feared that even more-prohibitive customs barriers would be erected against Russian grain imports, or that foreign grain purchasers would buy Russian grain cheaply and build up vast stockpiles. Eventually this stockpiling would cut European dependence on foreign grain suppliers, and Russian growers would find themselves without European customers. Alternatively, the existence of vast grain reserves within Europe might serve to depress cereal prices on the international market for years. In any event, the majority was convinced that Russian railroad tariff reductions would do little to preserve Russian agriculture and the Russian nobility from the inglorious ruin predicted by the committee minority and by noble groups.

The majority decided to examine the argument of the minority and of the Special Committee concerning the fate of the central provinces. This argument could be summarized in three propositions: (1) tariffs on short export shipments were too high and tariffs on long domestic shipments too low; (2) this tariff structure was advantageous to peripheral producing areas and disadvantageous to producers who lived nearer major domestic markets; (3) the peripheral regions, taking advantage of the differential tariff, were devastating agriculture in the central and western regions by their competition.

The majority believed that statistical data proved these propositions incorrect. The amount of grain shipped to domestic markets on railroads increased 118.7 million poods between 1890 and 1895. About 42 percent of this increase was hauled less than 400 versts; 27 percent was hauled from 400 to 1,000 versts, and 31 percent was shipped over 1,000 versts. These statistics suggested that domestic markets were increasingly supplied by local producers who were not being driven away by higher tariff rates.

Next the majority turned to the Moscow market, one of the nation's major domestic centers. Statistics indicated that in 1895 the central provinces supplied 69 percent of all grain sold, while the peripheral provinces supplied only 4.1 percent.[20] The central provinces sold fully 76 percent of the rye and 93 percent of the oats traded in Moscow province. The peripheral areas sold 18 percent of the wheat, but the central provinces still outbalanced this figure by selling 28 percent of the wheat purchased in Moscow province.[21] This latter statistic was impressive since the central areas were traditionally rye and oat producers, not wheat producers. The central provinces were certainly not being overwhelmed by competition from the periphery, at least if the Moscow market was an adequate guide.

Aggregate statistics showed that the central region received only 12 million poods of grain from other regions and sent out ten times more to other markets. Even then, 8 million poods of the grain from outside were milled into flour and then shipped on to other regions.[22]

These statistics convinced the majority that competition from eastern and southern provinces did not crowd producers from the center out of domestic markets. The final report of the Tariff Committee flatly asserted that all agricultural regions were "sufficiently and equitably protected from the competition of other regions." In the committee's opinion, existing tariffs "managed to achieve all the goals set in the 1893 review."[23] The committee determined not to set special rates for gray cereal shipments, as opposed to red cereal shipments.[24]

Having decided that the old tariff schedules should be preserved, the committee delivered a ringing endorsement of differential tariffs. Differential rates were used not only in Western Europe but also in North America. "The fact that differential rates are universally accepted is proof in itself that differential rates are closely tied to the very existence of railroad transport; without them the productive forces of railroad enterprises could not be fully developed and railroads could not provide the economy with those benefits which it rightly demands from modern communications in the nineteenth century." To reject differential tariffs would be, in the committee's words, "an extremely dangerous shock to the entire national economy."[25]

Witte was not satisfied with the Tariff Committee's report. On 21 February 1897 he asked that a Council on Tariffs (*Sovet po tarifnym delam*) reexamine the whole issue. Again there was substantive disagreement over the proper policy to be followed. One group, including members of the Ministries of Internal Affairs, Communications, and State Control, plus spokesmen for private railroads, one industrialist, and one representative of the mining industry, concluded that the 1893 system needed no substantive changes. A second group, consisting of members from the Ministries of Finance, Agriculture, and State Domains, three railroad company spokesmen, and one industrialist, suggested that the 1893 system be retained with two small changes. First tariffs on grain exports should be decreased by about five kopecks per pood on shipments of intermediate and long distance. Second, tariffs on certain grades of flour and groats should be raised as much as 10 percent over the normal rates on unrefined grain shipments.[26]

The divided opinion of the Council on Tariffs meant that further debate on the tariff problem was likely in the Joint Bureau of the Committee of Ministers and the Department of State Economy in the State Council. Although the Council on Tariffs was much closer than earlier committees to a full endorsement of the Ministry of Finance's tariff policies, Witte was worried that his program might be altered in the final stage of consideration. Accordingly, he prepared a position paper for use by the Committee of Ministers and the State Council.

In the position paper Witte minimized the claims of damage to agriculture made by opponents of his tariff policy, and he argued that differential tariffs were a logical consequence of railroad building in Russia:

The essence of the complaints against our railroads and grain tariff is that the central and western provinces do not now enjoy the same advantages and dominance over grain sales that they once possessed. . . . To a certain extent those complaints are factually correct, but to attribute [the changed position of these regions] to the 1893 tariffs is far from just. The present position of the central and western provinces relative to other agricultural regions is the natural and inevitable result of the construction of our railroad net, which has exerted such a profound influence on the entire economic life of Russia and on the very structure of the national economy. Thanks to the fundamental superiority of railroad shipments . . . railroad construction always brings regions into closer contact, equalizes market conditions, and leads to a general reduction of prices. These results are not only natural and inevitable, they are the direct purpose for railroad construction.

The preservation of the central and western regions' former unchallenged superiority, due to their geographic proximity to market centers, would be possible only if we rejected the advantages of those modern means of transport without which the cultural development of our nation would be completely impossible.[27]

Having asserted that differential tariffs were essential to a modern economy and perforce to the cultural development of Russia, Witte turned to his opponents' claims. He wrote that the influence of tariffs on growers' incomes had often been exaggerated. He observed that railroad tariffs in Russia and in America had dropped, and so had grain price levels. Tariff reductions had brought no increase in farmers' income. Witte mentioned other economic factors that outweighed tariffs in influence on grain prices: the disposition of the world market, the size of the domestic harvest, economic events such as monetary or industrial depressions, import tariffs, new railroad building, improvements in other means of transport for export.

Witte cited the conclusions of the majority on the Tariff Committee that statistics did not support the notion that peripheral regions had flooded central market areas with grain. He argued that virtually every grievance of his opponents was exaggerated or based on improper statistical inference.

Witte was willing to make two policy changes. First, he would not object to a 10 percent increase in duties on flour and groats. Second, he gave lukewarm support to a plan to lower export duties to 0.01 kopecks per pood/verst. Witte had rejected this plan a year earlier, but now he would bend to the prevailing political winds. His memorandum suggested that the plan would not be of much help to producers since their small financial gains "would be dissipated into the hands of numerous middlemen", yet he thought the plan might be passed anyway "so as not to give growers the impression that the government was unwilling to help them."[28]

To accompany his position paper on tariffs, Witte prepared a second document that responded to the marshals' 1896 memorandum as a whole. Since the marshals had made a change in tariff rates a key item on their economic agenda, Witte devoted a long section of his response to a forceful rebuttal of the marshals' position.

Witte asserted that Russian railroad tariffs were not high by any standard; in fact, they were lower than the tariffs in Europe and equal to North American rates. He noted that since 1880 the treasury had spent 640 million rubles to cover the deficits run up by railroad companies. "This means that 640 million rubles, collected by ordinary means from the taxpayers, were spent to assist those individuals served by the railroads."[29] Witte made it clear that any further tariff reductions on the order of those contemplated by noble grain producers "would lay a new burden on the state budget."

On the question of differential rates and the problem of central Russia, Witte was less flexible than he had been in his special memorandum on tariffs for the State Council. He wrote that neither the 1889 nor the 1893 tariffs "had produced a radical change in the existing system of railroad grain tariffs." The differential principle had been operative on certain lines even before the government had intervened with its national tariff schedule. According to Witte, the 1893 tariff had been designed "to facilitate the sale of grain from the central provinces. . . . The 1893 tariff did not give the periphery any special advantages over central Russia; in fact, the center achieved . . . dominance in grain sales, particularly in domestic markets."

Witte then referred to the Special Committee convened by the Railroad Department of the Ministry of Finance in October 1896 to discuss railroad tariffs. He said bluntly that the conclusions drawn by the Special Committee were one-sided because areas like Ufa, Orenburg, Perm, western Siberia, and the Northern Caucasus had been unrepresented in its deliberations. Moreover, farmers who were actual participants in the Special Committee debate "were far from unanimous" in their opinions, while "representatives of other industries—trade, flour milling, railroads—were for the most part in favor of the existing tariff system."[30] Witte implied that the position of noble landowners needed no special protection from the government since the nobles themselves were not uniformly opposed to the tariff system. By pointing to the alleged lack of harmony among the nobility on the Special Committee of October 1896, Witte hoped to minimize the impact of the provincial marshals' joint memorandum of March 1896.

In sessions on 27 May and 3 July 1897, the Joint Bureau of the Committee of Ministers and the Department of State Economy of the State Council studied Witte's two memoranda and considered the Council on Tariffs' recommendations. The Joint Bureau decided that to reduce tariffs on export shipments over 1,000 versts would be economically harmful, but it did recommend a change in domestic tariffs and in duties on flour and groats. The Joint Bureau became convinced that lower domestic rates on short distances would favor producers in the central provinces by making it difficult for peripheral producers to sell grain on the domestic market at cut prices. The Joint Bureau went so far as to agree that "while grain shipments [from peripheral areas] are not especially large, the very opportunity [for buyers] to receive grain from distant areas at cut prices definitely reduces prices on the domestic market." The Joint Bureau contended that "it would be very desirable to eliminate this problem."[31]

The Joint Bureau's decision was a partial defeat for Witte on the question of domestic shipments because the Bureau acted explicitly out of sympathy for growers in the central region. Witte's attempt to minimize the grievances of farmers in that area had failed. However, the Joint Bureau did not specify how the tariff schedule was to be altered; this "technical" matter was left to the Tariff Committee of the Ministry of Finance.

It would appear that Witte used the responsiblity to establish a new tariff on domestic shipments to undermine the Joint Bureau's intentions. The Tariff Committee had two choices before it: to raise rates on long domestic shipments—a measure that would benefit the central provinces by making it more expensive for Siberian producers to compete on the central market—or to reduce rates on short- and medium-distance shipments. The first option was rejected, ostensibly because it would have harmed the flour industry by reducing the amount of wheat available for milling. The Tariff Committee therefore reduced rates on shipments less than 540 versts, and it also reduced rates on medium-distance shipments (800–1,120 versts). However, it did not reduce these rates sufficiently to eliminate competition from Siberia. Thus, while making a few minor concessions, Witte had preserved his basic tariff policy.

The debate over tariff policy in 1896 and 1897 demonstrated the limits of the marshals' power in the tsarist state. On the one hand, by exercising their right to petition, the marshals could place an issue on the government's political agenda. In the absence of the marshals' 1896 memorandum it is extremely unlikely that Witte would have authorized a full-scale bureaucratic review of the differential tariffs. He was already aware that the 1893 tariffs put a certain financial pressure on the traditional grain-producing regions, and he himself had acted to prevent Siberian grain from being dumped on the central Russian market. Apart from the marshals' forceful representations for change in the 1896 memorandum, there was nothing new in the political or economic realm to cause the government to reconsider its tariff policy. Moreover, the marshals could dictate, within certain limits, the terms on which the government policy would be debated. The 1896 memorandum argued that differential tariffs were a problem for the central agricultural areas of the Empire. The governmental review at every instance naturally focused on the regional impact of the tariffs. Finally, the marshals could achieve at least a low level of representation in the review of government policy. The Ministry of Finance set up the ad hoc Special Committee on Tariffs in 1896 precisely in order to accommodate the marshals. This was a concession of some significance because representation on policy decisions had been almost entirely ruled out under Alexander III. Now Nicholas II, faced with a situation in which the nobility struggled for economic survival, granted the marshals a new forum for the expression of their concerns.

On the other hand, the nobility had no substantive power beyond that of supplication, no positive power to make and execute policy. There is an old Russian saying that "man proposes, but God disposes." This saying could easily be modified to describe Russian politics: "The nobility propose, but the tsar and the bureaucracy dispose." In the case of tariff policy, power to dispose remained from beginning to end in the hands of Nicholas and his ministers, particularly Witte. With each successive stage of tariff review by the Finance Ministry, the bureaucrats' conclusions came to resemble ever more closely the original policy of the Minister of Finance. Only in the Joint Bureau did Witte sustain a partial defeat, and even this defeat he managed to neutralize through the Tariff Council which made only the most moderate adjustments in domestic tariff rates. Thus, when the marshals confronted a determined minister who had the tsar's confidence, they would be defeated no matter what passion or reason brought them to the clash.

In addition, one should note that the marshals' influence was limited by the degree of unity they could muster. The 1896 memorandum was a rare showing of unanimity on important questions facing the nobility, but this unity could not long be maintained. The greater the number and variety of nobles speaking on a given issue, the greater the disagreements among them. In the case of the tariff question, Witte justifiably observed that not all representatives of agriculture on the ad hoc committee disagreed with government tariff policy, and Witte was absolutely correct to say that nobles and other grain producers from peripheral provinces would have favored the 1893 policy if they had attended the 1896 committee meetings. This disunity within the nobility was an inevitable consequence of the diversity within the First Estate, and it was a serious political liability whenever certain nobles were pressing the government for reform. Of course, it is difficult to say what would have happened if the government had been criticized on the tariff issue by a truly unified nobility. Even then Witte would probably not have backed off from his differential tariffs. What is clear is that convincing displays of unity by the nobility were never the rule, always the exception, and that ministers could take advantage of noble disunity in planning and justifying their political strategy.

In the final analysis, marshals of the nobility could speak for themselves and, to a more limited degree, for nobles of a certain province, or of a certain occupation or economic category. A government minister could speak for himself, for his agency, for the tsar, and for the nation. Thus, as the marshals implored assistance for the central provinces and agriculture in the name of the First Estate, Witte denied that assistance in the name of other provinces, the economy as a whole, and the national welfare. The marshals' defeat in 1896/97 was, therefore, galling and inevitable.

The Reaction of the Provincial Nobility to the Tariff Review

The marshals' failure to secure a radical change in the government's policy on agricultural trade was a pill too bitter to be swallowed. Having made a new approach toward tariffs a key element of their political designs, the marshals could not simply shrug their shoulders and walk away from their defeat. Yet if it was evident that some nobles would resist the continuation of the Finance Ministry's distasteful policies, it was by no means clear what form their resistance would take. There were basically two alternatives: discontented nobles could continue to express their grievances through officially sanctioned channels; or they could organize themselves in clandestine groups to work against the Ministry of Finance and, if necessary, the regime itself. The former alternative did not promise to be any more successful than the 1896 memorandum, though through it the marshals could hope to keep the tariff question alive. The latter alternative was risky, perhaps criminal, and could not be effective in the absence of pressure on the government from other sources. Furthermore, it raised the possibility of replacing existing government agencies, perhaps even with a new regime. In 1897 only the bravest of nobles could contemplate such a dangerous course. Heretofore, dissatisfied nobles had pursued the politics of accommodation with the new society and the government, not the politics of revolution.

Despite the dim prospects of success, most nobles chose the first alternative. This option was made more attractive by the government, which went out of its way to provide convenient legal avenues for the expression of noble grievances. Indeed, one might almost suspect the government of seeking to control dissent among the nobility by channeling its expression.

One channel the government opened was an appeal sent to the provincial zemstvos for information and suggestions on the future conduct of agricultural policy. In late 1894 the Ministry of Agriculture and State Domains posed five questions to the zemstvos:

1. What needs of agriculture in the province are so acute and crucial that they demand immediate attention?
2. What measures seem most advisable to solve these problems in view of local conditions?
3. Which agricultural problems are most amenable to solution in view of local circumstances?
4. What needs of agriculture, presently neither crucial nor difficult to solve, deserve future attention?
5. What measures to benefit local agriculture may be implemented by the zemstvo and require the participation or cooperation of the Ministry of Agriculture?[32]

Over the next three years the zemstvo responses to this questionnaire were sent directly to the Ministry. Thirty-three provinces had responded by 1898; only Saratov failed to answer before the Ministry published the responses in 1899.[33]

Nearly all the zemstvos touched on the question of grain tariffs, and certain assemblies analyzed the issue in great detail. The most rigorous criticisms of government tariff policy came from two regions: the south/southwestern periphery and the blacksoil center. Provincial assemblies from the south and southwest—for example, in Ekaterinoslav, Khar'kov, Kherson, and Bessarabia—complained that their export tariffs were so high they could no longer compete on the European market. In these peripheral provinces, grain production costs were relatively high because labor and machinery were both expensive. When the cost of short-distance export tariffs was added to production costs, growers could not comfortably compete with other nations on the world grain market. In blacksoil central provinces such as Voronezh, Simbirsk, Kursk, Orel, Riazan', Tula, and Tambov, the zemstvos complained that agriculture was being undermined by grain sent from the eastern periphery. Typical of such complaints was the response of the Simbirsk assembly to the government questionnaire:

> Thanks to the tariff, on the eastern periphery, where there is still virgin soil even though it is naturally of inferior quality when compared to soil in central Russia, grain can be sown successfully on such a scale that it may have a devastating impact on grain prices. If one keeps in mind that the value of land is many times less in the eastern provinces than in central Russia, then this danger will be all the more intelligible. The rapacious farming of the periphery may serve as a serious brake on the development of a more rational agriculture in central Russia. Of course, that cannot be desirable.[34]

The other channel that the government opened for grievances was the Special Commission on the Nobility which sent to marshals and noble assemblies a questionnaire on the needs of agriculture. The marshals who answered the questionnaire repeated the complaints made by the zemstvos, but they also added two new concerns. First, the marshals made explicit their contempt for Minister of Finance Witte, whom they saw as the chief obstacle to Russian agriculture. In a letter posted in February 1898, Riazan' provincial marshal L. M. Muromtsov criticized Witte's reaction to the marshals' 1896 memorandum:

> Since then [1896] not a single step has been taken on the road indicated by the convocation. In his remarks on the marshals' memorandum the Minister of Finance has proven with figures and other clever formulations that the nobility are far from impoverished, that only a small percentage has been ruined in the economic crisis. His Excellency does not wish to agree with the obvious fact that the reform of 1861 was a difficult experience for the noble Estate. As a person who knew all the figures of the epoch well, as a member of the Provincial Bureau on Peasant Affairs, as someone who has survived all the economic dislocations of that period, I cannot agree with the Minister of Finance's conclusions. This is especially true because the notions of this talented statesman have an undesirable effect on many noble causes that are quite dear to me.[35]

Another example of the high feelings against Witte was an 1897 speech to the Riazan' nobility by V. S. Buimistrov. Buimistrov asserted that the universally recognized source of Russia's agricultural problems was the Great Depression, a fact rejected by the Minister of Finance in spite of overwhelming evidence. Indeed, Buimistrov depicted Witte as the only person who failed to agree with the marshals' analysis of the agrarian crisis. What could the nobility do in response to Witte's obstructionism? Buimistrov answered as follows:

> Above all, one must always remember what our 27 provincial marshals
> have said, not in private, but before the tsar to whom the nobility
> have always spoken the truth: that high prices will solve all our prob-
> lems. All the necessary steps must be taken to raise prices, so that
> agricultural Russia will not be the slave of Western Europe.[36]

Buimistrov's analysis was simplistic, but his language was blunt and his tactics intriguing. He suggested that the nobility take advantage of their close historical connection with the throne and convince the tsar of the rightness of their cause. The implication was that nobles should no longer try to sway the Minister of Finance, but should deal directly with Nicholas. If one could not break down Witte's obstructionism, one should simply bypass him altogether. Buimistrov did not explain how, given the structure of the state, such a feat could be achieved.

Second, the marshals argued bitterly against what they saw as the unfair advantages that industry enjoyed over agriculture. The marshals' tactics were to portray government policy, in the words of Khar'kov provincial marshal Kapnist, as "one-sided protectionism" which stimulated industry while depressing agriculture and the nobility.[37] For example, in a document submitted by Kazan' provincial marshal N. M. Galuzin to the Special Commission, the Kazan' landowner Prince Pavel Ukhtomsky attacked agriculture's allegedly excessive fiscal obligations to the state. Ukhtomsky noted that while industry paid 183 million rubles of taxes on a gross income of 2.1 billion rubles, agriculture paid 543 million rubles on a gross income of 1.5 billion rubles. The conclusion to be drawn was obvious: agriculture was still Russia's leading source of revenue because it was taxed more heavily than industry. Ukhtomsky also pointed to other sources of fiscal pressure on agriculture. Storage charges, import duties, freight bills, insurance premiums, and other miscellaneous expenses amounted to 38 percent of the average sale price of Kazan' grain. "In most cases [growers] get less than half the sale price of grain on the international market [as net income]." Yet the government did nothing to cut expenses for growers or to raise grain prices. The government was again acting in the interest of industry, Ukhtomsky charged, because low grain prices meant cheap bread prices—and cheap bread meant factory owners could pay low wages to their factory workers. Ukhtomsky proposed to rectify the imbalance between industry and agriculture by increasing taxes for industry, dropping protective tariffs on iron imports, and cutting railroad tariffs on grain exports.[38]

Another marshal who condemned the one-sidedness of government policy was Orel provincial marshal Stakhovich, the man whose 1896 personal audience with Nicholas had been an important part of the campaign for lower bank interest rates. On 24 May 1898 Stakhovich reviewed government inaction on the marshals' proposals and concluded: "Now in Spring 1898, one must repeat the same statement: until there is a change in current financial policy in Russia, one cannot expect the impoverishment of the nobility to be arrested, much less for the nobility's welfare to improve." Stakhovich believed that everyone connected with agriculture—grain firms, bank debtors, peasants, and especially nobles—were being ruined. "The landed nobility are the first [among the victims] because they have invested their lives, their work, their capital in the land. The more money and energy they devote to agriculture, the worse off and poorer they are." Why was this so? According to Stakhovich, industry could always turn to the Ministry of Finance for protection from competition and for solid, often generous financial support. Yet agriculture had "neither advocates nor vigilant protectors of its interests when they are violated by the general course of recent financial politics." Stakhovich demanded that the Finance Ministry stop ignoring agriculture and the nobility, that it decrease railroad tariffs and drop protectionist tariffs on agricultural goods.[39]

Perhaps the most eloquent criticism of alleged bias in government financial policy came from the pen of Nikolai Novosil'tsev, the Pskov provincial marshal. On 9 October 1898 Novosil'tsev completed his answer to the Special Commission questionnaire with the following words:

> Agriculture now represents the sole means of material support and tax payments for ninety percent of the population of the Russian Empire. It would seem very logical for the government to devote all its resources to the support of this enterprise. The nobility, the zemstvo, and various societies have been talking about this for a long time.
>
> In fact, the [government's] main effort has been directed toward the development and support of manufacturing production. Yet the

products of industry, as a result of protectionism, have not gotten
much cheaper, and when complaints are heard about this there
is always the same answer: competition will develop and goods will get
cheaper. I suggest this answer obscures one important consideration—that by the time the golden era of competition has arrived, the
ninety percent of Russia who live by the land and who constitute
the chief consumers [of manufactured goods] will be so impoverished
that they will be unable to buy even the cheapest goods.

Now it is essential, without losing a single minute, to direct all
resources to the support of agriculture. Only when this concern [for ag-
riculture] becomes the dominant concern of economic policy will
[we] arrive [at] the complete equilibrium, whose absence is now felt by
everyone. Only then will the anomaly of agricultural poverty and
15–20 percent industrial dividends be destroyed.[40]

What had begun as a campaign against government trade policy
now threatened, in the hands of certain marshals, to become a vendetta against the Minister of Finance and a crusade against Russian
industry. While it was conceivable that the vendetta could be waged
victoriously, the crusade was obviously a lost cause. The marshals'
failure to alter tariff policy in 1896/97 drove them to rhetorical excess
and political shortsightedness in 1897 and 1898.

GOVERNMENT TARIFF POLICY,
1900–1902

The opposition of the nobility to the 1897 confirmation of Witte's
tariff policy did not compel the government to abandon that policy,
but it did lead to a series of new tariff reviews. In July 1900 the
government established a new special committee to review tariff
rates. Like its predecessors, the committee included spokesmen for
agricultural interests, but this time the spokesmen were not selected
to represent their respective provinces, but to represent their regions.
This new principle of selection was the government's concession to
noble agitation on the tariff question since the mid-1890s. In the
event, it also proved a clever way to isolate defenders of central
Russian regional interests.

The committee held preliminary sessions from 21 through 24 July
1900. It tentatively resolved that in view of the harvest and prevailing prices, railroad tariffs on export shipments could remain stable.
Long-distance domestic shipments might be subject to higher rates
in order to assure that domestic markets be supplied with grain from
nearby growers. By the time the committee held its final sessions in

October 1900, there had developed a split between members from the central provinces and those from other regions.

Representatives of the central provinces offered a new tariff formula designed to distinguish domestic shipment rates from export rates. Rather than significantly increased prices on long-distance domestic hauls, the central provincial group proposed lower tariffs on intermediate-distance export shipments (a reduction of 2 kopecks per pood) and on intermediate-distance domestic shipments (a rate of 0.02 kopecks per pood/verst on hauls up to 1,000 versts). Tariffs on domestic shipments of 100 versts or more would be increased slightly. The goal of the central provincial group was to achieve the same price differentials recommended by the committee majority in July by different means: by selective price reductions rather than by a large increase in tariff costs on long-distance domestic hauls.

Other members of the special committee disputed the wisdom of the central provincial group proposal. Spokesmen from the eastern and southern provinces rejected lower tariffs on intermediate-distance hauls because they feared that such tariffs would make it harder for growers from southern and eastern provinces to sell grain in northern and western Russian markets.

In the end, the special committee endorsed the existing tariff schedule on unrefined grain, but made several minor changes in tariff rates on milled grain. For example, the cost of shipping rye and wheat flour within Russia was to be increased to 10 percent above the rate on unrefined grain. This change was supported by most nobles on the committee, but it was unpopular with the flour industry and industrial spokesmen.[41] Still this dispute was a trivial matter compared to the earlier confrontation of central provincial interests with those of southern and eastern provinces.

The special committee forwarded its recommendations to the Tariff Committee in the Ministry of Finance. The Tariff Committee agreed with most of the special committee program, but it rejected the proposed tariff increases on high grades of flour. In short, the Tariff Committee defended the status quo. The designs of growers from central Russia were again frustrated.

By the beginning of 1902, the political climate of Russia had grown still more threatening to the autocracy. One of the leading zemstvo activists, D. N. Shipov, summarized his impressions of the gathering storm as follows:

It had become transparently clear that if the government did not soon renounce its unfriendly and negative attitude toward social forces and if it did not create favorable conditions for cooperation with activist elements on the basis of moral solidarity and a mutual understanding of the needs and goals of the state, then there would inevitably be a radical reform of our government system under the influence of the swiftly developing opposition, and soon there would be thought of popular rule.[42]

The yawning gap between society and the state made discussion of the government's financial politics a matter of significance and urgency. On 22 January 1902, Nicholas II ordered the creation of a Special Commission on the Needs of Agriculture. Witte had been the driving force behind the creation of the Special Commission, and Nicholas made Witte chairman. The commission developed an extensive program of discussion: forty issues were put on the commission agenda, and these issues were to be considered by committees in every district and province of Russia. The very organization of these local committees became a matter of controversy; the zemstvo chairmen challenged the government's formula for committee selection, and some chairmen wanted to boycott the discussions altogether.[43] Eventually this crisis was resolved, and preparations to analyze the needs of agriculture continued.

One of the problems on the commission agenda was the tariff question. Just before the tariff question was turned over to the Special Commission, there was a private conversation on railroad tariffs in the Railroad Department of the Ministry of Finance.[44] This conversation is interesting because it illustrates the government's disharmony on the tariff issue and shows the degree to which the noble agitation had influenced the thinking of some powerful officials in the Finance Ministry.

The private conversation occurred on 17 May 1902, and the following persons participated in it: Senator I. I. Kabat; Privy Counsellors I. A. Zvegintsov and V. V. Maksimov; Acting State Counsellors Prince O. S. Golitsyn, A. A. Shul'ts, A. M. Terne, D. P. Semenov; State Counsellors N. E. Giasintov, K. Ia. Zagorsky, M. P. Fedorov, P. A. Skal'kovsky; and E. K. Tsigler.

Senator Kabat began by noting that the government had just reviewed the tariff question in 1900, and he found the recently published tariffs adequate. Kabat said that if it should become necessary to assist agriculture, especially in the central provinces, then he would recommend a reduction in tariffs on shipments longer than 200 versts. That reduction would mean a net gain for farmers of two kopecks per pood on shipments averaging 540 versts.

Privy Counsellor Zvegintsov recommended that tariffs be reviewed every year so that transportation costs could be coordinated with harvest information and production costs. Zvegintsov said that reduced tariffs alone would not suffice to improve Russian grain trade; other measures would have to be introduced simultaneously. He argued for special rapid delivery of agricultural products by the railroads, the design of special railroad cars for grain shipments and for cattle transport, and improved organization of grain elevators. He also called for special seasonal tariff rates. During the two or three months following the harvest, rates would be reduced on grain shipments for the farmers' benefit.

Acting State Counsellor Prince O. S. Golitsyn thought that the existing tariff system deserved support. He contended that a new tariff schedule alone could scarcely be expected to help agriculture very much, and he added that most landowners were coming to accept this view. He asserted that while reduction of one or two kopecks per pood in tariff levels would not benefit the farmer, it would subject railroads to sizable losses. Turning to Zvegintsov's idea of seasonal tariffs, Golitsyn argued that the disposition of markets was the most crucial variable in grain trade; a seasonal reduction in tariffs would mean a possible delay in sales of grain, since prices would be driven down to artificially low levels by the glut of grain on the market. Golitsyn also rejected a yearly tariff review. He said that annual tariff adjustments "would be fatal for the grain trade; the simplicity, clarity, and stability of the existing tariffs are their finest qualities."

E. K. Tsigler summarized the operation of tariffs in the United States. He noted that the average charge for shipments from western states to Chicago and from Chicago to New York was 1/82 kopecks per pood/verst. Russian railroads could make shipments over similar distances for 1/73 kopecks per pood/verst. In absolute figures, Russian grain could be shipped to London cheaper than American grain could be shipped from New York. Shipments from Odessa were 5 kopecks per pood cheaper, and those from Baltic ports were up to 15 kopecks cheaper than American shipments. Tsigler concluded from these comparisons that Russian transportation costs were not only comparable to the low American rates, but actually cheaper. Tsigler also noted that many American railroad companies had become financially unstable because competition between railroads was so brutal. The Russian system of railroad tariffs was far superior to the American one so often held up as a model.

Privy Counsellor V. V. Maksimov began his commentary by referring to the problem of tariff stability and simplicity. He observed that the 1889 tariff plan had tried to create an optimal distribution of grain among exporting facilities through a complicated system that gave substantial reductions on certain railroad lines. This plan did not achieve its goals, and therefore the principle of optimal distribution and the complex tariff scheme were abandoned in 1893 in favor of a simpler, more stable differential scheme. Maksimov noted that comprehensive and invariable tariffs were preferable to fluctuations and annual reviews, which would be "very harmful for commerce."

Concerning changes that would assist the agricultural center, Maksimov advised caution. He said that some measures that would help central Russia would damage grain production in other regions. Maksimov also warned that the government would have to define carefully the meaning of "the center" because the term had been used sloppily in debates in agricultural questions.

Maksimov raised a more global question about international competition. He said that the United States, through its domination of sea transport and its railroad trusts, may have ushered in a new phase in the world grain trade. The new American technology and economic organization created "a growing danger" to Russia, which might have to respond by building its own commercial fleet.

Acting State Counsellor A. A. Shul'ts pronounced himself an opponent of major changes in tariffs. He rejected the concept of annual reviews and other measures that would lead to a fluctuation in tariff rates. He said that if tariffs must be reduced, these reductions should be uniform for all regions. Shul'ts said that a partial rate cut on intermediate-distance shipments, one of the favorite proposals of central Russian producers, would be especially undesirable; it would harm the northern nonblacksoil provinces, which lived on their own grain production. Shul'ts reminded his colleagues that the central provinces' complaints against the periphery were ironic, since some peripheral provinces like Ufa and Samara had suffered from central competition. Shul'ts had in mind the grain export shipments of the Volga provinces down the river system to ports; these water shipments became less profitable after the railroad system was built. In effect, the railroads radiating from central Russia had taken away from the peripheral areas a profitable outlet for grain. Finally, Shul'ts announced that tariff reductions subsidized by the treasury would be against the national interest, since the subsidy would come from taxes on the general population, some of whom did not benefit from the railroads.

Acting State Counsellor D. P. Semenov put his hopes on a dual system of grain tariffs—one set of tariffs for red cereals and another set for gray cereals like rye and oats. Semenov wanted to revive a proposal made in the 1896 review; export shipments of gray cereals would cost up to five kopecks per pood less on hauls of 500 to 800 versts. The Semenov plan would have been advantageous to central Russian producers and to some western provincial producers, since gray cereals tended to dominate agriculture in these regions.

A. M. Terne admitted that Russian railroad tariffs did not have a decisive impact on international grain market sales, but he did believe that reduced tariffs, in conjunction with other changes, might have some effect on sales. Terne was worried about the American ascendancy in the grain market, and he was anxious lest Russia lose its share of the international commerce altogether. Terne warned his colleagues that in 1901 America had sold twice as much grain as Russia and that the Americans were now selling more rye and corn than before. This latter phenomenon was particularly disturbing since Russia had traditionally dominated the European rye market. In response to fears that reduced tariffs would mean economic losses for Russian railroad companies, Terne said that the government would have to weigh those losses against the consequences of losing a major share in the grain commerce business. For Terne, defeat on the international market represented a devastating prospect, unacceptable to the national interest.

M. P. Fedorov was unwilling to gamble on reductions of export tariffs. He thought that each cut in export tariffs would bring a corresponding drop in the international market price of grain; this would bring no net benefit to Russian producers. Federov observed that American, Canadian, and Argentine reserves were large enough to withstand Russian attempts to take over the world grain market by a price war. In addition, Fedorov found export tariff cuts undesirable for another reason: he was convinced that reductions would harm Russian railroads, particularly the Riazan'-Ural company. In fact, Fedorov recommended an increase in export tariffs.

Fedorov did concede that some alteration of domestic rates might be necessary to help the central region. He proposed a "demarcation line" running though Kovel', Briansk, L'gov, Kursk, and Tsaritsyn that would increase tariffs in such a way as to impede shipments from southern Russia to the west and north. Fedorov said that his scheme would assist the central Russian provinces, and it would not entail those disadvantages for the northern nonblacksoil region that might have followed a reduction in intermediate-distance tariffs.

Fedorov's call for increased export tariffs was rejected by other participants in the conversation. K. Ia. Zagorsky went so far as to argue that "an increase in tariffs would inevitably reduce our exports and harm [Russian] producers."

P. A. Skal'kovsky sought to raise domestic tariffs to the level of export tariffs, and thereby to equalize all the rate structures in a single workable system. In his view, any cut in internal tariffs would harm the railroads, and eventually grain producers would suffer too. Skal'kovsky sought to assist the central provinces by increasing the tariffs on flour shipments so as to discourage southern and western producers from selling flour in central provincial markets. Skal'kovsky's plan would not have helped farmers in central Russia, but it was welcome news for the flour industry there.

The 17 May conversation showed how divided government officials were on the railroad tariff issue. Senator Kabat, Privy Counsellor Semenov, M. P. Fedorov, and P. A. Skal'kovsky were attracted to different plans for reducing internal tariffs. Prince Golitsyn, E. K. Tsigler, V. V. Maksimov, and A. A. Shul'ts opposed cuts in domestic shipment rates. A. M. Terne defended reduced export tariffs, while M. P. Fedorov stood at the other extreme in his defense of increased export tariffs. Zvegintsov was virtually alone in his sponsorship of seasonal rates and annual rate reviews, proposals that other members of the committee thought irresponsible and potentially harmful to agriculture. While there was no consensus on what changes were desirable, participants in the conversation did seem to be uneasy with the status quo. Maksimov, Terne, and Fedorov were very concerned about foreign competition on the international market, particularly American competition. These officials recognized the regional factor in Russian grain trade. Kabat, Semenov, Fedorov, and Skal'kovsky offered plans to help the central provinces. Maksimov and Shul'ts rejected assistance for the agricultural center on the grounds that proposed assistance would harm grain producers in other regions. It was clear that the government had accepted the terms of the debate set by the landed nobility from central Russia.

The steering committee of the Special Commission met on 18 and 21 May 1902. The committee reached three conclusions: (1) agricultural interests did not necessitate another review of the 1889 tariff statute; (2) existing tariffs satisfied the general needs of agriculture, thus a general restructuring of the tariff schedule was not necessary in 1902; and (3) if there was sentiment for change in the local committees, the Minister of Finance would turn the matter over to the tariff agencies for study. These agencies would then make recommendations to the Special Commission.[45]

THE WITTE COMMITTEES AND THE
TARIFF PROBLEM, 1902–03

In the deliberations of local and provincial committees on the needs of agriculture there was strong sentiment for a general reduction of railroad tariffs. Fourteen provincial committees called for cheaper tariff rates; these committees included nobles from Bessarabia, Voronezh, Ekaterinoslav, Kazan', Kostroma, Nizhny-Novgorod, Penza, Perm, Saratov, Simbirsk, Smolensk, Tauride, Tambov, and Iaroslavl' provinces. Ninety-two district committees endorsed tariff reductions. All told, there was some sentiment for lower tariffs in forty-one provinces of European Russia.[46]

In the campaign against high tariffs it became evident that some committees were motivated by regionalism. The Podolia provincial committee argued that Russian agriculture was differentiated by regional specialization and that in future reviews of railroad tariffs, these regional specializations should be stimulated as much as possible. Berdichev district in Kiev province made a similar argument: it was desirable to set domestic railroad tariffs so that separate regions could ship those products which were naturally grown in their areas "without competing with each other by virtue of lower, regionally-specific, tariffs."[47] Konstantinograd district in Poltava province recommended the abolition of tariffs which "produce a breakdown in agriculture despite the natural conditions of various localities."[48]

Several committees, including the Chernigov, Kazan' and Tambov provincial committees, recommended that tariff policy be altered to protect the interests of central Russia. Birsky district in Ufa province asked that tariff advantages of northeastern Russia be preserved, even if it were impossible to reduce existing tariffs still further.

Opinions on the differential tariff were divided. Provincial committees in six provinces—Orenburg, Penza, Poltava, Volynia, Viatka, and Khar'kov—asserted that the differential tariff was desirable "in general."[49] Provincial committees in Minsk, Mogilev, and Tambov believed that differential tariffs should be applied only to export shipments and that proportional tariffs should be exacted on domestic grain shipments.[50] The Chernigov provincial committee petitioned for a "softening" of the differential rates in order to protect the central provinces against competition from the periphery. The Kazan' provincial committee said that the differential system was "generally undesirable and should be replaced by a pood/verst (proportional) system."[51]

At the district level there was greater evidence of a desire to change the existing system. While four district committees expressed satisfaction with the differential tariff,[52] forty-three district committees argued for some form of change in the existing differential formulae.[53] Twenty-seven of these district committees called for a complete abolition of the differential tariffs.

The pattern of opposition to railroad tariffs was complex, and it its often impossible to say why a given position on the tariff question prevailed in one area, but not in another. In Kursk and Volynia provinces, for example, district committees disagreed sharply with one another about the needs of their respective regions. There was no unity of opinion within these provinces, even though one might have expected nobles to have worked out a common position by 1903. However, it is apparent that most opposition to the differential tariff came from districts in central blacksoil provinces (Tula, Riazan', Tambov, Nizhny-Novgorod, Penza, Khar'kov, Chernigov, Orel, Kursk), from the southern and southwestern steppe provinces (Kherson, Tauride), and from the western provinces (Bessarabia, Kov'no, Vil'no, Grodno, Minsk, Mogilev). These areas were affected negatively, at least to some extent, by the differential rate system, and there had been periodic complaints against government policy from the center and south since the inception of the tariff system. The western provinces had not been as active earlier in the agitation against the railroad system perhaps because they lacked the political institutions that made such agitation possible: zemstvos and elected marshals.

The Witte committees, like so many of their predecessors, ended their deliberations without changing government tariff policy, and so a substantial segment of the Russian nobility remained frustrated by the treatment it had received from the government since 1896. The failure of the nobility to alter government policy can be attributed to several factors: divisions among the landed nobles from different regions of the country; the steadfastness of Witte in the pursuit of his policies; the 1897 decision by most nobles to persevere in the politics of accommodation, which made it easier for the government to control dissent within the nobility. In retrospect, the campaign against the Ministry of Finance's policies seems doomed from its inception.

Yet those who spoke out against differential tariffs learned two invaluable lessons. First, they learned that political organization was an effective though not lethal weapon in the struggle against distasteful policies. When the twenty-seven provincial marshals had spoken with one voice against agricultural trade regulations, the government had responded—not by changing regulations, to be sure, but by a series of official policy reviews in which nobles were sometimes represented. What nobles had to ponder now was how to increase the scale of their political organization and the effectiveness of their representations. Second, nobles learned that the politics of accommodation could dislodge neither ministers nor policies that had the tsar's approval. In order to have their way in the future, nobles might have to abandon accommodation in hopes of changing the regime itself.

*Whether or not the estate is sold today—does it
really matter? That's all done with long ago; there's
no turning back, the path is overgrown. Be calm, my dear.
One must not deceive oneself; at least once in one's life
one ought to look the truth straight in the eye.*
                                    —*A. P. Chekhov,*
                              The Cherry Orchard, *Act III*

C H A P T E R   9
The Peasant Question

There are really only two kinds of political issues: those susceptible of solution given the existing resources and structure of the state, and those vexed questions which are not susceptible of solution. In the twenty years following 1881 noble petitioners had assumed that the noble question fell into the former category for two reasons: first, they thought that the accommodation of the nobility to new Russian social conditions could be accomplished through modest financial subsidies from the treasury and through changes in the law codes; second, they supposed that the Russian government would ultimately find the preservation of the landed nobility to be in the interests of the state. By the turn of the twentieth century, both assumptions had been seriously shaken. It was not at all clear that any inexpensive, yet effective subsidy for the nobility could be invented, or that, once invented, nobles could fashion a consensus durable enough to guarantee its adoption. Nor was it evident that the Finance Ministry's hostility toward subsidizing the nobility could be overcome or circumvented. Thus, the noble question began to look intractable.

Yet if the noble question was intractable, it was also, observers now realized, a *question mal posée*. For the nobility's proper place in Russian society could not be determined without a prior resolution of the peasant question, a problem vexed and damnable in every sense. How could one decide the fate of noble landownership without first deciding how to provide the peasantry with enough land to feed themselves and to satisfy their material needs? How could one settle the problem of the legal privileges of one hundred thousand noble families without prior determination of the legal status of one hundred million peasants? Should one attempt to accommodate the landed nobility to the autocracy if the price for that accommodation were the alienation of the peasantry from both nobility and autocracy? These were the riddles of the peasant question, each one more devilish than the next. Yet one could not untangle one riddle without having to puzzle out the answers to them all. The noble question, then, turned out to be not an independent issue, but one facet of an immense, complex, and explosive problem.

NOBLE ATTITUDES TOWARD THE PEASANTRY BEFORE 1900

During the Great Depression there were at least three different approaches to the peasant question current among the Russian nobles.[1] The most traditional approach was the patriarchal one expressed so forcefully by A. D. Pazukhin in 1885.[2] Too frequently Pazukhin is remembered only as the right-hand man of D. A. Tolstoy in the elaboration of the counterreforms; one forgets that Pazukhin's views on the peasantry were formed while he was Alatyrsky district marshal of the nobility in Simbirsk province, and that his views were more typically provincial than they were the product of the St. Petersburg official milieu. For Pazukhin the peasant question was not primarily an economic one; instead it was a moral and political issue. In a well-ordered hierarchical society there are harmonious relations between nobles and peasants: nobles enjoy the peasants' trust because nobles protect peasants against unwarranted government interference in peasant life and against the peasants' own cupidity and moral weakness. Pazukhin believed that Alexander II's reforms threatened the harmony of the rural order by undermining the separation of the social Estates. By allowing the lower orders to involve themselves in all-Estate institutions like the zemstvo, and by permitting judicial organs to try cases of nobles and non-nobles alike, the reformers had encouraged the peasants to see themselves as equals to the nobility and had thus undercut patriarchal authority. If something were not done soon to restore this authority and to separate the Estates, the peasantry would be left defenseless against the kulaks and merchants who were bent on destroying the commune. Pazukhin's program, of course, consisted in the restoration of the political and legal authority of the nobility over the peasantry. It was, therefore, a classic example of the tendency so widespread in the 1880s to see the peasants' future as contingent on that of the nobility, not vice versa.

We have already encountered a variant of the patriarchal approach to the peasant question in the 1887 speech of Makarievsky district marshal Khvoshchinsky to the Nizhny-Novgorod noble assembly. Like Pazukhin, Khvoshchinsky saw the nobility as the necessary link between the tsar and people in the hierarchically ordered Russian society, and as the protector of the peasantry and conservative values. Unlike Pazukhin, however, Khvoshchinsky looked on the destruction of partriarchal authority as an economic problem, as well as a moral and political one. "The new, self-appointed leaders of the people—the kulak, tavern owner, and clerk—oppress the peasantry more than serfdom did" and were "already forcing the nobility off their [the nobles'] lands."[3] The implication of Khvoshchinsky's argument was that by acting to preserve noble landownership, the government would simultaneously solve the peasant question, because nobles would again be able to protect the peasants from these "self-appointed leaders." Like Pazukhin, Khvoshchinsky put the noble cart in front of the peasant horse.

Another, and very curious variant of partriarchalism linked the peasant question with the Jewish question. Adherents to this brand of patriarchalism blamed the Jews for oppressing the peasantry in the western provinces. They also tended to associate the nobility's economic and political difficulties with the alleged power of the Jews over sources of credit and with a Jewish "plot" to create a constitution that would give moneylenders and kulaks a free hand. Anti-Semitic patriarchalism was particularly virulent in high court circles in Alexander III's reign. Alexander, as Hans Rogger has demonstrated, "accepted the judgment of his first Minister of the Interior [N. P.] Ignatiev that the simple Christian folk of Russia, meaning primarily the peasants, needed protection from the economic domination of the Jews."[4] These sentiments were propagated publicly by V. P. Meshchersky in *Grazhdanin* and by Katkov in *Russky vestnik*. In the 1890s, at the height of the Great Depression, radical rightists gathered around Sergei Sharapov, a bitter opponent of Witte's economic policies, who saw Witte as part of an international Jewish conspiracy to "destroy the producing classes and break down the old Christian structure of Europe."[5] The remedy for the peasantry's problems proposed by anti-Semitic patriarchalists was to return to the system in which social Estates were separate, the nobility controlled the countryside and the Jews were restricted in their places of residence and their occupations.

It is difficult to judge how widespread anti-Semitic partriarchalism was among the provincial landed nobility.[6] Few petitions from noble assemblies alluded to the Jewish problem, and those which did commented only superficially. There were, however, complaints lodged by marshals against alleged Jewish manipulation of the grain trade. For example, Kursk provincial marshal Durnovo claimed in an 1896 memorandum that "the entire grain trade has fallen into the hands of Jews [*zhidov*], exporters, and selling agents." Durnovo accused the Jews of deliberately mixing sand and other nonfood additives with Russian export grain, thus reducing demand for the grain abroad and cutting Russian producers' profits.[7] There were also attacks on the Jews published by nobles acting independently of corporative institutions. Between 1896 and 1903, F. D. Glinka, a retired naval lieutenant and landlord in Smolensk province, wrote a series of pamphlets against Witte's economic policies. Typical of them was a long leaflet published in 1899 that accused the Jews of exploiting the peasantry and trying to overthrow the Russian state through monometallism.[8] Thus, anti-Semitic patriarchalism had a definite, but apparently limited currency among the provincial nobility.

Common to all variants of patriarchalism was a refusal to concede to the peasant question anything but a contingent status in politics, and an insistence that noble status and authority, now threatened by external factors, must be restored.

The second approach to the peasant question might be called the meliorative approach. Those who embraced it saw the economic positions of nobility and peasantry alike as discrete parts of a broader question—the agrarian question. In order to solve the agrarian question, the government would have to devote attention to the needs of all social groups living in the countryside, and would have to adopt reforms to ameliorate the difficulties peculiar to each. Thus, as the government worked with one hand to shore up the nobility, it could work with the other hand to provide the peasants with a higher standard of living. In this approach the interests of nobility and peasantry were not perceived as competitive or contingent one on the other, but as compatible with and independent of one another. Meliorism was the approach to the peasant question most typically taken by provincial elites during the second phase of the Great Depression.

The tamest variant of the meliorist approach to the peasant question was that adopted by the twenty-seven provincial marshals who participated in the 1896 St. Petersburg convocation. For the marshals the key problem facing Russian peasants was the disastrously low price of grain. "Low grain prices damage not only large landowners, as the Ministry of Finance has stated, but also everyone who sells grain . . . and everyone involved in its production, since payments to sharecroppers and the quality of harvests cannot be completely independent of grain prices." The marshals admitted that the peasants had insufficient land to cultivate and were compelled to buy or rent more land in order to survive. "Given the increasing pressure on the land supply since the emancipation, the allotments that barely suffice to feed a peasant and his family, the peasants get by only by acquiring more land through purchase or rent, and by selling the harvest in order to meet taxes and other obligations." Peasant renters were in a particularly difficult position, according to the marshals: "The security and price of rented land are correlated with the income of renters, who possess no capital whatsoever. Their only resource is income from the sale of grain."[9]

Because the price of grain was not high enough to guarantee peasant producers an income adequate to meet their fiscal obligations, arrears on redemption payments grew throughout Russia. "Arrears have sky-rocketed, especially in the last few years. They have now reached 85.7 percent of the annual payment for the whole of Russia, but in certain provinces arrears have reached 300 and even 435 percent. (They have been especially high in agricultural provinces— Samara, Simbirsk, Ufa, Kazan', Nizhny-Novgorod, Penza, Voronezh, Orel, Tula, and others.)" Rural Russia was declining and becoming impoverished. Landowners, peasants, grain traders alike were "lost in a maze of debts and arrears, with no way out, because no one pays attention to their problems."[10]

According to the marshals, the peasants' problems could be alleviated if Minister of Finance Witte would reduce the fiscal pressure on the rural sector and abandon his artificial support for the industrial economy. More concretely, the marshals argued that an end to high import tariffs and a change in the differential export tariff would help the peasant grain producers as well as the nobles. In addition, a decrease in rural taxation would mean more money available to peasants for land purchases and increased consumption. The marshals did not provide a very sophisticated analysis of the peasant land question, and they ignored entirely the juridical and legal position of peasants. However, the marshals did acknowledge the peasant question as an independent issue, and noted the need for policy changes.[11]

A second variant of the meliorist approach to the peasant question was that espoused by zemstvo reformists in the wake of the 1891/92 famine.[12] The zemstvo reformists agreed with the marshals that Witte's differential tariff policy as well as his policy of taxing the rural sector to pay for industrial development should be abandoned.[13] However, zemstvo activists were more specific in their proposals to ameliorate the peasants' economic situations, and more comprehensive in that they treated the legal and cultural problems of the peasantry as well. In 1893, at the first so-called zemstvo congress to meet after the famine, the insufficiency of the peasant land fund was a major item of discussion. The congress formulated the following resolution:

> Recognizing land shortage as one of the most fundamental factors
> in the decline of peasant welfare, [we must] stimulate petitions on the
> necessity of reforming the Peasant Bank: reduction of interest rates;
> the abolition of penalty payments; the issuance of loans primarily to
> peasant associations and societies; the collection of payments on
> loans to be like that for redemption payments and the abolition of the
> sale of lands bought by peasants in instances of non-payment; di-
> rection of the bank's activity toward independent purchase of estates,
> both in private sales and at public auction, for the purpose of sell-
> ing parts of them to the peasants, in which cases it must bear in mind
> the new settlement and resettlement of peasants; credit for newly
> settled peasants and advantages to them. Where it is possible, the zem-
> stvo itself should act according to the same program. . . . [We must]
> petition for the abolition of all restrictions and limitations on reset-
> tlement. [We must] petition: 1) for the demarcation of a land fund for
> colonization; 2) for credit to aid resettlement; 3) for the constant
> dissemination of information among the people concerning resettle-
> ment; 4) for the creation of resettlement offices.[14]

At the 1894 zemstvo congress, discussion of the land question continued and there were again suggestions that peasant land credit be improved and that peasant resettlements be arranged. However, as N. M. Pirumova has demonstrated, there were also arguments that "the existing impoverishment of the populace is due to deeper causes than those that can be affected by agronomic measures."[15] Certain participants at the 1894 congress hinted that the cultural level of the peasantry would have to be raised as a prerequisite to the solution of the peasant question. "Not only certain agronomic improvements, but also all questions of economic welfare may be properly and successfully solved only if there is a development of personal independence and a corresponding degree of moral self-consciousness."[16] Thus, the zemstvo reformists had begun to see the peasant question as an issue of broad scope indeed.

The agreements reached by the zemstvo leadership at the 1893 and 1894 congresses contributed to a generally deeper consciousness in provincial zemstvo assemblies of the need for reform in the peasant economy. In analyses of the needs of Russian agriculture submitted to the government between 1894 and 1899, twenty-one provincial zemstvo assemblies recommended some form of change in government policy toward the peasantry.[17] There was strong sentiment, especially in the nonblacksoil north and in the heavily populated Right-bank Ukraine, that the peasant problem be solved by settling peasants on sparsely populated or virgin territory. There was also some pressure from the politically influential zemstvos in Moscow and St. Petersburg to reform the Peasant Bank. However, the most interesting treatments of the land question suggested that nothing less than the abandonment of the Witte system and the abolition of the peasant commune could solve the land question.

The Nizhny-Novgorod zemstvo presented a long analysis of peasant poverty that touched on the questions of landlessness, the lack of work animals on many communal holdings, and the increase in peasant arrears on redemption payments. The zemstvo noted that statistics "proved the extremely impoverished condition of the rural populace in Nizhny-Novgorod and the extremely primitive level of agriculture," and confessed that in recent times there had been "a sharp deterioration in the standard of living of the population and in the position of agriculture."[18] One way of reducing peasant poverty, the zemstvo argued, was to reduce direct and indirect taxes falling on the peasants. The zemstvo rejected the frequently cited arguments against reduced indirect taxes by indicating that these taxes fell hardest on items most necessary to the peasants (kerosine, matches, tea, sugar). The zemstvo also expressed annoyance over customs duties on imported agricultural machinery, because these duties were, from their point of view, an indirect tax on the rural populace.[19] The Nizhny-Novgorod zemstvo thus presented a direct attack on the Witte system.

Questions about the organization of the peasant economy were raised in several assemblies. It was standard communal practice to separate allotments of individual peasants into narrow strips, which were often located in different fields held by the commune. Communal parcellization of land was sometimes reinforced by landowners who preferred to intersperse peasant allotments with seigneurial arable. The practice of irregular distribution of communal land with noble land and the parcellization of peasant allotments was called *cherespolosnost'*. Zemstvo assemblies in Vladimir, Tauride, Kursk, Perm, Smolensk, Ufa, and Khar'kov provinces complained about *cherespolosnost'* and recommended a consolidation of peasant field strips into single pieces of land.[20] The St. Petersburg zemstvo assembly asked that peasants be permitted to transfer from communal tenure to individual tenure by a majority vote of commune members, instead of by a two-thirds majority.[21] Both the St. Petersburg plan and the attacks against *cherespolosnost'* by other assemblies were signs of declining sympathy for contemporary peasant communal practice, and they anticipated some features of the Stolypin land reform, promulgated on 9 November 1906.

It should also be noted that the zemstvos did not limit their discussions of the peasant problem to economic reform. Almost universally, they supported measures to improve the cultural level of the peasantry. Eighteen assemblies advocated universal primary education, and twenty-four advocated the foundation of agricultural schools that would instruct peasants in the rudiments of technical farming.[22]

While zemstvo reformists committed themselves to the amelioration of peasant economic and cultural problems, they did not pursue programs incompatible with the survival of the Russian nobility. True, their solutions to the peasant question distinguished them from the marshals, who were far more tight-lipped concerning the peasantry. Nevertheless, none of the zemstvo programs—not the Peasant Bank reform, not peasant resettlement, not reduction of indirect taxes, not abolition of the commune, not the foundation of new schools—would have precluded the continued existence of the nobility. One of the best-known zemstvo leaders, D. N. Shipov of Moscow province, was quite self-conscious in his attempt to balance what he thought were the legitimate interests of the nobility and the peasantry.[23] A man genuinely devoted to popular welfare, an advocate at the 1896 zemstvo congress of economic reforms and better schools for the peasantry, Shipov was also a firm believer in noble property rights and in the monarchy. His basic political faith was, in Leonard Schapiro's words, "that the aim of politics should never be the conflict of rights, but always the harmonization of interests."[24]

The third approach to the peasant question was one that envisioned the eventual abolition of barriers between social groups, and thus the dissolution of the peasantry as a separate Estate. For want of a better term, one might call this approach egalitarian, although certain thinkers with this orientation would have been irritated at being so classified. One variant of this approach to the peasantry was represented in the work of B. N. Chicherin, who stood for legal, as opposed to social, egalitarianism. The twin principles on which Chicherin based his peasant program were equality before the law and the sanctity of private property.

Since 1855, Chicherin had argued for freedom of speech, religion, and assembly; for the gradual integration of the peasantry with educated society; for the eventual introduction of a constitution in Russia and a system of government based on election and representation.[25] In an article published in 1897 Chicherin criticized members of the nobility who wanted to "preserve those barriers which were characteristic of the serf system." Now, Chicherin warned, "conditions and attitudes are quite different; the ground on which the old structure rested has disappeared. The fall of the old structure may not occur suddenly—that would not even be desirable—but it is inevitable."[26]

If Chicherin wanted to introduce legal equality in Russia, he had no intention of introducing equality in the economic sphere. Chicherin thought that property rights must remain intact, whatever the risks of social inequality in the countryside.[27] Like Locke and Burke, Chicherin saw property as an absolute necessity for a stable political order; indeed, he thought that the Russian nobility's contributions to public life were made possible by their status as independent landholders. In Chicherin's view, the problem of the Russian peasantry was not so much that peasants were compelled to live side by side with large estate owners, but rather that the peasants had been prevented by the commune from acquiring a genuine respect for property rights. If the commune were abolished simultaneously with the introduction of legal equality, then there would develop in rural Russia a class of independent property owners—a class that would include both former nobles and former peasants. Throughout his adult life Chicherin was a determined opponent of the commune and of those who saw the commune as a unique institution rooted in the national character. For Chicherin, the commune was a historical institution that had long ago outlived its usefulness and, by the turn of the century, had become a danger to the state.[28]

The second variant of egalitarianism was the reformulated version of Tolstoy's Christian anarchism. Tolstoy had long been tempted to "seek salvation in a peasant hut," but it was not until the 1880s and 1890s that he succeeded in elaborating a convincing philosophical justification for his beliefs. On the one hand, Tolstoy gradually worked out the connection between the existence of private property and economic justice. An encounter with the peasant Shutaev in 1881 convinced Tolstoy that it was actually possible to live without private property, and the failure of his private philanthropy among the Moscow poor in 1882 led Tolstoy to see that charity alone could not cure poverty. In 1884 he read Henry George's *Progress and Poverty* and became an advocate of the nationalization of land. But it was not until 1886 when he finished *What Then Must We Do?* that Tolstoy systematically exposed money and property as the root of all evil, and suggested a simple Christian life without property as the answer to evil. On the other hand, Tolstoy struggled to come to terms with the value of government in society. In *An Examination of Dogmatic Theology* (1880), Tolstoy first proclaimed his notion of nonresistance to evil, with its implication that Christians must avoid military duty and all activities of government founded on compulsion. Yet only in 1893 did he arrive at his final verdict on modern governments as essentially immoral agencies that exist to maintain the privileges of the rich, and that persecute the people by warfare, taxes, and prisons.

Tolstoy's denunciations of social injustice and government violence would probably have been dismissed without comment by the censor if the Russian rural economy had not been prone to sudden disasters like the famine of 1891/92. The state could ill afford the scandal caused by Tolstoy's "Letters on the Famine," where he proclaimed to the educated public: "All our theaters, museums, all this stuff, these riches of ours we owe to the effort of these same hungry people who made these things, which are useless to them, simply because they are fed by these means—that is, they will always be obliged to do this kind of work to save themselves from the death by starvation that constantly hangs over their heads."[29] Nothing could have more clearly echoed Lavrov's thesis that civilization depends on the blood, sweat, and exploitation of the masses. No wonder Pobedonostsev wrote to Alexander III in 1891 that "Tolstoy is a fanatic in the matter of his insane ideas, and unfortunately attracts and leads to madness thousands of giddy people."[30]

What made Chicherin and Tolstoy so disturbing to the government was their attempt to disregard the noble question as irrelevant and to see the peasant question in terms most disadvantageous to the government—i. e., as a problem inherent in the existing sociopolitical structure and therefore as impossible to solve without a change in the political order.

Thus, before the turn of the twentieth century the nobility held at least three different attitudes toward the peasant question, not one rigidly classbound perspective, and there was very little solace for the government in any of these attitudes. The egalitarian approach was obviously subversive. The meliorist approach, while not necessarily inconsistent with autocracy, was critical of the Witte system, of the commune, and of peasant culture. Even patriarchalism had its dangers, for a patriarchal system can be maintained only if the patriarchs have a sure economic footing and a sense of self-confidence, neither of which existed by the turn of the century. In addition, anti-Semitic patriarchalism was explicitly critical of the Ministry of Finance in the 1890s, and it was at best a most dubious basis on which to rest internal politics.

TABLE 9.1

Peasant Disturbances, 1881–1900[a]

Year	Number of disturbances	Year	Number of disturbances
1881	47	1891	37
1882	58	1892	53
1883	93	1893	54
1884	110	1894	31
1885	60	1895	28
1886	58	1896	113
1887	75	1897	83
1888	46	1898	51
1889	38	1899	52
1890	45	1900	32

SOURCE: AN SSSR, *Krest'ianskoe dvizhenie v Rossii v 1881–1889 gg.* (Moscow, 1960), pp. 788–830; *Krest'ianskoe dvizhenie v Rossii v 1890–1900 gg.* (Moscow, 1959), pp. 601–648.
[a]Total number of disturbances, 1881–1900 = 1,164.

The Revival of the Peasant Movement

It is no easy task to explain to what extent the nobility viewed the peasantry as a revolutionary threat, if only because the character of the peasant movement varied sharply over time and was generally localized rather than national in scope. Indeed, there are major disagreements among historians about the extent of the peasant movement during the Great Depression. In 1909 the Menshevik historian Vladimir Gorn wrote that the years 1885 to 1895 "mark an almost complete collapse of the peasant movement."[31] However, Soviet scholars have disputed Gorn's analysis. For example, P. N. Pershin counted more than 1,600 peasant disturbances between 1881 and 1900, although he did admit that the troubles "were scattered over a huge territory and had a solitary and episodic character."[32]

My own study of peasant disturbances in the Great Depression suggests that Pershin overestimated their number (see Table 9.1). Moreover, it must be remembered that the bulk of peasant disturbances involved short-term disputes over matters such as timbercutting rights, rights to pasturage and water, and peasant transit across estate boundaries. Such disputes, by their very nature, were local in character and usually involved small peasant groups against one or more local estate owners. Hence, as P. A. Zaionchkovsky has argued, it is wrong for historians to take the quantity of peasant disturbances in a single year as a true index of the state of tensions in the countryside.

Nevertheless, the best evidence indicates that at the turn of the century, peasant restiveness was a serious problem in the blacksoil center and in the New Russian provinces of the southern steppes. In 1899 over one hundred peasants from Tauride province were brought to trial over grazing rights; the peasants had armed themselves with pitchforks and guns to enforce their claims.[33] In May 1898 a crowd of two hundred peasants in Zolotaia Balka village in Kherson offered armed resistance to a noble landowner trying to enforce meadow rights. The peasants broke down a gate to the landowner's home, entered, and destroyed much of the interior. They shouted: "How long can we stand it? We are already ruined!"[34] According to one observer writing in November 1901, many peasants hoped for a swift and radical change in social and political relations. "In various places they make predictions that this change will occur within three to seven years."[35] Even without this change, the observer noted that there was a "constant silent struggle of peasants against landowners."[36] The most recent full-scale investigation of peasant discontent, by the French historian Sylvain Bensidoun, agreed with the contemporary assessment. Bensidoun has shown that in certain districts of the blacksoil center and New Russia, "there was a quasi-permanent agitation" which caused the government grave concern.[37] As early as 17 July 1898 the Minister of Internal Affairs distributed a circular to provincial governors deploring the new developments in the southern steppes and instructing authorities to "take the most decisive steps to avoid and suppress these disorders."[38]

If the peasant movement before 1902 was a matter of some concern to officials in the Ministry of Internal Affairs, the events in Poltava and Khar'kov provinces in the spring of 1902 were cause for national alarm.[39] In March 1902 peasants on the Karlovka estate of Duke Meklenburg-Strelitsky assumed control of over two thousand desiatins of land. They opened up the seigneur's warehouses, took seed grain, and began the spring planting. Between 9 and 26 March, the peasants took potatoes from various potato cellars on the domain; these raids culminated on the night of 26 March when peasants carried off potatoes and 800 poods of animal fodder. By 28 March, peasants had begun to seize fodder and grain on neighboring estates. By 31 March, fifteen estates had been raided in Konstantinograd and Poltava districts of Poltava provinces.[40]

By the end of March the situation had become serious. The peasants had acted earlier in small groups of fifty or more; now they were moving in huge masses. On 31 March over one hundred peasants from various volosts fell upon the Durnovo estate in the village Chutovo, near the Poltava-Khar'kov border. On the same day the movement spread into Valkov and Bogodukhov districts in Khar'kov. Once in Khar'kov, the peasants turned more violent; they drove off the seigneurs' cattle and set fire to a number of estates. It was reported that one estate house was pulled apart board by board for lumber.[41] Before the army had suppressed the uprising, fifty-six estates in Poltava province (seventeen in Konstantinograd, thirty-nine in Poltava district) and twenty-four in Khar'kov had suffered damage.[42]

The uprising was remarkable not only for its breadth of appeal among the peasantry, but also for its deliberateness. According to one contemporary source, the peasants acted "calmly with complete confidence that they were right. With the village elder and hundred man in the lead they approach manors and estate headquarters and ask for the keys to the warehouse and storage areas. Usually the landowner is notified a day in advance that the peasants are coming after the grain."[43] The peasants managed such deliberation because they had convinced themselves "that soon there will be a time when there will be no more nobles and no more peasants."[44] Even when faced by army detachments, peasants insisted on their rights. One captain informed a group of peasants that his orders were to shoot if they did not disperse. The peasants answered: "You are lying. You would not dare shoot. The tsar did not give you that order." After several of the peasants were shot dead, the survivors warned the captain that "officers will be held strictly responsible by His Majesty, the Emperor."[45]

In the face of peasant resistance to military detachments, the provincial elite in Khar'kov and Poltava provinces panicked. In Khar'kov province large numbers of landowners took their valuables, abandoned their estates, and went to the provincial capital where "all the hotels were crowded with noble landowners."[46] In Poltava province the governor summoned all the district marshals to discuss methods "to prevent and suppress dissent among the people." On 6 April 1902 the marshals petitioned the government to enforce an emergency alert throughout Poltava province—that is, to declare martial law.[47]

Provincial governors, whose responsibility it was to establish order, relied on force. Governor Obolensky of Khar'kov province was particularly brutal. He toured the disorderly areas with an infantry detachment and several hundred mounted cossacks, and ordered the troops to apply corporal punishment to rebel peasants. In one village Obolensky had all the male peasants kneel from 8 A.M. to 3 P.M., while his troops periodically whipped them with birch rods that had been soaked in a saline solution. *Iskra*, the Social-Democratic journal, called Obolensky "the Russian Kitchener."[48] In Konstantinograd district, Poltava province, authorities were not more humane. One peasant named Shchetin was given 200 lashes by the army and later was beaten again by village police.

Shortly after the disorders had been suppressed, the government brought 1,092 peasants to trial for their alleged parts in the rebellion.[49] One hundred twenty-seven peasants were sentenced to loss of rights and privileges and were handed over to the Corrections Department for terms of 1 to 4.5 years. Six hundred eighteen peasants were sentenced to prison and were deprived of their rights for periods of 4 months to 1.5 years. Ninety-one peasants were imprisoned for 2 months to 1 year, but were not otherwise deprived of their rights. Peasants were also forced to pay a tax surcharge of 800,000 rubles as restitution for damages.[50]

Even as the peasants were being punished in Poltava and Khar'kov, disorders occurred in neighboring Kherson, Ekaterinoslav, and Bessarabia, and in the Volga provinces of Saratov and Tambov.[51] In Saratov the favorite tactic of the peasants was systematic arson, used to compel a recalcitrant landowner to rent his land to peasants on favorable terms, or even to force the sale of land to the peasants. The Saratov peasants also employed the tactics of boycotting and striking against noble landowners. The coordination of peasant activity and the high level of consciousness necessary to carry out such tactics were the result of a "chronic state" of struggle against Saratov landowners, revolutionary literature read by the peasants, and peasant discussion of the Khar'kov-Poltava disorders.[52] In Tambov the mood of the peasantry was so angry that one landowner wrote: "There is occurring some kind of *Pugachevshchina* [massive peasant rebellion]; you can't pass through the countryside without hearing a threat. Nearby they burn all the grain of the land captain. They say that it is no use to hope; they have to go themselves and take the land from the rich."[53]

The growth of an apparently revolutionary movement among the peasantry of southern and central blacksoil Russia indicated that the ground was trembling beneath the feet of the Russian nobility. This development had a profound impact on noble politics.

THE PATRIARCHAL NOBILITY AND THE PEASANT QUESTION

The adherents of Russian patriarchalism seemed to have lost their confidence after the turn of the century. On the one hand, they watched the gradual revival of the peasant movement in the countryside. On the other hand, they witnessed the autocracy being buffeted by urban opposition: the assassinations of Minister of Education Bogolepov in 1901, and of Minister of Internal Affairs Sipiagin in 1902; the student disorders in Moscow and St. Petersburg in 1901; the May Day clash between Shlisselburg workers and the police in 1901 that ended in gunfire. Many patriarchalists suddenly came to see that the survival of the nobility required reforms that would improve peasant standards of living, and perhaps a substantial moderation of autocractic authority.

In the pages of former State Secretary Polovtsov's diary for 1901 there is a remarkable letter which Polovtsov sent to Nicholas II. Polovtsov warned the tsar that without reform the fate of the regime was in jeopardy:

> Over the course of many centuries glorious in our history the government relied for support on large noble property. In 1861 that property was not only shaken, but sent on an ever widening path to destruction. This fact is most lamentable, but it cannot be corrected. Bureaucratic efforts to help the noble class are no more than phrases incapable of achieving genuine results. Perhaps over many years a reliable class of landowners will be created, but that is far away, and, in any case, nothing is being done now to bring this about. And meanwhile, the peasant masses, once led by the nobility but now placed in a somewhat hostile relationship to them, lives, multiplies, moves under the influence and leadership of all kinds of wild men, who pursue mainly their own personal, avaricious, and in most cases subversive ends. . . .
>
> More than once I have heard from peasants that if their father or grandfather had been allotted so much land in 1861, then the government was now obliged to give their sons and grandsons plots of the same size.
>
> What will happen if such a conviction leads from words to deeds, as there were attempts to do in the seventeenth and eighteenth centuries? The former soldier, torn from his milieu for 25 years of service, no longer exists. The soldier now so brave before foreign enemies abandons his family only for a short period and keeps solidarity with his family's interests, especially in land. On whose side will he stand in a contest of this sort over land?[54]

Polovtsov's solution to this problem was to abolish the commune and transfer peasants to household and personal ownership. He believed that the landless nobility should be "stricken out of legislative calculations," and the right to own property should be opened to all groups in the population. He also warned that the sphere of

205

bureaucratic officials' activity should be narrowed.[55] Yet despite his very courageous and forthright letter to Nicholas, Polovtsov was pessimistic that the tsar would make the proper decisions. A month after the letter was sent, he confided to his diary: "The young tsar is more and more contemptuous of the organs of his authority, and begins to believe in the efficacious force of his own autocratic power. . . . It is terrible to say, but under the influence of Shil'der's recently published book [on Paul I] one begins to sense something similar to Paul's time."[56] The dark hint here is to tyranny, madness, and regicide.

Polovtsov's letter to Nicholas was a sign that patience with the regime had worn thin by 1901. A year later, in the wake of the Poltava-Khar'kov uprising, there was new evidence that patriarchalists were not happy about government policy toward the peasantry. In Konstantinograd district, Poltava province, the district committee on the needs of agriculture compared the secure position of Western European landowners with the unfortunate position of the Russian nobility:

> The position of the landowners in the Russian Empire, and in particular, in Konstantinograd district, can scarcely be called satisfactory. Those landowners who have gone abroad in order to acquaint themselves with agriculture in other nations . . . have been struck by the order which exists in the countryside, even in states with such institutions as France.
>
> You travel down fine roads, down alleys of fruit trees bearing great loads of fruit, and it never occurs to anyone to knock down some one else's fruit. On the roadsides you see wonderful rows of grain, marvelous artificial meadows . . . and nowhere is there evidence of illegal pasturing. There are not even any guards or horse patrols. Everywhere you see cattle and horses, and when you ask if there is a problem with theft, you encounter surprised and uncomprehending expressions; nothing of the sort occurs here [in Western Europe]. You are not a little surprised by their discipline in these matters, despite liberal institutions.[57]

In Russia, even in years when there was no threat of peasant uprising, order and discipline were characteristically absent in the countryside. The Konstantinograd landowners devoted long, censorious passages of their report to description of the endemic disorder of rural society. These passages deserve citation because they highlight the problem of landowners everywhere in southern and central Russia.

The Peasant Question

Let us examine how our landowners live in the countryside. During four months of winter, one month of spring and one of fall—six months altogether—the roads of the district are completely or partially impassable; to try to secure supplies during this period is very risky. Recently, when the zemstvos began to spend highway funds, they built bridges and gates at the worst places on the roads. . . . One cannot fail to mention that the peasants mercilessly destroy these bridges and gates, which swiftly disappear. The peasants carried away one bridge almost entirely, and the vandalism only stopped after guards were posted.

The winter has ended and the landowner has finished planting crops, and there begins for him a difficult and sad situation. Every landowner hires someone to patrol his fields on horse; but if the landowner really wants to save his pasture and grain, the guard must patrol every night. Often the guard encounters gangs of poachers, so the landowner is glad if he drives them away from his crops and prevents illegal grazing. If the landowner has the misfortune to own an orchard, and if there is an especially good year for fruit, then he is threatened by another disaster: they [the peasants] will not only pick these fruits before they ripen, but will break off branches from the valuable trees to get an apple or pear. The garden plot of the landowner must be guarded with special care, or he will wind up without one.

The harvest of grain begins. Every landowner makes up his budget: he gives so much land in return for labor in harvesting season. According to his calculation he hires workers and rents machines. But his sharecroppers do not show up at his summons, since they are harvesting their own grain, and meanwhile the grain spoils and the landowner suffers great losses. It is disadvantageous for him to give out land in return for harvest labor, because it would be very easy to harvest grain by machine, and more profitable to plant the land now let out to peasants himself. But he knows that to deprive the peasant of this land would be to put him [the peasant] in an impossible position, which would cause an undesirable strain of social relations. The landowner must let out land and take his losses.

They have gathered the grain, and put it in sheeves, and again the landowner must guard it so that the peasants do not haul it away. The whole summer a landowner must be on guard so that they don't steal his horses, and the better the horses, the greater the chance of theft. And if they steal the horses, you can never find them, and it hardly pays to search for the lost horses, God knows. Yet to be in the middle of work season without draft animals is not desirable.

And so the landowner spends more than half his energy in guarding his estate during these six months. . . . Yet if he becomes a stingy master and makes the defense of his estate the most important thing, then fate prepares a terrible revenge. One of his threshing rooms will be turned into ashes, or a barn with cattle will be reduced to cinder.[58]

In the opinion of Konstantinograd landowners, farming conditions in their district were so bad that it no longer made sense to make capital improvements on an estate. The children of the nobility were leaving the countryside for a better life in the cities, and the older generation of landowners, despairing of a brighter future and tired of long and unprofitable work, would sooner or later be forced to sell their estates to the local peasantry. If noble agriculture was to survive at all, then the central government would have to improve security measures. One suggestion was that the government create a new rural police modeled after the French gendarmes or Austrian police force. "Living in the countryside the police would know every peasant and would prevent trespassing and theft." The landowners called on the land captains "to deal more objectively with landowners' interests, and with peasant interests." They also demanded strict enforcement of work contracts made with peasants. Aside from these repressive measures, the landowners petitioned the government to regulate the grain trade in favor of the Russian producers, and to reduce tariffs.[59]

Yet despite their obvious patriarchal inclinations, the Konstantinograd landowners realized that there had to be substantive reforms of the peasant economy and the peasants' political status if the problems of Poltava province were ever to be solved. They sent the government a second memorandum that dealt exclusively with the peasant question.[60] The second memorandum began with the observation that the decline of peasant agriculture after 1861 was the inevitable result of inadequate administrative supervision of the countryside and of the "ignorance and helplessness" of the peasantry. Turning to the economic reasons for the shortcomings of peasant agriculture, the document mentioned irrational farming techniques (the improper use of fallow, waste of seed, lack of fertilization) and the inefficient organization of arable (*cherespolosnost'*, parcellization, and distance from peasant villages). The committee concluded that a viable peasant economy was "impossible, given such antiquated systems." One solution for the problem was to hire a district agronomist, who would be responsive to local needs and to an agency of the central government concerned with agriculture. The committee called on the Peasant Bank to acquire property to rent to the poor peasants and on peasant resettlement programs to deal with the lower strata of the peasantry as well as the kulaks. The committee endorsed the construction of grain elevators for peasant produce and criticized the Ministry of Finance for not acting on a similar proposal by the Konstantinograd zemstvo.

In the third section of the memorandum, the committee attacked limitations on peasants' civil and juridical rights. The committee contended that "the main impetus for progress in industry and other enterprises was always personal initiative and independence, based on freedom of the individual and the right of property, the right to possess and freely to dispose of one's property. Without that freedom and certainty of his rights a person's endeavors [*predpriimchivost'*] are paralyzed and his energy is diminished."[61] The committee recommended the abolition of communal obligations, of limitations on individual landownership, and of travel restrictions. It demanded that peasants be made legal equals of the rest of the population. This proposal would have destroyed the communal system in Russia, thereby releasing considerable energy in the private economic sector.

It may be worthwhile to note that one result of the Konstantinograd committee's proposal would have been the end of corporal punishment in Russia. Liberals had been campaigning for decades to do away with corporal punishment, but the Konstantinograd committee was not dominated by liberals. It is especially significant that such a short time after the government had brutally suppressed the 1902 peasant rising, nobles in the very province where the rebellion occurred asked the government to abolish corporal punishment. This step may be interpreted as indicating disapproval of the government's methods of dealing with disorder.

The Poltava district committee on the needs of agriculture followed a different procedure than the Konstantinograd committee in preparing recommendations to the government. The chairman of the Poltava committee, Marshal M. A. Eristov, managed to divide participants into three commissions: one on technical problems of farming, one on general and juridical issues, and one on economic questions. Each commission presented recommendations to the district committee. The conclusions of the latter two commissions were interesting because they were similar to the decisions reached in neighboring Konstantinograd, although they were more elaborate and perhaps even more radical.

The conclusions of the general-juridical commission indicate that commission members made the restoration of social order their primary objective. They asserted:

Neither technical nor economic reforms will help the countryside unless a reliable system for the suppression of crime can be established. Today the people neither respect nor value other people's prop-

erty, and they light-heartedly steal from melon patches and vegetable gardens. They take fruit from the orchards and gather others' grain. This is done by professional thieves, and not out of need, and by ordinary people just for amusement. [Under such circumstances] no technical improvements can be introduced on a broad scale. . . .
The absence of respect for law places a limit on the introduction of cultural reforms.[62]

Like their counterparts in Konstantinograd, the Poltava commissioners contrasted the lawlessness of Russia with the order of Western European agriculture, and they petitioned for a reorganization of Russian rural police at the treasury's expense. Yet the Poltava commissioners did not consider repression an adequate answer to rural problems:

To eliminate the current rural disorders we need an extensive educational program, a constant flow of knowledge into the countryside, the equalization of the peasantry with other Estates in legal, juridical, and administrative affairs, the inculcation of respect for one's rights and the rights of others, and an understanding of one's responsibilities. We need a forum in which legal rights can really be protected. . . . To guard property and the general order in the countryside we do not require [so much] police reorganization, as general cultural measures.[63]

Turning to specific proposals, the commissioners asked that the government abolish limitations on the peasants' rights to own and dispose of private property. They urged the government to build more roads for general use, and they called for greater expenditures on resettlement of surplus peasant populations. Perhaps the most important proposal made by the Poltava juridical commission was for greater independence for the district zemstvo. The commission linked agricultural progress to local self-government and described the zemstvo "as the only competent agency for the implementation of measures aimed at the development and improvement of agriculture." The commission attacked the government for restricting zemstvo jurisdiction and suggested a number of changes in the current law. The first change was the elimination of noble predominance in the zemstvo by arranging elections so that the people would be more strongly represented. The peasants would elect their representatives directly, and the property requirement for other delegates would be reduced substantially. The second major change was the elimination of restrictions on zemstvo jurisdiction over education, food procurement, and local public works. Zemstvos would also be authorized to cooperate among themselves to fight disasters such as epidemics and crop failures. The commission also proposed to create "an inter-zemstvo agency for the discussion and debate of questions relevant to zemstvo activity."[64] While this proposal was not a constitutional project, it did suggest some sort of national assembly to deal with internal affairs.

The commission on economic questions also emphasized the import of education and respect for property, both of which were conditions sine qua non for agricultural improvement. The commission said that "the general forms of economic life . . . have not improved, productivity has not increased. New shortages have appeared and the needs of the countryside have not diminished; they have grown." Of particular concern to the commission members was the lack of land for peasant cultivation. "The problem of land shortage is crucial for Poltava district, since more tillers of the soil have insufficient land. . . . Many peasants cannot find work near home and every year are forced to look for work in the south—an unproductive waste of time and resources." This problem could only be solved by a government program to relocate the poor peasantry as well as the prosperous, and by a new set of bank regulations that would permit loans to poor families. The Peasant Bank and the Noble Land Bank would be combined in an All-Estate Land Bank which would give greater attention to the needy. The commission recommended that the government abandon taxation that harmed rural Russia and benefited industry; such unfair taxes included customs duties, excessive railroad tariffs, and high indirect taxes on sugar and alcohol. Redemption payments were also criticized as burdensome to the peasantry and unnecessary from a budgetary standpoint.[65]

The Poltava district committee accepted most recommendations of the general-juridical and economic commissions. This acceptance was further proof that even Poltava's conservative nobles considered fundamental reform of the social and economic system a necessity.

Two districts in Khar'kov province, Bogodukhov and Valkov, were affected directly by the 1902 peasant uprising. The Bogodukhov district committee on the needs of agriculture met in October 1902 and formulated eleven proposals for economic and social change. It is difficult to tell what ideological factors contributed to the committee's conclusions because the minutes of the meeting were not published.[66] However, the proposals themselves seem to combine repression and reform. One committee suggestion was that any seizure of land for personal use be considered a violation of criminal law. Another idea was that two police officers be assigned to the location and recovery of stolen horses in every community [*stan'*]. These

defenses of a more powerful police presence were balanced by proposals to abolish the communal system of cultivation, to resettle
peasants with plots of less than three desiatins, to found an agricultural bank for persons from all Estates, and to lower interest rates
in the Peasant Bank. The Bogodukhov district committee did not
advocate major political reforms, but it mentioned that agriculture
in Russia suffered from the absence of an institution that would
defend its interest at the highest bureaucratic level.

The Valkov district committee endorsed a report written by the
committee chairman, district gentry marshal V. V. Shirkov.[67] Shirkov
asserted that improvements in material conditions and legal reforms
were not sufficient to solve the problems of rural Russia. What Russia
needed was a peasantry that believed deeply in fundamental moral
principles. According to Shirkov, this moral education could never
be achieved by law "which operates in a strict and therefore narrow framework of demonstrable right and wrong." Nor could it be
achieved by schools "which observe their students only a few hours
of the day, and for only a few years in their lives." Moral education
could be directed only by the Church. "The Russian people have the
real treasure of a true church, whose schools are the only genuine
source of moral goodness."[68]

But the church was unable to fulfill its mission because priests,
especially in rural areas, were not salaried. The priests were caught
up in the difficult battle to survive and could not devote sufficient
attention to preaching. Shirkov's solution for this problem was to
pay priests an annual salary from the state treasury. This material
support would be justified by a decrease in peasant crime, because
religious instruction would make "falsehood and crime unthinkable."

Shirkov's ideological standpoint was obviously conservative and
patriarchal. He thought religion was the most effective means of
social control and recommended close cooperation between the Orthodox Church and the state. Yet Shirkov was also a realist. He
knew that religious instruction about the sacred nature of property
would not make the peasants respect property. Religious reform and
secular reform would have to occur simultaneously. Therefore, Shirkov called for the abolition of the peasant communes and the creation of a class of small proprietors. To the criticism that this would
transform many peasants into a rural proletariat, Shirkov answered:
"This will not worsen the situation, since the members of communes
are now nothing other than proletarians. . . . They will be the inevitable victims in the relentless march of progress. With time they
will find their places in the new order."[69] The proposal for abolition
of the commune was accompanied by petitions to reform the Noble

and Peasant Land Banks and to reduce indirect taxes on items such as sugar and beer.

It should be apparent from the preceding discussion that in the four districts most affected by the spring 1902 peasant uprising, the landed nobility favored major economic reform. The noble leaders in these districts were most concerned that order be established in the countryside. Yet they realized that neither repression nor religion could insure social stability, and so they urged the government to deal constructively with the peasant question. Real stability would require the abolition of communal tenure, the reorganization of the credit system, and the reduction of the peasants' tax burden. These reforms implied a complete break with the old governmental procedure of overtaxing rural Russia to pay for industrial development, and they suggested that the government would have to rethink all its outmoded assumptions about the relationship between the commune, the peasant mentality, and rural law and order.

The Khar'kov-Poltava committee reports were most significant as symbols of a far-reaching change within the patriarchal nobility. Earlier these nobles had supposed that the key to the agrarian problem was government aid to the nobility; it was now evident that neither government nor nobility could survive without a prior resolution of the peasant question. As N. N. Kovalevsky wrote in a report suppressed by the governor of Khar'kov province: "We cannot begin to battle the mosquitoes until we have dealt with the vampires. . . . The agricultural industry cannot be improved to any appreciable degree without first eliminating the main causes of the present condition in the villages."[70] Thus, in the 184 district committees on agriculture to debate the value of the peasant commune, some 125 opposed its retention.[71] Many traditional, patriarchal Russian nobles had defected from support of the social status quo.

It must be noted, however, that certain adherents of Russian patriarchalism refused to abandon the peasant commune and wished to maintain or restore the old ascendancy of the nobility in the countryside. This disposition was especially strong inside the Ministry of Internal Affairs before Plehve's death. In October 1903 the Ministry finished a draft project that would have maintained the commune, while allowing peasants greater freedom to leave it for economic reasons. The draft project also endorsed preservation of Estate divisions in Russia's legal order and declared peasant allotments inalienable.[72] In early 1904 the Ministry presented its draft project to provincial committees composed mostly of nobles who gave the main principles outlined above preliminary approval. However, Plehve's assassination and the general growth of anti-government sentiment permitted these same committees to back away from the project's principles in the summer and fall of 1904.[73] In the end, Plehve's project was a dead letter.

By 1905 the defenders of the peasant commune and of old-style patriarchal relationships in the countryside were a small minority of nobles on the extreme right wing of the political spectrum. These nobles looked on the commune as a uniquely Russian institution under attack by liberals, "cosmopolitans," and Witte. The patriarchalists made their last bureaucratic stand on behalf of the commune in late 1904 and early 1905 during meetings of the Special Commission on the Needs of Agriculture. Senator N. A. Khvostov, a larger landowner and fervent nationalist, told the commission that "a group of true Russian people could never accept the abolition of the commune, nor the destruction of the family life of the peasants."[74] Although two other commission members shared his view, the majority sided against Khvostov. After this defeat, unreconstructed patriarchalists had nowhere to turn except to the extragovernmental, anti-Semitic pressure groups of the radical right.[75] Unfortunately for the patriarchalists, few of these groups were hospitable to purely nobiliary ambitions.

THE PEASANT QUESTION
IN THE EMERGENCE
OF RUSSIAN LIBERALISM

While the revival of the peasant movement forced many patriarchalists to acknowledge the need for peasant reform, it strengthened the resolve of meliorists and egalitarians to persuade the government to change its peasant policies. The attempts at persuasion took the form of personal appeals to the tsar and royal family; the extralegal organization of reformers and the coordination of their efforts; and finally, the foundation of the Russian liberation movement.

Of the personal appeals to the tsar and royal family on the peasant question the most noteworthy were Tolstoy's letters to Nicholas II and the Grand Duke Nikolai Mikhailovich in 1902. Tolstoy wrote bluntly to the tsar that "autocracy is an obsolete form of government which may suit the needs of a people somewhere in Central Africa, cut off from the whole world, but not the needs of the Russian people."[76] Autocracy, Tolstoy reasoned, depended on violence for its perpetuation. Yet, he told the tsar, "the people can be oppressed by violent measures, but they cannot be governed by them." The way of redemption lay in the tsar's renunciation of violence as well as in renunciation of the principle of private property. "I personally think that the private ownership of land is just as obvious and as crying an injustice as serfdom 50 years ago. I think that its abolition will place the Russian people on a high level of independence, well-being, and contentment."[77] Surprisingly, Nicholas II did not react to Tolstoy's effrontery by ordering the writer's arrest. Instead, Grand Duke Nikolai Mikhailovich, a friend of Tolstoy's, sent a private rejoinder. Tolstoy responded with a second letter, this time addressed to the grand duke, in which he defended himself against the charge of being an unrealistic idealist. "The realization of my idea which seems so unrealizable to you is incomparably more possible than what they are trying to do now—support an obsolete autocracy without any higher idea, but only autocracy for the sake of autocracy."[78]

The positions taken by Tolstoy in his 1902 letters were nothing new; what was new and quite extraordinary was Tolstoy's presumption that he, as a citizen equal to the emperor, could tell the emperor to abolish private property and renounce violence. Twenty-one years earlier Tolstoy's letter of advice to Alexander III was addressed to "Your Imperial Majesty." Tolstoy's 1902 letter to Nicholas was addressed "Dear Brother." These two salutations represented two different sociopolitical worlds: the world of 1881 in which deference and patronage were the lubricants of all social interactions, and the world after 1900 in which equality and fraternity were being born. Tolstoy was both an instrument and a recorder of this seismic shift.

A second form of pressure on the government was the extralegal organization of reformists against peasant policy. After the zemstvo congress of 1896, the government forbade meetings of the national zemstvo leadership to coordinate zemstvo activity. However, zemstvo leaders soon found ways to circumvent the prohibition. In 1899 a circle of zemstvo and noble activists met in the so-called Beseda circle.[79] The purpose of Beseda included discussion of certain aspects of zemstvo affairs and "the facilitating of unanimous and authoritative declarations by zemstvo and noble assemblies on urgent questions."[80] Beseda made several contributions to the agrarian reform movement by sponsoring publication of books and articles on the peasant question.[81]

The Beseda group was also responsible for circulating the 1901 "Letter from Zemstvo Veterans" which urged zemtsy to demand political and economic reforms at the winter sessions of the provincial zemstvo assemblies. The letter was a moral indictment of government policies toward the peasantry: "Chronic harvest failures and unbearable taxation in the form of redemption payments and direct taxes have literally ruined the people, causing their physical degeneration." The letter asked: "Is it possible to remain politically inactive and to participate passively in the progressive impoverishment and corruption of the Motherland?"[82] The zemstvo veterans expressed frustration that their own efforts to help the peasantry had been blocked by the central government's constant interference. "Every step of the zemstvo as a public agency is bound by a spider's web of numerous circulars by various ministers."[83] The solution to the problems of the people was to sweep away the spider's web. The zemstvo charter should be changed to broaden the zemstvo's powers and jurisdiction, to give it unfettered powers of taxation, to eliminate administrative supervision over local decisions. Simultaneously, the zemstvo veterans recommended the equalization of peasant rights with those of other social Estates and the abolition of the Estate, or curial system of zemstvo elections.[84] As Schmuel Galai has noted, the "Letter from Zemstvo Veterans" had little immediate effect on zemstvo assemblies[85] but, by mid-1902 after the Poltava-Khar'kov uprising, the letter found a more receptive audience.

The delayed impact of the 1901 letter illustrated the strengths and liabilities of Beseda. On the one hand, Beseda was an important forum for discussion. Its deliberate avoidance of members "with a marked party coloration"[86] certainly facilitated the free exchange of opinions by its members and the charting of long-term strategy. On the other hand, Beseda tended to be aloof from the day-to-day struggles of the zemstvos, and hence its recommendations did not always have the desired immediate impact. Moreover, nonpartisanship meant that Beseda publications on the peasant question did not reflect a single point of view, but rather the opinions of individual authors. Hence, Beseda seemed to speak to the public and the crown in a divided counsel.[87] Ultimately, Beseda's contribution to the liberation movement was that of midwife to other, more effective political organizations.

Another effort at political mobilization of reformists occurred in 1902 in the wake of the government's announcement of district and provincial meetings of the Special Convocation on the Needs of Agriculture. D. N. Shipov, a member of Beseda, wrote a letter to all provincial zemstvo board chairmen asking them to meet at his apartment in Moscow in order to consider the zemstvo response to the government announcement. Fifty-two zemstvo leaders met with Shipov between 23 and 25 May 1902.[88] The group was unanimous in its conviction that the Witte committees represented an attempt by the government to deal with the fundamental questions of rural life without consulting the zemstvos directly. In fact, as Shipov reported, the government had put the question: "Is the zemstvo to be—or not to be?"[89] Having thus interpreted the government's intentions, the zemstvo activists debated whether to protest by boycotting committee sessions or to participate with the intention of compelling the government to consider local needs from the zemstvo perspective. After considerable debate the group decided that zemtsy should participate in the Witte committees as private individuals, but that they should press for the adoption of a five-point program: (1) to guarantee the peasant legal rights, including equality with other classes, freedom from administrative supervision [*opeka*], proper trials in courts of law, and freedom from corporal punishment; (2) to provide universal access to public education, to raise the intellectual level of schools, and to eliminate obstacles to education outside public schools; (3) to eliminate the Estate principle in zemstvo organization, to bring zemstvos closer to the people, and to guarantee zemstvos economic and political independence; (4) to solve the problems of contemporary government economic and fiscal policy, such as high indirect taxes and a budget too great for the nation to support; (5) to allow freedom to debate these matters in the local committees on the needs of agriculture.[90]

The Shipov group program was interesting for two reasons. First, it interpreted the needs of the local population as primarily cultural and political. Thus, considerable attention was paid to legal reforms such as the elimination of Estate barriers, guarantees of equal rights under the law, and freedom of speech. Second, the Shipov program was surprisingly vague on economic issues. Except for a fleeting reference to the dangers of overtaxing the peasantry, the zemtsy were silent about the national economy. The vital matter of land reform was not mentioned at all.

The Shipov program helped set the agenda for moderate reformists in the Witte committees.[91] The Soviet historian M. S. Simonova, who studied all the proposals introduced in 1902/03, cited the deliberations of the Sudzha district committee in Kursk province as typical of the moderate reformists.[92] The Sudzha committee began by rejecting the government's technical orientation to the agrarian crisis and by asserting that the primary problems of rural Russia were the regime's political shortcomings. One step toward elimination of the peasant economic crisis was to give peasants equal rights. Another was to transform the peasant commune "into a voluntary association for the cultivation of allotments." This latter would be accomplished by canceling the legal and fiscal obligations that characterized existing communal life.

The chairman of the Sudzha committee, district marshal A. V. Evreinov, thought that the tragedy of the 1861 peasant reform was that while the peasants were given some personal rights, they were left dependent upon noble landowners. The redemption payments required by the reform were one symptom of this dependence, thus Evreinov wanted to eliminate such payments. He also urged the government to broaden the resettlement program for land-poor peasants. The committee under Evreinov's guidance criticized Witte's forced industrialization plan and asked the government to lower indirect taxes that burdened the peasantry.

The committee also complained about the counterreforms of the 1890s and attacked government interference with the zemstvo. In general, the committee was desirous of a more decentralized system of government that would allow zemstvo activists freedom of initiative in local matters.[93]

As Simonova showed, liberal journalists were delighted by the Sudzha program, but Minister of Internal Affairs Plehve was not. On 15 July 1902 Plehve wrote to Witte: "I am inclined to be especially hard on Sudzha, because it is one of several focal points of the zemstvo revolution."[94] Plehve and Nicholas II administered personal reprimands to Evreinov and district zemstvo chairman P. D. Dolgorukov. On 14 September 1902 Evreinov announced to the Sudzha committee that he had been forbidden to discuss questions connected with zemstvo independence, freedom of speech and religion. Plehve then sacked Evreinov as district marhsal of the nobility and had Dolgorukov dismissed from all official posts and banned from public activity for five years.[95]

In retrospect, it is clear that these harsh reprisals were undeserved. Evreinov and his colleagues said nothing that had not been said before in zemstvo and noble assemblies. The Sudzha program was not much different than the reform programs advocated by patriarchalist nobles in Poltava and Khar'kov, though it is clear that Evreinov did not devote as much attention to the restoration of order as did the southerners. In addition, the evidence suggests that the government's harshness backfired: a large number of district and provincial committees embraced aspects of the Shipov May 1902 program. Table 9.2 shows Galai's calculations of levels of support for four main points in Shipov's recommendation.

Thus, the reformists had strong support for universal education and broadened zemstvo rights, and some support for changes in the legal and financial position of the peasantry. Given the regime's openly declared hostility to the mere discussion of such reforms, the reformists had every reason to rejoice over Shipov's achievement in guiding committee deliberations.

However, not every reform-minded committee followed Shipov's

TABLE 9.2
Support of Shipov's 1902 Program
in the Witte Committees

Main points of reform	District number	Percent of total (N = 586)	Provincial number	Percent of total (N = 82)
Peasant rights	134	25	13	15
Education	234	43	49	60
Zemstvo rights	202	37	25	30
Financial policy	104	19	12	14

SOURCE: Schmuel Galai, *The Liberation Movement in Russia 1900–1905* (Cambridge, 1975), p. 153; S. N. Prokopovich, *Mestnye liudi o nuzhdakh Rossii* (St. Petersburg, 1904), p. 259.

moderate program. A much more radical approach to the peasant question was apparent in the Voronezh district committee, which met in August 1902. The stage was set for debate by two firebrands: a seventy-year-old schoolteacher and populist, N. F. Bunakov, and a physician, S. V. Martynov. Bunakov excoriated the government for its timid approach to contemporary problems, for its interest in "agricultural institutes and cooperatives, experimental farms, and the control of land erosion." These technical problems only drew attention from the real issue: the need for a fundamental change in the Russian way of life.[96] Catalyzed by Bunakov's comments, the Voronezh committee set up a commission to formulate a program of action. The commission made the usual criticisms of the educational system, the legal order, and Witte's industrialization plan; it called for familiar reforms in each area. Yet the Voronezh commission went beyond its counterparts in two respects. First, it urged the government to reform the political system from top to bottom. At the local level there would be an elected all-Estate government [*mel'-kaia zemskaia edinitsa*]; at the district and provincial levels there would be elected zemstvos. At the national level there would be an all-Russian zemstvo with the right to initiate legislation. This, according to Simonova, was to be a kind of constituent assembly under the tsar. Second, the Voronezh commission advocated the nationalization of land. There would be a state land fund consisting of treasury land and additional land bought by the Peasant Land Bank; land from this fund would be distributed to poor peasants. The commission justified its position on land reform as follows: "It is impossible to convince the peasant that there is no land for him, because his [belief] is not the result of outside influences, but is his own deep conviction . . . that a tiller of the soil cannot live without land."[97]

Compared with the Shipov program, the Voronezh program was a signficant shift to the left. It envisioned more sweeping political reforms than did Shipov, and it addressed the question of land reform. The Voronezh plan anticipated the Constitutional-Democratic idea of a national land reserve. Minister Plehve was so upset by the Voronezh deliberations that he arrested Martynov and Bunakov, and disciplined others on the committee.[98]

In April 1903 Shipov made still another attempt to strengthen the zemstvo role in solving local problems, including the peasant question. On 24 and 25 April he invited twenty-eight provincial zemstvo activists to a private meeting in St. Petersburg to discuss zemstvo problems. The participants debated two proposals: the Shipov proposal that any legislation affecting local needs be turned over to provincial zemstvo assemblies for preliminary approval; and a proposal by K. K. Arseniev of St. Petersburg that elected zemstvo representatives be invited to participate in the central government's discussions of laws entailing local reforms. Shipov's proposal was approved, but Arseniev's idea was narrowly defeated by a vote of 15 to 13.[99]

The results of this meeting show that by April 1903, the movement to reform peasant life was on the brink of becoming a movement to reform the structure of the central government. Shipov himself opposed a collision with the government over reform of the central apparatus, yet his political-cultural interpretation of the peasant question and his efforts to build a united zemstvo front had led to precisely such a collision.

The third form of pressure on the government was the effort to build a Russian liberation movement through the agency of the newspaper *Osvobozhdenie*. A newspaper of the united opposition was by no means a new idea, but previous newspaper projects in the 1880s and 1890s had failed.[100] The success of Struve in establishing *Osvobozhdenie* owed much to the generally recognized need for local reform, and particularly for a solution to the peasant question. *Osvobozhdenie* was financed by Russians of noble and professional backgrounds who wanted an organ in which all oppositional and reform groups could freely discuss these issues. In his first editorial, Struve did not deal with the agrarian question, except indirectly. Describing the liberation movement, Struve wrote:

> This movement, by its nature, is liberal and democratic: liberal because it aims to win freedom, and democratic because it defends the vital interests, material and spiritual, of the masses. Even the extreme Russian parties do not go beyond broad political and economic reforms in the democratic spirit. These goals unite all Russians, aside from the selfish partisans of the existing bureaucratic nightmare.[101]

Struve's editorial was a guarded statement of the general principles informing the liberation movement; it hinted at a radical position on the peasant question, but remained extremely vague.

The same issue of *Osvobozhdenie* contained two other statements— one by constitutionalists and the other by zemstvo activists. The constitutionalist statement was a programmatic document in favor of individual rights, equality before the law, civil freedom, and popular representation. The constitutionalists tried to finesse the land issue by pleading that there was no sense in writing a catalog of popular grievances. These grievances would be taken up by the legislature when political freedom had been won.[102] The second statement, an "Open Letter from Zemstvo Activists," represented the views of nonconstitutionalist liberals. While these moderate liberals failed to provide a well-fashioned economic reform program, they did comment on recent peasant disorders. It is clear that government interference with zemstvo operations, the recent student disorders, and strikes had frightened the moderate liberals, but not nearly so much as agrarian uprisings. "The recent agrarian disorders, which produced so many victims and so much violence, especially force us to melancholy reflections. The disorders occurred in a milieu that we know well, and the reasons for their development are clear and understandable.

"Obviously, revolutionary propaganda had great effect on the soil of popular impoverishment, ignorance, incomprehension of the elementary bases of civil rights, lawlessness, and the estrangement of educated elements from the people." The zemtsy continued: "All of this has been caused by our financial and economic politics, which squeeze the last juices out of the countryside; by the obstacles to popular education; by the absence of order; by the popular distrust of the courts."[103]

The vagueness of Struve's editorial, the avoidance of the land issue by constitutionalists, and the hand wringing of the zemtsy over recent peasant disorders indicated that there was much nervousness about the agrarian situation, but no disposition to fashion a common agrarian program. This early reticence gradually disappeared as it became obvious that radical intellectuals, members of the third element, and the continuation of peasant violence made declaration of a land program imperative. The growing conviction of the need for a clear position on the peasant question coincided with pressure from Miliukov and others to create a liberal political party.[104] Both matters were discussed in the summer of 1903 when leaders of the liberation movement convened in a summit meeting at Schaffhausen, Switzerland.[105]

The Schaffhausen conference resolved to found a Union of Liberation to coordinate liberal activity and communicate with the masses. It also decided to issue a policy statement on social issues. The statement appeared in *Osvobozhdenie* under the title "On the Agrarian Question."[106]

The article commenced with a comment on the close historical relationship between Russian liberalism and socialism. There was no divorce between the two concepts in Russia, as there had been in England; indeed, the concepts were identical and inseparable in their basic ethical intent—human liberation.[107] Therefore, it was quite natural for liberals to adopt an agrarian reform program. Next, the liberals noted that "the whole structure of the national and state economy—directly and indirectly—rests on the broad back of the peasant, and the structure will be shaken if the peasant cracks or falters." In short, said the liberals, the Physiocrats were right: *pauvres paysans—pauvre royaume.*[108] Yet the autocracy was powerless to solve the peasant question; in fact, it was "the main obstacle to agricultural progress in Russia." To overturn the autocracy would mean to move toward a solution of the peasant question, even as the French Revolution had been a giant step toward economic justice.[109]

According to the liberals there were two paths available for the rural economy: the peasant-democratic path, and the class-aristocratic path. The autocracy had followed the second path, which the liberals described as profoundly immoral and economically senseless. The first steps down the immoral road had been taken in 1861, when the peasant emancipation freed the serfs legally but victimized them economically. Then in the reign of Alexander III, the autocracy had inaugurated "an era of open, even cynical, support for the nobility." This era had led from the Noble Land Bank to the counterreforms, and to the pro-noble legislation of Nicholas II's reign. Pursuit of privilege and class rule had damaged the rural economy and prevented the adoption of genuine local self-government which would have been more responsive to the needs of the people.[110] Continuation of autocratic rule would inevitably mean the perpetuation of an immoral, inefficient, cynical, and undemocratic rural regime.

The liberals would end political injustice and follow the peasant-democratic path of development. Their first priority would be "the democratization of landownership," and the "completion of the peasant emancipation, based on the principle of personal ownership of the land one cultivates." This program would mean "abolition of all the privileges of the nobility and of noble landowning that have been created in modern times."

Here the Russian liberation movement must take as its model the Great French Revolution, which destroyed the vestiges of feudalism. First of all, the privileges of the nobility in the area of cheap and accessible credit must be destroyed by the closure and liquidation of the Noble Land Bank. . . . It is also desirable to abolish limitations on the mobilization of noble land, which, as the experience of England and Prussia show, have a very reactionary political and economic impact. Generally the fall of the autocracy must be accompanied, in our opinion, by the eradication of the very terms "nobility" and "peasantry." All social barriers must be broken categorically.[111]

In order to aid the transfer of land to the needy peasants, the liberals would have had the state purchase property then at the disposal of the Noble Land Bank. The state would also assume the role of middleman in the land market; it would buy land from private parties to distribute later to the peasantry. If the state land fund proved inadequate to meet popular needs, then the government would exercise the right of compulsory alienation of private land. It would, of course, compensate former owners for their losses. The state would also create a "democratic right to rent land," patterned perhaps on the Ulster covenant in Ireland. The liberals ended with a rhetorical flourish:

Our countryside is like a sick person, afflicted with several illnesses and stuck in a dark and dank cellar, where neither light nor air penetrate. It is useless to treat the sick person while he lacks the conditions in which a healthy person can survive. But give him a proper environment, and many afflictions will disappear without any medical treatment, and it will become possible to diagnose the other illnesses. Our sick person needs light and freedom. Give him these priceless blessings. And . . . *let Carthage be destroyed!*[112]

The agrarian policy of the Russian liberation movement was in every sense a historical landmark. It declared for the first time that meliorism and egalitarianism, liberalism and socialism were fully compatible one with the other, and that their logical culmination was peasant-democratic revolution against the autocracy. More importantly, the new agrarian policy signified the end of noble politics as such for the reformist nobility. Henceforth, in choosing to be a Russian liberal, one buried one's identity as a noble: one chose citizenship and with it the eradication of all privileges of the nobility, of the very terms "nobility" and "peasantry." The pursuit of political liberty and social justice left no room for the selfish interests of the First Estate.

The danger of the new agrarian policy was that it would be too radical for its constituency among the nobility. In the short run, that was not the case for three reasons. First, the immediate problem facing the liberation movement by late 1903 was how to win a constitution. When the leadership of the liberation movement returned home from Schaffhausen, they worked hard to establish coherent liberal organizations so that constitutional agitation would be possible. Thus, the Union of Zemstvo Constitutionalists, convened in November 1903, concentrated on organizational tasks and even put off the beginning of pro-constitutional work in the zemstvos until 1904.[113] Second, the beginning of the Russo-Japanese War in January 1904 distracted attention from the social front. Through much of 1904, liberals debated whether constitutional demands could be pressed legitimately in wartime. Third, most nobles with leadership positions in the liberation movement believed that they were morally obliged to stand behind social justice, whatever the personal cost. Even Shipov, who was so careful not to offend the central government by demanding a constitution, looked on the equalization of Estates and land redistribution as ethically desirable. Thus in November 1904, when the Union of Liberation announced its existence and published its "declaration of intent" on social policy, there was no desertion by liberal nobles.

By the time the banquet campaigns had begun in the winter of 1904/05, the Russian nobility were disaffected from the central government. Patriarchal nobles were convinced that the government had to change its policies toward the rural sector to ward off revolution and to preserve the First Estate. Meliorists and egalitarians had raised successively the banners of economic reforms, structural political reform, and constitutionalism. At a time when Nicholas II needed the firm support of the landed elite to master popular unrest, he could not command it. It was James Harrington, a historian and pioneer social scientist, who wrote of England's seventeenth-century crisis in government: "A monarchy divested of its nobility has no refuge under heaven but an army." In 1905 Nicholas II found himself with no refuge under heaven but his army. He had no choice but to purchase the survival of his dynasty with rivers of blood.

Conclusion:
Noble Politics
in Comparative Perspective

In the quarter-century between 1881 and 1905, members of the Russian landed nobility sought to reconcile the continued existence of the First Estate with a changing social and political environment. At first, in the wake of the terrorist campaign from 1878 to 1881, there were hopes for a political resolution of Russia's crisis that would have incorporated the nobility into the central government's decision-making apparatus. Zemstvo liberals called for the convocation of a zemsky sobor in which the Russian land would "merge closely with the Sovereign," but the zemtsy failed to press the government for a formal limitation of the autocrat's prerogatives. Meanwhile, the Holy Retinue posed as prospective guardian of the national interest. It demanded that propertied elements of the nobility be given an advisory role in the fight against terrorism, a statutory right to sit on the State Council, and an undefined role in the zemsky sobor. When Alexander III's ministers recovered their courage after the regicide of 1 March, they disbanded the Holy Retinue and forbade zemstvos to raise sensitive political issues. This reassertion of the central government's traditional authority pushed liberalism and aristocratic-conservatism out of Petersburg political life for a generation.

The beginning of the Great Depression turned the attention of the landowning nobility to the problem of economic survival. Indeed, the Great Depression, which seriously affected the estates of the noble political leadership, transformed economic issues into the preoccupation of noble assemblies until after the turn of the century. Thus, the politics of structural political change was displaced by the politics of economic interest.

In the initial stage of the Great Depression lasting until 1891, noble interest politics was animated by resistance to the market economy. In a phrase that might have been used by Karl Marx, Iu. D. Rodionov complained that "money is faceless." Rodionov and other marshals worried that faceless capital would drive nobles from their ancestral homes and replace them with greedy predators who, caring only for profit, would one day turn Russia into a desert. Concerned marshals from the blacksoil belt and southern steppes petitioned the government to create a Noble Land Bank that would avert the ruin of the First Estate by offering loans at rates of interest lower than private banks. Marshals from seventeen provinces also advocated the adoption of new entail legislation that would legally obstruct the sale of noble land to other social groups. Unfortunately for the nobility, the provincial advocates of these new laws failed to agree on a common version of the proposed changes, thus making it easier for opponents of change to water down the final legislation. To the chagrin of Meshchersky and Katkov, the Noble Bank Statute provided for a commercially run operation that would grant loans only to hereditary nobles. The entail law, promulgated after twelve years of debate in 1899, was so weak that only one noble took advantage of its provisions in 1900.

By the late 1880s there were disturbing signs that noble resentment against the market and its surrogates might spill over into a frontal attack on government policy. In fact, that did occur during the second phase of the Great Depression after 1891, when some provincial nobles became convinced that economic pressures on the First Estate could not be alleviated without changes in existing government programs and agencies. Between 1891 and 1895 certain provincial marshals criticized the government's decisions to centralize the Noble Land Bank's operations and to run the bank as a competitive business charging high interest rates. In 1893 nobles from the central agricultural area and the Volga Basin became anxious over the government's new differential tariff policy, which facilitated export trade partly by attracting grain shipments from the eastern periphery and so allegedly threatened the ascendancy of central producers on the domestic market. These two issues led angry nobles to launch a general attack on the central government's agrarian policies, thus signaling the beginning of a struggle with Minister of Finance Witte over the fate of rural Russia.

From the tactical perspective this struggle was very interesting. Politically active nobles made a serious attempt to align themselves in a united front against Witte. The joint memorandum of January 1895, signed by eleven marshals and three private landowners from eight provinces, was the first example of concerted action. Then in early 1896, twenty-seven provincial marshals met in St. Petersburg and collaborated on a seventy-page memorandum concerning the needs of the nobility. From 1896 to 1902 nobles sat on government commissions formed to consider agrarian policies, among which the most notable were the Special Commission on the Nobility (1897–1899) and the Special Commission on the Needs of Agriculture. Despite the aggrieved nobles' attempts to coordinate their efforts and their use of new political forums, all the advantages in bureaucratic struggle lay with Witte. By his mastery of economic fact, the force of his office and personality, and his adroit political maneuvers, Witte divided his critics and took advantage of their disagreements. Although the government made minor adjustments in its bank and tariff policies, Witte managed to preserve intact the principles of differential tariffs and a centralized commercial Noble Land Bank. Despite the slow recovery of grain price levels following the nadir of the depression, Witte's victory in agrarian politics dashed the nobility's hopes for economic accommodation to the new order.

The turn of the century found Russian peasants in the blacksoil center and New Russia engaged in a serious struggle against local landlords. The 1902 uprisings in Poltava and Khar'kov and the high level of tension elsewhere in southern and central Russia led to a complete reassessment of political assumptions. The patriarchal nobility, who formerly had granted the peasant question only a contingent status, now recognized the necessity of peasant reforms, especially the abolition of the commune. Those nobles who formerly had recognized the need for peasant reforms were driven to demand structural political changes either to accompany economic reform or to serve as a precondition for economic reform. Among the structural changes advocated were the granting of zemstvo autonomy, the equalization of peasant civil rights with those of other social groups, the abolition of legally delimited Estates, and the adoption of a constitution. Here was the end of economic accommodation and the climax of the nobility's confrontation with the central government.

With the support for the Russian liberation movement by a substantial minority of provincial noble landowners and their allies in the intelligentsia, noble politics came full circle. After a quarter-century in which the politics of economic interest had displaced the advocacy of structural political change, the question of how Russia should be governed now returned to its rightful place on the national agenda. Yet there were important differences between the advocates of political change in 1881 and 1905. In 1881 both zemstvo liberals and the Holy Retinue portrayed themselves as saviors of the autocracy from terrorism. In 1905 liberal nobles joined with the intelligentsia and popular radicals in a united front against the autocracy. In 1881 political reform was not firmly connected with a concrete program of peasant reform; indeed, the Holy Retinue's bias was to preserve large landownership. In 1905 there was at least a temporary linkage between political and economic reform, although this linkage would later be broken. In 1881 the emphasis of zemstvo liberals was on the cooperation of social Estates in the zemstvo milieu; in 1905 liberals looked forward to the effacement of all legal barriers between Estates and the building of an egalitarian society. For liberal nobles in 1905, an egalitarian civil order was the end of their identity as nobles and the beginning of their life as citizens—the culmination of a dream born with the emancipation. As former Kozlov district marshal Alexander Ivanovich Novikov wrote in memoirs published in 1905: "I was able to kill off the man of *high life*, the landlord, the nobleman, and the land captain. I was able to become simply a human being, and there is nothing higher than that on this earth.[1]

NOBLE POLITICS AS AGRARIANISM

How did the reaction of Russian nobles to the depression compare with the reactions of grain producers in other nations? Let us take the examples of the United States, a net grain exporter and Russia's chief competitor on the world wheat market, and of Germany, a nation that became a net grain importer during the depression. In both cases farmers organized themselves into politically significant groups and attempted to win major economic and political reforms from the government. Both cases are well known in historical literature and thus are convenient for comparative purposes.[2]

American populism was an anti-hierarchical agrarian movement with a broad and heterogeneous social base. The roots of populism can be traced to the deep South and Texas, where cotton farmers struggled to liberate themselves from the so-called crop-lien system that forced them into perpetual debt, land tenancy, or land sale. These farmers joined together in a Farmers' Alliance, the goals of which included formation of purchasing and merchandising cooperatives that would break the power of farm creditors, and the creation of a political coalition that would insure the protection of popular interests. Between 1886 and 1892 the Farmers' Alliance underwent a significant transformation: on the one hand, its membership grew to encompass wheat farmers of the West and Midwest who were affected by the Great Depression, labor organizations, and also blacks in Texas and the deep South; on the other hand, its ideology was altered from a fairly parochial defense of Texan and southern farming interests into a comprehensive political platform the centerpiece of which was Charles W. Macune's "sub-treasury system." After a brief experience as a third party, the leadership of the populists decided to support William Jennings Bryan in the 1896 election. This decision to fuse populism with the Democratic ticket is usually interpreted as the end of populism as an independent national political force, though populist demands and the "populist style" continued to have resonance in American political life.

For two generations American historians have debated the nature of populism as a political movement. One camp of historians has argued that the populists were democratic, tolerant of racial and religious diversity, and progressive on economic and racial issues; other historians have accused the populists of racism, anti-Semitism, nativism, anti-intellectualism, and political reaction.[3] Whatever the ultimate resolution of this fierce debate, I should think it clear that the heart of populism was resistance to market institutions as constituted in the last third of the nineteenth century. From the beginning the populists worked against a commercial credit system which, in the words of one contemporary, "has brought about a state of dependence that reduces the great body of agricultural people to a condition of serfs."[4] In the cotton South, farmers depended for their very livelihood on the mercies of local store owners and other private lenders. In wheat- and corn-raising states like Kansas, farmers argued that "as for the interest rates, usury penalties and foreclosure provisions, 'creditors have had the laws their own way for a long time,' resulting in a system designed to benefit the lender not the borrower."[5]

A recent study has shown that in statewide elections in Kansas in 1890, counties with high proportions of mortgaged farmers tended to vote populist.[6] Populists from the West and Midwest also complained loudly about what they saw as excessively high rates charged by railroad shipping firms. Farmers from eastern Iowa were angered when they paid higher freight bills for shipments to Chicago than did farmers from Council Bluffs on Iowa's western border.[7] Kansas populists made reduction of railroad freight rates a standard item in their political platform between 1882 and 1897.[8] High and allegedly inequitable freight bills were the more galling to farmers where they had few grain elevators in which to store grains while awaiting favorable market prices; these farmers had to sell crops soon after harvest to commercial agents. Thus, all the market agencies with which farmers had to deal—banks, private lenders, the railroads, purchasing agents from the great grain-exporting firms—seemed to thwart what the farmers saw as their legitimate interests.

The desire of farmers to emancipate themselves from the hold of these market institutions led them in two directions. On the one hand, the Farmers' Alliance worked to establish cooperatives to buy necessary machinery and farm supplies in volume at low prices and to sell produce at advantageous prices. Lawrence Goodwyn, the leading contemporary historian of populism, has seen the cooperative movement as an attempt to create a democratic economy. According to Goodwyn, the cooperative experience was, in fact, the essence of populism.[9] On the other hand, the failure of the cooperatives in the late 1880s and the deepening of price depression compelled the populists to search for political solutions to their economic problems. The populists pressed state and federal governments for effective controls over credits and for even tighter regulation of the railroads. Eventually, dissatisfaction with the government's response to their grievances and disappointment over the lack of sympathic understanding by the two major political parties led the populists to question whether their goals could be achieved at all within the confines of the existing economic and political system.

By the early 1890s, populist theoreticians were elaborating an ever more sweeping indictment of the nation's monetary system, of industry, and of capitalism in general.[10] In 1892 when the People's Party constituted itself, leading populists not only backed Macune's subtreasury plan to restore agricultural income to pre-depression levels, they listened with sympathy to Ignatius Donnelly's fulminations about a conspiracy threatening mankind. In his famous preamble to the People's Party platform, Donnelly asserted:

> the supply of currency is purposely abridged to fatten usurers, bankrupt enterprise, and enslave industry. A vast conspiracy against mankind has been organized on two continents and it is rapidly taking possession of the world. If not met and overthrown at once it forebodes terrible social convulsions, the destruction of civilization, or the establishment of an absolute despotism.[11]

Suspicion of a plot against the common people was part of what Richard Hofstadter has called the populists' "social dualism."[12] History, in the words of populist Sockless Jerry Simpson, was "a struggle between the robbers and the robbed."[13] The robbers included bankers, industrialists, railroad owners, and anyone in a position to exploit farmers, laborers, petty merchants, and others who produced the wealth of America. During the mid-1890s some populists, such as Donnelly, Mary E. Lease, and Coin Harvey, engaged in rhetorical anti-Semitism, whereby the Rothchilds and other European Jewish financiers were blamed for the farmers' economic woes.[14] The Jews too were evidently seen as enemies of the common man.

To Populist anti-capitalism and anti-Semitism was added an element of nativism which held recent European immigrants responsible for the decline in the American standards of living. Nativism was by no means universal among populists;[15] however, certain leaders and propagandists of the movement did condemn "the dangerous and corrupting hordes of the old World."[16]

Populist conspiracy theories, anti-Semitism, and nativism were the negative sides of a retrospective agrarian utopia. If the enemies of the farmer could be conquered, America might return to a harmonious and blissful state in which the common man would prosper. In order for populism and virtue to triumph, however, the populists would have to win the adoption of their reforms through the political process. For many reasons this victory was never attained. The farmer-laborer coalition was too tenuous, the nation's farming interests too varied, the tasks of political organization too formidable for a third party to defeat Democrats and Republicans in a national election. Consequently, when William Jennings Byran and the Democrats offered partnership in an anti-gold and anti-industrialist campaign in 1896, the Populist leadership succumbed to temptation: they abandoned utopia to destroy a cross of gold.

German agrarianism distinguished itself from American populism in its economic origins, social roots, and political impact. The danger facing German grain producers in the late 1870s was that Russian and American grain sold on the European market would drive domestic German prices below the cost of production. An obvious remedy against foreign competition on the domestic market was the adoption of a protective tariff. In December 1878 over two hundred deputies of the Reichstag called on Bismarck for economic protection, and in spring 1879 Bismarck introduced a package of tariffs that would restore duties on iron and introduce a small levy on grains. The passage of this modest tariff in 1879 proved insufficient to protect German growers against worsening economic circumstances, and so Bismarck asked the Reichstag for more precipitate tariff hikes in 1885 and 1887.[17]

However, Bismarck's fall from power in 1890 and the accession of Caprivi as chancellor led to the gradual abandonment of agrarian protection in the early 1890s. In December 1891 the Reichstag accepted a treaty that significantly reduced agricultural tariffs levied on Austro-Hungarian imports, and in July 1892 Caprivi allowed Romanian wheat to enter Germany for duties comparable to those imposed on Austrian goods. The climax of Caprivi's anti-protectionist policy was the passage of the Russian trade treaty in 1894: in return for a reduction of customs duties imposed by Russia on industrial goods, the Germans agreed to allow Russian grain imports to pass with lower tariffs.[18]

Caprivi's "new course" set off a storm of protests from German growers. In February 1893 Caprivi's most determined opponents formed a new organization to fight him—the Bund der Landwirte, or League of Farmers. The Bund claimed an initial membership of 180,000. Half the membership and 141 of 250 local committees came from eastern Germany—the area traditionally dominated by the Junkers.[19] Although the Bund did publicize the needs of peasant smallholders in its daily newspaper, it was from the beginning a pressure group run by wealthy conservative Junkers mainly for the benefit of East Elbian estate owners.

At first the Bund der Landwirte concentrated its energies on winning economic concessions from the government. The 1893 program of the Bund called on the central government to raise import duties on agricultural commodities and especially to avoid commercial trade treaties with Russia and other nations who competed against German agricultural produce. It also asked that peasant tax burdens be decreased and that the central govenment carefully supervise the grain futures market in order to avoid arbitrary price fixing that would harm grain producers and consumers alike. The 1893 program reminded the government that "German agriculture is the first and most significant enterprise, the strongest support of the German Reich and its separate states."[20]

However, the Bund soon changed the focus of its attention from the narrow economic demands of 1893 to the broadest questions of German national identity. There are four aspects of the Bund's ideology that deserve attention. First, the Bund embraced the traditional German political and social order. Its members were monarchists who rejected modern representative government as a dangerous threat to the spiritual values of the German people. The leadership of the Bund may be described as authoritarian patriarchalists who fully subscribed to the view that the Junkers should govern the peasantry and provide the leadership of the state under the aegis of the Kaiser.[21] Second, the Bund combined the principles of modern nationalism with its traditional conservatism. As H.-J. Puhle has demonstrated, the Bund's nationalism was heavily influenced by social Darwinism and the racial thought of the nineteenth century. The Bund's leaders saw themselves as participants in a constant struggle for a "healthy national egoism" that would preserve the German masses from corrupting foreign elements as well as from racial and biological impurity.[22] Third, the Bund was characterized by its militant anti-Semitism. It accused the Jews of usury and of unfair banking practices, but also warned that Jews would infiltrate the officer corps of the German army and would even help lead Germans toward a liberal or socialist state. This economic and political anti-Semitism also had a clearly racial element. As the *Berliner Blatt* reported in 1910: "The struggle between the Bund der Landwirte and international finance capital that has raged for more than a decade is—one must not be deceived about this—in no way a purely economic struggle; at least as it is seen on Jerusalem Street it is not purely economic. Racially-conscious Jewry sees in the agrarians the true representatives of the German race."[23]

The fourth aspect of the Bund's ideology was its anti-industrial, anti-capitalist bias. The Bund quickly went beyond the defense of agrarian interests listed in the 1893 program to an attack against the capitalist ethos. Banks, industry, commerce, the stock exchange, all threatened the life blood of Germany and the stability of the German state itself. "There is today no conservative [*staatserhaltende*] politics that is not bound up with an anti-capitalist economic politics," noted a Bund publication in 1905.[24] The Bund's anti-capitalism was part of a wider German movement against modernity. In many ways the Bund's anti-capitalism fitted in comfortably with the more scholarly criticisms of capitalism produced by the economists Karl Oldenburg, Adolf Wagner, and Max Sering.[25]

The Bund der Landwirte's struggle against the perceived enemies of German agriculture escalated quickly into a struggle for control of the German state. Caprivi understood that the agrarians would never be satisfied by his own removal from the political scene and a change in economic policy: what they wanted was a conservative revolution to restore old Germany. "In regard to the [agrarians]," Caprivi wrote a friend, "I see only evil, and it appears to me that a revolution by the agrarians is not impossible and for the moment is more dangerous than a Social Democratic revolution."[26]

The Bund der Landwirte never achieved all its ideological objectives. Nevertheless, in 1894 the Bund played a major role in obtaining Caprivi's dismissal from office. The Bund's constant agitation against the Caprivi trade agreements led to the 1902 tariff legislation which restored high import duties on grain. The Bund also succeeded in transforming the Conservative Party into a willing parliamentary instrument for carrying out the Bund's policies. Finally, the Bund's nationalism, conservatism, and anti-Semitism helped poison the German political atmosphere in the two decades before the Great War. The Bund der Landwirte was simultaneously one of the most influential public mass organizations working against the German government's policies and the most influential pressure group within the German Reichstag.[27]

If one compares the Russian, German, and American responses to the Great Depression, one cannot fail to notice certain similarities. In all three cases agrarian movements began with protests against economic conditions, and it may be said that the essence of each lay in resistance to the market. Whereas the grain-exporting nations (Russia and America) witnessed complaints about expensive credit and rail transport, the grain importer, Germany, had an agrarian movement initially concerned about tariff protection. However different the specific issues addressed locally, the impulse of resistance to the market was common. In all three cases complaints about market conditions were accompanied by attacks on market institutions: banks, merchants, purchasing agents, the stock exchanges. Moreover, after an initial period of concentration on more or less parochial economic issues, all three movements entered a second, politically confrontational stage. In Russia before the turn of the century, the struggle was fought out bureaucratically with the Minister of Finance. In Germany and America the battle was waged openly in the arena of electoral politics. All three agrarian movements culminated in a threat to the established political order. In Russia conservative nobles became disaffected from the monarchy at a crucial moment, whereas liberals tried deliberately to limit the monarch's prerogatives through self-government and constitutionalism. In America aggrieved farmers created a third party to challenge the two entrenched anti-agrarian parties. The Bund der Landwirte, after sacking Caprivi and winning a reversal of his tariff policies, pressed for what can only be described as a conservative revolution against industrial capitalism.

The three agrarian movements also have much in common when viewed as social phenomena. It is true that the movements had different social roots: the Russian agrarians were nobles; the Germans were led by the Junkers, although the mass component consisted of peasants; the American agrarians were farmers who eventually aligned themselves with labor organizations and blacks. However, all three movements manifested genuine status anxiety. In the early stages of the depression, status anxiety showed among the Russian nobility in the form of anger about merchant and peasant land purchases; in the second stage of the depression, status anxiety took the form of anti-industrialism and then of a "crisis of confidence" over the peasant question. Among the patriarchal nobility there was a limited growth of anti-Semitism in the 1890s. In America status anxiety took the form of anti-industrialism, anti-Semitism, and nativism. However, in the American case status anxiety was counterbalanced by a strain of economic democracy plus a certain tolerance toward blacks and poor laborers. Germany presented the clearest example of status anxiety in the Bund der Landwirte's anti-industrialism, illiberalism, nationalism, and race-oriented anti-Semitism.

Marc Bloch once observed that comparative history, properly understood, should serve to point out the originality of individual cases as well as to enumerate similarities.[28] What then was unique about Russian agrarianism? If one studies the forms taken by the three protest movements in question, it is immediately obvious that the Russian movement was almost certainly entirely corporate in form, whereas the American and German cases were mass movements. Russian grievances during the depression were discussed either in local assemblies dominated by the nobility (noble assemblies and the zemstvos) or in governmental commissions and committees designed as channels for the expression of provincial noble opinion. The Russian movement departed from its corporate framework only partially after the turn of the century when reform-minded nobles made league with the intelligentsia against the autocracy and its peasant policy. The Bund der Landwirte, though dominated by Junkers and animated by a corporate spirit, nevertheless organized itself as a parliamentary pressure group and an extraparliamentary mass movement. American populism can be understood almost exclusively as an anti-hierarchical mass movement operating in the realm of elective politics. The restricted form of Russian agrarianism can be attributed to the absence in Russia of noncorporate mechanisms for the resolution of political problems, to the Russian traditions of patronage politics and deference to the crown. It should be added that most nobles preferred accommodation with the regime to confrontation: in this sense the corporate nature of Russian agrarianism was the result of conscious choice.

The second major difference between the Russian case and the two others was that the Russian movement was politically and ideologically incoherent. Even though American populism drew on people from different backgrounds and from many states, its ideology was relatively clear. Populism as a political program can be traced from the demands of the Farmers' Alliance in the 1880s directly to the platform of the People's Party in 1892. Only after the decline of populism as an independent political force did the term "populism" become vague and inexact. The Bund der Landwirte's ideology was a classic example of anti-modernism, and no educated German had difficulty distinguishing its tenets. However, the politics of the Russian nobility was an interest politics only weakly connected with articulated ideology. Unlike their American and German counterparts, Russian agrarians never succeeded in creating a political program that could command national support. Nor was there a single dominant ideology current among the nobility that might have served as a basis for such a program.

Therefore, viewed against the American and German backgrounds, the politics of the Russian nobility appears as a variant of agrarianism, distinguished by its corporate character and its ideological and programmatic incoherence.

ESTATE POLITICS

If at one level Russian noble politics was a variant of agrarianism, at another level it was an example of Estate politics in the context of a failing monarchical absolutist regime. When Russian liberals took as their model the great French Revolution of 1789, they did so not only because Nicholas II's methods of governing reminded them of Louis XVI's sullen despotism, but also because they recognized a similarity between the plight of Russian nobles and those of France.

Like the Russian nobility, the French *noblesse* was a legally delimited social order of extreme complexity.[29] There was the ancient *noblesse de race*, a court nobility in Versailles, a nobility connected with civil officeholding and with the army officers corps, a provincial nobility grouped around the *parlements*, and a pretentious nobility in Paris. There were nobles who were supported by traditional peasant dues, others who made money from commercial agriculture, and still others who drew on investments in business, government loans, and real estate.[30] As in Russia, the political position of the French nobility was unsettled. The French crown had engaged in a long struggle against the Paris *parlement*—a fight that grew more intense in the late 1780s. The crown was also dismissive of provincial pre-rogatives: when provincial *parlements* failed to register the central government's decisions, the parlements were overridden by *lits de justice*, temporarily transported to new locations, or even dismissed and forbidden to reassemble. The exasperating struggle between crown and *parlements* climaxed under the ministers Calonne and Brienne in 1787/88 when the central government, frustrated in its attempts to win the *parlementaires'* consent for fiscal and admini-strative reforms, unilaterally cancelled the *parlementaires'* supreme judicial status and abolished their right to remonstrate against the crown.[31] Yet the crown was not set in principle against the nobil-ity; indeed, the monarchy had a direct stake in the survival of noble spirit in the army and in the nobility's continued purchase of office—not to mention, in the persistence of nonpolitical privilege and social order.

The difficult political challenge facing the French nobility was complicated by pressure against the nobility exerted by other social groups. Although the peasantry had been relatively quiet, rural dis-order was always a possibility, especially in years of harvest short-falls. The rural panic of summer 1789 illustrated the potential for anti-nobiliary violence lurking below the apparently tranquil sur-face of village life.[32] Non-noble elites constantly sought access to the privileges of nobility and were disappointed by legislative barriers to their advancement such as the Ségur Ordinance of 1781 limiting the army officer corps to those with four quarters of nobility.[33] Yet the pressure of the non-noble elites for entrance into the nobility was so intense that many social barriers were eroded or destroyed. In a sense, as François Furet has indicated, the key to the political-social crisis of the eighteenth century was not the closing of the noble Estate to new members, but its opening: "too broad to main-tain the cohesion of the order, and too narrow for the prosperity of the century."[34] Thus, French nobles, like the Russian nobility a cen-tury later, constituted a complex social order undergoing a serious political crisis in an unstable, even threatening social environment.

It is interesting that the French nobility responded to the dan-gerous political crisis of the late 1780s by embracing several different political strategies. The notables summoned in 1787 at the insistence of Calonne were willing to support basic financial and political re-forms and to cooperate with the crown, provided its ministers were more candid and less highhanded than Calonne. The Paris *parlement* was more difficult to please than the hand-picked notables: indeed, the Court of Peers in the Paris *parlement* demanded a monarchy under the tutelage of the *parlement* and the Estates General—that is, in effect, an aristocratic revolution. Most provincial *parlements* resisted the government's proposed reforms in the name of regional prerogatives. As an anti-reformist publicist wrote:

> The Kingdom comprises so many diverse peoples, it includes provinces so distant from one another and so dissimilar in their customs, their products, their interests, that the wisest and most vigilant administration cannot avoid making mistakes in trying to govern them all on the same basis, being the sole judge of their political needs. . . . From that derives . . . the provinces' possession of local courts charged with looking after their interests, and the right inherent in those courts of being guardians of the laws and debating their registration.[35]

This was a defense of regional *parlements*, pure and simple.

To the reformers of 1787, the aristocratic revolutionaries and defenders of particularism in 1788, must be added the radical liberals who desired a merger of social orders and a republican government. The radical liberals had their roots in a small minority of provincial nobles and in the so-called National party in the capital. The spirit of the National Party can be gauged from the recommendations of Comte d'Antraigues that noble fiscal privileges be abolished:

> Those privileges that isolate us and have cost us so dear have become odious to us. Past centuries have taught us that levies imposed by the Estates General should be borne by all orders of the state. They have taught us that privileges, contrary to the interests of all, are snares that prevent healthy coalitions, and that [we] should have only one and the same interest as the people, in order to make freedom and laws always triumphant, and save the republic.[36]

The model for the radical liberals was England. As one member told the *parlement* in Dauphiné: "England would still be under the sway of despotism if there had been privileged classes on the eve of their revolution; the great adventure was that of the nation, which was not stymied and opposed by frivolous disputes and petty interests."[37]

There was, of course, a direct connection between the radical liberalism of 1788 and the activity of those nobles in 1789 who joined the Third Estate in the Estates General and who supported the abolition of seigneurial dues on the night of 4 August.

If no Russian noble of liberal persuasion could fail to be impressed by the example of the French nobility in 1788 and 1789, no historian should ignore the similarities between the French and Russian experiences. In both France and Russia members of a diversified social order, faced with a political crisis in an uncongenial social environment, answered political challenge in a variety of ways. Neither the Russian nor the French case can be understood in terms of class analysis, which would demand greater social homogeneity and a narrower range of responses to the social crisis. The French and Russian experiences should be seen as examples of privileged Estates fragmenting under enormous historical pressure, not as decaying and parasitic classes vainly resisting the rise of the bourgeoisie.

The main difference between the French and Russian cases was in their institutional context. In France the *parlements* had a tradition of partial independence from the crown, and the right of remonstrance. When the crown requested *parlements'* registration of financial legislation in order to balance the budget, the *parlements* resisted, thereby provoking a near bankruptcy of the treasury; in effect, the *parlements* had a veto power over the king's immediate financial plans. Control over the royal purse strings meant that the *parlements* were on nearly equal terms with the crown in the struggle for political power, and that *parlementaires* could be quite assertive in criticizing the king's nonfinancial policies. Russian nobles had no such control over the royal budget, were overmatched in disputes with the crown, and thus, were generally more deferential than the French in their attitudes toward royal authority.

That Russian noble politics was at once a variant of agrarianism and of Estate politics in a dying monarchy enables us to understand its historical peculiarities. The crisis of the Russian nobility at the end of the nineteenth century was a dual crisis: the question of the nobility's place in Russia's social and economic order and the question of the nobility's proper political role in the state were raised almost simultaneously. An economic and social crisis was superimposed on a political crisis. Agrarianism was the response to the social-economic crisis, but it was insufficient as an answer to the political crisis, hence the transcendence of narrow economic issues and mere status anxiety by global social and political issues after the turn of the century. In both the economic and political realms, the nobility's reaction to crisis was complex and contradictory rather than simple and consistent. An effective economic and political program to preserve the nobility never appeared in Russia because there was no noble class to save, only an Estate of nobles. In 1896 Novgorod's provincial marshal B. A. Vasil'chikov explained to the Special Commission on the Nobility the characteristic problem of the nobility:

Our Russian nobility encompasses persons so diverse in religious, national, economic, and territorial relations that it is impossible to unite them at the present time. The interests of each individual noble are closer to the interests of his profession than to the interests of the Estate as a whole. It is inconceivable that one should expect in the late nineteenth century the awakening of Estate consciousness and solidarity in this diverse mass.[38]

Notes
Selected Bibliography
Index

Notes

Introduction

1. Stephen Spender, *Collected Poems*, p. 49.
2. The best account of the peasant revolution is J. L. H. Keep, *The Russian Revolution of 1917*.
3. Vladimir Nabokov, *Speak, Memory*, pp. 30–31.
4. Ibid., p. 30.
5. My fellow historians will recognize that certain important issues have been excluded from this book. Among them are the origins of Alexander III's counterreforms, Russian liberal constitutionalism on the eve of 1905, the move for reform of local government before 1905, the nobility in the 1905 revolution, and the role of the nobility in the development of political parties in Russia. All the issues enumerated above have been or soon will be the subject of exhaustive monographs by Western or Soviet historians.
6. Anyone who has read Cobb's footnotes cannot fail to be impressed by the lengths to which Cobb has gone to trace individual stories through Parisian and provincial archives. See, for example, *The Police and the People*.
7. Theodore Zeldin, *France 1848–1945*, vol. 2, *Intellect, Taste, and Anxiety*, p. 1156.
8. See Thompson's preface to *The Making of the English Working Class* for his strictures on the meaning of class.
9. Soboul's objectionable textbook has been translated into English by Alan Forest and Colin Jones as *The French Revolution 1787–1799*. For Furet's objection, see "Le catéchisme révolutionnaire," pp. 255–289. See also T. B. Bottomore, *Elites and Society*, pp. 7–92 for a general review of the literature on class.
10. Peter N. Stearns, "The Middle Class," pp. 377–396.
11. But see the objections of Lenore O'Boyle, "The Classless Society," p. 412.

12. Nicholas Riasanovsky refers to the "gentry class" and the "landlord class" in his textbook *A History of Russia*, p. 469. Iu. B. Soloviev uses *klassovoe* and *soslovnoe* as synonyms in his *Samoderzhavie i dvorianstvo v kontse XIX veka*, p. 165.
13. See Iu. B. Soloviev, *Samoderzhavie i dvorianstvo v 1902–1907 gg.*, p. 4.
14. The egregious example discussed in Chapter 3 below is A. M. Davidovich, *Samoderzhavie v epokhu imperializma*, p. 59.
15. A. Ia. Avrekh, "Russky absoliutizm i ego rol' v utverzhdenii kapitalizma v Rossii," pp. 89–101; V. S. Diakin, *Samoderzhavie, burzhuaziia i dvorianstvo v 1907–1911 gg.*, pp. 3–4.
16. For example, Richard Pipes in *Russia under the Old Regime*.
17. P. G. Ryndziunsky, "Rossiiskoe samoderzhavie i ego klassovye osnovy (1861–1904 gg.)," p. 37.

CHAPTER 1

1. *Svod zakonov Rossiiskoi imperii*, vol. 9, stat'ia 15.
2. A. P. Korelin, "Dvorianstvo v poreformennoi Rossii (1861–1904 gg.)," pp. 116–135.
3. Population figures from A. G. Rashin, *Naselenie Rossii za 100 let (1813–1913 g.)*, p. 45.
4. Statistics on the first half of the nineteenth century have been compiled by V. M. Kabuzan and S. M. Troitsky, "Izmeneniia v chislennosti, udel'nom vese i razmeshchenii dvorianstva v Rossii v 1782–1858 gg.," pp. 162–165.
5. Korelin, "Dvorianstvo," pp. 116–135.
6. Ibid., p. 99; original data in TsGIA, fond 1283, opis' 1, 1 delo-vo, 1897 g., delo 5, chast' 1, l. 13; TsGIA, fond 1343, opis' 57, delo 585, l. 3.
7. Hugh Seton-Watson, *The Russian Empire, 1801–1917*, p. 240; P. I. Savvaitov, "Obozrenie Kievskoi, Podol'skoi i Volynskoi gubernii s 1830 po 1850 god," pp. 13–15.
8. Korelin, "Dvorianstvo," pp. 136–139.
9. Ibid., pp. 137–138.
10. Ronald Grigor Suny, "The Peasants 'Have Always Fed Us,'" pp. 27–51.
11. See *Trudy mestnykh komitetov o nuzhdakh sel'skokhoziaistvennoi promyshlennosti*, vol. 4, *Vilenskaia guberniia*, p. 22.
12. Robert Edelman, "The Nationalist Party and the Western Zemstvo Crisis of 1909," pp. 22–54.
13. V. Levitsky, "Pravye partii," *Obshchestvennoe dvizhenie v Rossii s nachala XX veka*, vol. 3, 347–472.
14. Marc Raeff, *Origins of the Russian Intelligentsia*.
15. B. N. Chicherin, *Vospominaniia*, p. 114; quoted in Nicholas Riasanovsky, *A Parting of the Ways*, pp. 265–266.

16. P. A. Zaionchkovsky, *Pravitel'stvenny apparat samoderzhavnoi Rossii v XIX v.*, p. 221.
17. Ibid., pp. 106–142, esp. pp. 141–142.
18. Ibid., pp. 179–224, esp. pp. 198–208.
19. Alexander Vucinich, *Science in Russian Culture, 1861–1917*, p. 100.
20. L. P. Minarik, "Proiskhozhdenie i sostav zemel'nykh vladenii krupneishikh pomeshchikov Rossii kontsa XIX–nachala XX v.," p. 357.
21. L. P. Minarik, "Kharakteristika krupneishikh zemlevladel'tsev Rossii kontsa XIX–nachala XX v.," p. 694.
22. Ibid.
23. Minarik, "Proiskhozhdenie," pp. 359–360; *Adres kalendar' i pamiatnaia knizhka Permskoi gubernii na 1902 g.*, pp. 83–105.
24. A. M. Anfimov, "Maioratnoe zemlevladenie v tsarskoi Rossii," pp. 151–159.
25. Ibid., p. 155.
26. Robert E. Jones, *The Emancipation of the Russian Nobility, 1762–1785*, p. 59.
27. V. V. Vorovsky has estimated that 26 percent of hereditary nobles were illiterate at the end of the nineteenth century; *Sochineniia*, 1: 218.
28. Richard Pipes, *Russia under the Old Regime*, p. 175.
29. Thomas Stewart Hause, "State and Gentry in Russia, 1861–1917," p. 26n.
30. One of the most interesting fictional attempts to reconstruct life on a small estate is Ivan Bunin's "Sukhodol," a *povest'* written in 1911. For Bunin, the old pre-emancipation estates were decaying physically and morally; thus, on the "slanting floor boards," on the "grayish-blue terrace crumbling with age," inside the "warped glass doors," alongside the dusty piano with its "yellowed music," lords and house-serfs lived fearful, obsessive, unproductive, and—above all—neurotic lives. Yet Bunin was so troubled by this corrupt condition and found it so alien that he admitted: "We have no clear conception, not even a slightly accurate idea of the life of our great-grandfathers, to say nothing of our earlier ancestors . . . with every day we are finding it more difficult to picture things that took place a mere fifty years ago" (see I. A. Bunin, *Sobranie sochinenii v deviati tomakh*, 3: 133–187).
31. Pipes, *Russia*, p. 189.
32. Proskuriakova, "Razmeshchenie i struktura dvorianskogo zemlevladeniia Evropeiskoi Rossii v kontse XIX–nachale XX veka," pp. 55–75.

CHAPTER 2

1. Daniel Field, *The End of Serfdom*, p. 13.
2. Donald MacKenzie Wallace, *Russia on the Eve of War and Revolution*, p. 117.

3. Ibid., p. 161.
4. I have followed Alexander Gerschenkron's summary of the emancipation settlement in "Agrarian Policies and Industrialization in Russia, 1861–1917," pp. 727–729.
5. P. A. Zaionchkovsky, *Otmena krepostnogo prava v Rossii*, pp. 206–207; Gerschenkron, "Agrarian Policies," p. 729.
6. Zaionchkovsky, *Otmena*, chap. 4; B. G. Litvak, *Opyt statisticheskogo issledovaniia krest'ianskogo dvizheniia XIX veka.*
7. A. I. Gertsen, *Sobranie sochinenii v 9-i tomakh*, vol. 7, pp. 367–371.
8. P. A. Valuev, TsGIA, fond Glavnogo komiteta ob ustroistve sel'skogo sostoianiia, no. 1181, op. XV, 1863, delo 38, l. 3; quoted in P. A. Zaionchkovsky, *Providenie v zhizn' krest'ianskoi reformy 1861 g.*, p. 366.
9. Ibid., p. 391. There is no data given for Mogilev.
10. Ibid., p. 412.
11. Ibid., p. 181.
12. Geroid Tanquary Robinson, *Rural Russia under the Old Regime*, pp. 87–88.
13. D. I. Budaev, *Krest'ianskaia reforma 1861 goda v Smolenskoi gubernii*, p. 202.
14. A. N. Engel'gardt, *Iz derevni*, p. 350. Zaionchkovsky cites an example for Moscow province where a landowner named Meshchersky excluded from peasant allotments streams, roads, and paths in the knowledge that peasants would have to pay him for the use thereof (*Providenie*, p. 182).
15. B. G. Litvak, "Ustavnye gramoty Moskovskoi gubernii kak istochnik po istorii realizatsii Polozheniia 19 fevralia 1861 g.," pp. 192–193.
16. One landowner who learned the hard way was Ivan Ivanovich Stankevich of Iukhnovsky and Viazemsky uezds in Smolensk province. In 1892 Stankevich tried to end a boundary dispute with local peasants by calling in a surveyor. Two years later, in 1894, a government surveyor appeared to carry out the survey. As Stankevich described the scene: "As long as there were clear signs: pastures, hedges, the peasants indicated the boundaries correctly; when we came to ponds and uncultivated areas, they started to claim [*zakhvatyvat'*] my land. I argued because the boundaries were well known to me. Who was correct—the peasants or I? There is no living witness who would testify that I, having given out to the peasants every year as pasture, under newly formulated oral agreements, watering and uncultivated lands beyond the allotments' boundaries, had given out [land] from such and such a point to another point; it is obvious that the silent witness in this case could only be the allotment plan, which, to my surprise, had been completely ignored. I limited myself to protests, desiring to see the survey to some sort of conclusion." When Stankevich checked his allotment plan, he discovered that in addition to the 17 desiatins "shamelessly seized by the peasants" in front of the surveyor, there were another 28 desiatins of seigneurial land under unauthorized use by the peasants. The confused situation became

more confused when peasants demanded redrawing of boundaries at a stream. The result was a three-year civil suit over boundaries of the estate.

Stankevich was so upset by this whole affair that in 1897 he wrote an indignant letter to the Special Commission on the Nobility. His letter ended in exasperation: "All this torture of embittered relations between peasants and landowners, the torture of endless and expensive legal redtape, forced me to contemplate throwing over the whole case, to give up the land to the peasants, if only to disentangle myself. . . . Here is the sad position of the noble landowner. Here one thinks about improvements in farming while farming is not consolidated, not secure, when a legal survey itself, designed to bring order, drags on as if on purpose. Having lived my life in the country, to my old age I have lived as a proper noble with neighbor peasants. Now relations have gotten hostile and God knows to what limits this hostility will reach" ("Dokladnaia zapiska Smolenskogo dvorianina Iukhnovskogo i Viazemskogo uezda, Ivana Ivanovicha Stankevicha," 1 maia 1897 goda, TsGIA, fond 1283, opis' 1, delo 1, t. 3. ll. 282–284).

17. This debate is analyzed by P. A. Zaionchkovsky in *The Russian Autocracy in Crisis, 1878–1882*, pp. 217–219 ff.

18. P. I. Liashchenko, *A History of the National Economy of Russia to the 1917 Revolution*, p. 387.

19. George Pavlovsky, *Agricultural Russia on the Eve of the Revolution*, p. 100.

20. S. N. Terpigoriev, *Oskudenie, Sobranie sochinenii v 6-i tomakh*, vol. 1, p. 4.

21. Ibid., pp. 16–17.

22. Ibid., pp. 4–36.

23. See letters 1–5 in M. E. Saltykov-Shchedrin, *Pis'ma o provintsii, Sobranie sochinenii v 6-i tomakh*, vol. 3, pp. 235–286. The original letters were published between 1868 and 1870 in the journal *Otechestvennye zapiski*.

24. Pavlovsky, *Agricultural Russia*, pp. 108–111.

25. Terpigoriev, *Oskudenie*, chap. 2, "Rational Agriculture."

26. Wallace, *Russia*, pp. 142–143.

27. These criticisms are misleading in two ways. First, they imply that most machinery used on Russian farms in the post-emancipation period was foreign-made, whereas by 1880 domestic manufacture of agricultural equipment had equaled imports. Second, they imply that Russian nobles enterprising enough to import foreign equipment were ill informed about the operation of the machinery under Russian conditions; that may have been true immediately after the emancipation, but certainly was not true after a few landowners had experimented with the new machinery. So on a growing number of noble estates mechanized agriculture was introduced.

28. P. I. Liashchenko, *A History*, p. 465.

29. A vivid account of work on an estate in Tauride province told from

a worker's perspective is in Praskovia Ivanovskaia's biography in Barbara Alpern Engel and Clifford N. Rosenthal, eds., *Five Sisters: Women against the Tsar*, pp. 105–112.

30. P. I. Liashchenko, "Mobilizatsiia zemlevladeniia v Rossii i ego statistika," p. 10; N. A. Egiazarova, *Agrarny krizis kontsa XIX veka v Rossii*, p. 45.
31. Pavlovsky, *Agricultural Russia*, p. 100.
32. V. I. Lenin, *Collected Works*, vol. 3, pp. 194–195n.
33. Liashchenko, *A History*, p. 466.
34. Robinson, *Rural Russia*, p. 99; A. M. Anfimov, *Zemel'naia arenda v Rossii v nachale XX veka*, p. 14. Anfimov repeats his estimate concerning the amount of rented land in *Krest'ianskoe khoziaistvo Evropeiskoi Rossii 1811–1904*, pp. 116–118. Thus, in 1905 peasants rented 37 million desiatins out of the 191 million desiatins that they cultivated. However, Anfimov has been accused of exaggerating the extent of peasant renting. S. M. Dubrovsky believes that a more reasonable estimate of the amount of land rented to peasants is 25 million desiatins. See his strictures in *Sel'skoe khoziaistvo i krest'ianstvo Rossii v period imperializma* (Moscow, 1975), pp. 144–154, esp. p. 151.
35. N. M. Druzhinin, "Pomeshchich'e khoziaistvo posle reformy 1861 g. (Po dannym Valuevskoi komissii 1872–1873 gg.)," pp. 187–230.
36. Pavlovsky, *Agricultural Russia*, pp. 43–46.
37. Druzhinin, "Pomeshchich'e," pp. 194–201.
38. A. S. Nifontov, *Zernovoe proizvodstvo Rossii vo vtoroi polovine XIX veka po materialam ezhegodnoi statistiki urozhaev Evropeiskoi Rossii*, p. 207.
39. See table in A. P. Korelin, *Dvorianstvo v poreformennoi Rossii 1861–1904 gg.*, p. 56.
40. N. A. Proskuriakova, "Razmeshchenie i struktura dvorianskogo zemlevladeniia Evropeiskoi Rossii v kontse XIX–nachale XX veka," p. 63.
41. Pavlovsky, *Agricultural Russia*, pp. 48–50.
42. Druzhinin, "Pomeshchich'e," pp. 201–205.
43. Ibid., pp. 206–207.
44. Nifontov, *Zernovoe*, p. 207.
45. Ibid., p. 167.
46. Ibid., p. 192.
47. Korelin, *Dvorianstvo*, p. 56.
48. See his letter to A. A. Tolstaia, 15 August 1874, in R. F. Christian, ed., *Tolstoy's Letters*, vol. 1, *1828–1879*, pp. 271–272.
49. Lenin, *Works*, vol. 3, pp. 242–243.
50. Ibid., pp. 245–248.
51. Druzhinin, "Pomeshchich'e," p. 211.
52. Nifontov, *Zernovoe*, p. 207.
53. Ibid., pp. 296–297.
54. Korelin, *Dvorianstvo*, p. 56.
55. Pavlovsky, *Agricultural Russia*, p. 47.
56. Nifontov, *Zernovoe*, p. 207.

57. Ibid.
58. Ibid., pp. 207, 296–297.

CHAPTER 3

1. George Rudé, *Revolutionary Europe, 1783–1815*, p. 29.
2. Protocols of the Unofficial Committee in Veliky kniaz' Nikolai Mikhailovich, *Graf Pavel Aleksandrovich Stroganov (1774–1814)* (St. Petersburg, 1903), vol. 2, pp. 111–112.
3. Alexander Herzen, *My Past and Thoughts*, vol. 3, p. 1153.
4. A recent example is A. M. Davidovich, *Samoderzhavie v epokhu imperializma*, p. 59. Davidovich followed Lenin's dictum that until February 1917 "sovereign power in Russia was in the hands of a single old class, namely: the feudal-noble-landowner class, led by Nikolai Romanov."
5. For a discussion of the premises of Soviet historiography of absolutism, see A. Gerschenkron, "Soviet Marxism and Absolutism," pp. 853–869.
6. See P. A. Zaionchkovsky, *The Russian Autocracy in Crisis, 1878–1882*; Iu. B. Soloviev, *Samoderzhavie i dvorianstvo v kontse XIX veka*; V. G. Chernukha, *Vnutrenniaia politika tsarizma s serediny 50-kh do nachala 80-kh gg. XIX veka*; N. M. Pirumova, *Zemskoe liberal'noe dvizhenie*.
7. V. Zhukovsky, *Polnoe sobranie sochinenii v odnom tome*, p. 171; Nicholas Riasanovsky, *Nicholas I and Official Nationality in Russia, 1825–1855*, pp. 73–183.
8. L. V. Cherepnin, *Zemskie sobory russkogo gosudarstva v XVI–XVII vv.* The American historian Richard Hellie has dismissed Cherepnin's work as "highly tendentious" and tainted with mysticism (see *Russian Review* 39, no. 2 (April 1980): 238–239). Hellie is certainly correct to say that Cherepnin overstated the frequency of assemblies and exaggerated their political impact.
9. David L. Ransel, *The Politics of Catherinian Russia*.
10. Nikolai Gogol', *Dead Souls*, pp. 58–59.
11. F. M. Dostoevsky, *Sobranie sochinenii v desiati tomakh*, vol. 6, pp. 9–10.
12. For an excellent discussion of the 1785 charter, see Baron S. A. Korff, *Dvorianstvo i ego soslovnoe upravlenie za stoletie 1762–1855 godov*, pp. 136–183. Two solid treatments of the background to the charter are: Robert E. Jones, *The Emancipation of the Russian Nobility, 1762–1785* and Ransel, *Politics of Catherinian Russia*.
13. A thorough discussion of the requirements is provided by A. P. Korelin, *Dvorianstvo v poreformennoi Rossii 1861–1904 gg.*, pp. 137–143.
14. Ibid., p. 142; original data in TsGIA, fond 1283, opis' 1, I delo-vo, 1897 g., delo 217, l.9. "Spravka o sostave gubernskikh dvorianskikh sobranii."
15. S. N. Terpigoriev, *Oskudenie*, vol. 1, pp. 120–121.

16. A. P. Korelin, "Rossiiskoe dvorianstvo i ego soslovnaia organizatsiia (1861–1904 gg.)," p. 73.
17. Terpigoriev, *Oskudenie*, vol. 1, pp. 120–121.
18. TsGIA, fond 1343, opisi 16–36, 46, raznye dela. For all 83 families the average (mean) = 2,344; standard deviation = 3,935. For the 72 families who were less wealthy than magnates, average (mean) = 1,045 male souls; standard deviation = 1,068.
19. Ibid. For all 37 marshals the average land owned was 74,193 desiatins; standard deviation = 243,182. For the least wealthy 25 marshals in the sample, the mean number of desiatins owned was 3,990; standard deviation = 2,575.
20. *Vsia Rossiia*. For the least wealthy 21 owners, average (mean) = 5,512 desiatins; standard deviation = 4,097. This excluded the largest estate of 75,719 desiatins.
21. Ibid. Mean = 3,478; standard deviation = 4,882.
22. On Kholodkovsky, see TsGIA, fond 1343, opis' 31, delo 2756, ll. 4–13.
23. On Arapov, see TsGIA, fond 1343, opis' 16, delo 2500, ll. 52–57.
24. TsGIA, fond 1343, opis' 25, delo 6276, ll. 157–164.
25. For a substantial discussion of these three service patterns and list of examples, see G. M. Hamburg, "Land, Economy, and Society in Tsarist Russia: Interest Politics of the Landed Gentry during the Agrarian Crisis of the Late Nineteenth Century" (Ph.D. diss., Stanford, 1978), pp. 28–40; 308–310.
26. N. M. Pirumova, *Zemskoe liberal'noe dvizhenie*, p. 84.
27. Ibid., p. 83.
28. M. E. Saltykov-Shchedrin, *Pis'ma o provintsii, Sobranie sochinenii*, vol. 3, p. 237.
29. TsGIA, fond 593, opis' 1, delo 103, Ob uchrezhdenii Gosudarstvennogo dvorianskogo pozemel'nogo banka 1883–1892 gg., "Khodataistvo Orlovskogo dvorianstva," ll. 7–9.
30. Andrzej Walicki, *The Slavophile Controversy*, p. 450.
31. V. A. Kitaev, *Ot frondy k okhranitel'stvu*, p. 49.
32. Letter dated 4 January 1858 in R. F. Christian, ed., *Tolstoy's Letters*, vol. 1, p. 115.
33. Daniel R. Brower, *Training the Nihilists*, p. 42.
34. Ibid., p. 47.
35. D. I. Pisarev, "Pchely," *Sochineniia v 4-kh tomakh*, vol. 2, pp. 100–101.
36. Ibid., p. 105.
37. Curiously enough, Pisarev rejected the necessity for rudeness. See his criticism of *Fathers and Sons* in "Bazarov," *Sochineniia*, vol. 2, pp. 12–13.
38. For Gleason's comments on style, see his *Young Russia*, pp. xi, 290–291. The phrase "flower of the conservatory" was Nechaev's.
39. Brower, *Training*, p. 42.
40. P. L. Lavrov, *Historical Letters*, esp. pp. 129–140.
41. James H. Billington, *Mikhailovsky and Russian Populism*, p. 91.

42. Terence Emmons, *The Russian Landed Gentry and the Peasant Emancipation of 1861*, pp. 381–385.
43. B. N. Chicherin, *Golosa iz Rossii*, vol. 4, pp. 112–126.
44. See his pamphlets *Kakoi iskhod dlia Rossii iz nyneshnogo ee polozheniia?* and *Konstitutsiia, samoderzhavie i zemskaia duma.*
45. An excellent analysis of Cherkassky's path to democratic reform is Richard Wortman, "Koshelev, Samarin, and Cherkassky and the Fate of Liberal Slavophilism," pp. 273–277.
46. Ibid., pp. 277–278.
47. The affinities between Koshelev and Shipov were first pointed out by P. N. Miliukov, "Novy variant slavianofil'skoi politicheskoi doktriny." See most recently Walicki, *Slavophile Controversy*, pp. 474–494, esp. pp. 490–492.
48. V. A. Kitaev, *Ot frondy k okhranitel'stvu.*
49. Ibid., p. 101. See Chicherin's article in *Atenei* 1858, no. 12: 219.
50. Kitaev, *Ot frondy*, p. 91. See Katkov's review of Tocqueville in *Russky vestnik*, 1857, ianvar', kn. 1, "Sovremennaia letopis'," pp. 1–2.
51. N. Barsukov, *Zhizn' i trudy M. P. Pogodina*, vol. 14, p. 211; Daniel Field, "Kavelin and Russian Liberalism," pp. 63–64.
52. The best summary of Kavelin's politics is Field, "Kavelin and Russian Liberalism." See also D. P. Hammer, "Two Russian Liberals."
53. Emmons, *Russian Landed Gentry*, pp. 367–368.
54. On the position of these aristocrats in the emancipation debate, see ibid., pp. 294–298; on the fate of their political proposals, especially the 1861 Bezobrazov memoir and petition, see pp. 376–381.
55. For a brilliant discussion of the Shuvalov plan, see Chernukha, *Vnutrenniaia politika tsarizma*, pp. 67–118.
56. Saltykov-Shchedrin, *Pis'ma o provintsii*, pp. 276–277.
57. For a discussion of the theme of nobility in *The Adolescent*, see Konstantin Mochulsky, *Dostoevsky*, pp. 525–528.
58. L. N. Tolstoy, *Polnoe sobranie sochinenii v 90-i tomakh*, vol. 19, pp. 222–239.
59. Ibid., vol. 18, pp. 321–322.
60. Ibid., vol. 19, p. 232.
61. Ibid., vol. 23, pp. 1–60.

CHAPTER 4

1. Graf P. A. Valuev, *Dnevnik 1877–1884*, p. 36.
2. See diary entries for 16 May 1879; 15 February, 22 April, 8 and 18 September 1880; 18 February 1881 in ibid.
3. Diary entry for 16 November 1882 in ibid.
4. On Petrunkevich's role in framing the zemstvo petitions, see N. M. Pirumova, *Zemskoe liberal'noe dvizhenie*, pp. 127–138, and Charles E. Timberlake, *Essays on Russian Liberalism*, pp. 18–41.
5. Cited in Pirumova, *Zemskoe liberal'noe*, p. 137.

6. V. L. Burtsev, *Za sto let (1800–1896)* p. 214.
7. Ibid., pp. 215–216.
8. M. M. Stasiulevich, *Poriadok* no. 61, 3 March 1881.
9. K. P. Pobedonostsev, *Pis'ma K. P. Pobedonostseva k Aleksandru III*, vol. 1, pp. 318–319. Letter dated 11 March 1881.
10. V. Ia. Bogucharsky, "Iz istorii politicheskoi bor'by v 80-kh godakh," pp. 10–11.
11. N. A. Sadikov, "Obshchestvo 'Sviashchennoi druzhiny,'" pp. 200–217; Stephen Lukashevich, "The Holy Brotherhood: 1881–1883," pp. 491–509.
12. Valuev recorded in September 1882 that the Retinue hired 6,000 temporary guards to protect Alexander III in Moscow. After noting the exertions of the Holy Retinue and official police, Valuev asked: "How long are such measures feasible? And what outcome can one foresee?" (*Dnevnik*, p. 206). Lukashevich mentions this diary entry, but misdates it as 19 September 1881 and does not quote Valuev's skeptical conclusions ("Holy Brotherhood," pp. 497–498).
13. Sadikov, "Obshchestvo," p. 206.
14. Lukashevich, "Holy Brotherhood," pp. 493–495; the Moscow membership was published by M. Fedorova, "Moskovsky otdel Sviashchennoi druzhiny."
15. On the hundred families, see L. P. Minarik, *Ekonomicheskaia kharakteristika krupneishikh zemel'nykh sobstvennikov Rossii kontsa XIX–nachala XX v.*
16. "Iz dnevnika V. N. Smel'skogo," p. 226.
17. "Konstitutsionnye proekty nachala 80-kh gg. XIX veka," pp. 118–139.
18. Ibid., p. 132.
19. Ibid., pp. 132–133.
20. Ibid., p. 135.
21. Ibid., p. 142.
22. Ibid., p. 140.
23. P. A. Zaionchkovsky, *The Russian Autocracy in Crisis*, p. 297. Zaionchkovsky thinks that Vorontsov-Dashkov favored the sobor only as a quid pro quo for earning Ignatiev's blessing on the Holy Retinue.
24. Sadikov, "Obshchestvo," p. 211.
25. Schmuel Galai, "Early Russian Constitutionalism, 'Vol'noe Slovo' and the 'Zemstvo Union,'" p. 37.
26. Arkhiv Akademii nauk (Moscow), f. 518 (V. I. Vernadsky), op. 5, no. 68, p. 22. I wish to thank Professor Terence Emmons for drawing my attention to this source.
27. B. N. Chicherin, *Vospominaniia Borisa Nikolaevicha Chicherina*, pp. 221–222.
28. Ibid., p. 223.
29. Lord Ernle, *English Farming Past and Present*, 6th ed. pp. 380–381.
30. Robert Estier, "La Dépression agricole de la fin du XIXe siècle," pp. 299, 306.

31. Wilhelm Roessle, *Bismarcks Politik nach seinen Staatsschriften und Reden*, pp. 552–553.
32. Edward C. Kirkland, *Industry Comes of Age*, p. 46; George Rogers Taylor and Irene D. Neu, *The American Railway Network, 1861–1890*.
33. Sir Robert Ensor, *England, 1870–1914*, p. 115.
34. V. K. Iatsunsky, "Osnovnye momenty istorii sel'skokhoziaistvennogo proizvodstva v Rossii do 1917 goda," p. 58.
35. I. D. Koval'chenko and L. V. Milov, *Vserossiisky agrarny rynok XVIII–nachalo XX veka*, p. 211.
36. Ibid., p. 381.
37. P. I. Liashchenko, *A History of the National Economy of Russia*, p. 503.
38. Jacob Metzer, "Railroad Development and Market Integration, p. 548.
39. Ibid.
40. Ibid., p. 544.
41. V. K. Pleve, *Doklad predsedatelia Vysochaishe uchrezhdennoi v 1881 godu komissii po povodu padeniia tsen na sel'skokhoziaistvennye proizvedeniia v piatiletie 1883–1887*, p. 61.
42. Ibid., p. 66.
43. Ibid., p. 59.
44. P. I. Liashchenko, *Russkoe zernovoe khoziaistvo v sisteme mirovogo khoziaistva*, pp. 311–314.
45. Ministerstvo zemledeliia i gosudarstvennykh imushchestv. Otdel sel'skoi ekonomii i sel'skokhoziaistvennoi statistiki, *Svod statisticheskikh svedenii po sel'skomu khoziaistvu Rossii k kontsu XIX veka*, Vypusk II, pp. 22–41.
46. *Otchety gosudarstvennogo zemel'nogo banka*. Calculations by A. M. Anfimov, *Krupnoe pomeshchich'e khoziaistvo Evropeiskoi Rossii*, p. 318.
47. *Materialy Vysochaishe uchrezhdennoi 16 noiabria 1901 g. komissii*, Chast' 1, pp. 306–307.
48. *Vestnik finansov, promyshlennosti i torgovli*, no. 2 (1902), p. 82.
49. Departament zemledeliia i sel'skoi promyshlennosti, *Sel'skokhoziaistvennye i statisticheskie svedeniia po materialam poluchennym ot khoziaev*, Vypusk III, pp. xxii–lvii.
50. *Vestnik finansov*, p. 82.
51. Departament zemledeliia, *Sel'skokhoziaistvennye i statisticheskie svedeniia*, Vypusk III, pp. xii–lvii.
52. N. A. Egiazarova, *Agrarny krizis kontsa XIX veka v Rossii*, p. 78.
53. Ibid., p. 79.
54. *Vestnik finansov*, p. 82.
55. Departament zemledeliia, *Sel'skokhoziaistvennye i statisticheskie svedeniia*, Vypusk III, pp. xxii–lvii.
56. Ibid., Vypusk XI, pp. 129–131.
57. Koval'chenko and Milov, *Vserossiisky agrarny*, pp. 327–328.
58. *Vestnik finansov*, p. 82.
59. Departament zemledeliia, *Sel'skokhoziaistvennye i statisticheskie svedeniia*, Vypusk III, pp. xxii–lvii.

60. A. S. Nifontov, *Zernovoe proizvodstvo Rossii vo vtoroi polovine XIX veka po materialam ezhegodnoi statistiki urozhaev Evropeiskoi Rossii*, p. 272.
61. P. I. Liashchenko, "Mobilizatsiia zemlevladeniia v Rossii i ego statistika," pp. 59–60.
62. A. P. Korelin, *Dvorianstvo v poreformennoi Rossii 1861–1904 gg.*, pp. 60–67.

CHAPTER 5

1. S. N. Terpigoriev, *Sobranie sochinenii v shesti tomakh*, vol. 1, p. 180.
2. Ibid., pp. 180–181.
3. On Shidlovsky, see the brief account in A. P. Korelin, *Dvorianstvo v poreformennoi Rossii 1861–1904 gg.*, pp. 255–256. See also Shidlovsky's 1881 petition: "Predstavlenie A. R. Shidlovskogo ministru vnutrennikh del ot 28 maia 1881 g." in TsGIA, fond 1284, opis' 91, 1881 g., delo 53, ll. 1–6.
4. Korelin, *Dvorianstvo*, pp. 256–257; Korelin found a letter from Shidlovsky to Moscow provincial marshal A. V. Bobrinsky calling for support. TsGAM, fond 380, opis' 1, delo 1317, ll. 22–24. "Pis'mo A. R. Shidlovskogo moskovskomu predvoditeliu A. V. Bobrinskomu ot 7 fevralia 1883 g."
5. Noble petitions or marshals' memoranda came from: Smolensk, Orel, Voronezh, Kostroma, Bessarabia, Chernigov, Penza, Samara, Kaluga, Orenburg, Kazan', Khar'kov, and Ufa. Zemstvo assemblies in Orel, Tambov, Kaluga, Poltava, Penza, and Saratov also supported a central land bank for the nobility. Korelin lists only the first eight noble assemblies as defenders of a noble bank (*Dvorianstvo*, pp. 256–257).
6. TsGIA, fond 593, opis' 1, delo 103, ll. 245–246. "Khodataistvo Ufimskogo gubernskogo predvoditelia dvorianstva ministru vnutrennikh del 8-ogo maia 1885."
7. Ibid., l. 15. "Khodataistvo Kaluzhskogo dvorianstva dekabria 1883."
8. Ibid., ll. 56–63. "Khodataistvo Bessarabskogo gubernskogo predvoditelia dvorianstva 24 aprelia 1884 g."
9. Ibid., l. 8. "Khodataistvo Orlovskogo dvorianstva dekabria 1883."
10. Ibid., l. 13. "Khodataistvo Voronezhskogo chrezvychainnogo gubernskogo sobraniia dekabria 1883."
11. Ibid., ll. 56–63. "Khodataistvo Bessarabskogo gubernskogo predvoditelia dvorianstva 24 aprelia 1884 g."
12. Ibid.
13. Ibid., l. 9. "Khodataistvo Orlovskogo dvorianstva dekabria 1883 g."
14. Ibid., l. 10.
15. Ibid., l. 11.
16. See entry for 14 October 1884 in A. A. Polovtsov, *Dnevnik gosudarstvennogo sekretaria A. A. Polovtsova v dvukh tomakh*, vol. 1, p. 248.
17. TsGIA, fond 593, opis' 1, delo 103, ll. 51–52. "Zapiska zemlevladel'tsev-dvorian Gdovskogo uezda S-Peterburgskoi gubernii."

18. TsGAOR, fond 677, opis' 1, delo 108, l. 18. "Pis'mo V. P. Meshcherskogo Aleksandru III ot 11 iiunia 1884 g."; cited in Iu. B. Soloviev, *Samoderzhavie i dvorianstvo v kontse XIX veka*, p. 171.

19. TsGAOR, fond 677, opis' 1, delo 108, l. 22.

20. See Soloviev's account in *Samoderzhavie i dvorianstvo*, pp. 172–173. Meshchersky recorded his version of the audience in his so-called "secret diary" which he sent to Alexander III for the latter's edification.

21. TsGIA, fond 593, opis' 1, delo 103, l. 143. "Zhurnal Osobogo soveshchaniia dlia obsuzhdeniia Polozheniia o gosudarstvennom zemel'nom banke."

22. Ibid., l. 147. "Osoboe mnenie Penzenskogo gubernskogo predvoditelia dvorianstva kniazia A. D. Obolenskogo i Eletskogo uezdnogo predvoditelia dvorianstva S. S. Bekhteeva po voprosu o soedinenii Gosudarstvennogo zemel'nogo banka s krest'ianskim."

23. Ibid., l. 149. "Osoboe mnenie Khar'kovskogo gubernskogo predvoditelia dvorianstva A. R. Shidlovskogo po voprosu ob organizatsii zemel'nogo kredita."

24. For Russian budgetary information, see *Ministerstvo finansov 1802–1902*, vol. 1, pp. 632–639; vol. 2, pp. 640–649.

25. Soloviev, *Samoderzhavie i dvorianstvo*, p. 174.

26. Polovtsov, *Dnevnik gosudarstvennogo sekretaria A. A. Polovtsova*, vol. 1, pp. 308–309.

27. This was not achieved without bitter disagreement between Ostrovsky and Pobedonostsev. On 9 April "Ostrovsky by trivial, so-to-speak bureaucratic changes spoils what was written by Pobedonostsev, who, of course, agrees to all changes that affect only his authorial *amour propre*, and not the essence of the matter." And again on 13 April: "We read in committee the project rescript to the nobility. Two or three expressions that had been inserted by Ostrovsky are changed to his extreme displeasure. They discuss whether to leave the words 'to the nobility belongs the preeminent place in military action'; whether this does not contradict the statute on military obligations. Pobedonostsev heatedly insists on the preservation of this expression" (ibid., pp. 310–312). The struggle between Ostrovsky and Pobedonostsev was part of the ongoing struggle between bureaucratic liberals and conservatives. Ostrovsky was a fair-weather liberal, at this point a protege of the liberal Minister of Justice, Nabokov. Incidentally, the final version of the rescript wishes "the nobility to preserve the preeminent place in military leadership."

28. TsGIA, fond 593, opis' 1, delo 103, ll. 1–2. "Vysochaishy reskript. Vsemilostiveishy ego Imperatorskogo Velichestva reskript blagorodnomu Rossiiskomu dvorianstvu."

29. Polovtsov, *Dnevnik gosudarstvennogo sekretaria A. A. Polovtsova*, VOL. 1, p. 316.

30. Ibid., pp. 314–315.

31. B. N. Chicherin, *Vospominaniia Borisa Nikolaevicha Chicherina*, p. 279.

32. Soloviev, *Samoderzhavie i dvorianstvo*, pp. 186–187.
33. Ibid., p. 187.

CHAPTER 6

1. See J. R. Jones, *Country and Court*, p. 76.
2. On the failure of the 1714 statute, see V. O. Kliuchevsky, *Sochineniia v 8-i tomakh*, vol. 4, pp. 87–91, 317.
3. TsGIA, fond 593, opis' 1, delo 307 ("Po komissii pod predsedatel'- stvom N. S. Abazy o merakh k podderzhaniiu dvorianskogo zem- levladeniia"), l. 13. "Zapiska o zapovednykh imeniiakh gubernskogo predvoditelia dvorianstva kniazia Meshcherskogo ot 29 maia 1887 g."
4. Those provinces joining the entail campaign were: Petersburg, Pskov, Smolensk, Tula, Kaluga, Riazan', Penza, Kursk, Nizhny-Novgorod, Kazan', Simbirsk, Ufa, Poltava, Khar'kov, Ekaterinoslav, Kherson, and Tauride.
5. TsGIA, fond 593, opis' 1, delo 307, ll. 8–9.
6. TsGIA, fond 593, opis' 1, delo 307, l. 36. "Doklad Simbirskomu gubernskomy dvorianskomu sobraniiu po voprosu o svobode zave- shchanii zapovednykh imenii." This speech evidently served as the model for a memorandum submitted by R. K. Zmeev and A. N. Pareny to the Tula provincial nobility in 1891. Zmeev and Pareny quoted the Simbirsk speech of 1888 almost verbatim on the govern- ment's stake in noble landownership. See TsGIA, fond 593, opis' 1, delo 307, l. 91. "Mneniia o nedelimykh dvorianskikh uchastkakh chlenov komissii po voprosu o zapovednykh imeniiakh R. K. Zmeeva, A. N. Parenago i Iu. V. Arsenieva, predstavlennyia ocherednomu Tul'skomu gubernskomu dvorianskomu sobraniiu 13 dekabria 1891 goda."
7. Ibid., ll. 16–17. "Zapiska Nizhegorodskomu sobraniiu dvorianstva 1887 goda Makarievskogo uezdnogo predvoditelia dvorianstva Vla- dimira Vasilievicha Khvoshchinskogo."
8. Ibid., l. 27. "Zapiska Suzhanskogo uezdnogo predvoditelia dvo- rianstva S. Zhekulina, 30 oktiabria 1888 g."
9. Ibid., l. 41. "Vypiska iz postanovleniia Pskovskogo gubernskogo dvorianskogo sobraniia 31 ianvaria 1889 g."
10. In the Kherson noble assembly there were 27 votes against the entail petition (out of 102 cast), and in Penza province 26 negative votes (out of 210).
11. TsGIA, fond 593, opis' 1, delo 307, ll. 272–276. "Zapiska o sposobe uchrezhdeniia dvorianskikh neotchuzhdaemykh i nedelimykh uchast- kov. Predvoditel' dvorianstva Romenskogo uezda Poltavskoi gubernii Grigory Navritsky 4 maia 1892 g."
12. Ibid., l. 315. "Soderzhanie zapiski zemlevladel'tsa Smolenskoi gu- bernii M. A. Liagotino."
13. Ibid., l. 343. "Zapiska dvorianina—Senatora Printsa."

14. For a discussion of the statute's history, see Iu. B. Soloviev, *Samoderzhavie i dvorianstvo v kontse XIX veka*, pp. 203–212. My account is based on Soloviev and on my own reading of archival sources. For a description of the statute itself, see Thomas Stewart Hause, "State and Gentry in Russia, 1861–1917," pp. 119–124.

15. Soloviev, *Samoderzhavie i dvorianstvo*, pp. 204–205. TsGIA, fond 1151, opis' tom XII, 1896 g., delo 1, l. 118. "Kratky istorichesky ocherk uchrezhdenii, ustanavlivaiushchikh nedelimost' i neotchuzhdaemost' zemel'noi sobstvennosti."

16. The commission evidently had in mind the approximately 35,000 landowners who held lands of that value in the 100 to 5,000 desiatin range. See Soloviev, *Samoderzhavie i dvorianstvo*, pp. 205–206.

17. Ibid., p. 207.

18. Ibid., p. 208; TsGIA, fond 1151, opis' tom XII, 1896 g., delo 1, ll. 221, 231–233.

19. Soloviev, *Samoderzhavie i dvorianstvo*, p. 317; TsGIA, fond 1283, opis' 1, delo 229, l. 80. "Protokol zasedaniia 21 fevralia 1898 g."

20. Ibid., l. 146. "Protokol zasedaniia 25 aprelia 1898 g."

21. TsGIA, fond 1283, opis' 1, delo 6, chast' 1, l. 512.

22. Soloviev, *Samoderzhavie i dvorianstvo*, p. 325.

CHAPTER 7

1. TsGIA, fond 593, opis' 1, delo 47, "Po khodataistvam dvorianskikh sobranii ob izmeneniiakh nekotorykh statei ustava banka," l. 118. "Zapiska chlenov ot dvorian v Khar'kovskom otdelenii Gosudarstvennogo dvorianskogo zemel'nogo banka I. I. Karazina i I. P. Sarandinaki."

2. Ibid., l. 118. "Pis'mo Khar'kovskogo gubernskogo predvoditelia dvorianstva Grafa V. Kapnista M. A. Venevitinomu, Voronezhskomu gubernskomu predvoditeliu dvorianstva 8 ianvaria 1892 g."

3. See, for example, D. N. Shipov, *Vospominaniia i dumy o perezhitom*, pp. 150–151. Without pressing the point too far, one might study the logic of Shipov's justification for electing representatives from "public institutions." Shipov was most upset over the government's distrust of society, which led to "administrative centralization in all spheres of government." Noble criticisms of the bank had a similar logic. The bank's directorship did not trust branch offices, so everything had to be centralized in Petersburg—an unwarranted and dismaying development.

4. TsGIA, fond 593, opis' 1, delo 47, ll. 276–278. "Pis'mo Khar'kovskogo gubernskogo predvoditelia dvorianstva Kapnista Grafu A. A. Golenishchevu-Kutuzovu 18 sentiabria 1893 goda."

5. Ibid., l. 280. "Pis'mo Khar'kovskogo predvoditelia dvorianstva Kapnista Grafu A. A. Golenishchevu-Kutuzovu 22 oktiabria 1893 goda."

6. Ibid., ll. 523–526. "Vypiski iz protokola chrezvychainogo obshchego

sobraniia Bessarabskogo dvorianstva ot 9 oktiabria 1896 goda." Here l. 523.

7. Ibid., ll. 525–526. The government had introduced a vodka monopoly and limited the wine trade. It had permitted the import of seedless grapes [*korinki*] without any customs duties and had proposed establishment of an excise tax on wine. These government measures, according to the assembly chairman, had reduced the price of wine despite a low harvest and high quality grapes.

8. Ibid., l. 521. "Khodataistvo Bessarabskogo gubernskogo predvoditelia dvorianstva Ivana Egoricha Katarzhi ot 14 oktiabria 1896 g."

9. In 1895 and 1896 the harvests of grain in Samara were poor. In August 1896 the Samara provincial marshal, Count N. A. Tolstoy, wrote to the director of the Noble Land Bank asking that emergency provisions of the Bank Charter be applied to affected estates. After a review of the situation by bank authorities, Minister of Finance Witte made the final decision to grant aid to estate owners who had suffered because of the poor harvest. See ibid., ll. 493–504. "Pis'mo ot Samarskogo gubernskogo predvoditelia dvorianstva upravliaiushchemu Gosudarstvennym dvorianskim zemel'nym bankom 23 avgusta 1896 goda."

10. Ibid., l. 292. "Pis'mo ot Poltavskogo gubernskogo predvoditelia dvorianstva S. Brazola Grafu A. A. Golenishchevu-Kutuzovu ot 14 oktiabria 1893 goda."

11. Ibid. According to Brazol, only the large landowners with mechanical reapers had managed to harvest their crops before the rainy season.

12. Ibid., l. 293.

13. Ibid., ll. 315–318. "Mnenie komissii, izbrannoi Poltavskim dvorianskim sobraniem, po voprosu ob oblegchenii polozheniia zaemshchikov Gosudarstvennogo dvorianskogo zemel'nogo banka."

14. Ibid., ll. 323–325. "Pis'mo ot Poltavskogo gubernskogo predvoditelia dvorianstva S. Brazola tsariu." The Poltava petition was forwarded together with the undated Brazol letter and an explanatory document which will be discussed below.

15. Ibid., l. 323. Incidentally, Brazol was wrong to claim that the noble population had declined.

16. Ibid., ll. 326–330. "Ob"iasnitel'naia zapiska Poltavskogo khodataistva."

17. Ibid., ll. 326–327.

18. Ibid., l. 329.

19. Ibid., l. 330.

20. Ibid., l. 359. "Osoboe mnenie k zhurnalu chrezvychainogo Samarskogo dvorianskogo sobraniia 30 iiulia 1894 g."

21. This action was alluded to in ibid., l. 378. "Dokladnaia zapiska," dated 24 January 1895.

22. Ibid. The report was signed by: Orel marshal S. N. Shenig; Dmitrovsky district (Orel province) marshal N. V. Vashich; Podolia marshal N. I. Vinogradsky; Ol'gopol'sky district (Podolia province) marshal A. N. Volzhin; Chernigov marshal G. A. Miloradovich; Soroksky dis-

trict (Bessarabia province) marshal Prince P. M. Kantakuzin; Courland marshal Count G. K. Kaiserling; Tula marshal A. A. Arseniev;
deputy of the Tula nobility A. Ofrosimov; Tula landowner Prince
D. Obolensky; Khar'kov marshal Count V. A. Kapnist; Volkovsky
district (Khar'kov province) marshal V. V. Shirkov; Karsunsky district
(Simbirsk province) marshal Iu. D. Rodionov; Tula land captain Baron
A. A. Del'vich.
23. TsGIA, fond 593, opis' 1, delo 47, ll. 393–401. "Vsepoddaneishaia
dokladnaia zapiska predvoditelia dvorianstva Valkovskogo uezda
Khar'kovskoi gubernii, Valeriana Shirkova fevralia 1895 goda."
24. Ibid., l. 393.
25. Iu. B. Soloviev, *Samoderzhavie i dvorianstvo v kontse XIX veka*, p. 219.
26. Ibid., pp. 219–220. Original in Manuscript Section, Lenin Library,
fond 126, k. 12, dnevnik A. A. Kireeva, zapis' 31 ianvaria 1896 g.,
l. 48.
27. TsGIA, fond 593, opis' 1, delo 351 ("O merakh k oblegcheniiu polozheniia zaemshchikov dvorianskogo banka i ob izmenenii poriadka
ikh otvetstvennosti po zaimam 1896–1911 gg."), ll. 1–3. "Zapiska gubernskikh predvoditelei dvorianstva, vyzvannykh s Vysochaishego
ego Imperatorskogo Velichestva soizvoleniia g. ministrom vnutrennikh del v soveshchanii o nuzhdakh dvorianskogo zemlevladeniia."
28. Ibid. There were paper rubles and gold rubles in circulation until the
1897 currency reform under Witte. Gold rubles were worth more in
real terms because they had a fixed value in precious metal, whereas
the value of paper rubles was subject to some fluctuation.
29. Ibid., l. 4.
30. Ibid., l. 12. The loans in question were obviously short-term loans.
The institution that most frequently granted this kind of loan to
nobles was the State Bank.
31. Ibid., l. 13.
32. Ibid., ll. 35–37.
33. See I. F. Gindin and M. Ia. Gefter, "Trebovaniia dvorianstva i finansovo-ekonomicheskaia politika tsarskogo pravitel'stva v 1880–
1890-kh godakh, pp. 122–155.
34. Ibid., pp. 125–126.
35. Ibid., pp. 131–132.
36. Ibid., pp. 128–129.
37. Ibid., pp. 135.
38. Ibid., p. 129.
39. Ibid., p. 147.
40. Ibid., pp. 147–152.
41. Soloviev, *Samoderzhavie i dvorianstvo*, p. 229. Soloviev points out that
"from the factual point of view, the marshals' memorandum cannot
even be seen as a caricature of reality, with large distortions and
exaggerations. . . . The memorandum was distinguished precisely
by the complete absence of even the flimsiest link with reality."

While it is true that the marshals' perspective was biased and many of their arguments faulty, Soloviev goes too far to assert that the marshals' grievances had not the flimsiest justification.

42. TsGIA, fond 593, opis' 1, delo 351, l. 111. "Dokladnaia zapiska Vitte Nikolaiu II o merakh k oblegcheniiu polozheniia zaemshchikov Gosudarstvennogo dvorianskogo banka i ob izmenenii poriadka ikh otvetstvennosti po ssudam." Soloviev, *Samoderzhavie i dvorianstvo*, pp. 234–235.
43. TsGIA, fond 593, opis' 1, delo 351, l. 155. "O merakh k oblegcheniiu polozheniia zaemshchikov Gosudarstvennogo dvorianskogo banka i ob izmenenii poriadka ikh otvetstvennosti po zaimam 7 aprelia 1897 g."
44. Ibid., ll. 169–170.
45. Soloviev, *Samoderzhavie i dvorianstvo*, p. 237.
46. Graf S. Iu. Vitte, *Vospominaniia tsarstvovaniia Nikolaia II*, vol. 1, p. 181.
47. This would have meant 12 million rubles in the first year.
48. TsGIA, fond 593, opis' 1, delo 351. "Soobrazheniia stats-sekretaria Durnovo po proektu o merakh k oblegcheniiu polozheniia zaemshchikov Gosudarstvennogo dvorianskogo zemel'nogo banka 27 aprelia 1897 g."
49. Witte's marginalia on ibid., l. 225; also cited in Soloviev, *Samoderzhavie i dvorianstvo*, p. 239.
50. TsGIA, fond 593, opis' 1, delo 351, l. 255. "Zakliuchenie predvoditelei po proektu ministra finansov ot 7 aprelia 1897 goda."
51. Ibid., l. 257.
52. Ibid., ll. 258–259.
53. Soloviev, *Samoderzhavie i dvorianstvo*, p. 243.
54. TsGIA, fond 593, opis' 1, delo 351, ll. 292–294, here l. 294. "Soobrazheniia po povodu doklada ministra finansov finansovomu komitetu o merakh k oblegcheniiu polozheniia zaemshchikov Gosudarstvennogo dvorianskogo zemel'nogo banka."
55. Ibid.
56. Ibid., l. 292.
57. Soloviev, *Samoderzhavie i dvorianstvo*, p. 242.
58. TsGIA, fond 593, opis' 1, delo 351, l. 295. "Soobrazheniia po povodu predstavlennogo ministrom finansov proekta o merakh k oblegcheniiu polozheniia zaemshchikov Gosudarstvennogo dvorianskogo zemel'nogo banka."
59. Ibid., l. 297. "Zapiska Khar'kovskogo gubernskogo predvoditelia dvorianstva Grafa V. A. Kapnista."
60. Soloviev, *Samoderzhavie i dvorianstvo*, p. 243.
61. Ibid., p. 249.
62. Ibid., p. 250.
63. TsGIA, fond 593, opis' 1, delo 351, l. 337. "Protokoly zasedanii komiteta finansov, 9 maia 1897 goda."
64. Ibid.
65. Ibid., l. 338.

66. Ibid., l. 339.
67. Ibid., ll. 340–341.
68. Ibid., l. 339.
69. Soloviev, *Samoderzhavie i dvorianstvo*, p. 245.
70. These provinces included Kaluga, Vladimir, Kursk, Nizhny-Novgorod, Penza, Poltava, Chernigov, Tauride, Ekaterinoslav, Bessarabia.
71. TsGIA, fond 1283, opis' 1, 1897 g., delo 2, tom 2, l. 267. "Doklad chrezvychainomu Suzhanskomu dvorianskomu sobraniiu."
72. Ibid., l. 273. "Zhurnal sobraniia dvorianstva Suzhanskogo uezda 28 aprelia 1898 g."
73. TsGIA, fond 1283, opis' 1, delo 1, tom 1, l. 26. "Pis'mo Penzenskogo predvoditelia dvorianstva ot 12 marta 1898 g., No. 42 s prilozheniem."
74. Ibid., l. 66. "Pis'mo Vladimirskogo predvoditelia dvorianstva ot 12 marta 1898 g., No. 194."
75. Ibid., l. 158. "Otnoshenie Chernigovskogo dvorianstva ot 7 sentiabria 1898 g., No. 817."
76. TsGIA, fond 1283, opis' 1, delo 1, tom 2, l. 14. "Otnoshenie Ekaterinoslavskogo gubernskogo predvoditelia dvorianstva ot 10 fevralia 1898 g., No. 79."
77. Ibid., l. 257. "Pis'mo Nizhegorodskogo gubernskogo predvoditelia dvorianstva ot 26 aprelia 1898 g. No. 755."
78. TsGIA, fond 1283, opis' 1, delo 1, tom 1, l. 66. "Pis'mo Vladimirskogo predvoditelia. . . ."
79. Ibid., l. 212. "Pis'mo Kaluzhskogo gubernskogo predvoditelia dvorianstva ot 24 noiabria 1898 g. No. 395."
80. Ibid.
81. Ibid., ll. 193–194. "Pis'mo Iaroslavskogo predvoditelia dvorianstva ot 25 iiulia 1898 g. No. 192."
82. TsGIA, fond 1283, opis' 1, delo 1, tom 3, l. 30. "Pis'mo Ufimskogo gubernskogo predvoditelia dvorianstva ot 27 maia 1898 g. No. 36."
83. TsGIA, fond 1283, opis' 1, delo 1, tom 2, l. 221. "Zakliucheniia soveshchaniia gg. predvoditelei i deputatov dvorianstva Khersonskoi gubernii, sostoiavshego 2 i 3 dekabria 1897 i 20 fevralia 1898 goda dlia obsuzhdeniia proekta dvorianskikh kass vzaimopomoshchi."
84. Ibid., l. 79. "Pis'mo Riazanskogo gubernskogo predvoditelia dvorianstva ot 22 fevralia 1898 g. No. 21 s prilozheniem."
85. Ibid.
86. Ibid., l. 84.

Chapter 8

1. Letter to P. I. Evropeitsev, 26 July 1861, in V. O. Kliuchevsky, *Pis'ma. Dnevniki*, p. 19.
2. TsGIA, fond 1233, opis' 1, delo 68, l. 3. "Spravka po voprosu o zheleznodorozhnykh tarifakh na perevozku khlebnykh gruzov."

3. Ibid., l. 12.
4. Ibid., l. 14.
5. Ibid.
6. The surcharge was introduced on grain shipped through the town of Cheliabinsk on the trans-Siberian railroad; the amount of the surcharge was from 8 to 10 kopecks per pood of grain. This levy was referred to as the "Cheliabinsk break."
7. TsGIA, fond 593, opis' 1, delo 351, ll. 1–3.
8. Ibid., l. 8.
9. Ibid., l. 9.
10. The logic of the marshals was specious because most Western European growers actually faced higher production costs than did Russians, and thus Russian grain undercut European prices on the international market.
11. TsGIA, fond 593, opis' 1, delo 351, l. 8.
12. I. F. Gindin and M. Ia. Gefter, "Trebovaniia dvorianstva i finansovo-ekonomicheskaia politika tsarskogo pravitel'stva v 1880–1890-kh godakh," pp. 122–155. Original document entitled "Zamechaniia ministra finansov S. Iu. Witte na zapisku gubernskikh predvoditelei dvorianstva o nuzhdakh dvorianskogo zemlevladeniia," p. 146.
13. TsGIA, fond 1233, opis' 1, delo 68, l. 27.
14. "Zamechaniia ministra," p. 146.
15. TsGIA, fond 1233, opis' 1, delo 68, l. 19.
16. Ibid., l. 20.
17. It is not clear why producers who used canals and waterways for grain shipments would have suffered under the minority plan. If water transportation remained cheaper than railroad rates, then these producers would presumably have continued to use their old methods of transport. Otherwise, these producers would switch to railroad transport, if railroad junctions were reasonably convenient.
18. TsGIA, fond 1233, opis' 1, delo 68, l. 20.
19. Ibid., ll. 20–21.
20. Central provinces included in the committee's study were Kursk, Orel, Tula, Tambov, Riazan', and Voronezh. Peripheral provinces included Orenburg, Ufa, Samara, and the Ural region.
21. These data begged the crucial question of production costs. The central producers surely had a high share of local markets, but their production costs were higher than those for Siberia. Moreover, Siberian grain did drive prices down in central markets, although one cannot say how much.
22. TsGIA, fond 1233, opis' 1, delo 68, ll. 22–23.
23. Ibid., l. 23.
24. Ibid., ll. 25–26.
25. Ibid., l. 29.
26. Ibid., l. 30.
27. Ibid., l. 31.
28. Ibid., l. 34.

29. "Zamechaniia ministra," pp. 143–44.
30. Ibid., pp. 145–147.
31. TsGIA, fond 1233, opis' 1, delo 68, l. 35.
32. Ministerstvo zemledeliia i gosudarstvennykh imushchestv, *Nuzhdy sel'skogo khoziaistva i mery ikh udovletvoreniia po otzyvam zemskikh sobranii*, pp. 4–5.
33. Responses were so slow because "in most cases . . . zemstvo assemblies sent the questionnaire to district zemstvos for preliminary consideration; in provinces where there exist special zemstvo agricultural agencies, provincial and district agricultural committees or commissions, the questions of the Ministry were also examined by these agencies . . . in certain provinces zemstvo assemblies created special commissions for this purpose." Besides these administrative reasons for slow responses, many zemstvos prepared statistical materials for the use of the government (Ibid., pp. 5–6). The original zemstvo responses were summarized in issues of *Izvestiia ministerstva zemledeliia i gosudarstvennykh imushchestv*, 1896, nos. 14–41; 1897, nos. 6–44; 1898, no. 7. Thus, some zemstvo responses occurred concurrently with the 1896–97 tariff review; others were composed and published after the review's conclusion.
34. Ministerstvo zemledeliia, *Nuzhdy sel'skogo*, pp. 175–176.
35. TsGIA, fond 1283, opis' 1, delo 1, tom 2, l. 81. "Pis'mo Riazanskogo gubernskogo predvoditelia dvorianstva ot 22 fevralia 1898 g., No. 21 s prilozheniem."
36. TsGIA, fond 1283, opis' 1, delo 1, tom 3, l. 75. "Zapiska dvorianina Vladimira Stepanovicha Buimistrova chrezvychainomu Riazanskomu gubernskomu dvorianskomu sobraniiu 15 fevralia 1897 g.
37. TsGIA, fond 1283, opis' 1, delo 1, tom 2, ll. 163–164. "Pis'mo Khar'-kovskogo predvoditelia dvorianstva ot 3 aprelia 1898, No. 161 s prilozheniem."
38. For Galuzin's statement and Ukhtomsky's memorandum, see ibid., ll. 46–71. "Pis'mo Kazanskogo gubernskogo predvoditelia dvorianstva ot 11 fevralia 1898, no. 190"; "Zapiska kniazia Pavla Ukhtomskogo Kazanskoi gubernii."
39. TsGIA, fond 1283, opis' 1, delo 1, tom 3, ll. 51–55. "Pis'mo Orlovskogo gubernskogo predvoditelia dvorianstva ot 24 maia 1898 g., No. 320 s prilozheniem."
40. TsGIA, fond 1283, opis' 1, delo 1, tom 1, ll. 79–81. "Otnoshenie Pskovskogo predvoditelia dvorianstva ot 9 oktiabria 1898 g., No. 334 s prilozheniem."
41. TsGIA, fond 1233, opis' 1, delo 68, ll. 39–40.
42. D. N. Shipov, *Vospominaniia i dumy o perezhitom*, p. 157.
43. Ibid.
44. TsGIA, fond 1233, opis' 1, delo 68, ll. 81–84. "Materialy po voprosu o zheleznodorozhnykh tarifakh na perevozku khlebnykh gruzov i zhurnaly zasedanii osobogo soveshchaniia po etomu voprosu."
45. Ibid., l. 160. "Zhurnal Vysochaishe uchrezhdennogo Osobogo sove-

shchaniia o nuzhdakh sel'skokhoziaistvennoi promyshlennosti, no. 4, zasedaniia 18 i 21 maia 1902 g."

46. Vysochaishe uchrezhdennoe Osoboe soveshchanie o nuzhdakh sel'-skokhoziaistvennoi promyshlennosti, *Svod trudov mestnykh komitetov po 49 guberniiam Evropeiskoi Rossii. Zhelezkye dorogi i tarify.*, pp. 221–224.

47. Ibid., p. 221.

48. Ibid., p. 222.

49. Ibid., p. 248.

50. Ibid. Proportional tariffs were calculated according to the number of pood/versts on the basis of a flat rate.

51. Ibid., p. 249.

52. Ibid., p. 248. Nolinsky (Viatka province), Starooskol'sky (Kursk province), Gaisinsky (Podolia province), and Romensky (Poltava province) districts favored the differential tariff "in general."

53. Ibid., pp. 248–249. Vilensky (Vil'no province), Kosel'sky (Kaluga province), Vilkomirsky (Kov'no province), Igumensky and Minsky (Minsk province), Ranenburgsky (Riazan' province), Kirsanovsky and Shatsky (Tambov province), Krapivensky and Tul'sky (Tula province) districts defended the differential tariff on exports but wanted a proportional tariff on domestic shipments.

L'govsky and Novooskol'sky (Kursk province), Bolkovsky (Orel province), Khar'kovsky (Khar'kov province), and Starodubsky (Chernigov province) districts petitioned for a "softening" of differential rates to protect the center against competition from the peripheral provinces.

Bendersky (Bessarabia province), Vladimir-Volynsky, Lutsky, and Starokonstantinovsky (Volynia province), Pruzhansky (Grodno province), Laishevsky (Kazan' province), Kovensky (Kov'no province), L'govsky, Putivl'sky, and Fatezhsky (Kursk province), Chausky (Mogilev province), Serchansky (Nizhny-Novgorod province), Livensky, Maloarkhangel'sky, and Mtsensky (Orel province), Pronsky and Sapozhkovksy (Riazan' province), Melitopol'sky (Tauride province), Elatomsky, Lipetsky, Morshansky, and Temnikovsky (Tambov province), Epifansky, Efremovsky (Tula province), Ananevsky (Kherson province), Glukhovsky and Ostersky (Chernigov province) districts said that differential tariffs were generally undesirable and recommended a pood/verst (proportional) system.

CHAPTER 9

1. There were doubtless as many different attitudes toward the peasantry as there were noble landowners, and it would be wrong for a historian to pretend that these attitudes may be described comprehensively. In this section I shall treat only the most common

varieties of public sentiments concerning the peasantry, that is, those more or less articulate and systematic public expressions of attitudes that were of significance politically.

2. Pazukhin's original article was published by Katkov in *Russky vestnik* in December 1885. It appeared almost immediately as a separate booklet. See A. D. Pazukhin, *Sovremennoe sostoianie Rossii i soslovny vopros.*

3. See n. 7, Chapter 6.

4. Hans Rogger, "Russian Ministers and the Jewish Question," pp. 16–22; here, p. 17.

5. Heinz-Dietrich Loewe, *Antisemitismus und reaktionaere Utopie*, p. 26.

6. The first serious study of anti-Semitism in the Russian press, including the provincial press, is being conducted by John D. Klier. So far Klier has investigated the Jewish question during the reform era. See "The Jewish Question in the Reform Era Russian Press, 1855–1865," pp. 301–319. Of related interest is David I. Goldstein, *Dostoevsky and the Jews*, which, unfortunately, does not treat the critical reception of Dostoevsky's anti-Semitism in the provinces.

7. TsGIA, fond 1283, opis' 1, delo 3, ll. 32–40. "Zapiska o merakh k podderzhaniiu dvorianskogo zemlevladeniia 2 marta 1896 g."

8. Fedor Konstantinovich Glinka, *K voprosu ob uluchshenii polozheniia zemel'nogo dvorianstva.*

9. TsGIA, fond 593, opis' 1, delo 351, l. 4.

10. Ibid.

11. In the months following the 1896 convocation, the question of the effect of low prices on the peasantry became a matter of bitter public dispute. In 1895 Witte had commissioned a study of prices, harvest levels, and the peasant standard of living. It was published in 1897 under the editorship of A. I. Chuprov and A. S. Posnikov, *Vliianie urozhaev i khlebnykh tsen na nekotorye storony russkogo narodnogo khoziaistva.* The introduction by Chuprov argued that only 9 percent of the peasantry produced marketable surpluses and that the rest of the peasantry either subsisted on their own grain or purchased grain for domestic consumption. It followed that low grain prices were beneficial to most of the peasantry who were net grain purchasers. Witte had advance knowledge of the book's conclusions and used them to justify his policies in the 1895 and 1896 annual reports on the budget. See S. S. Ol'denburg, *Last Tsar*, vol. 1, pp. 92–94. Witte also defended low grain prices in his criticism of the marshals.

The conclusions of the Chuprov-Posnikov study were publicly debated at a session of the Imperial Economic Society held in March 1897. Here Chuprov tried to defend himself against the devastating criticism of the Marxists M. I. Tugan-Baranovsky and P. B. Struve, and against a number of academics. See *Vliianie urozhaev i khlebnykh tsen na raznye storony ekonomicheskoi zhizni. Doklad Prof. A. I. Chuprova.*

The criticisms at the Free Economic Society were followed by printed attacks by noble marshals. For example, in 1899 D. F. Samarin published an article in *Novoe vremia* arguing that the peasantry were producers of grain first and consumers second, that the Chuprov-Posnikov volume had greatly underestimated the volume of grain sold by peasants at market. This article was reprinted as a pamphlet: D. F. Samarin, *O nizkikh tsenakh na khleb.* Prince A. G. Shcherbatov also addressed the price issue. He argued that "a good harvest and high prices on grain, moderately low prices on grain in bad harvest—that is the interest of all agricultural Russia—that is, of the entire nation," (see Kniaz' A. G. Shcherbatov, *Po povodu knigi Vliianie urozhaev i khlebnykh tsen na nekotorye storony russkogo narodnogo khoziaistva,* p. 14). Thus, the marshals' seemingly tame position on the peasant question put them squarely in the center of a bitter controversy.

12. Contemporaries seem to have been shocked by the extent of the famine and to have blamed the government for it. Liberals in particular associated the famine with a revival of reformist sentiment. For two reactions to the famine see Kniazhna Ol'ga Trubetskaia, *Kniaz' S. N. Trubetskoi,* pp. 19, 177–178; and A. A. Kizevetter, *Na rubezhe dvukh stoletii.*

13. Iu. B. Soloviev has written that "there is no difference at all between the attitude toward protectionism taken by the reactionary and the liberal zemstvo nobility" (*Samoderzhavie i dvorianstvo v kontse XIX veka,* p. 253). For a review of zemstvo liberal positions on the peasant question, see N. M. Pirumova, *Zemskoe liberal'noe dvizhenie,* pp. 138–157.

14. Arkhiv Akademii Nauk SSSR, fond 518, opis' 4, delo 198 (Programma chastnogo zemskogo s"ezda 1893 g.) ll. 100–101; cited in ibid., p. 144.

15. Ibid., p. 145. Original in Arkhiv Akademii Nauk SSSR, fond 518, opis' 4, delo 198.

16. There is a minor disagreement between Pirumova and P. I. Shlemin about the cultural question. Shlemin argues in his dissertation that the zemtsy used their observations about the ignorance of the peasantry to turn attention away from the possibility of allotting peasants more land. Pirumova argues that at this stage, the zemtsy had not yet reached consensus on the need to allot more land to the peasantry; they still hoped to solve the land question by resettlement and more credit. The zemtsy, in Pirumova's view, were not trying to divert attention from anything. I believe that Pirumova is right. Unfortunately, Pirumova also contends that those who mentioned the need for cultural improvement were in disagreement with those who advocated material reforms only. It seems to me that this is a curious and unnecessary, not to say misleading distinction. See P. I. Shlemin, "Zemsko-liberal'noe dvizhenie na rubezhe XIX–XX vekov," p. 69; Pirumova, *Zemskoe liberal'noe,* p. 145, n. 54.

17. The provincial assemblies included eight nonblacksoil provinces

(Vladimir, Vologda, Kostroma, Moscow, Pskov, St. Petersburg, Smolensk, Iaroslavl'); six blacksoil provinces (Voronezh, Kursk, Riazan', Tula, Khar'kov, Chernigov), all five southern steppes provinces, two provinces from the eastern periphery (Viatka, Perm), and none from the western periphery (where, except in Bessarabia, there were no zemstvos) (Ministerstvo zemledeliia i gosudarstvennykh imushchestv, *Nuzhdy sel'skogo khoziaistva i mery ikh udovletvoreniia po otzyvam zemskikh sobranii*, pp. 158–169).

18. Ibid., pp. 280–282.
19. Ibid., pp. 284–285.
20. Ibid., pp. 158–167.
21. Ibid., p. 165.
22. M. F. Tolmachev, *Krest'iansky vopros po vzgliadam zemstva i mestnykh liudei*, p. 62; Pirumova, *Zemskoe liberal'noe*, p. 151.
23. The best source on D. N. Shipov is his own memoirs, *Vospominaniia i dumy o perezhitom*, which constitute an indispensable guide to the history of zemstvo activism.
24. Leonard Schapiro, *Rationalism and Nationalism in Russian Nineteenth-Century Political Thought*, p. 162.
25. At various points in his long career, Chicherin opposed the immediate introduction of a constitution, but he always maintained that Russia was evolving toward constitutionalism.
26. B. N. Chicherin, "Eshche neskol'ko slov o sovremennom polozhenii russkogo dvorianstva. (Otvet kniaziu P. N. Trubetskomu)," *Voprosy politiki*, p. 28.
27. Chicherin detested those political doctrines and all political thinkers who wished to level social inequality in the name of liberty. See his brilliant, ill-tempered, and quite devastating critique of German socialism in *Sbornik gosudarstvennykh znanii*, vol. 5, pp. 1–71; vol. 6, pp. 1–39. Chicherin regarded economic egalitarianism as fanatical utopianism.
28. Chicherin, Peresmotr zakonodatel'stva o krest'ianakh," *Voprosy politiki*, pp. 52–69.
29. L. N. Tolstoy, "O golode," *Polnoe sobranie sochinenii* vol. 29, p. 106.
30. Quoted by Ernest J. Simmons, *Leo Tolstoy*, p. 440.
31. V. Gorn, "Krest'ianskoe dvizhenie do 1905 goda," in L. Martov et al., eds., *Obshchestvennoe dvizhenie v Rossii s nachala XX veka*, vol. 1, p. 230.
32. P. N. Pershin, *Agrarnaia revoliutsiia v Rossii*. Soviet documentary publications on the peasant movement are surveyed by E. S. Paina, *Krest'ianskoe dvizhenie v Rossii v XIX–nachale XX vv.*
33. S. Nechetny, "U zemli," pp. 43–44.
34. Ibid., p. 44; Gorn, "Krest'ianskoe dvizhenie," p. 243.
35. Nechetny, "U zemli," p. 65.
36. Ibid., p. 39.
37. Sylvain Bensidoun, *L'agitation paysanne en Russie de 1881 à 1902*, pp. 444–445.

38. Gorn, "Krest'ianskoe dvizhenie," pp. 241–242.
39. The documents on the 1902 Poltava and Khar'kov uprisings are published in *Krest'ianskoe dvizhenie v Poltavskoi i Khar'kovskoi guberniiakh v 1902 g. Sbornik dokumentov.* The best article on the uprisings is L. E. Emeliak, "Krest'ianskoe dvizhenie v Poltavskoi i Khar'kovskoi guberniiakh v 1902 g.," pp. 154–175. See also Gorn, "Krest'ianskoe dvizhenie," pp. 245–248; Pershin, *Agrarnaia revoliutsiia,* pp. 227–229; Maureen Perrie, *The Agrarian Policy of the Russian Socialist-Revolutionary Party from Its Origins through the Revolution of 1905–1907,* pp. 53–57. Bensidoun, *L'agitation paysanne,* pp. 426–429.
40. Emeliak, "Krest'ianskoe dvizhenie," pp. 163–164.
41. Ol'denburg, *Last Tsar,* vol. 2, p. 15. However, Bensidoun implies that peasants only burned estates of landowners whom they had reason to detest. Bensidoun, *L'agitation paysanne,* p. 427.
42. Emeliak, "Krest'ianskoe dvizhenie," p. 165.
43. *Iskra,* 1902, no. 20.
44. Gorn, "Krest'ianskoe dvizhenie," p. 247.
45. Ibid., p. 248.
46. Emeliak, "Krest'ianskoe dvizhenie," p. 170; *Iskra,* 1902, no. 21.
47. Emeliak, "Krest'ianskoe dvizhenie," p. 170; TsGIA, fond 1405, opis' 103, 1902 g., delo 9342, l. 44.
48. *Iskra,* 1902, no. 23.
49. In Khar'kov province 493 peasants were tried; in addition, 254 peasants in Konstantinograd district and 345 in Poltava district, Poltava province, were tried. TsGIA, fond 1405, opis' 103, 1902 g., delo 9342, l. 162.
50. Senate ukase on 11 May 1902; TsGIA, fond 1291, opis' 46, No. 221, l. 37.
51. Gorn, "Krest'ianskoe dvizhenie," pp. 249–252; Perrie, *Agrarian Policy,* p. 57.
52. Gorn, "Krest'ianskoe dvizhenie," p. 249.
53. Ibid., p. 250.
54. A. A. Polovtsov, "Dnevnik A. A. Polovtsova," pp. 98–99, entry for 20 June 1901.
55. Ibid., p. 96, entry for 12 June 1901.
56. Ibid., p. 99, entry for 22 July 1901.
57. *Trudy mestnykh komitetov o nuzhdakh sel'skokhoziaistvennoi promyshlennosti,* vol. 32, *Poltavskaia guberniia,* p. 256.
58. Ibid., pp. 257–258.
59. Ibid., pp. 259–264.
60. "Zapiska Konstantinogradskogo uezdnogo komiteta o nuzhdakh krest'ianskogo khoziaistva," in ibid., pp. 293–305.
61. Ibid., p. 301.
62. Ibid., p. 749.
63. Ibid.
64. Ibid., pp. 750–755.
65. Ibid., pp. 736–742.

66. The eleven proposals can be found in *Trudy mestnykh*, vol. 45, *Khar'kovskaia guberniia*, pp. 181–182.
67. "Doklad Valkovskogo komiteta po voprosu o denezhnykh sredst-vakh, neobkhodimykh dlia vozrozhdeniia sel'skokhoziaistvennoi promyshlennosti," in ibid., pp. 183–193.
68. Ibid., p. 191.
69. Ibid.
70. Ol'denburg, *Last Tsar*, vol. 2, p. 20.
71. Ibid., p. 21.
72. TsGIA, fond 1263 Komiteta ministrov, opis' alfavit k zhurnalam komiteta, delo 5630, l. 95.
73. M. S. Simonova, "Politika tsarizma v krest'ianskom voprose naka-nune revoliutsii 1905–1907 gg.," pp. 221–222.
74. Ibid., p. 230.
75. The history of the radical right has been explored by Hans Rogger, "The Formation of the Russian Right, 1900–1906," pp. 66–94.
76. R. F. Christian, ed., *Tolstoy's Letters*. Vol. 2, *1880–1910*, p. 611, Letter dated 16 January 1902.
77. Ibid., pp. 612–613.
78. Ibid., p. 617, letter dated 25 April–1 May 1902.
79. Terence Emmons, "The Beseda Circle, 1899–1905," pp. 461–490.
80. Ibid., p. 465; D. I. Shakhovskoi, "Soiuz osvobozhdeniia," p. 103.
81. Emmons, "Beseda Circle", pp. 482–483, n. 69—a bibliography of Beseda publications.
82. V. I. Lenin, *Polnoe sobranie sochinenii*, vol. 6, pp. 349–355.
83. Ibid., p. 350.
84. Ibid., pp. 353–355.
85. Schmuel Galai, *The Liberation Movement in Russia, 1900–1905*, pp. 133–136.
86. Shakhovskoi, "Soiuz osvobozhdeniia," p. 103.
87. Emmons, "Beseda Circle," p. 488. See also E. D. Chermensky, "Zemsko-liberal'noe dvizhenie nakanune revoliutsii 1905–1907 gg.," pp. 41–60.
88. For a list of participants and an account of the meeting, see D. N. Shipov, *Vospominaniia i dumy o perezhitom*, pp. 159–168.
89. Ibid., p. 162.
90. Ibid., pp. 167–168.
91. It should be noted that under questioning by Plehve in March 1903, Shipov denied his influence on the Sudzha committee. This denial was obviously disingenuous (Ibid., pp. 208–209).
92. M. S. Simonova, "Zemsko-liberal'naia fronda (1902–1903 gg.)," pp. 150–216.
93. Ibid., pp. 164–170.
94. TsGIA, fond 1233, opis' 1, delo 110, l. 2.
95. See Galai, *Liberation Movement*, pp. 154–155.
96. Simonova, "Zemsko-liberal'naia fronda," pp. 174–175.
97. Ibid., pp. 177–178; TsGIA, fond 1282, opis' 2, delo 1005, l. 28.

98. Simonova, "Zemsko-liberal'naia fronda," p. 179.
99. Shipov, *Vospominaniia*, pp. 217–220.
100. See G. M. Hamburg, "The London Emigration and the Russian Liberation Movement," pp. 321–339.
101. "Ot redaktora," *Osvobozhdenie*, no. 1 (18 June 1902), p. 5.
102. "Ot russkikh konstitutsionalistov," in ibid., pp. 7–12.
103. "Otkrytoe pis'mo ot gruppy zemskikh deiatelei," in ibid., p. 13.
104. Galai, *Liberation Movement*, p. 171–176.
105. On this meeting, see K. F. Shatsillo, "Formirovanie programmy zemskogo liberalizma i ee bankrotstva nakanune pervoi russkoi revoliutsii (1901–1904 gg.)," p. 72.
106. "K agrarnomu voprosu," *Osvobozhdenie*, no. 33 (19 October 1903), pp. 153–158.
107. Ibid., p. 153.
108. Ibid., p. 154.
109. Ibid., p. 155.
110. Ibid., p. 155–156.
111. Ibid., p. 157.
112. Ibid., p. 158.
113. Galai, *Liberation Movement*, pp. 187–188.

CONCLUSION

1. A. I. Novikov, *Zapiski gorodskogo golovy*, p. 252. I owe this reference to Samuel C. Ramer of Tulane University.
2. There is no systematic comparative history of agrarian politics in late nineteenth-century Europe and America. In a recent book Margaret Canovan has treated all the variants of populism to have influenced European and American life, but her book is mainly a political taxonomy, not a history of social movements. Moreover, she ignores agrarian movements of a nonpopulist nature (see Canovan, *Populism*). I am grateful to Vincent DeSantis of Notre Dame for this reference.

   There are two brief treatments of the depression which mention the European variants of agrarianism, but they have little to say about the social roots of agrarian movements (see C. P. Kindleberger, "Group Behavior and International Trade," and Michael Tracy, *Agriculture in Western Europe*). There is one comparative study of European landed elites in the nineteenth century, but it has virtually nothing to say about the impact of the depression and is very disappointing on political matters generally (David Spring, ed., *European Landed Elites in the Nineteenth Century*). Any systematic comparative history will have to await monographic research on the French landed elite on which almost no monographic research has been done for the nineteenth century. Thus, the historian is drawn—almost by necessity—to the American and German cases.
3. A very useful, albeit irritatingly partisan overview of this debate

can be found in Lawrence Goodwyn, *Democratic Promise: The Populist Movement in America*, pp. 600–614. I am also indebted to my colleague Vincent DeSantis who shared with me his knowledge of the debate on populism.

4. Charles H. Otken, *The Ills of the South or Related Causes Hostile to the General Prosperity of the Southern People*, pp. 15–25.
5. Peter H. Argersinger, *Populism and Politics*, p. 5.
6. Ibid., pp. 58–65.
7. N. S. Ashby, *The Riddle of the Sphinx*, pp. 128–142.
8. Argersinger, *Populism and Politics*, pp. 2, 7, 283–285.
9. Goodwyn, pp. 109–153.
10. As Goodwyn notes, "in its underlying emotional impulses, Populism was a revolt against the narrowing limits of political debate within capitalism as much as it was a protest against specific economic injustices," p. 358.
11. *The World Almanac*, pp. 83–85.
12. Richard Hofstadter, *The Age of Reform*, p. 64.
13. Elizabeth N. Barr, "The Populist Uprising," in William E. Connelley, ed., *A Standard History of Kansas and Kansans*, vol. 2, p. 1170.
14. Hofstadter, *Age of Reform*, pp. 77–81. Goodwyn tries, unsuccessfully in my opinion, to deny the link between populism and anti-Semitism.
15. Walter T. K. Nugent in *The Tolerant Populists* denies that nativism was prevalent in Kansas.
16. Hofstadter, *Age of Reform*, pp. 82–85.
17. On the impulses behind German protectionism, see Hans-Ulrich Wehler, *Bismarck und der Imperialismus*, pp. 87–95; Hans Rosenberg, *Grosse Depression und Bismarckzeit*, pp. 178–187.
18. A convenient summary of Caprivi's policies and the opposition to them is Kenneth D. Barkin, *The Controversy over German Industrialization 1890–1902*, pp. 44–102.
19. See ibid., pp. 60–67.
20. The program of the Bund der Landwirte is reprinted as an appendix to Hans-Jurgen Puhle, *Agrarische Interessenpolitik und preussischer Konservatismus im Wilhelminischen Reich (1893–1914)*, p. 314.
21. Ibid., pp. 85–89.
22. Ibid., pp. 89–94.
23. *Berliner Blatt*, no. 257 (2 November 1910); on anti-Semitism, see Puhle, *Agrarische Interessenpolitik*, pp. 125–140.
24. *Korrespondenz der Bundes der Landwirte*, no. 13 (15 February 1905), cited in ibid., p. 95.
25. See Barkin's admirable exposition of their attack on capitalism in *Controversy*, pp. 131–185.
26. Ibid., p. 102.
27. Puhle, *Agrarische Interessenpolitik*, pp. 288–289.
28. See Marc Bloch, "A Contribution towards a Comparative History of European Societies," p. 38.
29. An introduction to the French nobility in the eighteenth century

may be found in Albert Goodwin, ed., *The European Nobility in the Eighteenth Century*. A monumental study of the French society of orders has just appeared in English translation: Roland Mousnier, *The Institutions of France under the Absolute Monarchy 1598–1789*.

30. On the social and economic life of provincial nobles, see J. Meyer, *La noblesse brétonne au XVIIIᵉ siècle*; Robert Forster, *The Nobility of Toulouse in the Eighteenth Century*. On the *parlementaires*, see François Bluché, *Les magistrats du Parlement du Paris au XVIIIᵉ siècle (1715–1771)*; William Doyle, *The Parlement of Bordeaux and the End of the Old Regime, 1771–1790*.

31. Jean Egret, *The French Prerevolution 1787–1788*, pp. 144–178.

32. The classic discussion of peasant violence in the early revolutionary period is Georges Lefebvre's *The Great Fear of 1789*.

33. The Ségur Ordinance, usually cited as the chief example of aristocratic reaction, was actually adopted against the advice of the great aristocracy and of the War Office. G. Six, "Fallait-il quatre quartiers de noblesse pour être officier à la fin de l'Ancien Régime?" pp. 42–56; see also David Bien, "La réaction aristocratique avant 1789," pp. 23–48.

34. See François Furet, "Le catéchisme révolutionnaire," pp. 255–289.

35. Egret, *French Prerevolution*, pp. 157–158.

36. Ibid., p. 195.

37. Ibid., p. 177.

38. TsGIA, fond 1283, opis' 1, deloproizvodstvo 1, 1897, delo 231, l. 159; also quoted in A. P. Korelin, "Dvorianstvo v poreformennoi Rossii (1861–1904)," p. 173.

Selected Bibliography

Archives

Tsentral'ny Gosudarstvenny Istorichesky Arkhiv (TsGIA) [Central State Historical Archive]:

Fond 593. Gosudarstvenny dvoriansky zemel'ny bank.

Fond 1184. Osobaia komissiia po delam zemel'nogo kredita.

Fond 1233. Osoboe soveshchanie o nuzhdakh sel'skokhoziaistvennoi promyshlennosti.

Fond 1282. Kantseliariia Ministerstva vnutrennikh del.

Fond 1283. Kantseliariia Ministerstva vnutrennikh del po delam dvorianstva.

Fond 1284. Departament obshchikh del Ministerstva vnutrennikh del.

Fond 1343. Upravliaiushchy senat. Departament gerol'dii.

Books, Articles, Manuscripts

Adres kalendar' i pamiatnaia knizhka Permskoi gubernii na 1902 g. Perm, 1902.

Adres-kalendar'. Obshchaia rospis' nachal'stvuiushchikh i prochikh dolzhnostnykh lits po vsem upravleniiam v Rossiiskoi imperii na [1859–1916] g. St. Petersburg, 1859–1916.

Anfimov, A. M. "Karlovskoe imenie Meklenburg-Strelitskikh v kontse XIX–nachale XX v." *Materialy po istorii sel'skogo khoziaistva i krest'ianstva SSSR.* Moscow, 1962. Vol. 5, pp. 348–376.

———. "Khoziaistvo krupnogo pomeshchika v XX veka." *Istoricheskie zapiski* 71 (1962): 43–73.

———. *Krest'ianskoe khoziaistvo Evropeiskoi Rossii 1881–1904.* Moscow, 1980.

———. *Krupnoe pomeshchich'e khoziaistvo Evropeiskoi Rossii.* Moscow, 1969.

———. "K voprosu o kharaktere agrarnogo stroia Rossii v nachale XX v." *Istoricheskie zapiski* 65 (1959): 119–162.

———. "Maioratnoe zemlevladenie v tsarskoi Rossii." *Istoriia SSSR,* 1962, no. 5: 151–159.

———. "Prussky put' razvitiia kapitalizma v sel'skom khoziaistve i ego osobennosti v Rossii." *Voprosy istorii* 1965, no. 7: 62–76.

———. "V. I. Lenin o kharaktere agrarnykh otnoshenii v Rossii nachala XX veka." In AN SSSR. Institut istorii. *Osobennosti agrarnogo stroia Rossii v period imperializma,* pp. 64–85. Moscow, 1962.

———. *Zemel'naia arenda v Evropeiskoi Rossii v nachale XX veka.* Moscow, 1961.

Argersinger, Peter H. *Populism and Politics: William Alfred Peffer and the People's Party.* Lexington, 1974.

Ashby, N. S. *The Riddle of the Sphinx.* Des Moines, 1890.

Atkinson, Dorothy Grace Gillis. "The Russian Land Commune and the Revolution." Ph.D. diss., Stanford University, 1971.

Avrekh, A. Ia. "Russky absoliutizm i ego rol' v utverzhdenii kapitalizma v Rossii." *Istoriia SSSR,* 1968, no. 2: 89–101.

Barkin, Kenneth D. *The Controversy over German Industrialization, 1890–1902.* Chicago, 1970.

Barsukov, N. *Zhizn' i trudy M. P. Pogodina.* St. Petersburg, 1900.

Bensidoun, Sylvain. *L'agitation paysanne en Russie de 1881 à 1902.* Paris, 1975.

Bien, David. "La réaction aristocratique avant 1789: l'example de l'armée." *Annales; économies, sociétés, civilisations* 29 (1974): 23–48.

Billington, James H. *Mikhailovsky and Russian Populism.* Oxford, 1958.

Bloch, Marc. "A Contribution towards a Comparative History of European Societies." In *Land and Work in Medieval Europe.* New York, 1969.

Bluché, François. *Les magistrats du Parlement de Paris au XVIIIe siècle (1715–1771).* Paris, 1969.

Blum, Jerome. *Lord and Peasant in Russia from the Ninth to the Nineteenth Century.* Princeton, 1961.

Bogucharsky, V. Ia. "Iz istorii politicheskoi bor'by v 80-kh godakh." *Russkaia mysl',* 1910, no. 9, pt. 2: 1–31.

Bottomore, T. B. *Elites and Society.* New York, 1964.

Brower, Daniel R. *Training the Nihilists: Education and Radicalism in Tsarist Russia.* Ithaca, 1975.

Budaev, D. I. *Krest'ianskaia reforma 1861 goda v Smolenskoi gubernii.* Smolensk, 1967.

Bulygin, I. A.; Indova, E. I.; Preobrazhensky, A. A.; and Tikhonov, Ia. A. "Problema formirovaniia vserossiiskogo rynka v sovremennoi sovetskoi istoriografii." In *Aktual'nye problemy istorii Rossii epokhi feodalizma. Sbornik statei,* edited by L. V. Cherepnin, pp. 200–223. Moscow, 1971.

Bunin, I. A. *Sobranie sochinenii.* 9 vols. Moscow, 1965.

Burtsev, V. L. *Za sto let (1800–1896). Sbornik po istorii politicheskikh i obshchestvennykh dvizhenii v Rossii v dvukh chastiakh.* London, 1897.

Canovan, Margaret. *Populism*. New York, 1981.

Chekhov, A. P. *Seven Short Novels*. Translated by Barbara Makanowitzky. New York, 1963.

Cherepnin, L. V. *Zemskie sobory russkogo gosudarstva v XVI–XVII vv.* Moscow, 1978.

Chermensky, E. D. "Zemsko-liberal'noe dvizhenie nakanune revoliutsii 1905–1907 gg." *Istoriia SSSR*, 1965, no. 5: 41–60.

Chernukha, V. G. *Vnutrenniaia politika tsarizma s serediny 50-kh do nachala 80-kh gg. XIX veka*. Leningrad, 1978.

Chicherin, B. N. "Dopolnitel'naia zametka o narodnosti v nauke." *Atenei*, 1858, no. 5: 41–60.

———. "Nemetskie sotsialisty." *Sbornik gosudarstvennykh znanii*, 1878, vol. 5: 1–71; vol. 6: 1–39.

———. "Sovremennye zadachi russkoi zhizni." In *Golosa iz Rossii*, edited by Alexander Herzen, Vypusk IV: 51–129. London, 1857.

———. *Voprosy politiki*. Moscow, 1904.

———. *Vospominaniia Borisa Nikolaevicha Chicherina. Zemstvo i Moskovskaia duma*. Moscow, 1934.

———. *Vospominaniia. Moskva sorokovykh godov*. Moscow, 1929.

Christian, R. F., ed. *Tolstoy's Letters*. 2 vols. New York, 1978.

Chuprov, A. I., and Posnikov, A. S., eds. *Vliianie urozhaev i khlebnykh tsen na nekotorye storony russkogo narodnogo khoziaistva*. 2 vols. St. Petersburg, 1897.

Cobb, Richard. *The Police and the People: French Popular Protest, 1789–1820*. Oxford, 1972.

Confino, Michael. *Systèmes agraires et progrès agricole. L'assolement triennal en Russie aux XVIIIᵉ–XIXᵉ siècles. Étude d'économie et de sociologie rurales*. Paris, 1969.

Connelley, William E., ed. *A Standard History of Kansas and Kansans*. 2 vols. Chicago, 1918.

Davidovich, A. M. *Samoderzhavie v epokhu imperializma*. Moscow, 1975.

Deich, G. M. "Osoboe soveshchanie o nuzhdakh sel'skokhoziaistvennoi promyshlennosti." Ph.D. diss., Leningrad, 1946.

Departament sel'skogo khoziaistva Ministerstva gosudarstvennykh imushchestv. *Ob''iasneniia k khoziaistvenno-statisticheskomu atlasu Evropeiskoi Rossii*. St. Petersburg, 1857.

Departament zemledeliia i sel'skoi promyshlennosti. *Sel'skokhoziaistvennye i statisticheskie svedeniia po materialam poluchennym ot khoziaev. Vypusk III*. St. Petersburg, 1890.

Derenkovsky, G. M. "Leninskaia 'Iskra' i krest'ianskoe dvizhenie v Poltavskoi i Khar'kovskoi gub. v 1902 g." *Doklady i soobshcheniia instituta istorii AN SSSR* 2 (1954): 53–73.

Diakin, V. S. *Samoderzhavie, burzhuaziia i dvorianstvo v 1907–1911 gg.* Leningrad, 1978.

Dostoevsky, F. M. *Sobranie sochinenii*. 10 vols. Moscow, 1957.

Dovzhenok, V. I. "K istorii zemledeliia i vostochnykh slavian v 1 tysiache-letii n. e. i v epokhu Kievskoi Rusi." *Materialy po istorii zemledeliia SSSR* 1 (1952): 157–159.

Doyle, William. *The Parlement of Bordeaux and the End of the Old Regime, 1771–1790.* London, 1974.

Druzhinin, N. M. "Pomeshchich'e khoziaistvo posle reformy 1861 g. (Po dannym Valuevskoi komissii 1872–1873 gg.)." *Istoricheskie zapiski* 89 (1972): 187–230.

———. *Russkaia derevnia na perelome 1861–1880 gg.* Moscow, 1978.

Dubrovsky, S. M. "K voprosu ob urovne razvitiia kapitalizma v sel'skom khoziaistve Rossii i kharaktere klassovoi bor'by v derevne v period imperializma." In AN SSSR. Institut istorii. *Osobennosti agrarnogo stroia Rossii v period imperializma,* pp. 5–44. Moscow, 1962.

Edelman, Robert. *Gentry Politics on the Eve of the Russian Revolution: The Nationalist Party, 1907–1917.* New Brunswick, N.J., 1980.

———. "The Nationalist Party and the Western Zemstvo Crisis of 1909." *Russian Review* 34, no. 1 (January 1975): 22–54.

Egiazarova, N. A. *Agrarny krizis kontsa XIX veka v Rossii.* Moscow, 1959.

Egret, Jean. *The French Prerevolution, 1787–1788.* Chicago, 1977.

Emeliak, L. E. "Krest'ianskoe dvizhenie v Poltavskoi i Khar'kovskoi guberni-iakh v 1902 g." *Istoricheskie zapiski* 38 (1951): 154–175.

Emmons, Terence. "The Beseda Circle, 1899–1905." *Slavic Review* 32, no. 3 (September 1973): 461–490.

———. "The Peasant and the Emancipation." In *The Peasant in Nineteenth-Century Russia,* edited by Wayne S. Vucinich, pp. 41–71. Stanford, 1968.

———. *The Russian Landed Gentry and the Peasant Emancipation of 1861.* Cambridge, 1968.

———. "The Russian Landed Gentry and Politics." *Russian Review* 33, no. 3 (July 1974): 269–283.

———. "Russia's Banquet Campaign." *California Slavic Studies* 10 (1977): 45–86.

———, ed. *Emancipation of the Russian Serfs.* New York, 1970.

Engel, Barbara Alpern, and Rosenthal, Clifford N., eds. *Five Sisters: Women against the Tsar.* New York, 1975.

Engel'gardt, A. N. *Iz derevni. 12 pisem.* Moscow, 1937.

Ensor, Sir Robert. *England, 1870–1914.* Oxford, 1938.

Ernle, Rowland. *English Farming, Past and Present.* 6th ed. Chicago and London, 1961.

Estier, Robert. "La Dépression agricole de la fin du XIXᵉ siècle." In *Histoire des paysans français du XVIIIᵉ siècle à nos jours.* Roanne, 1976.

Fedorov, V. A. "Pomeshchich'i krest'iane tsentral'no-promyshlennogo raiona Rossii nakanune otmeny krepostnogo prava." Ph.D. diss., Moscow, 1969.

Fedorova, M. "Moskovsky otdel Sviashchennoi druzhiny." *Golos minuvshego*, 1918, nos. 1–3.

Field, Daniel, *The End of Serfdom: Nobility and Bureaucracy in Russia, 1855–1861*. Cambridge, 1976.

———. "Kavelin and Russian Liberalism." *Slavic Review* 32, no. 1 (March 1973): 59–78.

Fletcher, T. W. "The Great Depression of English Agriculture, 1873–1896." *Economic History Review*, 2d s., 13, no. 3 (April 1961): 417–432.

Forster, Robert. *The Nobility of Toulouse in the Eighteenth Century: A Social and Economic Study*. Baltimore, 1971.

Freeze, Gregory. "A National Liberation Movement and the Shift in Russian Liberalism, 1901–1903." *Slavic Review* 28, no. 1 (March 1969): 81–91.

Furet, François. "Le catéchisme révolutionnaire." *Annales; économies, sociétés, civilisations* 26 (1971): 255–289.

Galai, Schmuel. "Early Russian Constitutionalism, 'Vol'noe Slovo' and the 'Zemstvo Union': A Study in Deception." *Jahrbuecher fuer Geschichte Osteuropas*, n.F., 22, no. 1 (1974): 35–55.

———. *The Liberation Movement in Russia, 1900–1905*. Cambridge, 1973.

Genovese, Eugene. *Roll, Jordan, Roll: The World the Slaves Made*. New York, 1976.

Gerschenkron, A. *Agrarian Policies and Industrialization in Russia, 1861–1917*. Cambridge Economic History of Europe, vol. 6, part 2: 706–800. Cambridge, 1965.

———. "Soviet Marxism and Absolutism." *Slavic Review* 30, no. 4 (December 1971): 853–869.

Gertsen, A. I. *Sobranie sochinenii*. 9 vols. Moscow, 1958.

Gindin, I. F. *Gosudarstvenny bank i ekonomicheskaia politika tsarskogo pravitel'stva, 1861–1892 gody*. Moscow, 1960.

Gindin, I. F., and Gefter, M. Ia. "Trebovaniia dvorianstva i finansovo-ekonomicheskaia politika tsarskogo pravitel'stva v 1880–1890-kh godakh." *Istorichesky arkhiv*, 1957, no. 4: 122–155.

Gleason, Abbott. *Young Russia: The Genesis of Russian Radicalism in the 1860s*. New York, 1980.

Glinka, Fedor Konstantinovich. *K voprosu ob uluchshenii polozheniia zemel'nogo dvorianstva. Zavisimost' voprosa ot sushchestvuiushchego napravleniia ekonomicheskoi i finansovoi politiki strany*. Mogilev na Dnepre, 1899.

Gogol', Nikolai. *Dead Souls*. Translated by D. Magarshack. Baltimore, 1961.

Goldstein, David I. *Dostoevsky and the Jews*. Austin, 1981.

Goodrich, Carter. *Government Promotion of American Canals and Railroads, 1800–1890*. New York, 1960.

Goodwin, Albert, ed. *The European Nobility in the Eighteenth Century*. London, 1953.

Goodwyn, Lawrence. *Democratic Promise: The Populist Movement in America*. New York, 1976.

Gradovsky, A. D. *Kurs russkogo gosudarstvennogo prava.* 3 vols. St. Petersburg, 1883.
Grazhdanin.

Haimson, Leopold H., ed. *The Politics of Rural Russia, 1905–1914.* Bloomington, 1979.
Hamburg, G. M. "The London Emigration and the Russian Liberation Movement: The Problem of Unity, 1889–1897." *Jahrbuecher fuer Geschichte Osteuropas* 25, H. 3 (1977): 321–339.
Hammer, D. P. "Two Russian Liberals: The Political Thought of B. N. Chicherin and K. D. Kavelin." Ph.D. diss., Columbia University, 1962.
Hause, Thomas Stewart. "State and Gentry in Russia, 1861–1917." Ph.D. diss., Stanford University, 1973.
Herzen, Alexander. *My Past and Thoughts: The Memoirs of Alexander Herzen.* New York, 1968.
Hexter, J. H. *On Historians: Reappraisals of Some of the Makers of Modern History.* Cambridge, Mass., 1979.
Hicks, John D. *The Populist Revolt.* Minneapolis, 1931.
Higgs, Robert. *The Transformation of the American Economy, 1865–1914: An Essay in Interpretation.* New York, 1971.
Hofstadter, Richard. *The Age of Reform: From Bryan to F. D. R.* New York, 1955.

Iatsunsky, V. K. "Osnovnye momenty istorii sel'skokhoziaistvennogo proizvodstva v Rossii s XVI veka do 1917 goda." In AN SSSR. Institut istorii. *Ezhegodnik po agrarnoi istorii Vostochnoi Evropy 1964,* pp. 44–64. Kishinev, 1966.
Ikonnikov, N. F. *La noblesse de Russie: Éléments pour servir à la reconstitution des registres généalogiques de la noblesse d'après les actes et documents disponibles complètes grâce au concours dévoué des nobles russes.* 1st ed., 26 vols. Paris, 1957–1966.
Iskra.
Issledovanie ekonomicheskogo polozheniia tsentral'no-chernozemnykh gubernii. Trudy osobogo soveshchaniia 1899–1901 gg. Moscow, 1901.
"Iz dnevnika V. N. Smel'skogo." *Golos minuvshego,* 1916, no. 1.
"Iz perepiski zemskikh deiatelei 70–80-kh godov." *Golos minuvshego,* 1915, no. 12: 211–212.

Jones, J. R. *Country and Court: England, 1658–1714.* Cambridge, Mass., 1978.
Jones, Robert E. *The Emancipation of the Russian Nobility, 1762–1785.* Princeton, 1973.

Kabuzan, V. M., and Troitsky, S. M. "Izmeneniia v chislennosti, udel'nom vese i razmeshchenii dvorianstva v Rossii v 1782–1858 gg." *Istoriia SSSR,* 1971, no. 4: 162–165.

Kadomtsev, B. P. *Professional'ny i sotsial'ny sostav naseleniia po perepisi 1897 g.* St. Petersburg, 1903.

Kafengauz, B. B. *Ocherki vnutrennego rynka Rossii pervoi poloviny XVIII v. (Po materialam vnutrennikh tamozhen).* Moscow, 1958.

Katkov, M. N. *Sobranie peredovykh statei "Moskovskikh vedomostei."* Moscow, 1898.

Keep, J. L. H. *The Russian Revolution of 1917: A Study of Mass Mobilization.* New York, 1976.

Kelly, William J. "Railroad Development and Market Integration in Tsarist Russia: Evidence on Oil Products and Grain." *Journal of Economic History* 36, no. 4 (December 1974): 908–916.

Kindleberger, C. P. "Group Behavior and International Trade." *Journal of Political Economy* 59, no. 1 (February 1951): 30–46.

Kirkland, Edward C. *Industry Comes of Age: Business, Labor, and Public Policy.* Chicago, 1967.

Kitaev, V. A. *Ot frondy k okhranitel'stvu. Iz istorii russkoi liberal'noi mysli 50–60-kh godov XIX veka.* Moscow, 1972.

Kizevetter, A. A. *Na rubezhe dvukh stoletii. (Vospominaniia 1881–1914).* Prague, 1929.

Klier, John D. "The Jewish Question in the Reform Era Russian Press, 1855–1865." *Russian Review* 39, no. 3 (July 1980): 301–319.

Kliuchevsky, V. O. *Pis'ma. Dnevniki. Aforizmy i mysli ob istorii.* Moscow, 1968.

———. *Sochineniia v 8-i tomakh.* Moscow, 1958.

"Kolichestvo zemli zadolzhennoi v zemel'nykh bankakh, summa ssudy i razmer platezha protsentov na desiatinu po guberniiam." *Vremennik Tsentral'nogo statisticheskogo komiteta Ministerstva vnutrennikh del,* 1889, no. 8.

"Konstitutsionnye proekty nachala 80-kh gg. XIX veka." *Krasny arkhiv* 31 (1928): 118–139.

Korelin, A. P. "Dvorianstvo v poreformennoi Rossii (1861–1904 gg.)" *Istoricheskie zapiski* 87 (1971): 91–173.

———. *Dvorianstvo v poreformennoi Rossii 1861–1904 gg. Sostav, chislennost', korporativnaia organizatsiia.* Moscow, 1979.

———. "Rossiiskoe dvorianstvo i ego soslovnaia organizatsiia (1861–1904 gg.)." *Istoriia SSSR,* 1971, no. 5: 56–81.

Korelin, A. P., and Tiutiukin, S. V. "Revoliutsionnaia situatsiia nachala XX veka v Rossii." *Voprosy istorii,* 1980, no. 10.: 4–24.

Korf, Baron S. A. *Dvorianstvo i ego soslovnoe upravlenie za stoletie 1762–1855 godov.* St. Petersburg, 1906.

Koshelev, A. I. *Kakoi iskhod dlia Rossii iz nyneshnego ee polozheniia?* Leipzig, 1862.

———. *Konstitutsiia, samoderzhavie i zemskaia duma.* Leipzig, 1862.

Koval'chenko, I. D. "Agrarny rynok i kharakter agrarnogo stroia Evropeiskoi Rossii v kontse XIX–nachale XX v." *Istoriia SSSR,* 1973, no. 2: 42–74.

———. *Krest'iane i krepostnoe khoziaistvo Riazanskoi i Tambovskoi gubernii v pervoi polovine XIX v. (K istorii krizisa feodal'no-krepostnicheskoi systemy khoziaistva).* Moscow, 1959.

———. "O tovarnosti zemledeliia v Rossii v pervoi polovine XIX v." In AN SSSR. Institut istorii. *Ezhegodnik po agrarnoi istorii Vostochnoi Evropy 1963,* pp. 469–486. Vil'nius, 1964.

———. *Russkoe krepostnoe krest'ianstvo v pervoi polovine XIX v.* Moscow, 1967.

Koval'chenko, I. D., and Milov, L. V. *Vserossiisky agrarny rynok XVIII–nachalo XX veka. Opyt kolichestvennogo analiza.* Moscow, 1974.

Krest'ianskoe dvizhenie v Poltavskoi i Khar'kovskoi guberniiakh v 1902 g. Sbornik dokumentov. Khar'kov, 1961.

Krest'ianskoe dvizhenie v Rossii v 1881–1889 gg. Moscow, 1960.

Krest'ianskoe dvizhenie v Rossii v 1890–1900 gg. Moscow, 1959.

Laverychev, V. Ia. "Obshchaia tendentsiia razvitiia burzhuazno-liberal'nogo dvizheniia v Rossii v kontse XIX–nachale XX v." *Istoriia SSSR,* 1976, no. 3: 46–65.

Lavrov, P. L. *Historical Letters.* Translated by James P. Scanlan. Berkeley and Los Angeles, 1967.

Lefebvre, Georges. *The Great Fear of 1789.* New York, 1973.

Leikina-Svirskaia, V. R. *Intelligentsiia v Rossii vo vtoroi polovine XIX veka.* Moscow, 1971.

Lenin, V. I. *Collected Works.* 4th ed. Moscow and London, 1960.

———. *Polnoe sobranie sochinenii.* 4th ed., 38 vols. Moscow, 1941–1956.

Liashchenko, P. I. *A History of the National Economy of Russia to the 1917 Revolution.* New York, 1949.

———. *Istoriia narodnogo khoziaistva SSSR.* 3 vols. Moscow, 1956.

———. "Mobilizatsiia zemlevladeniia v Rossii i ego statistika" *Russkaia mysl',* fevral' 1905, kn. 2: 1–26.

———. *Ocherki agrarnoi evoliutsii Rossii.* St. Petersburg, 1908.

———. *Russkoe zernovoe khoziaistvo v sisteme mirovogo khoziaistva.* Moscow, 1927.

Litvak, B. G. *Opyt statisticheskogo issledovaniia krest'ianskogo dvizheniia XIX veka.* Moscow, 1967.

———. "Ustavnye gramoty Moskovskoi gubernii kak istochnik po istorii realizatsii Polozheniia 19 fevralia 1861 g." Ph.D. diss., Moscow University, 1956.

Loewe, Heinz-Dietrich. *Antisemitismus und reaktionaere Utopie: Russischer Konservatismus im Kampf gegen den Wandel von Staat und Gesellschaft, 1890–1917.* Hamburg, 1978.

Lukashevich, Stephen. "The Holy Brotherhood: 1881–1883." *Slavic Review* 18, no. 4 (December 1959): 491–509.

Makovsky, D. P. *Razvitie tovarno-denezhnykh otnoshenii v sel'skom khoziaistve russkogo gosudarstva v XVI veke.* Smolensk, 1962.

Manning, Roberta Thompson. "The Liberals and the Landed Gentry, 1905–07." Manuscript, 1975.

———. "The Noble Oppositions and the Emergence of a Provincial Gentry in Russia, 1861–1905." Manuscript, 1975.

———. "The Russian Provincial Gentry in Revolution and Counterrevolution, 1905–07." Ph.D. diss., Columbia University, 1975.

Martov, Iu. et al. *Obshchestvennoe dvizhenie v Rossii s nachala XX veka.* 5 vols. St. Petersburg, 1908–1911.

Materialy Vysochaishe uchrezhdennoi 16 noiabria 1901 g. komissii. St. Petersburg, 1903.

Metzer, Jacob. "Railroad Development and Market Integration: The Case of Tsarist Russia." *Journal of Economic History* 34, no. 3 (September 1974): 529–550.

———. "Reply to Kelly. Railroad Development and Market Integration in Tsarist Russia. A Rejoinder." *Journal of Economic History* 36, no. 4 (December 1976): 917–918.

Meyer, J. *La noblesse brétonne au XVIIIe siècle.* 2 vols. Paris, 1966.

Miliukov, P. N. *Gosudarstvennoe khoziaistvo v Rossii v pervoi chetverti XVIII stoletiia i reforma Petra Velikogo.* 2d ed. St. Petersburg, 1905.

———. "Novy variant slavianofil'skoi politicheskoi doktriny." *Russkoe bogatstvo*, 1905, no. 4.

———. *Russia and Its Crisis.* London, 1962.

Minarik, L. P. *Ekonomicheskaia kharakteristika krupneishikh zemel'nykh sobstvennikov Rossii kontsa XIX–nachala XX v. Zemlevladenie, zemlepol'zovanie, sistema khoziaistva.* Moscow, 1971.

———. "Kharakteristika krupneishikh zemlevladel'tsev Rossii kontsa XIX–nachala XX v." In AN SSSR. Institut istorii. *Ezhegodnik po agrarnoi istorii Vostochnoi Evropy 1963*, pp. 693–708. Vil'nius, 1964.

———. "Ob urovne razvitiia kapitalisticheskogo zemledeliia v krupnom pomeshchich'em khoziaistve Evropeiskoi Rossii kontsa XIX–nachala XX v." In AN SSSR. Institut istorii. *Ezhegodnik po agrarnoi istorii Vostochnoi Evropy 1964*, pp. 615–626. Kishinev, 1966.

———. "Proiskhozhdenie i sostav zemel'nykh vladenii krupneishikh pomeshchikov Rossii kontsa XIX–nachala XX v." In AN SSSR. Institut istorii. *Materialy po istorii sel'skogo khoziaistva i krest'ianstva SSSR* 6 (1965): 356–395.

Ministerstvo finansov 1802–1902 g. 2 vols. St. Petersburg, 1902.

Ministerstvo zemledeliia i gosudarstvennykh imushchestv. *Nuzhdy sel'skogo khoziaistva i mery ikh udovletvoreniia po otzyvam zemskikh sobranii.* St. Petersburg, 1899.

Ministerstvo zemledeliia i gosudarstvennykh imushchestv. Otdel sel'skoi ekonomii i sel'skokhoziaistvennoi statistiki. *Svod statisticheskikh svedenii po sel'skomu khoziaistvu Rossii v kontse XIX veka.* St. Petersburg, 1903.

Mironov, B. N. "O kriterii edinogo natsional'nogo rynka." In AN SSSR. Institut istorii. *Ezhegodnik po agrarnoi istorii Vostochnoi Evropy 1968*, pp. 180–188. Leningrad, 1972.

Mochulsky, Konstantin. *Dostoevsky: His Life and Work.* Princeton, 1967.

Moskovskie vedomosti.

Mousnier, Roland, *The Institutions of France under the Absolute Monarchy, 1598–1789.* Chicago, 1979.

Nabokov, Vladimir. *Speak, Memory: An Autobiography Revisited.* New York, 1966.

Nechetny, S. "U zemli." *Vestnik russkoi revoliutsii. Sotsial'no-politicheskoe obozrenie,* 1902, no. 2, pt. 2: 43–44.

Nifontov, A. S. *Zernovoe proizvodstvo Rossii vo vtoroi polovine XIX veka po materialam ezhegodnoi statistiki urozhaev Evropeiskoi Rossii.* Moscow, 1974.

North, Douglas. "Ocean Freight Rates and Economic Development, 1750–1913." *Journal of Economic History* 18 (December 1958): 537–555.

Novikov, A. I. *Zapiski gorodskogo golovy.* St. Petersburg, 1905.

Nugent, Walter T. K. *The Tolerant Populists: Kansas Populism and Nativism.* Chicago, 1963.

O'Boyle, Lenore, "The Classless Society: Comment on Stearns." *Comparative Studies in Society and History,* 1979, pp. 397–413.

Ocherki istorii SSSR, period feodalizma. Vtoraia chetvert' XVIII v. Moscow, 1950.

Ol'denburg, S. S. *Last Tsar: Nicholas II. His Reign and His Russia.* 4 vols. Gulf Breeze, Fla. 1975.

Osvobozhdenie.

Otchety gosudarstvennogo zemel'nogo banka. St. Petersburg, 1888–1902.

Otken, Charles H. *The Ills of the South or Related Causes Hostile to the General Prosperity of the Southern People.* New York, 1894.

Paina, E. S. *Krest'ianskoe dvizhenie v Rossii v XIX–nachale XX vv.* Moscow, 1963.

Pavlovsky, George. *Agricultural Russia on the Eve of the Revolution.* London, 1930.

Pazukhin, A. D. *Sovremennoe sostoianie Rossii i soslovny vopros.* Moscow, 1886.

Perrie, Maureen. *The Agrarian Policy of the Russian Socialist-Revolutionary Party from Its Origins through the Revolution of 1905–1907.* Cambridge, 1976.

Pershin, P. N. *Agrarnaia revoliutsiia v Rossii.* 2 vols. Moscow, 1966.

Pipes, Richard. *Russia under the Old Regime.* New York, 1974.

Pirumova, N. M. *Zemskoe liberal'noe dvizhenie. Sotsial'nye korni i evoliutsiia do nachala XX veka.* Moscow, 1977.

Pisarev, D. I. *Sochineniia v 4-kh tomakh.* Moscow, 1955.

Pleve, V. K. *Doklad predsedatelia Vysochaishe uchrezhdennoi v 1888 godu komissii po povodu padeniia tsen na sel'skokhoziaistvennye proizvedeniia v piatiletie 1883–1887.* St. Petersburg, 1892.

Pobedonostsev, K. P. *Pis'ma K. P. Pobedonostseva k Aleksandru III.* 2 vols. Moscow, 1925–1926.

Polnoe sobranie zakonov Rossiiskoi imperii. Sobranie 3-e. 33 vols. St. Petersburg, 1885–1916.

Polovtsov, A. A. "Dnevnik A. A. Polovtsova." *Krasny arkhiv* 3 (1923): 75–172.

————. *Dnevnik gosudarstvennogo sekretaria A. A. Polovtsova v dvukh tomakh.* Moscow, 1966.

Popov, P. I. "Khlebno-furazhny balans 1840–1924 gg.," in Komissiia SNK SSSR po izucheniiu sovremennoi derevni. *Sel'skoe khoziaistvo na putiakh vosstanovleniia.* Moscow, 1925.

Pravitel'stvenny vestnik.

Preobrazhensky, A. A., and Tikhonov, Iu. A. "Itogi izucheniia nachal'nogo etapa skladyvaniia vserossiiskogo rynka (XVII veka)." *Voprosy istorii,* 1961, no. 4: 80–109.

Principes et autorités contre l'édit de la Cour plénière. Paris, 1788.

Proskuriakova, N. A. "Razmeshchenie i struktura dvorianskogo zemle-vladeniia Evropeiskoi Rossii v kontse XIX–nachale XX veka." *Istoriia SSSR,* 1973, no. 1: 55–75.

Puhle, Hans-Jurgen. *Agrarische Interessenpolitik und preussischer Konservatismus im Wilhelminischen Reich (1893–1914).* Hannover, 1966.

Pushkin, A. S. *Eugene Onegin.* Translated by Sir Charles Johnston. New York, 1978.

Raeff, Marc. *Origins of the Russian Intelligentsia: The Eighteenth-Century Nobility.* New York, 1966.

Rakhmatullin, M. A. "Khlebny rynok i tseny v Rossii v pervoi polovine XIX v." In *Problemy genezisa kapitalizma. Sbornik statei,* edited by S. D. Skazkin et al., pp. 334–442. Moscow, 1970.

Ransel, David L. *The Politics of Catherinian Russia: The Panin Party.* New Haven, 1975.

Rashin, A. G. *Naselenie Rossii za 100 let (1813–1913 g.). Statisticheskie ocherki.* Moscow, 1956.

Riasanovsky, Nicholas. *A History of Russia.* 3rd ed. New York, 1977.

————. *Nicholas I and Official Nationality in Russia, 1825–1855.* Berkeley, 1969.

————. *A Parting of the Ways: Government and the Educated Public in Russia, 1801–1855.* Oxford, 1976.

Riha, Thomas. *A Russian European: Paul Miliukov in Russian Politics.* South Bend, Ind., 1969.

Robbins, Richard Gardner, Jr. *Famine in Russia, 1891–1892: The Imperial Government Responds to a Crisis.* New York, 1975.

————. "The Russian Famine of 1891–1892 and the Relief Policy of the Imperial Government." Ph.D. diss., Columbia University, 1970.

Robertson, Ross M. *History of the American Economy.* 3d ed. New York, 1973.

Robinson, Geroid Tanquary. *Rural Russia under the Old Regime: A History of the Landlord-Peasant World and a Prologue to the Peasant Revolution of 1917.* Berkeley, 1969.

Roessle, Wilhelm. *Bismarcks Politik nach seinen Staatsschriften und Reden.* Jeden, 1943.

Rogger, Hans. "The Formation of the Russian Right, 1900–1906." *California Slavic Studies* 3 (1964): 66–94.

————. "Russian Ministers and the Jewish Question." *California Slavic Studies* 8 (1975): 15–76.

Romanov, Nikolai Mikhailovich. *Graf Pavel Aleksandrovich Stroganov (1774–1814)*. St. Petersburg, 1903.

Romanovich-Slaviatinsky, A. *Dvorianstvo v Rossii ot nachala XVIII veka do otmeny krepostnogo prava*. 2d ed. Kiev, 1912.

Rosenberg, Hans. *Grosse Depression und Bismarckzeit: Wirtschaftsablauf, Gesellschaft und Politik in Mitteleuropa*. Berlin, 1967.

Rubinshtein, N. L. *Sel'skoe khoziaistvo Rossii vo vtoroi polovine XVIII veka. (Istoriko-ekonomichesky ocherk)*. Moscow, 1957.

Rudé, George. *Revolutionary Europe, 1783–1815*. New York, 1964.

Rudnev, V. *Krest'ianskoe dvizhenie v nachale XX v.* Moscow, 1929.

Ryndziunsky, P. G. "Rossiiskoe samoderzhavie i ego klassovye osnovy (1861–1904 gg.)." *Istoriia SSSR*, 1977, no. 2: 34–52.

———. *Utverzhdenie kapitalizma v Rossii 1850–1880 gg.* Moscow, 1978.

Sadikov, N. A. "Obshchestvo 'Sviashchennoi druzhiny.'" *Krasny arkhiv* 31 (1928): 200–217.

Saltykov-Shchedrin, M. E. *Sobranie sochinenii*. 6 vols. Moscow, 1951.

———. *Sobranie sochinenii*. 20 vols. Moscow, 1969.

Samarin, D. F. *O nizkikh tsenakh na khleb*. Moscow, 1902.

Savvaitov, P. I. "Obozrenie Kievskoi, Podol'skoi i Volynskoi gubernii s 1830 po 1850 god." *Russky arkhiv*, 1884, no. 5: 13–15.

Schapiro, Leonard. *Rationalism and Nationalism in Russian Nineteenth-Century Political Thought*. New Haven, 1967.

Scheibert, Peter. *Die russische Agrarreform von 1861: Ihre Probleme und der Stand ihrer Erforschung*. Cologne, 1973.

Schmoller, G. "Die amerikanische Konkurrenz und die Lage der mitteleuropaischen, besonders der deutschen Landwirtschaft." *Schmollers Jahrbuch* 6 (1882): 247–284.

Sel'skokhoziaistvennye i statisticheskie svedeniia po materialam, poluchennym ot khoziaev. Vol. 3. St. Petersburg, 1890.

Selunskaia, N. B. "Istochnikovedcheskie problemy izucheniia pomeshchich'ego khoziaistva Rossii kontsa XIX–nachala XX veka." *Istoriia SSSR*, 1973, no. 6: 81–95.

———. "Modelirovanie sotsial'noi struktury pomeshchich'ego khoziaistva Rossii kontsa XIX–nachala XX veka." In AN SSSR, Otdelenie istorii, *Matematicheskie metody v issledovaniiakh po sotsial'no-ekonomicheskoi istorii*, pp. 151–179. Moscow, 1975.

Seton-Watson, Hugh. *The Russian Empire, 1801–1917*. Oxford, 1967.

Shakhovskoi, D. I. "Soiuz osvobozhdeniia." *Zarnitsy* no. 2 (1909): 81–171.

Shannon, Fred A. *The Farmer's Last Frontier: Agriculture 1860–1897*. The Economic History of the United States, vol. 5. New York, 1961.

Shapiro, A. L. "O roli Peterburga v razvitii vserossiiskogo rynka v XVIII–pervoi polovine XIX veka." In *Goroda feodal'noi Rossii*, edited by V. I. Shunkov, pp. 386–397. Moscow, 1966.

Shatsillo, K. F. "Formirovanie programmy zemskogo liberalizma i ee bankrotstva nakanune pervoi russkoi revoliutsii (1901–1904 gg)." *Istoricheskie zapiski* 97 (1976): 50–98.

————. "Taktika i organizatsiia zemskogo liberalizma nakanune pervoi russkoi revoliutsii." *Istoricheskie zapiski* 101 (1978): 217–270.

Shcherbatov, A. G. *Po povodu knigi Vliianie urozhaev i khlebnykh tsen na nekotorye storony russkogo narodnogo khoziaistva.* Moscow, n.d.

Shipov, D. N. *Vospominaniia i dumy o perezhitom.* Moscow, 1918.

Shlemin, P. I. "Zemsko-liberal'noe dvizhenie na rubezhe XIX–XX vekov." Ph.D. diss., Moscow University, 1972.

Simmons, Ernest J. *Leo Tolstoy.* Boston, 1946.

Simms, James Young, Jr. "The Impact of the Russian Famine of 1891–2: A New Perspective." Ph.D. diss., University of Michigan, 1976.

Simonova, M. S. "Politika tsarizma v krest'ianskom voprose nakanune revoliutsii 1905–1907 gg." *Istoricheskie zapiski* 75 (1965): 212–242.

————. "Problema 'oskudeniia' tsentra i ee rol' v formirovanii agrarnoi politiki samoderzhaviia v 90-kh godakh XIX–nachale XX v." In *Problemy sotsial'no-ekonomicheskoi istorii Rossii,* edited by L. M. Ivanov et al., pp. 236–263. Moscow, 1971.

————. "Zemsko-liberal'naia fronda (1902–1903 gg.)." *Istoricheskie zapiski* 91 (1973): 150–216.

Six, G. "Faillait-il quatre quartiers de noblesse pour être officier à la fin de l'Ancien Régime?" *Révue d'histoire moderne* 4 (1929): 42–56.

Smith, Peter. *History of Transportation in the United States before 1860.* Washington, D.C., 1948.

Soboul, Albert. *The French Revolution, 1787–1799: From the Storming of the Bastille to Napoleon.* Translated by Forest and Jones. New York, 1974.

Soloviev, Iu. B. *Samoderzhavie i dvorianstvo v kontse XIX veka.* Leningrad, 1973.

————. *Samoderzhavie i dvorianstvo v 1902–1907 gg.* Leningrad, 1981.

Spender, Stephen. *Collected Poems.* New York, 1955.

Spring, David, ed. *European Landed Elites in the Nineteenth Century.* Baltimore, 1977.

Stearns, Peter N. "The Middle Class: Toward a Precise Definition." *Comparative Studies in Society and History,* 1979, pp. 377–396.

Steingel', E. A. *O nekotorykh sushchestvennykh prichinakh nyneshnego khlebnogo krizisa i vozmozhnogo ego ustraneniia v budushchem.* St. Petersburg, 1895.

Stover, John F. *The Railroads of the South, 1865–1900: A Study in Finance and Control.* Chapel Hill, N.C., 1955.

Struve, P. B. *Krepostnoe khoziaistvo. Issledovaniia po ekonomicheskoi istorii Rossii v XVIII i XIX vv.* St. Petersburg, 1913.

Suny, Ronald Grigor. "The Peasants 'Have Always Fed Us': The Georgian Nobility and the Peasant Emancipation, 1856–1871." *Russian Review* 38, no. 1 (January 1979): 27–51.

Svod zakonov Rossiiskoi imperii. 16 vols. St. Petersburg, 1832–1917.

Tarnovsky, K. N. "Problemy agrarnoi istorii Rossii perioda imperializma v sovetskoi istoriografii (1917–nachalo 1930-kh godov)." *Istoricheskie zapiski* 78 (1965): 31–62.

————. "Problemy agrarnoi istorii Rossii perioda imperializma v sovetskoi istoriografii (konets 1930-kh–pervaia polovina 1950-kh godov)." *Istoricheskie zapiski* 83 (1969): 196–221.

————. "Problemy agrarnoi istorii Rossii perioda imperializma v sovetskoi istoriografii (Diskussiia nachala 1960-kh godov)." In *Problemy sotsial'no-ekonomicheskoi istorii Rossii*, edited by L. M. Ivanov et al., pp. 264–310. Moscow, 1971.

Taylor, George Rogers. *The Transportation Revolution, 1815–1860*. The Economic History of the United States, vol. 4. New York, 1951.

Taylor, George Rogers, and Neu, Irene D. *The American Railroad Network, 1861–1890*. Cambridge, 1956.

Terpigoriev, S. N. *Sobranie sochinenii*. 6 vols. St. Petersburg, 1899.

Thompson, E. P. *The Making of the English Working Class*. New York, 1963.

Timberlake, Charles E. *Essays on Russian Liberalism*. Columbia, Mo., 1972.

Tolmachev, M. F. *Krest'iansky vopros po vzgliadam zemstva i mestnykh liudei*. Moscow, 1903.

Tolstoy, L. N. *Polnoe sobranie sochinenii*. 90 vols. Moscow, 1930–1958.

Tracy, Michael. *Agriculture in Western Europe: Crisis and Adaptation since 1880*. London, 1964.

Trubetskaia, Ol'ga. *Kniaz' S. N. Trubetskoi. Vospominaniia sestry*. New York, 1953.

Trudy mestnykh komitetov o nuzhdakh sel'skokhoziaistvennoi promyshlennosti. 58 vols. St. Petersburg, 1903.

Trudy Vserossiiskogo s"ezda sel'skikh khoziaev. Vypusk 5. Moscow, 1896.

Tsentral'ny statistichesky komitet. *Statistika zemlevladeniia 1905 g. Svod dannykh po 50 guberniiam Evropeiskoi Rossii*. St. Petersburg, 1907.

Tsyzarev, I. "Preddverie agrarnoi revoliutsii 1905 g. Opyt kharakteristiki agrarnogo dvizheniia 1902 g." *Arkhiv istorii truda v Rossii*, 1923, no. 9: 99–124.

Valuev, P. A. *Dnevnik 1877–1884*. Petrograd, 1919.

Veselovsky, B. B. *Istoriia zemstva za sorok let*. 4 vols. St. Petersburg, 1911.

Vestnik finansov, promyshlennosti i torgovli.

Vitte, S. Iu. *Vospominaniia tsarstvovaniia Nikolaia II*. Berlin, 1922.

Vliianie urozhaev i khlebnykh tsen na razlichnye storony russkogo narodnogo khoziaistva. 2 vols. St. Petersburg, 1897.

Vliianie urozhaev i khlebnykh tsen na raznye storony ekonomicheskoi zhizni. Doklad Prof. A. I. Chuprova i preniia v III Otdelenii Imperatorskogo vol'nogo ekonomicheskogo obshchestva, 1 i 2 marta 1897 g. (Stenografichesky otchet). St. Petersburg, 1897.

Vol'sky, M. *Ocherk istorii khlebnoi torgovli Novorossiiskogo kraia s drevneishikh vremen do 1852 g*. Odessa, 1854.

Vorovsky, V. V. *Sochineniia*. Moscow, 1933.

Vsia Rossiia. Russkaia kniga promyshlennosti, torgovli, sel'skogo khoziaistva i administratsii. St. Petersburg, 1895–1902.

Vucinich, Alexander. *Science in Russian Culture, 1861–1917*. Stanford, 1970.

Vysochaishe uchrezhdennoe Osoboe soveshchanie o nuzhdakh sel'skokhoziaistvennoi promyshlennosti. *Svod trudov mestnykh komitetov po*

49 guberniiam Evropeiskoi Rossii. Zheleznye dorogi i tarify. St. Petersburg, 1904.

Walicki, Andrzej. *The Slavophile Controversy: History of a Conservative Utopia in Nineteenth-Century Russian Thought.* Oxford, 1975.

Wallace, Donald MacKenzie. *Russia on the Eve of War and Revolution.* Edited by Cyril Black. New York, 1961.

Watters, Francis M. "The Peasant and the Village Commune." *The Peasant in Nineteenth-Century Russia,* edited by Wayne S. Vucinich, pp. 133–157. Stanford, 1968.

Wehler, Hans-Ulrich. *Bismarck und der Imperialismus.* Koeln, 1969.

Woodward, C. Van. *Tom Watson: Agrarian Rebel.* New York, 1938.

World Almanac. New York, 1893.

Wortman, Richard. "Koshelev, Samarin, and Cherkassky and the Fate of Liberal Slavophilism." *Slavic Review* 21, no. 2 (June 1962): 261–279.

Zaionchkovsky, P. A. *Krizis samoderzhaviia na rubezhe 1870–1880-kh godov.* Moscow, 1964.

———. *Otmena krepostnogo prava v Rossii.* 2d ed. Moscow, 1960.

———. *Pravitel'stvenny apparat samoderzhavnoi Rossii v XIX v.* Moscow, 1978.

———. *Providenie v zhizn' krest'ianskoi reformy 1861 g.* Moscow, 1958.

———. *The Russian Autocracy in Crisis, 1878–1882.* Edited by G. M. Hamburg. Gulf Breeze, Fla. 1979.

Zakharova, L. G. "Krizis samoderzhaviia nakanune revoliutsii 1905 g." *Voprosy istorii,* 1972, no. 8: 119–140.

Zeldin, Theodore. *France 1848–1945.* Vol. 2, *Intellect, Taste, and Anxiety.* Oxford, 1977.

Zhukovsky, V. *Polnoe sobranie sochinenii v odnom tome.* Moscow, 1915.

Index

Index

Budaev, D. I., 24
Buimistrov, V. S., 179
Bulgakov, A. N., 142
Bunakov, N. F., 219
Bund der Landwirte, 232–236
Bunge, N. Kh., 110–111, 113, 116
Bunin, I. A., 245n.30
Buzni, M. K., 137

Calonne, Charles Alexandre de, 237
Caprivi, Leo Count von, 232–234
Catherine II, 39, 44
Cherepnin, L. V., 42, 249n.8
Cherespolosnost', 24, 197, 208, 246–247n.16
Cherkassky, V. A., 61–62
Chernigov, 73, 188–189. *See also* Blacksoil belt provinces
Chernyshevsky, N. G., 58–60
Chicherin, B. N., 14, 61–62, 83–84, 116, 198–199, 267nn.25, 27
Chuprov, A. I., 265n.11
Class analysis, 3–4, 20, 68
Cobb, Richard, 3
Corporal punishment, 203, 209, 217
Council on Tariffs, 167, 171
Courland, 12. *See also* Western periphery provinces

Decembrist rebellion, 39–40, 47
Demidov, P., 77
Department of Railroad Tariffs, 163
Derozhinsky, M. L., 138
Dobroliubov, N. A., 58
Dolgorukov, A. M., 158
Dolgorukov, P. D., 218
Donnelly, Ignatius, 230–231
Dostoevsky, F. M., 44, 64–65
Druzhinin, N. M., 31–38
Durnovo, A., 153–154, 194
Durnovo, I. N., 150–152

Ekaterinoslav, 93, 188, 204. *See also* Southern steppes provinces
Emancipation: and capitalist relations, 140–141; and peasant land allotments, 22, 24, 148, 246n.14; and redemption payments, 25, 27, 195
Engel'gardt, A. N., 24
Entail: and impact of 1899 statute, 226; and *maioraty*, 18, 119–120; noble demands for, 119–127; types of, 118–119
Eristov, M. A., 209
Estates General, 237–238
Estland, 12. *See also* Western periphery provinces
Evreinov, A. V., 157, 217–218

Farmers' Alliance, 228–230, 236
Fedorov, M. P., 183, 186–187
Field, Daniel, 21
Frisch, L., 130
Furet, François, 4, 237

Gagarin, A. I., 111
Galai, Schmuel, 216, 218–219
Galuzin, N. M., 179
Gartman, Lev, 77
George, Henry, 199
Giasintov, N. E., 183
Gleason, Abbott, 59, 64
Glinka, F. D., 194
Gogol, N. V., 16, 19, 43–44
Golenishchev-Kutuzov, A. A., 136–137
Golitsyn, O. S., 183–184, 187
Goodwyn, Lawrence, 230
Gorchakov, I. A., 111
Goremykin, I. L., 145
Gorn, V., 201
Great Depression: causes of, 85–88; effects of, in France, 85; effects of, in Germany, 85, 231–232; effects of, in United States, 229; and noble landownership, 88–97; and noble politics, 107, 117, 132, 163, 167; and peasantry, 192–202; and railroad tariffs, 163, 167
Grodno. *See* Western periphery provinces